Y0-CAM-710

STUDIES IN EVANGELICALISM
edited by
Kenneth E. Rowe &
Donald W. Dayton

1. Melvin E. Dieter. *The Holiness Revival of the Nineteenth Century.* 1980.

2. Lawrence T. Lesick. *The Lane Rebels: Evangelicalism and Antislavery in Antebellum America.* 1980.

3. Edward H. Madden and James E. Hamilton. *Freedom and Grace: The Life of Asa Mahan.* 1982.

4. Roger H. Martin. *Evangelicals United: Ecumenical Stirrings in Pre-Victorian Britain, 1795-1830.* 1983.

5. Donald W. Dayton. *Theological Roots of Pentecostalism.* 1987.

6. David L. Weddle. *The Law as Gospel: Revival and Reform in the Theology of Charles G. Finney.* 1985.

7. Darius L. Salter. *Spirit and Intellect: Thomas Upham's Holiness Theology.* 1986.

8. Wayne E. Warner. *The Woman Evangelist: The Life and Times of Charismatic Evangelist Maria B. Woodworth-Etter.* 1986.

9. Darrel M. Robertson. *The Chicago Revival, 1876: Society and Revivalism in a Nineteenth-Century City.* 1989.

10. R. David Rightmire. *Sacraments and the Salvation Army: Pneumatological Foundations.* 1990.

11. Cornelis van der Laan. *Sectarian Against His Will: Gerrit Roelof Polman and the Birth of Pentecostalism in the Netherlands.* 1991.

Sectarian Against His Will:
Gerrit Roelof Polman
and the Birth of
Pentecostalism in
the Netherlands

by
CORNELIS VAN DER LAAN

Studies in Evangelicalism, No. 11

The Scarecrow Press, Inc.
Metuchen, N.J., & London
1991

Frontispiece: Gerrit R. and Wilhelmine Polman

BR
1644.5
.N4
L35
1991

British Library Cataloguing-in-Publication data available

Library of Congress Cataloging-in-Publication Data

Laan, Cornelis van der, 1948–
    Sectarian against his will : Gerrit Roelof Polman and the birth of
Pentecostalism in the Netherlands / by Cornelis van der Laan.
        p.   cm. — (Studies in evangelicalism ; no. 11)
    Originally presented as the author's thesis (Ph.D.)—University of
Birmingham, 1987.
    Includes bibliographical references and index.
    ISBN 0-8108-2412-4 (alk. paper)
    1. Polman, Gerrit Roelof, 1868–1932.   2. Pentecostal churches—
Netherlands—Clergy—Biography.   3. Pentecostal churches—
Netherlands—History.   I. Title.   II. Series.
BR1644.5.N4L35   1991
289.9'4'092—dc20
    [B]   91-18217

Copyright © 1991 by Cornelis van der Laan
Manufactured in the United States of America

Printed on acid-free paper

EDITORS' NOTE

The current resurgence of Evangelical religion has highlighted the important role of this force in the formation of American and European culture. The Studies in Evangelicalism series seeks to explore the movement's roots in the Evangelical Revival and Awakening of the eighteenth century, its nineteenth-century blossoming in revivalism and social reform, and its twentieth-century developments in both sectarian and mainline churches. We are concerned with emphasizing the diversity within Evangelicalism—the search for holiness, the Millennial traditions, Fundamentalism, and Pentecostalism in particular.

We are pleased to publish Cornelis van der Laan's study of Gerrit Roelof Polman and the birth of Pentecostalism in the Netherlands as number 11 in the series.

Cornelis van de Laan is General Secretary of the Broederschap van Pinkstergemeenten in Nederland (Assemblies of God in the Netherlands). He completed a doctorate in theology at the University of Birmingham in 1987.

DONALD W. DAYTON   KENNETH E. ROWE
Northern Baptist Theological   Drew University
  Seminary   Madison, New Jersey
Lombard, Illinois

CONTENTS

FOREWORD: THE HEART AND THE HEAD

Cornelis van der Laan is a first-generation Dutch Pentecostal. He is an ordained pastor, a leader, and a teacher in his native Pentecostal church. In this study he presents a meticulously researched and closely argued biography of the founder of Dutch Pentecostalism, G.R. Polman. Unlike many Pentecostal "historians" he places Pentecostalism in the context of social, political, and ecclesiastical history. He does not gloss over the deficiencies of the movement and its founder, but treats them with tact and frankness.

He searched for and found an amazing array of sources on Pentecostalism in public records, private collections, in the testimonies of eyewitnesses, in church periodicals, and in early Pentecostal publications, not only in his native Holland but also in Germany, Switzerland, England, the United States, and Sweden, thus demonstrating clearly that Pentecostalism was—at least in its formative years—a close international community.

On the basis of hitherto unknown documents, Van der Laan discovered that Polman was declared at his birth to be "onecht," a "not-genuine" or illegitimate child, because his mother was his father's stepdaughter who became the elder Polman's wife after the death of his first wife.

Van der Laan documents the struggle for survival of the Polman family in that small rural community of Westenholte, the early influences of the Salvation Army, and John Alexander Dowie on Polman, and brings to light many a detail on these revival movements which are not generally known. He describes how Polman discovered Pentecostalism as an ecumenical revival movement which was not called to build up its own church organization but to build up all the churches, including the ones that attacked him and his work. He was helped in this by one of the most lucid historians on early Pentecostalism, the Frisian pastor Dr. Wumkes, whose works are practically unknown outside Holland. Van der Laan used Wumkes' large collection of letters.

Van der Laan calls Polman a failed ecumenist, "a sectarian against his will." Certainly Polman was an ecumenist born before his time. He was a "go-between" for the German and the British during the First World War. Unlike many of the German and British Pentecostal leaders he was also a pacifist. For him the strident nationalism depicted in the pages of *Confidence* (the leading British Pentecostal periodical) and *Pfingstgrüsse* (the leading German Pentecostal periodical) was a denial of Christ's work of reconciliation. Consequently he visited German prisoners of war in England and British prisoners of war in Germany. He refrained from writing a declaration of faith because such a declaration would raise unnecessary walls between the churches. He gladly confessed that Pentecostalism was born in the crucible of the black slaves' suffering in the United States and rejected the fashionable claims that Pentecostalism was simply a development of America's white Holiness movement—I know of no other Pentecostal leader who puts himself so clearly on the side of the "onecht" (not-genuine) black citizens of America. But then he knew that in God's eyes the despised children of Israel were the people of God, the despised early Christian slaves were his church, the downtrodden descendants of America's slaves were the founders of the most vital 20th-century denominations, and he himself, the illegitimate son, was legitimate.

So why did Polman fail as an ecumenist? Van der Laan summarizes his dilemma succinctly: "Polman's ecumenical heart collided with his fundamentalistic Evangelical head. His Spirit baptism had generated a loving attitude towards all fellow-Christians, but he was unable to fully assimilate this ecumenical experience into his thinking. . . . Surely this was not his fault alone. He received no help from his Evangelical colleagues nor from the academic theologians." They were either too busy condemning the fledgling ecumenical movement or they simply ignored it.

Can the early ecumenical spirit of Dutch Pentecostalism be recaptured? This is no easy task. Van der Laan discusses the conditions which would make such a thing possible. In the first instance conflict must be recognized as a necessary context for innovative theology. "This requires an ecclesiology in which pluriformity becomes a hall-mark of the church; a dynamic pluriformity that allows room for conflict and change. It calls for a theology that refuses to make its own position normative; a theology that partakes in an intercultural learning process. A true Pentecostal-charismatic theology should welcome conflicts as being essential for the continuous work of the Spirit. Conflicts provide the context in which the charismata operate."

This is not an appeal for an "everything-goes" attitude. It is a theology which takes Paul seriously, where the heart pleads with the head and the head informs the heart—in fact a "body-of-Christ" theology which promises to rekindle in Dutch Pentecostalism that early ecumenical spirit.

This is only a beginning. Pentecostals and non-Pentecostals from other countries and other cultures have to enter the debate and make their contribution. "The promising ecumenical start failed, because on the one side the Pentecostals did have the right heart for the matter, but lacked the means to develop an adequate corresponding theology, while on the other side the (main-line) churches possessed the means, but lacked the necessary ecumenical heart." Is it not time to put the two together?

DR. WALTER J. HOLLENWEGER
Professor of Mission
University of Birmingham

ACKNOWLEDGMENTS

With the publication of my thesis "Gerrit Roelof Polman, Sectarian Against His Will: Birth of Pentecostalism in the Netherlands" (University of Birmingham, 1987), I would like to acknowledge those who helped me in various ways. In particular I am indebted to Professor Walter J. Hollenweger, who guided my study through its dissertation stage at the University of Birmingham. His numerous publications on Pentecostalism were largely responsible for arousing in me an interest for the subject dealt with in this present study, even before I met him. I am thankful for all those who have assisted me in making research material available, or with their advice. I am especially grateful to my brother Paul van der Laan, whose research on the ecumenical aspects of Dutch Pentecostalism has been completed at this same university, for his cooperation in finding sources in libraries and archives (like the correspondence of G.A. Wumkes and J.H. Gunning J.Hz. with G.R. Polman), and for his helpful remarks. I thank Jean-Jacques Suurmond for his comments while reading the manuscript. I owe much to the many eyewitnesses who were willing to share their memories with me, in particular the children of Polman. Much of my gratitude goes to my dear wife Willie who continually encouraged me to go ahead with my dissertation. Finally I want to give a thank-offering to our heavenly Father, without whose grace and provision I could not have succeeded.

INTRODUCTION

When the Pentecostal assembly of Amsterdam in 1981 commemorated its seventy-fifth anniversary, an American missionary recalled how the Pentecostal message started in the United States and from there came to Europe. The next speaker was Emmanuel Schuurman, the oldest Dutch Pentecostal pioneer still alive. The aged warrior corrected his American colleague by stating that Pentecost did not come from America, but from heaven. Although the sympathy of the audience was with the latter, for this study, neither of the two explanations suffice. The events of the Azusa Street revival in Los Angeles (1906) certainly influenced the start of Pentecostalism in Europe, and indeed the element of the supernatural must not be overlooked. Yet, religious revivals are not just the product of export, whether it is from America or from heaven. Revivalistic movements always arise within a historical context and as a rule are reactions against the status quo in church or society.

Pentecostalism today has conquered its ten thousands. David B. Barrett calculated in 1988 the global number of all Pentecostals at 176 million.[1] The majority of this figure comes from third-world countries, where Pentecostalism is fast becoming the dominant type of Christianity. Walter J. Hollenweger attributes the growth of Pentecostalism to its black roots, summarized as orality of liturgy; narrativity of theology and witness; maximum participation; inclusion of dreams and visions into personal and public forms of worship; an appreciation of the correspondence between body and mind—the most striking application being the ministry of healing by prayer.[2] Hollenweger further notes that in Europe and North America Pentecostalism is developing into a middle-class religion, following Evangelical traditions supplemented with the belief in a baptism of the Spirit. Many of the

1

elements vital for its rise and its expansion into the third world are disappearing. Therefore it is important that reliable accounts of the origins are written. Only recently have European Pentecostals become aware of their distinctive contribution to international Pentecostalism and have now started to seriously research their own heritage.[3]

In this study the birth of Pentecostalism in the Netherlands is discussed in its historical context with reference to church and society. The real growth of the Dutch Pentecostals only commenced during the 1950s. In early 1983 the Gereformeerd minister Bram Krol estimated the number of Pentecostals to be about 85,000 (including children).[4] Krol's figure might have been somewhat too high for 1983, but it is evident that Pentecostalism is becoming a stream to be reckoned with in the ecclesiastical map of the Netherlands. In order to understand a present phenomenon it is essential to be aware of its origin. To do justice to this point of departure and at the same time remain within manageable size, this research is limited to the first stage of Pentecostalism in the Netherlands, the period under the leadership of Polman (1907-1930). During this time, the main developments responsible for the shape of the movement took place. From an ecumenical renewal movement it evolved into a separate denomination. The concept of being the last outpouring of the Holy Spirit in the end time had to give way to a less urgent role in the plan of God.

Gerrit Roelof Polman (1868-1932) was the founder and undisputed leader of the movement during this period. He was an original and charismatic leader with an international reputation among the early Pentecostals. The Pentecostal assembly he founded at Amsterdam was a model for many Pentecostals in neighboring countries. In 1916 Netherlands Reformed minister G.A. Wumkes wrote *De Pinksterbeweging voornamelijk in Nederland*, the first scholarly account and analysis of the Pentecostal movement, which included a valuable but short sketch of Polman's life. Sixty years later another Reformed minister, J.J. Buskes, commented on Polman: "It is a pity that there, as yet, has not appeared a biography of this remarkable man."[5] This research seeks to redeem this omission.

For a proper understanding some of the terms used will be clarified now, while others will be explained as they are introduced. With "orthodox-reformed" are meant members within existing Protestant churches, who stress loyalty to the tradition and confessions of the reformation. With "Evangelicals" are meant members of the so-called free churches and free circles like the "Vrije Evangelischen," Baptists, (Plymouth) Brethren, the independent evangelists, the independent city missions, and the Salvation Army. All of them, including the orthodox-reformed, were more or less fundamentalist in their emphasis on the inerrancy and literal interpretation of the Bible and in their suspicion of academic (modern) theology. In agreement with the Evangelicals, the Pentecostals emphasized a personal faith in Jesus Christ on the basis of a radical conversion (rebirth). But, unlike the Evangelicals, the Pentecostals propagated a second crisis experience called the baptism with or in the Holy Spirit (shortened: Spirit baptism) subsequent to and distinct from conversion, usually accompanied by the speaking in tongues.

Most Evangelicals and clergy from existing churches soon branded Pentecostalism as a dangerous sect. The uneasy relationship between church and sect are reconsidered in the Conclusion. For the moment the theological definition of a sect given by F. Boerwinkel in *Kerk en Secte* will suffice:

> A sect is a group of people which, mainly out of a desire for purity and by making a part of the truth absolute, severs the solidarity with the greater whole of the group and no longer experiences this rupture as something to be regretted.[6]

Boerwinkel's emphasis is not on a transgression of doctrine, but on a transgression of solidarity. Not the separation in itself is disapproved, but the fact that the pain of the rupture is no longer felt and the "solidarity in guilt" is denied. In the course of this study it will be examined whether the early Pentecostals were rightly labeled "sectarian" by their contemporaries. The focus will be on Gerrit Roelof Polman as he in many ways was representative for early Pentecostalism in being a sectarian against his will.

NOTES

1. David B. Barrett, "The Twentieth-Century Pentecostal/Charismatic Renewal in the Holy Spirit, with Its Goal of World Evangelization," *International Bulletin for Missionary Research* 12 (1988),1.
2. Walter J. Hollenweger, "After Twenty Years' Research on Pentecostalism," *International Review of Mission* 75/297 (January 1986),6.
3. The best examples of this are the Conferences on Pentecostal and Charismatic Research in Europe, held in Leuven 1980 and 1981, in Birmingham 1984, and in Gwatt (Switzerland) in 1987. A collection of papers presented is forthcoming in W.J. Hollenweger, ed., *Pentecostal Research in Europe: Problems, Promises and People* (Frankfurt/Bern: Peter Lang). Another good example is the European Pentecostal Theological Association, with its quarterly *EPTA Bulletin.*
4. Bram Krol, "De groei van de Pinksterbeweging in Nederland," *Parakleet* 4/15 (Summer 1984),34-35.
5. J.J. Buskes, "1906: de eerste pinkstergemeente in Nederland," *Trouw,* 20 March 1976, p. 2.
6. F. Boerwinkel, *Kerk en Secte* 2d ed., (The Hague: Boekencentrum, 1956), p. 19.

1 HISTORICAL CONTEXT

The Netherlands Until 1848

The 17th century had been an age of great economic prosperity for the Netherlands not in the least due to the commercial and later also political dominion it obtained over the East Indies. The collapse that followed during the 18th century made the country unfit for an industrial revolution like that in England, but prepared it for the revolution under the French banner of 1795. In January 1795 French armies with support of the anti-Orange patriots captured the land and introduced the virtues of the French Revolution: freedom, equality, and brotherhood. Catholics and Protestant dissenters (Remonstrants, Mennonites, and Lutherans) welcomed the change in hope for more freedom. Indeed the privileged position of the Reformed church was abandoned and a formal equality of all churches stipulated.

After 18 years under French rule national independence was restored in 1813. William I became sovereign prince and from March 1815 king (1813-1840). By the constitution of 1815 the freedom of the existing religions was recognized, but the king obtained a formal right to intervene in church matters. The Reformed church was reorganized in 1816 under the name "Nederlandsche Hervormde Kerk." The form of government became more centralized and subject to state supervision. In 1814 Belgium was united with the Netherlands, but the union broke down with the Belgian revolt of 1830, finalized with the peace treaty of 1839.

The country was ruled by a small conservative aristocracy of nobility and notability. This same upper layer also governed the Reformed church and used it as a means to maintain peace and order in the state. They regarded the Netherlands as a Protestant nation in which the Catholics (one-third of the population!) could only have a second rate position.

The spirit of 18th-century Enlightenment that sought to replace God by man himself as center of the world and valued reason above revelation also penetrated the Reformed church. In the first part of the 19th century an enlightened theology was articulated by the "Groninger Richting," called after a group of theologians at the University of Groningen, among whom Petrus Hofstede de Groot was most important. The later "Moderne Theologie" came up at the University of Leiden in the 1840s. It aimed to make Christianity more relevant for the 19th-century civilization. The ministers influenced by this modern theology held "that it did not suit the modern Christian to believe in miracles, the divine inspiration of the Bible, hell, original sin, or all the other dualistic principles of ancient theology."[1] Protestants from the upper and more-or-less educated middle class welcomed this, in their eyes, more highly developed Christianity. When it came to nominations they took care that modernist ministers were appointed. This led to several countermovements of pietist and orthodox nature.

One of such reactions, known as the "Réveil," had much in common with the movement of the same name that was manifested in other parts of Europe. It found support among members of the aristocracy at Amsterdam and The Hague. Central figures were Willem Bilderdijk (1756-1831), Isaac da Costa (1798-1860), Abraham Capadose (1795-1874), Ottho Gerhard Heldring (1804-1876), and Guillaume Groen van Prinsterer (1801-1876). Seeking the restoration of the Reformed church, they combined an orthodox theology with deep personal faith and were active in areas of Christian education and charity. Noteworthy is the chiliasm of Da Costa and Capadose, two converted Jews, and Capadose's writings against vaccination.[2] Groen van Prinsterer became their political spokesman. He fought against the spirit of the French Revolution in which he saw a rebellion against God and constituted authority. Against the revolution he placed the gospel. His following became known as the "Anti-Revolutionairen." Abraham Kuyper would later work out the thoughts of Groen for a much broader circle.

Another, more radical, countermovement, known as the "Afscheiding" (Separation), led to a secession from the Netherlands Reformed church in 1834. It was initiated by the ministers Hendrik de Cock (1801-1842) and Hendrik P. Scholte (1805-1868) as a protest against the "false" Netherlands Reformed church and as a return to traditional Calvinism as stipulated by the synod of Dort (1618-1619). The separation found its following largely among the lower classes of society. During the first years the separatists were persecuted by state and church. Many of them, including Scholte, emigrated to North America, where they founded farming colonies in Michigan and Iowa.[3]

One factor that had contributed much to the success of the "Afscheiding" was the phenomenon of the so-called "conventikels" or "gezelschappen" (fellowships). Influences of Puritanism and Pietism and writings of the Dutch "Nadere Reformatie" had created a tradition of small fellowships within the Reformed church. These fellowships became a resort for orthodoxy, often combined with a strong experiential element. Here the "pure" believers assembled together in homes for edification and Bible readings exercised by lay-preachers called "oefenaars." Most of the more than 100 local churches that were established before 1840 as a result of the "Afscheiding" were in fact transformations of former fellowships.[4] Due to the acute shortage of ministers (only six ministers, aged between 24 and 34, had separated), a number of the "oefenaars" was ordained. A great number of internal conflicts led to several clusters of churches, all claiming to represent the true reformed tradition. Eventually the majority of the separatists united in the "Christelijke Gereformeerde Kerk" (1869).[5]

From a Protestant to a Neutral State

Revolutionary changes in other parts of Europe during 1848 brought about by the economical recession of 1847 caused enough commotion in the Netherlands to enable the upcoming liberals to come to government. William II (1840-1849) became so frightened that he turned liberal overnight![6]

Liberalism was a protest of a growing middle class and a class of intellectuals against the state and church of the ancien régime. It advocated the freedom of the individual and believed in the progress of humankind by use of modern science and technology.

With the new constitution of 1848, largely the effort of the liberal J.R. Thorbecke (1798-1872) from Zwolle, the power of the king was curtailed in favor of a constitutional government. Members of the parliament were from now on chosen directly by the voters, though the voting rights remained limited to a small part of the population, namely, the rich and educated males of 23 years and older. The privileges of the nobility were terminated and all religions were given the equal right to administer their own affairs. The latter assured the liberals of a strong Catholic support.

The years 1850 to 1870 formed a transitional period to the world of modern capitalism. Cabinets with alternate liberal and conservative signatures came and went. In spite of Protestant agitation the age-old assumption that held the Netherlands for a Protestant state had to give way to the liberal concept of a neutral state. Also in economic affairs the liberal policy prevailed. Following the example of England a free-trade economy was advanced and protectionism gradually abandoned. The process of industrialization, which would shift the economic framework from an agrarian-based structure towards an industrial one, slowly commenced. Compared with England the Dutch wheels of industry were turning at a low speed, but after 1890 the process accelerated.[7] With the growth of the population (2 million in 1800; 3 million in 1850; 5 million in 1900; nearly 8 million in 1930), an increasing number moved to the cities. The home-industry became largely replaced by the factories in the cities. Urbanization in the Netherlands, however, did not produce specific industrial cities; the large cities remained trade centers.[8]

The years 1870 to 1890 were a period of much activity, mobility, and progress, during which time the modern state was shaped. The conservatives disappeared to the background, while the confessionals came to the front in their fight against liberalism and the growing socialism. Though the conservatives as a political movement died out in the 1880s, their influence remained strong by means of the confessional parties and segments of the liberal party. The middle class in particular benefitted from the progress between 1850 and 1870 and were ready for a political emancipation.[9] Abraham Kuyper (1837-1920) became the spokesman of the so-called "kleine luyden": orthodox-Protestants from the working and lower-middle class (small craftsmen, shopkeepers, bargemen, small businessmen, but mostly farmers).[10]

Kuyper's Call for a Free Church

The constitution of 1848 compelled the Netherlands Reformed Church to adjust its form of government. By the regulation of 1852 representatives of the lower classes were given voting rights in the nominations of elders, deacons, and ministers. When in 1867 (15 years later!) the first nominations on this basis took place, it became apparent that even after the "Afscheiding" the orthodox still formed the hard core of the church members, if not the majority.[11] When in 1870 an orthodox majority in Amsterdam had the first opportunity to call a minister, they voted for Abraham Kuyper.

Kuyper had studied in Leiden, but was converted to dogmatic-Calvinism. He fervently opposed modernism, but he also opposed the synodical power within the church. He called for a "vrije kerk" (free church) with autonomy for the local churches. The matter divided the orthodox in two camps: supporters of the "vrije kerk" and supporters of the "volkskerk" (national church). In 1880 Kuyper founded the "Vrije Universiteit" at Amsterdam. When graduates from this university were not ordained by the Reformed synod, a conflict broke out.[12]

In 1886 the separation known as "Doleantie" under Kuyper began. The dissenters formed the "Nederduitsch Gereformeerde Kerken." In 1892 they united with the larger part of the "Christelijke Gereformeerde Kerk" from the Afscheiding. The new formation chose its present name: "Gereformeerde Kerken in Nederland."[13] The plural "kerken" fits in with Kuyper's model of a free church composed of autonomous local churches. Both separations "Afscheiding" and "Doleantie" were religious protests against unorthodox theology, but also social protests against the more privileged in the church. Kuyper affirmed that social and church principles intermingled. According to him it was more a fight of different classes than of different faiths.[14]

The ecclesiastical fragmentation had also given opportunity to the rise of a number of small denominations initiated by impulses from abroad, often more or less influenced by Methodism. Out of the "Afscheiding" some circles developed into Free Evangelical churches. They either remained independent or united in the "Bond van Vrije Christelijke Gemeenten," founded in 1881 and later renamed the "Bond van Vrije Evangelische Gemeenten."[15] Darbyism had already influenced some leaders of the Réveil. During the 1850s the first "Vergaderingen" of the "Broeders" (Plymouth Brethren) were established.[16] The Baptists arrived about the same time and in 1881 the "Unie van Gemeenten van Gedoopte Christenen," later renamed the "Unie van Baptisten Gemeenten" was formed.[17] The Irvingites were responsible for introducing three denominations that carried the name "Apostolische."[18] The Seventh-day Baptists came in 1877 and the Seventh-day Adventists in 1898.[19] Besides, there were the independent city missions and a number of missions that operated within the Netherlands Reformed church.[20]

Formation of the Confessional Parties

Also in social life Kuyper sought the liberation of his "kleine luyden." For this purpose he started a daily newspaper in 1872: *De Standaard*. With the formation of the "Anti-Revolutionaire Partij" in 1879, the first nationally organized political party in the Netherlands, Kuyper would also be their Moses in the political realm. He aimed to give his "kleine luyden" (the people behind the voters) a voice and therefore pleaded for extension of the electorate. Instead of the "Mammon suffrage" he asked for a "householder's suffrage," that is, voting rights for the male householders. Later he moderated this position. The Anti-Revolutionaire Partij was an active Protestant alliance between part of the ruling class, part of the farmers (that in majority was anti-liberal), and part of the urban lower-middle class.[21]

The Catholics would come to a similar political awareness under the priest Hermanus J.A.M. Schaepman (1844-1903). In the 1860s the Roman Catholics became alienated from the liberal party. Pope Pius IX in his *Quanta Cura* and *Syllabus Errorum* (1864) declared war on liberalism, enlightenment, and modern science. In 1868 the bishops in the Netherlands turned against neutral state education. For the first time the Catholic church in the Netherlands took a clear Catholic stand in a political issue. It meant a turning point in their position towards the state and altered their relation towards the Protestants.[22] In 1883 Schaepman wrote a program for a Catholic political party. Although it was only realized in the formation of the "Roomsch-Katholieke Staatspartij" of 1896, it in the meantime made it easier for Schaepman to come to terms with Kuyper. With the extension of the electorate in 1887 part of the lower-middle class became enfranchised. The election of 1888 gave the confessional parties (Protestants and Catholics) for the first time a majority in the parliament. Catholics and Protestants formed a coalition cabinet which produced a new education act (1889) allowing free schools to pass on one-third of the costs to the state.

In 1891 the liberals took power again until 1901. From then onwards it was very difficult to form a cabinet without the confessionals. A conflict between Kuyper and A.F. de Savornin Lohman led to a split within the Protestant side in 1898 that finally resulted in the formation of the "Christelijk-Historische Unie" of 1908. Next to the Anti-Revolutionaire Partij and the Christelijk-Historische Unie a number of small Protestant parties developed.

Awakening of the Working Class

Until the second part of the nineteenth century politics was a matter of a small elite. Up to this time the working class as such was still unknown. Wages were so low that laborers were

simply counted among the poor.[23] Trade unions did not exist.
The laborer rested in his fate, accepting it as the will of God
like he was taught by state and church.[24] The unemployed
were completely dependent on parochial relief, private
charity or begging.

The economic expansion had hardly improved life for the
lower classes. Poverty, long working hours, child labor, poor
housing, unemployment, and alcoholism were common features. The difference between the Netherlands and other West
European countries was not in the life situation of the workers,
but in the way they reacted to it.[25] Most of the Dutch laborers
accepted submissively their miserable condition. Towards the
end of the century, however, a growing labor movement arose
paired with an increasing unchurchliness.

Local labor unions appeared in the 1860s. Socialism, feared
by confessionals and liberals alike, entered when in 1869 a
subdivision of the "International Workingmen's Association"
(1864), better known as the First International, was founded
at The Hague. These most radical workers introduced direct
action (demonstrations and strikes), the doctrine of the class
struggle, and propagated the overthrow of the existing
order.[26] The effort failed due to lack of interest in socialism
and in international brotherhood by the working class.[27] It
hastened the formation of national trade unions: the neutral
"Algemeen Nederlandsch Werklieden Verbond" (ANWV)
of 1871 and of the Protestant "Patrimonium" of 1877.[28] A
socialist fraction within the ANWV stepped out in 1878 and
via the "Sociaal-Democratische Vereeniging" (1878) this led
to the "Sociaal-Democratische Bond" (SBD) of 1881.

Socialism had now permanently settled in the Netherlands.
A number of the first leaders had links with the atheistic
freethinker's movement "De Dageraad" (The Dawn). Early
socialism assumed an anti-religious character that greatly
worsened the controversy with the confessionals. In 1879
Lutheran pastor Ferdinand Domela Nieuwenhuis (1846-
1919) broke with his church; later he rejected religion
altogether, and became a prophet of the poor. In 1881 he
joined the SDB. Under his charismatic leadership large parts
of the working class were won for socialism. His influence was
so great that "drunkards became total abstainers and strong

smokers gave up their pipes, because Domela Nieuwenhuis was against the use of alcohol and tobacco; others became vegetarian, because the celebrated leader was."[29]
Domela Nieuwenhuis and other apostles of early socialism in the Netherlands were idealists. They dreamed of a socialistic paradise near at hand. Their chiliastic message promised a speedy deliverance and became a new gospel for the poor.[30] Universal suffrage was seen as an important means to establish the new order. In the 1880s large demonstrations were held to press the demand. The constitutional changes of 1887 were a disappointment for the labor movement as universal franchise was explicitly refused.

The "social issue" was hotly debated in Parliament. In 1887 a parliamentary inquiry committee visited factories and interviewed laborers, employers, medical inspectors, and others. The same year the report of the committee together with the complete text of all the interviews, numbering 1,100 pages, was published. A general cry of indignation broke out:

> The pretty self-made image that the bourgeoisie had been able to maintain so long, suddenly lay in pieces. Of the calm satisfied Netherlands where no abuses existed like in other countries, where no children were overdriven and where the labourers with cap in hand knew their place—of that Netherlands little remained.[31]

The new labor act of 1889, mainly concerned with female and child labor, was so meager that SDB spokesman W.H. Vliegen commented: "Is it accepted, then we have nothing, and is it rejected, then we have just as much!"[32] Nevertheless, with the act of 1889 the Netherlands was ahead of nearly all European countries.[33]
During this time Domela Nieuwenhuis was the only socialist member of Parliament (1888-1891). He and many other socialists with him lost faith in parliamentary politics and turned anarchist. When the high expectations of a socialistic order were not fulfilled disillusion set in. During the 1890s the early utopian socialistic movement declined, while the modern social-democratic movement came up.
In 1894 the "Sociaal-Democratische Arbeiders Partij"

(SDAP), modelled after the successful German social-democratic party, was founded. The SDAP repudiated the anti-parliamentary agitation of the SDB.[34] Though the new party spoke little about religion, socialism remained stigmatized as anti-religious by the confessionals. For great parts of the working class socialism had in fact replaced religion.[35] Socialism had little success in the Catholic South, where the laborers were used to obeying the clergy, who openly sided with the employers. On the other hand, some priests were much socially engaged and formed interconfessional labor unions, like "Unitas" by A.M.A.J. Ariëns (1895).

Increasing Unchurchliness

During the railway strike of 1903 it became evident how much the confessional trade unions, who did not join the strike, differed from the socialist unions. It also demonstrated a gap between the moderate and radical socialists. In January 1906 a strong central federation of the different socialist trade unions was founded, also modelled after the German example: the "Nederlandsch Verbond van Vakvereenigingen" (NVV). Started with 19,000 members it reached 160,000 in 1918 and 248,000 in 1920.[36] The NVV supported the SDAP in their campaign for universal suffrage that, at least for males, was finally reached in 1918. As the NVV with its moderate program and disciplined behavior also attracted confessional laborers, a reaction from the confessional side could be expected.

In 1909 the "Christelijk Nationaal Vakverbond" (CNV) that united the Protestant unions was founded. The initial interconfessional element soon disappeared. Started with fewer than 6,000 members it reached 28,000 in 1918 and 67,000 in 1920. The Roman Catholic unions were brought together in 1909 in the "Bureau voor de Roomsch-Katholieke Vakorganisaties." By this time the bishops had turned against the interconfessional labor unions. Started with 9,000 members, it reached 69,000 in 1918 and 141,000 in 1920.[37] The main groups of the Dutch labor movement, socialists, Protestants, and Catholics, were now definitively organized. All other trade unions, including the ANWV, declined.

In 1909 the still weak SDAP expelled part of its Marxist wing. The dissidents founded the "Sociaal-Democratische Partij"; with fewer than 200 members it was the first real communist party in Western and Central Europe.[38] After the split the SDAP grew rapidly from 10,000 members in 1910 to 25,000 in 1914. With the elections of 1913 the confessional parties lost 15 seats, while the socialists won 11 seats. The offer to join a cabinet with the liberals was however turned down by the socialists. Their next chance for government responsibility would only come in 1939.

The World War disturbed the general atmosphere of optimism and falsified the expectation that progress had annulled chances of war in Western Europe. The Dutch managed to remain neutral in spite of British pressure to side with the allies.[39]

During 1917 to 1918 supplies of food and goods became scarce. The condition of the workers was desperate. In July 1918 the first elections under universal male suffrage were held. The SDAP obtained 22 seats out of 100; the liberals were left with only 15; while the confessionals altogether had 50 seats. For the first time the communist party entered the parliament (2 seats). Strengthened by the Bolshevik revolution in Russia they demanded extreme state intervention in food supplies.[40]

On 11 November 1918, P.J. Troelstra, leader of the SDAP, made his dramatic error in declaring that the working class was now seizing power. The government immediately secured the support of the armed forces and mobilized their confessional following. With the help of Catholic and Protestant trade unions massive demonstrations of loyalty to state and crown were held.[41] The ideological controversies between the confessionals and socialists were, as in 1903, again sharpened. Though Troelstra admitted his mistake and most of his party members had not supported him in the adventure, the SDAP suffered a severe loss of prestige. For years they kept the reputation of being dangerous and unreliable. It also explains the great growth of the confessional labor unions after 1918. The unrest created did bring the government to quickly introduce universal female suffrage in 1919 (first elections on this basis were held in 1922) and the eight-hour working day.

For the coming period politics would remain in liberal-confessional hands. In economic matters the liberal views prevailed. The sharp antithesis between the confessionals and the liberals of the 19th century softened, while the antithesis between the confessionals and the socialists intensified. The Netherlands quickly recovered from the First World War. Late in 1920, however, a depression set in that lasted till 1924. The crisis of the 1930s became noticeable at the end of 1930 and then gradually worsened.

By 1920 a process of institutionalized segmentation of public life had developed. This process, called "verzuiling" (pillarization), was launched by Kuyper's call for "sovereignty in one's own sphere." It gave Dutch society an unusual heterogeneous character.[42] Protestants, Catholics, liberals, and socialists each created their own social world: from nursery school, via sporting club, trade union, university, hospital, broadcasting corporation, to burial society.[43] Pillarization was very successful among the working class. Since 1920 the confessional trade unions had at least 40% of the organized laborers. This was of great strategic value as it partly neutralized the feared class conflict.[44]

In the meantime the unchurchliness had taken mass proportions. The percentages of the Dutch population that at the ten-yearly census professed not to belong to any denomination or other religious community grew from 0.3% in 1879; to 1.5% in 1889; to 2.3% in 1899; to 5% in 1909; to 7.8% in 1920; to 14.4% in 1930.[45] By far the greatest loss was suffered by the Netherlands Reformed church, which after 1920 ceased to be the largest church. As of 1930 the three largest categories of the Dutch population were respectively the Roman Catholics, the Netherlands Reformed, followed by the unchurched. J.P. Kruijt in his authoritative dissertation *De onkerkelijkheid in Nederland* attributed the mass unchurchliness to:

1. Social dissatisfaction: as the church protected the bourgeoisie, a protest against the privileged implied a protest against the church;

2. Rationalization of economic life: better technology made humans less dependent on the supernatural;
3. Extension of natural scientific concepts: modernism and freethinkers movement caused a spirit of criticism to penetrate the mass;
4. Influence of urbanization: removal of social control as well as churches not being able to cope with the growth of the population, alienated many from the church;
5. Loss of function: modern social life, mass media, secularization of charity, loss of attachment to traditional forms, all deprived the church of its social significance other than being a community of believers.[46]

This pillared society with its fragmented ecclesiastical life and increasing unchurchliness forms the historical context in which the Dutch Pentecostal movement took shape. In the course of this study it will be examined how the Pentecostals relate to their contemporary church and society. First a number of religious streams and developments that are of special relevance for the inception of Pentecostalism will be discussed.

Notes

1. E.H. Kossmann, *The Low Countries 1780-1940*, Oxford History of Modern Europe (Oxford: Clarendon Press, 1978), p. 295.
2. The chiliasm of Da Costa and Capadose was however not identical and should not be equated with Darbyism. Darbyism did influence other friends of the Réveil, who subsequently left and joined the "Vergadering" (Brethren).

    C.A. Tukker, *Het Chiliasme van Reformatie tot Réveil* (Apeldoorn: Willem de Zwijgerstichting, 1981); W.J. Ouweneel, "Het Nederlandse Réveil en het zogenaamd Darbisme"; and Joh. Verhave and J.P. Verhave, "De vaccinatiekwestie in het Réveil," in *Aspecten van het Réveil*, ed. J. van den Berg, P.L. Schram, and S.L. Verheus (Kampen: J.H. Kok, 1980), pp. 189-209; 230-54.
3. Cf. Gerrit J. tenZythoff, *Sources of Secession: The Netherlands Hervormde Kerk on the Eve of the Dutch Immigration to the Midwest*, The Historical Series of the Reformed Church in America, no. 17 (Grand Rapids: Wm. B. Eerdmans, 1987).
4. H. Algra, *Het wonder van de negentiende eeuw*, 4th ed. rev., (Franeker: T. Wever, 1976), pp. 95-123.

5. First the majority of the separatists in 1839 had formed the "Christelijke Afgescheiden Kerk," in 1854 renamed as "Christelijke Afgescheiden Gereformeerde Kerk." In 1854 a theological school was founded at Kampen. In 1869 a fusion with most of the "Gereformeerde Gemeenten onder het Kruis" took place. This new formation was called "Christelijke Gereformeerde Kerk."

6. J.C. Boogman, "De politieke ontwikkeling in Nederland 1840-1874," in *Algemene Geschiedenis van Nederland*, vol. 12 (Haarlem: Fibula-Van Dishoeck, 1977), p. 334.

7. From 1859 to 1889 the number employed in industry increased annually by 5,000; from 1889 to 1909 by 12,000. It is evident how undramatic the development in the Netherlands was when compared with other countries. From 1880 to 1910 the proportion of employed persons in industry rose in the United States from 25% to 32%; in Belgium from 38.7% to 50.1%; in Germany from 36.5% to 52%; in Sweden from 14% to 30.8%; while in the Netherlands it grew from 30.8% to 33.4%. Kossmann, p. 416.

8. I.J. Brugmans, *Paardenkracht en Mensenmacht: Sociaaleconomische geschiedenis van Nederland 1795-1940* (The Hague: Martinus Nijhoff, 1976), pp. 313-15.

9. Cf. Jan Romein and Annie Romein, *De Lage landen bij de zee* (Amsterdam: Em. Querido, 1977), p. 479.

10. I. Lipschits, *De protestant-christelijke stroming tot 1940*, Ontstaansgeschiedenis van de Nederlandse politieke partijen, vol. 1 (Deventer: Kluwer, 1977), p. 22.

11. Kossmann, p. 295.

12. J.A. de Kok, "Kerken en godsdienst: De school als motor van de verzuiling," in *Algemene Geschiedenis van Nederland*, vol. 13 (Haarlem: Fibula-Van Dishoeck, 1978), p. 146.

13. Hereafter references to the "Gereformeerde Kerken in Nederland" will be with "Gereformeerde Kerk" or "Gereformeerd," while the terms "Netherlands Reformed Church," "Reformed Church," "Netherlands Reformed," or simply "Reformed" will always refer to the "Nederlandsche Hervormde Kerk."

14. Lipschits, p. 22. Concerning this aspect of the Afscheiding see L.H. Mulder, *Revolte der fijnen: De Afscheiding van 1834 als sociaal conflict en sociale beweging* (Kampen: J.H. Kok, 1973).

15. J. Karelse, *Zijn takken over de muur* (Utrecht: J. Bijleveld, 1956); H. Nijkamp, ed., *Ten antwoord op een stem* (Kampen: J.H. Kok, 1981).

16. W.J. Ouweneel, *Gij zijt allen broeders* (Apeldoorn: H. Medema, 1980).

17. J. van Dam, *Geschiedenis van het Baptisme in Nederland* 2d ed. (Bosch en Duin: Unie van Baptisen, 1978).

18. "Katholieke Apostolische Gemeenten," "Hersteld Apostolische Zendingsgemeente" and the "Hersteld Apostolische Zendingsgemeente in de Eenheid der Apostelen." M.J. Tang, *Het Apostolische werk in Nederland* (The Hague: Boekencentrum, 1982).

19. C.N. Impeta, *Kaart van Kerkelijk Nederland* 3d ed. (Kampen: J.H. Kok, 1972).

20. The "Vereeniging van leeraren en leden der Nederlandsche Hervormde Kerk tot verschaffing van hulp en leiding aan gemeenten en personen in de Nederlandsche Hervormde Kerk, die om des geloofs wil in nood verkeeren," or in short the "Confessioneele Vereeniging," founded in 1864 to renew the Netherlands Reformed church from within, was active in establishing and maintaining missions. In 1875 eleven evangelists were supported. J. Kuiper, *Geschiedenis van het Godsdienstig en Kerkelijk leven van het Nederlandsche Volk* (Utrecht: A.H. ten Bokkel Huinink, 1900), pp. 559-600.
21. Siep Stuurman, *Verzuiling, kapitalisme en patriarchaat* (Nijmegen: SUN, 1983), p. 134.
22. Ibid., pp. 127-28.
23. Brugmans noted that the "working-class grew up to an underfed, pithless mass, that lacked every knowledge and education and in alcohol abuse found the only pleasure of life." I.J. Brugmans, *Paardenkracht en Mensenmacht*, p. 192.
24. Public schools taught the children virtue, a sense of duty, willingness to submit to constitutional authority, and to accept the status into which one was born as God given. Kossmann, p. 289; Brugmans, p. 194.
25. J.P. Windmuller, C. de Galan and A.F. van Zweden, *Arbeidsverhoudingen in Nederland* (Utrecht/Antwerpen: Het Spectrum, 1983), p. 15.
26. Jacques Giele, "Arbeidersklasse en Arbeidersbeweging in 1887," in *Een kwaad leven: De arbeidsenquete van 1887*, vol. 1 (Nijmegen: Link,1981), pp. 316-17.
27. Windmuller, p. 17.
28. The ANWV rejected the theory of a class struggle and viewed strikes as more harmful than profitable for the laborer. Yet the Protestants considered the ANWV too subversive and formed the Patrimonium. Patrimonium was also open for membership of employers. It defended a patriarchal relationship between employer and worker and distrusted social legislation by the state. After 1890 Patrimonium altered its position in favor of the worker, also because the employers formed a separate union called "Boaz" in 1892. Only then did Patrimonium develop into a viable trade union. Windmuller, pp. 19-20, 29; R. Hagoort, *De Christelijke Sociale Beweging* (Franeker: T. Wever, 1955), pp. 202-04.
29. J.P. Kruijt, *De onkerkelijkheid in Nederland* (Groningen: P. Noordhoff, 1933), p. 178.
30. Ibid., p. 190.
31. Jacques Giele, "Een kwaad leven," in *Een kwaad leven: De arbeidsenquete van 1887*, vol. 1 (Nijmegen: Link, 1981), p. xii.
32. Ibid., 3:294.
33. Brugmans, p. 409.
34. When the SDB was declared illegal in 1894 it was immediately refounded as the "Sociale Bond." After a few years however the SB fell apart. Windmuller, p. 24.
35. Kruijt, p. 191.

36. Windmuller, p. 43; Kossmann, p. 509.
37. Stuurman, p. 183, for statistics.
38. Kossmann, p. 512. In 1918 the Sociaal-Democratische Partij was renamed "Communistische Partij Holland."
39. Kossmann, p. 546.
40. Ibid., p. 556.
41. Kossmann, pp. 557-60; Algra, 3:389-93; Stuurman, pp. 186-88.
42. Kossmann, p. 304.
43. Ibid.
44. Stuurman, p. 149.
45. H. Faber e.a., *Ontkerkelijking en buitenkerkelijkheid in Nederland* (Assen: Van Gorcum, 1970), p. 28.
46. Kruijt also discussed the possibility of relating the unchurchliness to the inborn character, but the conditions for a reliable conclusion were not met.

2 PRELIMINARY STREAMS

Salvation Army

William Booth (1829-1912), born Anglican, was a Methodist minister from 1852 till his resignation in 1861. In 1855 he married Catherine Mumford (1829-1890). At the time Mrs. Phoebe Palmer and her husband conducted revival meetings in England, Catherine wrote her first pamphlet defending women's right to preach (December 1859). On Sunday, 8 January 1860, she, while William was preaching, felt an inward urge to apply the conclusions of the pamphlet to herself and "to the astonishment of the congregation, and not in the least of her husband, she walked up the aisle as he was concluding his sermon and told him that she desired to speak."[1] Since then William shared the pulpit with his wife.

During the same period at Gateshead (1858-1861) they agreed to preach the doctrine of "Full Salvation." With John Wesley they concluded "that the very object of the Atonement was the conquest and removal of indwelling evil, and that the heart could be purified from its evil tendencies."[2] After some years of labor as itinerant evangelist, Booth in 1865 moved to London. In 1867 he established the East London Christian Mission, later called The Christian Mission and finally renamed: The Salvation Army.

Ninety percent of the poor working class that populated the East End of London had no church life whatsoever. Booth's first idea to get people converted and then send them to the churches proved impracticable because they would not go when sent, they were not wanted, and Booth needed the converts himself to help save others.[3] The Christian Mission had in- and outdoor meetings all year round. Prayer meetings at seven o'clock in the morning were known as "knee drills." From the beginning the penitent form (the "mourners" bench of Methodist camp meetings) was used. It provided for public declaration with subsequent counsel and registration.

The first constitution of the Christian Mission (1870) was based on Methodism, but with one important difference: women were admitted full participation, also in government.[4] Soon Booth felt that the democratic system was unfit for his purpose and a revision of the constitution was needed.[5] By 1878 everything was brought under control of one man: William Booth. The same time the new name The Salvation Army first appeared. The form of government became military. Army flag, army uniforms, and army ranks were introduced. William Booth had become General Booth.

The uniform proved helpful in that it did not identify the messenger of the gospel with a certain class of society. The flag carried the motto "Blood and Fire." Blood referring to the redemption in the blood of Jesus Christ. Fire referring to the fiery baptism with the Holy Spirit, which in the under-standing of the Salvation Army was an experience of sanctification. Accordingly the crimson field on the flag typified the blood of Christ (conversion) and its blue border symbolized purity (sanctification). Conversion and sanctifica-tion were taken as two separate crisis experiences. Field reports of the Salvation Army often included the number "sanctified" along with the number "saved." Salvation was available for anyone willing to put his or her trust in Jesus Christ, but could be lost by not persisting in the faith. Booth strongly opposed the Calvinistic teaching of election.[6]

With their rejection of the doctrine of election and with their ignoring of the sacraments (baptism and communion) the Salvation Army would clash with Dutch Calvinism.[7] Regarding the first they were informed by Methodism, while concerning the latter they resembled the Quakers. At first the sacraments were observed, but by 1882 they were aban-doned. Booth saw in the sacraments a source of disagreement and felt they were not intended as permanent ceremonies. For George Railton, who influenced Booth on this issue, there was only one baptism: "the baptism of the Holy Ghost"; and only one communion with Christ: "the communion of a cleansed heart devoted to His service."[8] In time the lack of infant baptism was substituted by the dedication of children under the flag—a practice that (apart from the flag) was later carried over in the Pentecostal movement, only not as a replacement of (infant) baptism, but in addition to (believer) baptism.

Working in the slums of industrial centers confronted the Army with the seamy side of society. Out of this need the social welfare program was born. Proclaiming the gospel went hand in hand with reaching out to the poor. In 1890 General Booth wrote his scheme for social reform *In Darkest England and the Way Out*. The same year his wife Catherine died. By this time the Army had become an international force. The "First International Congress" of 1886 emphasized the establishment of the Salvation Army as a world-wide movement. In 1887 it "opened fire" on the Netherlands, where it adopted the name "Leger des Heils."

Years before the Salvation Army officially entered the Netherlands, reports accusing the Army of Jesuitism or condemning it as a work of Satan had reached the Dutch press. Some, like P. Huet, Netherlands Reformed minister at Goes and editor of *Het Eeuwige Leven*, spoke favorably of "Het Reddingsleger," as it was usually called. Huet defended it against the criticism raised as early as May 1882.[9] The well-known Andrew Murray also commended the work of the Army and it was in his company that P. Huet visited the Army headquarters in London during October 1882.[10]

In September 1886 Jan van Petegem, minister of the Vrije Evangelische Gemeente, informed the general of his decision to establish a "Reddingsleger" in the Netherlands, but on his own terms. His soldiers would wear "R.L." (Reddingsleger) in place of "S.S." (Salvation Soldier) on the collar. "Trusting you are pleased we have started in Holland," he asked for a Dutch speaking officer or for the general himself to come and open the work. General Booth was not pleased and Van Petegem was informed that "only those who are authorized officers should operate in any way under our name."[11]

Before many months Captain and Mrs. Tyler were sent by headquarters to open fire on the Netherlands. On Sunday, 8 May 1887 the first meetings were held in a hall of the "Emmanual Mission" in the Gerard Doustraat at Amsterdam. Gerrit J. Govaars with C. Ferdinand Schoch and his wife

joined the work from the start.[12] After one year of labor
eleven corps had been opened, 3,000 seekers had knelt at the
penitent form, and more than 1,000 soldiers had been sworn
in, while the circulation of *De Heilssoldaat* (in 1890 renamed
Oorlogskreet and from 1897 *Strijdkreet*) had reached 14,000
copies per week.[13] The same year saw General Booth paying
his first visit to the Netherlands. Many visitations with
increasing success were to follow.

The Salvation Army introduced a number of novelties such
as knee drill; penitent form; clapping of hands; praying aloud
during meetings; shouting "hallelujah" or "praise the Lord";
women preaching; joyful singing of popular tunes; use of
musical instruments such as violin, mandolin, drum, trumpet,
and tambourine. Nearly all these features were also present in
the later Pentecostal movement.

The first years were troublesome. Meetings were disturbed. Soldiers were frequently molested. Many times the
police had to intervene. It brought the Army a lot of publicity
and gave them a reputation of courage and steadfastness.
Public repudiation of the Army changed when during the
extremely cold winter of 1890/91 many tramps in Amsterdam
were kept from freezing to death by the Army offering them
hot coffee and a warm shelter.[14] The Army proceeded to
open homes for unmarried mothers and for the homeless, as
well as labor yards for the unemployed. Due to their efforts
for social improvement of the poor the Army gradually
received more respect.[15]

Christian Catholic Apostolic Church in Zion

John Alexander Dowie was born 25 May 1847 in Edinburgh,
Scotland. With his parents he emigrated to Australia in 1860,
but returned to study at the University of Edinburgh during
1869 to 1871.[16] Thereafter he again went to Australia to be
ordained in the Congregational Church in 1872. He married
his cousin Jane Dowie in 1876. The same year, while he was
pastoring a church in Newton, a suburb of Sydney, a plague
struck the area. Within a few weeks he conducted over 40

funerals. Inspired by Acts 10:38, "Jesus went about doing good and healing all that were oppressed by the devil, for God was with him," and Hebrews 13:8, "Jesus Christ is the same yesterday and today and forever," he came to regard sickness as a work of Satan, that could be overcome by the prayer of faith. In answer to his prayers many were healed, which marked the beginning of his healing ministry.[17]

Dowie left the Congregational Church in 1878 to start an independent evangelistic work.[18] One time he ran for Parliament. He attributed his defeat to the liquor interests he had rallied against.[19] He moved to Melbourne, where he organized the International Divine Healing Association in 1882. Separate from Dowie similar ministries of healing were emerging in the American and British Holiness movements around men such as Charles Cullis, William E. Boardman, A.B. Simpson, R.K. Carter, and Andrew Murray; but also in Germany, Otto Stockmayer, and in the Netherlands, W. Hazenberg. Boardman, who kept a faith healing home in London, organized the International Conference on Divine Healing and True Holiness, held in London in 1886.[20] Dowie was invited to deliver an address, but was unable to come.[21]

In 1888 Dowie left Australia for America arriving at San Francisco in June. Some time after reaching the United States he took the title "Dr." In 1893, following a few years of itinerant ministry he decided to make Chicago his headquarters, where he established the Zion Publishing House. He started a new series, his weekly *Leaves of Healing,* from Chicago on 31 August 1894.[22] Multitudes of tracts and papers in various languages began to pour from the presses. Much of Dowie's success can be attributed to the wide circulation of his publications.[23] Remarkable healings attracted the attention of the newspapers and drew many people to his meetings.

In 1896 Dowie founded the Christian Catholic Church with himself as General Overseer. Later on more overseers as well as elders, evangelists, deacons, and deaconesses were added. All offices were open to women, but the only female to become overseer was Mrs. Jane Dowie.[24] The basis of fellowship required of the believers that:

1. they recognize the infallible inspiration and sufficiency of the Holy Scriptures as the rule of faith and practice;
2. they recognize that no persons can be members of the church who have not repented of their sins and have not trusted Christ for salvation;
3. such persons must also be able to make a good profession and declare that they do know in their own hearts that they have truly repented, and are truly trusting Christ, and have the witness, in a measure, of the Holy Spirit;
4. all other matters are matters of opinion.[25]

In the declaration of the constitution Dowie stated, "May this Church be divinely endowed with the nine gifts of the Holy Ghost, with the word of Wisdom, the word of Knowledge, Faith, Gifts of Healing, Workings of Miracles, Prophecy, Discerning of Spirits, Divers kinds of Tongues and Interpretation of Tongues."[26]

Initially Dowie had practiced single immersion for baptism, but after studying the subject again he reached the conclusion that the early apostolic practice of baptism was by triune immersion "into the name of the Father, and into the name of the Son and into the name of the Holy Spirit." Subsequently Dowie was rebaptized by triune immersion in May 1894.[27] From 14 March 1897 the names of the people baptized by triune immersion were listed in *Leaves of Healing*. In 1899 Dowie organized the "Seventies" who went out two by two in the cities and rural areas distributing literature and inviting people to the meetings. Later, in 1902, the Seventies were replaced by the "Zion Restoration Host."[28]

Dowie dreamed of a city, to be named Zion, where the social, political and religious life would be governed by the principles of the kingdom of God. He anonymously bought 6,500 acres of well-settled farm land 40 miles north of Chicago. During the annual all-night service on 31 December 1899, Dowie, at the stroke of midnight, unveiled his plans drawn on huge maps to an enthusiastic audience. Written across in bold letters was Zion's motto for 1900: "I WILL BRING YOU TO ZION."[29] Zion was to be an example to the world, "a city set on a hill." Forbidden were hospitals, doctors, drugs, tobacco, liquor, theaters, dance halls, secret societies, apostate churches, or "any of the curses or abominations which defile the spirits, souls and bodies of men."[30] With reference to Leviticus 25:23-24 the land belonged to God and was not to be sold. Instead the Zion land was leased from Dowie as landlord under God. The lease extended 1,100 years, a 100-year margin for the Lord's return and 1,000 years for the millennium![31] Prior to the Lord's return, which Dowie felt would be by the year 2000, the Christian Catholic Church was to build other Zion cities around the world, then reclaim Jerusalem, and literally establish the kingdom of God upon earth preparatory to the second coming of Christ.[32]

In August 1900 Dowie left for Europe to visit some of the Zion gatherings there. His stay in London was surrounded by riots, disorder, and inhospitable treatment. Upon his return to Chicago, January 1901, he reported that the Zion banner was also planted in Ireland, Scotland, France, and Switzerland.[33] Another world tour was made in 1904, when Dowie left for Australia in February and from there went to Europe in April, visiting France, Switzerland, Germany (Berlin), England, and France again, returning to America in June.[34]

The gates of Zion were opened in July 1901 and in August the first residence was ready for occupancy.[35] Population rapidly grew to about 6,000 by 1906. In order to provide for employment Dowie managed to have an entire lace factory moved from Nottingham, England, to Zion.[36] On 31 March 1902 the new Shiloh Tabernacle with 6,000 seats was opened in Zion. Just as in the other large tabernacles Dowie had opened in Chicago, it had across the front the words "Christ is All, and in All," framed by crutches, canes, trusses, bandages, and braces left by those who had been healed. Dowie often referred to them as "trophies." The words taken from Colossians 3:11, "Here there cannot be Greek and Jew, circumcised and uncircumcised, barbarian, Scythian, slave, free man, but Christ is all, and in all," found realization in Zion. There "neither race, nor colour, nor education, nor position, nor wealth" was a barrier to fellowship.[37] Dowie called for and practiced equal treatment of all races. He published notices of lynchings whenever they occurred.[38] He fought against white feelings of superiority: "The Great God will not tolerate this horrible, disgusting, disgraceful, and utterly unreasonable so-called 'race-prejudice.' There is only one race; but there are many families."[39]

The saints of Zion greeted each other with "Peace be to thee," to which was responded "Peace to thee be multiplied."[40] At nine o'clock in the morning and evening a whistle blew. People stopped whatever they were doing and bowed their head for two minutes of prayer until the whistle blew again. The central place of meeting was Shiloh Tabernacle. Several services on Sunday, starting at six-thirty in the morning, and several others during the week provided for plenty activity. The great Sunday afternoon service lasted four hours or more.[41] Dowie suppressed excessive emotionalism that could be expected in his meetings. He spoke informally, without notes, and had a highly retentive memory. Effortlessly he interspersed long passages of scripture verbatim in his discourse.[42] He liked to dialogue with his audience, but always directed them towards "yes" or "no" or "that's so" and the like. Applause was quite frequent and laughter sometimes vociferous.[43] The communion service was open to all Christians who wished to participate.[44] The city had a unique cosmopolitan character. About 70 nationalities were present in the small community. The use of native costumes often added color to the various church celebrations.[45]

Dowie used the Bible as a code of authority in a literal way. Statements from the Bible were regarded the infallible word of God and the ultimate explanation of any matter, whether scientific, ethical or religious.[46] Inconsistent with his literal approach to scripture Dowie much preferred the gospels over the epistles: "Sometimes I think we have too much written. I almost wish sometimes that Paul's Epistles were lost. I am sometimes tempted to wish that I had more gospel and less epistle."[47] He made a selective use of the Old Testament. On the one hand he used the laws of the Old Testament for society and thus condemned the eating of pork and oysters, while on the other hand he could say:

> Do you think I am going to follow Moses? Not one bit. I will follow Jesus (Amen). I do not believe in that talk about the Old Testament being inspired in the sense I have got to follow

everything some man said was inspired by God. God never said many things Moses said.[48]

Dowie's hermeneutical presupposition that all good derives from God and all evil from Satan brought him to alter passages of scripture that suggested differently. In the case of Abraham intending to sacrifice his son Isaac, Dowie, in spite of the biblical account, did not believe God as a loving father would tell Abraham to kill and sacrifice his son.[49] Dowie eventually came to feel that his *Leaves of Healing* were inspired by God and were in every respect a continuance of the gospels.[50]

Dowie preached a threefold gospel (also called "full gospel") of salvation, divine healing, and holy living.[51] He did not believe all humankind to be tainted by the sin of Adam. Sin was caused by Satan and all people were subject to it.[52] Salvation meant first repentance and then faith or trust in God, yet faith without work was of no value. A businessman, who underpaid his employees, was told, "When you pay your workmen and workwomen a fair wage for their labor, then you are saved and not till then, you wretch!"[53]

As to healing Dowie emphasized that Jesus Christ is still the healer, healing rests on Christ's atonement, and disease can never be God's will.[54] He did not allow the use of medicines or doctors and he condemned all healing evangelists who compromised on this issue. Dowie was careful only to pray for healing with Christians. In the healing room of the tabernacle, where Dowie prayed with the sick, people were admitted by tickets given only to professing Christians.[55] Healing required faith by the seeker: "Divine healing is the children's bread and it can not be given to those who are willfully children of the Devil, for these can not exercise faith."[56] Teaching formed an integral part of the healing process. It included repentance, the forsaking of sinful habits and practices; restitution of all wrongs as far as possible; acceptance that healing is included in the atonement; faith that Christ is able and willing to heal.[57] Dowie insisted upon clean living and often made healing depend on it.[58] He also posed tithing as a condition of God's continued blessing.[59]

As to demon possession Dowie spoke indiscriminately of

"devils" and of "having a devil." His references to devils making people sick or subjecting them to evil habits are numerous.[60] He further taught the trichotomy of man: body, soul and spirit, of which only the spirit is immortal.[61] Dowie believed that ultimately all humankind would be saved.[62] Concerning warfare he made clear that no one could participate in bloodshed and war and remain a member of the Christian Catholic Church.[63] His stand for pacifism seems to have been developed over time. Most likely he was influenced in his thinking by Arthur S. Booth-Clibborn.[64]

One central theme in Dowie's teaching was the "restoration of all things," which he saw against the background of Christ's imminent return. It included the restoration of spiritual gifts and apostolic offices. Dowie expected the gifts to become increasingly manifested in Zion.[65] In his determination to restore primitive Christianity he became more and more exclusivist and authoritarian. In relation to other churches Dowie came to regard all of them as apostasies and perverters of the gospel. He urged those that believed the full gospel to come out of the churches and join Zion.[66] Scarcely an address of his later ministry was free from some tirade against the denominations: "Let me put it simply and plainly. The purpose of the Christian Catholic Church is to smash every other church in existence."[67]

That pride goes before the fall is manifest in Dowie's life. Already in 1899 he had come to feel that he was the "Messenger of the Covenant" prophesied by Malachi.[68] But on 2 June 1901, he proceeded to declare himself to be "Elijah the Restorer." He explained that in the Old Testament Elijah had come as a destroyer; in John the Baptist he had come as a preparer; and now he had come as the restorer. The church was commanded to accept his claims: "I take my commission from God. I stand here and tell you, that you must obey God or perish."[69] The Elijah declaration met intense opposition from outside. Religious leaders all over the world denounced Dowie as an imposter and a fraud. Nevertheless the majority of his following went along with the declaration. For them the rise of the holy city authenticated the position of the prophet. Those that disagreed left, for dissenting voices were not tolerated in Zion.[70] By this time Dowie had achieved an international reputation. His spectacular and money-swallowing New York crusade in October 1903 was widely covered by the press.[71] Finally, on 18 September 1904, Dowie appeared in a highpriestly robe and appointed himself "First Apostle." At the same time he added the word "Apostolic" to the name of his church: Christian Catholic Apostolic Church.[72]

Besides his increasing self-exaltation Dowie seemed to believe that there was no limit to the finances of Zion. In spite of economic problems due to the New York visitation, which cost the church over $300,000, Dowie left for another costly world tour in 1904. When in 1905 he wanted to pursue his plans for a second Zion City in Mexico, the financial crisis was complete. On 2 September 1905, at the end of a service in Shiloh Tabernacle, Dowie suffered a stroke, followed by a second one in December. He left for the Caribbean to rest. On 2 April 1906, while Dowie was still away and now trying to purchase land in Mexico, the prophet was removed from office for reasons of financial mismanagement, "polygamous teachings and other grave charges," by the man he had put in charge over Zion during his absence: Wilburn Glenn Voliva.[73] Voliva succeeded Dowie as General Overseer. The people of Zion had been prepared by him for this move: "Hints as to the inconsistencies in the prophet's life style had been made in sermons in Zion for several months preceding the revolt."[74] When the change in leadership came the majority welcomed it. Although the accusations of polygamy and immorality were made without adequate foundation and were later remedied, the damage was done and Dowie had lost his flock.[75] The unity that had characterized the city before never returned. On 9 March 1907, Dowie died in his home in Zion, a broken-hearted man.

The dream of a city where sin would be destroyed proved untenable. Many Holiness and Pentecostal ministers continued to preach this dream, but, as W.J. Hollenweger noted, "they have lacked Dowie's strength and courage to put the dream to the test in real life."[76] A number of Dowie's followers later became leading Pentecostal preachers in North America, South Africa, Switzerland, and in the Netherlands. How many adherents the Zion church ever had in the Netherlands is unknown, probably not more than a few hundred. During 1904 A.S. Booth-Clibborn was the official representative of Zion.[77] In January 1906 G.R. Polman was to pick up the work left behind by Booth-Clibborn. The deposal and death of Dowie followed by the rise of the Pentecostal movement just about ended the Zion branch in the Netherlands. The message of divine healing had a much wider influence as it was also carried out by other evangelists not related to Zion, which will be dealt with hereafter.

Faith Healing

During the first half of the 19th century the official medical care in the Netherlands was of a low standard. There were plenty of general practitioners, but the majority lacked a proper education. Some could neither read nor write![78] Skilled physicians were few and very expensive. The situation changed when in 1865 academic training concluding with state examinations became compulsory. As a result the number of physicians dropped dramatically during 1865 to 1890, while the population grew rapidly. The shortage of practitioners was particularly felt in poor rural areas. Yet this was not the only reason that great parts of the population hardly made use of medical science.

For most of the working class medical treatment was too expensive. Only few of them could afford the high contribution to a sick fund. But even more important than the economic factor was the cultural barrier that prevented the lower classes from making use of the official medical care. The fast development of modern medical science did not keep pace with the slowly changing culture pattern of the people. The poor and the working man turned to a folk healer, whom they could understand, rather than to a learned physician who belonged to a different class and culture. Folk healing was part of their traditional way of life and the rational-scientific medicine was not.[79] The practice of faith healing that will be discussed hereafter can be compared with that of folk healing. Both formed a protest against the scanty accessibility of medical science due to its practical (shortage of doctors in rural areas), economic, social, and cultural barriers.

The message of divine or faith healing was put forward by a number of evangelists during the late 19th century. Mention has already been made of the American and British Holiness movements and of the International Conference on Divine Healing and True Holiness organized by William E. Boardman at London in 1886. Important for this development has been the ministry of Johan Christoph Blumhardt (1795-1880) who already in 1851 established a healing home in Bad Boll, Germany. The influence of Blumhardt and of Dorethea Trudel (1813-1863), a woman who was very effective in the ministry of healing at Mannedorf near Zurich, created a lot of interest within the Holiness movement and within the German Gemeinschaftsbewegung.[80]

Blumhardt never repudiated medical science. He saw two ways of healing: one by prayer and one by medical treatment. Andrew Murray (1828-1917), whose *Jezus de Geneesheer der Kranken, of de Geloofsgenezing naar Gods Woord* (Amsterdam: Hoveker & Zoon, 1885) was widely read in the Netherlands, also acknowledged the two ways of healing, but preferred the way by faith through prayer as being the only way for real blessing.

The following is a brief survey of some of the more radical faith healers who operated in the Netherlands. Like Dowie they refused to accept that God would heal by "means" such as medical science. All sickness was regarded as from the devil, therefore the only way to find healing was through the power of prayer and faith. Not being healed was seen as a sign of sin or a lack of faith on the patient's side.

The faith healer that caused most commotion in Dutch ecclesiastical life was W. Hazenberg. Hazenberg belonged to a church of the "Afscheiding" at Niezijl in Groningen. From his testimony it becomes apparent how important the role of the devil was in his life. While attending a church service around 1864 led by R. Duiker he received a vision. He saw two classes of men separated by a partition. One was still in the power of the devil, the other was delivered by the Son of God. Hazenberg belonged to the delivered ones and was assured that God would use him to deliver many from the power of Satan. Two weeks later Satan in person tempted him to forsake his divine calling. When he did not give in, the devil on several occasions tried to take his life.[81] Hazenberg started to study theology at Kampen. In 1868 he left for America where he finished his study at the theological school of the Christian Reformed Church and served that church as a minister for five years.[82] He married and had one daughter.

In 1880 he went to South Africa where he did missionary work among Muslims in Capetown. In order to win their trust he issued free homeopathic medicines to the sick. Soon he became convinced that God wanted to heal through prayer without the means of medicines. A number of healings did take place and before long Hazenberg was travelling throughout the country to pray for the sick.[83] In 1882 several letters by Hazenberg on the issue of faith healing were published in the Netherlands by P. Huet in *Het Eeuwige Leven*. From these letters it is apparent that already in 1882 Hazenberg took the extreme position to repudiate the use of medicines.[84] This makes it very unlikely that he had his message from Dowie as assumed by some later observers.[85] Huet continued to publish articles and letters from Hazenberg and others on the matter of divine healing. On a mission conference in Batavia (Java) in August 1885, missionary J.L. Zegers introduced the subject of faith healing which led to his publication *De Geloofsgenezing, hare leer en hare waarde*. Zegers did not doubt the reality of divine healing, but disapproved the radical teachings of Hazenberg. In his book he warned the Dutch Christians against Hazenberg who was planning to visit the Netherlands.

Around 1892 to 1893 Hazenberg moved from South Africa to the Netherlands. In Apeldoorn he founded a home for faith healing under the name "Beth-El." He issued a paper *Beth-El's Heilsbode* and had a number of booklets printed.[86] With his rather American approach in method and advertising he caught a lot of attention. His extreme position that all use of medical science was idolatry found support in circles of the strong orthodoxy and the pious, where he himself originated from, but was heavily attacked by the Christian press.[87] After a few turbulent years Hazenberg returned to South Africa in 1899.[88]

Another propagandist of faith healing was lay evangelist C.R. van Leeuwen who held meetings at Amsterdam. In 1901 he claimed nearly 4,000 healings in seven years of ministry! He published a paper called *Zion Boodschapper* and had a faith-home at Muiderberg under the name "Eben-Haezer." Van Leeuwen did not teach that all sickness came from the devil, but rather that it was a chastisement from God to bring men to repentance. By faith in the finished work of Christ one was healed. He distinguished between healing and restoration. By the prayer of faith one was always and immediately healed, but the complete restoration of the body could take a few years. In the meantime, no matter how sick one felt, one had to maintain having been healed and refrain from all medical help. Doubting your healing and turning to medicines again meant a certain return of the illness and a miserable death.[89] Medicines were only good for unbelievers and animals.[90] Van Leeuwen was acquainted with Dowie and supported him in his battle against the medical science, but operated independently.[91] He was against all institutional churches and each "spiritual joke," but expected his followers to faithfully attend his meetings, even if they lived outside of Amsterdam.[92] In 1910 the Netherlands Reformed church at Muiderberg issued a circular letter to their members warning them against the people of "Eben-Haezer." The warning was published in the weekly *De Gooilander*, to which Van Leeuwen wrote a reply. W.H. Lieftinck, pastor of the said church, responded in seven articles.[93]

It would seem that Amsterdam in particular was fertile soil for these kinds of propagandists. In 1899 the faith healing society "De Goddelijke Genezing" was founded there, seated on the Oude Waal.[94] The purpose of the society, according to the constitution, was to strengthen the faith of the members by holding meetings and spreading the gospel. Another faith healing society that also had domicile at Amsterdam was called "Geloofsvereeniging der Volheid van Christus in Nederland." Since 1899 they issued a paper entitled *Goddelijk Genezingsblad*. The society held meetings at Amsterdam, The Hague, Rotterdam, and Apeldoorn.[95]

In 1918 when Dr. B. Wielenga, Gereformeerd minister at Amsterdam, wrote his "Genezing op het Gebed"(*Schild en Pijl* 1/5) all of the above-mentioned ministries no longer existed. Yet Wielenga noted that the seed sown by these men had carried fruit.[96] The message of divine healing, in a slightly adapted form, was also cherished by the Pentecostals as it confirmed that miracles and spiritual gifts were still available here and now.

Holiness Movement

The North American 19th-century Holiness movement has been an important antecedent of the 20th-century Pentecostal revival. Inspired by Wesleyan Methodism the Holiness movement emphasized revivalism and holiness. It propagated two distinct crisis experiences in the Christian life: salvation and sanctification. Salvation or new birth was regarded as the first act of grace; it meant forgiveness of sins through faith in the redemptive act of Christ on the cross, and receiving a new nature. Sanctification was the second act of grace or second blessing and was supposed to eradicate the very root of sin in the life of the believer. This tendency towards perfectionism met with bitter opposition from the major denominations to which the Holiness movement initially was attached. Donald W. Dayton and others have demonstrated how this emphasis on the second blessing led to a new interest in the work of the Holy Spirit and to the introduction of the term: baptism with the Holy Spirit.[97] In 1870 Asa Mahan's *Baptism of the Holy Ghost* was published. The different terminology involved a shift from Christocentrism to an emphasis on the Holy Spirit, paired with "an almost complete shift in the exegetical foundations of the doctrine."[98] Instead of the usual passages that refer to cleansing and perfection, the most crucial texts in Mahan's *Baptism of the Holy Ghost* were taken from the book of Acts. This development was to be reinforced by the Keswick teachings from Britain.

American Holiness preacher Robert Pearsall Smith with his wife Hannah Whitall Smith accompanied by Moody and Sankey held successful Conventions for the Promotion of Holiness in Oxford (1874) and in Brighton (1875). A small number of Dutch ministers were present at Brighton, among whom were Abraham Kuyper and Pierre Huet. In *De Standaard* Kuyper wrote that Brighton had been a Bethel for him.

The "holy presence of the living God had been revealed to his soul more impressing than ever before."[99] During 1875 Pearsall Smith held meetings in the Netherlands, Germany, and Switzerland. His message that justification should be followed by sanctification and his emphasis on the work of the Holy Spirit aroused the interest of many. Kuyper tried to integrate this message into Dutch Calvinism.[100] However, immediately after the meetings the promoter of Holiness, Pearsall Smith, demonstrated improper conduct and fell into disgrace.[101] This unfortunate turn of events seems to have caused Kuyper to abandon his efforts to harmonize Methodism with Calvinism.[102] His interest in the work of the Holy Spirit developed along different lines and resulted in his three-volume *Het werk van den Heiligen Geest* (1888-1889).[103] Huet continued to propagate the Holiness message by means of his paper *Het Eeuwige Leven* and by revival meetings called "Samenkomsten tot opwekking van het geestelijke leven." J.G. Smitt (1845-1908) minister of the Christelijke Gereformeerde Gemeente (from the Afscheiding) in Amsterdam cooperated in these interdenominational meetings. When Smitt had to answer to charges of unorthodox teaching he left his denomination together with the nearly 1,000 members of his parish and formed a very active Free Evangelical church (Weteringskerk). Smitt expected a new baptism with the Holy Spirit for all Christians, the latter rain. He distinguished between the "work of the Holy Spirit" at conversion and the "fulfillment with the Holy Spirit" as a subsequent empowering for service.[104]

The above-mentioned Brighton convention gave rise to the annual Keswick conventions, initiated by vicar T.D. Harford-Battersby in 1875. Keswick became the center of British Holiness teaching. The American emphasis upon eradication of sin was substituted by an emphasis upon the power of the Spirit for Christian service.[105] To a large extent the Keswick teachers had embraced the dispensational premillennialism of John Nelson Darby, which added an eschatological tension to the holiness message.[106] They came to expect a great world-wide revival, a second Pentecost, to precede the premillennial coming of Christ. The Keswick views integrated and transformed large segments of the American Holiness movement. Important exponents were Dwight L.

Moody, Reuben A. Torrey, A.B. Simpson, A.J. Gordon, C.I.
Scofield, and Arthur T. Pierson. In 1895 Torrey in his *The
Baptism with the Holy Spirit* presented the Spirit baptism as a
definite experience for the purpose of empowering for
service, subsequent to regeneration. Both wings of the
Holiness movement, the Wesleyan wing and the (non-
Wesleyan) Keswick wing, obviously paved the way for the
later Pentecostal revival. Another area in which the Holiness
movement was a forerunner for Pentecostalism was in the
proclamation of faith healing. This message, though not
generally accepted, was put forward much in the line of later
Pentecostals by Charles Cullis, William Boardman, A.B.
Simpson, and others.[107]

The influence of the Holiness movement was strong in
Germany, where it combined with elements of Pietism and
gave rise to the Gemeinschaftsbewegung, which largely
operated within the state church.[108] Books by Finney, Mahan,
Torrey, and by the South African Andrew Murray appeared
in the German and Dutch languages. In the Netherlands the
influence was more limited to free missions and smaller
denominations. A new impulse arrived with the Welsh
Revival.

Welsh Revival

The Welsh Revival of 1904 to 1905 was so extraordinary that
it became known far beyond the borders of Wales. Most
remarkable among the leadership of the revival was the
26-year-old former miner, Evan John Roberts (1878-1951).
Since his "baptism with the Holy Spirit," as he called it
himself, during Spring 1904 his path was often led by visions
and revelations.[109] Eifion Evans described the part of Evan
Roberts as "a ministry of gifts rather than a ministry of the
Word."[110] His address was usually brief and not based on any
one text. Prominent in the meetings were singing, praying,
confessions, and testimonies. "The absence of liturgical order
or formality was based on two related ideas: the universality
of spiritual gifts, and the priesthood of all believers."[111]

The revival influenced the Pentecostal movement in

several ways. Some of the later British Pentecostal leaders were converted as a result of the Welsh Revival: George and Stephen Jeffreys, D.P. Williams, and Donald Gee.[112] Other future leaders of the Pentecostal movement were in touch with the revival. Alexander Boddy was with Evan Roberts in Tonypandy.[113] T.B. Barratt corresponded with Evan Roberts.[114] Joseph Smale from Los Angeles visited Wales. He and Frank Bartleman, who also corresponded with Roberts, inspired believers in Los Angeles to expect a similar revival in their midst.[115] Another significant contribution of the Welsh Revival was its emphasis on a special baptism with the Holy Spirit. J. Cynddylan Jones noticed, "The present Revival, however, whilst not obscuring the doctrine of the Cross, has brought into prominence the doctrine of the Spirit. Thousands of Christians, who had received the Christ, have now received the Holy Ghost."[116] In terms much familiar with the Holiness movement, but with an additional feature of fervent enthusiasm, the Welsh Revival intensified the existing expectation for a further outpouring of the Spirit among many circles of believers around the world.

In the Netherlands the expectancy was fed by enthusiastic reports in religious papers such as *De Nederlander*, *Maran-Atha*, *Jeruël*, and *Ermelosch Zendingsblad*. In February 1905 six men, among whom were two Netherlands Reformed ministers, Bähler and Kuijlman, and two lay evangelists, T. van Essen and Johan de Heer, spent one week in Wales. At London during meetings held by Torrey they met Jacob Vetter, co-founder with Jonathan Paul of the "Deutsche Zelt-Mission" in 1902. In Wales they were deeply touched by the ongoing revival. They conversed with Evan Roberts, who showed signs of overexertion.[117] L.H.A. Bähler described his experience thus:

> Among the wonderful things enjoyed in Wales one thing unforgettable to me is a church meeting, where in one corner was prayer, in another thanksgiving and elsewhere jubilation and singing. It all seemed confusing, but it was not. It was a great forest where one hears all kinds of birds singing and warbling together and yet there is no disharmony. And it was as if I saw a leading of the Holy Spirit from the beginning till the end.[118]

Back in the Netherlands Johan de Heer and T. van Essen were invited by different churches and circles to speak about their experiences in Wales. This led to numerous revival meetings throughout the country. As in the 1870s after Brighton these meetings were called "Samenkomsten tot opwekking van geestelijk leven." Netherlands Reformed minister M. ten Broek in his booklet *De Geestelijke Opwekking in Holland* described the spiritual awakening that followed the Welsh Revival. He saw two streams in the history of the church since the reformation that needed each other: dogmatism and Pietism. The first without the latter would become dry and dead, but the converse would lead to separatism and Methodism. In this context he welcomed the then-awakening as a move of God's Spirit. The blessing Ten Broek personally received he called his "Spirit baptism."[119] As a direct result some missions were formed and the "Nederlandsche Tentzending" (Dutch Tent Mission) was founded. With the help of Jacob Vetter a huge tent was bought (2,000 seats, costs ƒ10,000). The official opening was held in September 1906 at Apeldoorn in the presence of Queen Wilhelmina. The revival meetings were continued in the tent. Netherlands Reformed, Lutheran, Baptist, and Free Evangelical ministers worked together with lay evangelists like Johan de Heer and T. van Essen. In general, however, the Reformed and Gereformeerd clergy had no sympathy with the tent mission.

The intention was to evangelize the unbelievers. In practice those that were reached were for the most part faithful church-goers.[120] During the meetings those who were not certain of their salvation were invited to remain for the after-meetings, where many received the desired assurance. Believers that were blessed in this way were often no longer understood in their own church and therefore longed for fellowship with like-minded people. The smaller churches—Free Evangelical, Baptist, Darbyist, and free circles—were ready to welcome the converts in their midst, thus benefitting the most from the results. Of course this annoyed the ministers of the larger churches. H.J. Couvée, one of the Reformed ministers who cooperated with the tent mission, commented:

I have had so much sorrow from free circles and small churches, who very brotherly pray with you and evangelize with you, but behind your back take your church members, when they have come to the Saviour, away from your church, that although I believe that we will be able to live together in heaven, I do not believe that this is possible on this sinful earth.[121]

In December 1922, when the "Nederlandsche Tentzending" had declined, the "Nederlandsche Christelijke Gemeenschapsbond" was founded, modelled after the German "Gemeinschaftsbewegung." Having learned from the experience with the tent mission, it was decided to work strictly within the "churches of the Reformation," that is, Netherlands Reformed, Mennonite, Gereformeerd, Lutheran.[122] H.J. Couvée explicitly called the "Nederlandsche Christelijke Gemeenschapsbond" a direct result of the Welsh Revival.[123] The "Nederlandsche Tentzending" and the "Nederlandsche Christelijke Gemeenschapsbond" had close contacts with the German "Zelt-Mission" and "Gemeinschaftsbewegung." This greatly determined their negative attitude towards the Pentecostals.

Johan de Heer (1866-1961), son of a blacksmith, was brought up in the Netherlands Reformed church. He married in 1889. The death of his oldest daughter in 1896 led to his conversion. Through contact with the city mission "Jeruël" in Rotterdam he found peace with God. Nevertheless he first joined the Seventh-Day Adventists for a period of six and a half years. P.H. Ritter Jr. in his biography of Johan de Heer characterized this time with the legalistic Adventists as a period of penance and self-chastisement, which satisfied his need to bring sacrifices.[124] In 1902 De Heer broke with the Adventists and became an active helper of the city mission "Jeruël." It was an independent mission, founded in 1894, that, like the Salvation Army, paired proclaiming the gospel with social welfare work. De Heer noticed the lack of unity in song within the free circles to which "Jeruël" belonged. On some conferences one needed half a dozen different songbooks. From the English "Victory Songs" and the various songbooks used at "Jeruël" he compiled a new songbook that

was completed just before he visited the Welsh Revival in
February 1905.

In Wales he received a vision while sitting on the platform
during a meeting. Nearly 39 years of age he was called to
work as an evangelist in word and song.[125] With some Welsh
songs added to it his songbook became an immediate success
during the many revival meetings and conferences that
followed. On one of these meetings Arie Kok, the later
Pentecostal missionary to China who had also visited Wales,
gave his testimony.[126] With the outbreak of the First World
War the evangelist Johan de Heer transformed into a prophet
of the end time. His eschatology was taken from Darbyism,
rather than from Adventism. As of 1919 his "maranatha"
message was carried by his own paper "Het Zoeklicht"
followed by "Zoeklicht" conferences and tent crusades. He
saw his interdenominational work as a fruit of the Welsh
Revival.[127] Johan de Heer was among the first in the
Netherlands to write about the Pentecostal revival at Los
Angeles and Christiana. After his initial enthusiastic reports
the German evangelicals quickly informed him of the alleged
diabolic origin of the movement causing De Heer to
denounce his earlier statements.[128] Nevertheless, Johan de
Heer contributed much to the Dutch Pentecostals by means
of his songbook. From the start to this present day it has been
widely used, supplemented with specific Pentecostal songs.

In summary it can be said that the Welsh Revival led to a
spiritual awakening in the Netherlands during 1905 from
which in the end the smaller churches and free circles
benefitted the most. It also resulted in the founding of the
"Nederlandsche Tentzending," the "Nederlandsche Christelijke Gemeenschapsbond," and "Het Zoeklicht." The Pentecostal movement in the Netherlands, which began during
1907, was only affected indirectly.

NOTES

1. Robert Sandall, *The History of The Salvation Army*, vol. 1 (London:
   Thomas Nelson & Sons, 1947), p. 8; F. de Booth-Tucker, *The Life of
   Catherine Booth*, vol. 1 (London: International Headquarters, 1892),
   pp. 240-47.

2. Sandall, p. 9.
3. Ibid.
4. Ibid.
5. Booth-Tucker, p. 116.
6. In 1852 William Booth attempted to enter a college of the Congregational Church. He frankly stated his difficulty regarding the doctrine of election to the examining committee. The committee believed that after six months of study, he would be able to conform with the body and recommended him to read two books on the subject. On his way home Booth bought one of the books recommended. He had not read many pages before the book was flung across the room. Of course he did not pursue his efforts to enter the college: "It is one thing to forsake Methodism. It is quite another to abandon a doctrine which I look upon as a cardinal point in Christ's redemption plan: His universal love and the possibility of all being saved who will avail themselves of His mercy." Booth-Tucker, p. 74; cf. Harold Begbie, *Life of William Booth*, vol. 1 (London: Macmillan and Co., 1920), pp. 139-40.
7. For an early example of this see J. van Goverdinge Jr.'s lecture presented on the Noord- en Zuid-Hollandsche Conferentie voor Inwendige Zending, Delft, 18 May 1883: *Wat we weten van "Het Leger des Heils"* (Leiden: D. Donner, 1883).
8. Begbie, pp. 461-62. J.H. Gunning J.Hz., *William Booth* (Amsterdam: H.J. Spruyt, 1936), p. 120, attributed the same statement to Mrs. Booth.
9. *Het Eeuwige Leven* 2/12 (May 1882),201-07.
10. Ibid., 3/6 (November 1882),93-102; cf. A. Murray "Het Reddingsleger," *Stemmen van Waarheid en Vrede* (December 1882),749.
11. Arch Wiggens, *The History of The Salvation Army*, vol. 4 (London: Thomas Nelson & Sons, 1964), p. 16. Jan van Petegem was a carpenter who after his conversion and healing had become an evangelist. In 1882 he became minister with the Vrije Evangelische Gemeenten. Together with a certain Van Urk, a chemist at Steenwijk, he founded the "Reddingsleger" in 1887. It was an imitation of the Salvation Army, which in the eyes of Van Petegem was too British. Some corps were started, but not for a long time. The *Reddingsbode* appeared as the official organ for about 13 years. J.G. Muller, *Leven en werken van wijlen Ds. Jan van Petegem verteld door zijn kleinzoon J.G. Muller* (n.p.: by author, n.d.).
12. Govaars was already acquainted with the Salvation Army for several years. In 1886 he met George Railton and helped him in translating the Army's hymnbook into Dutch for use in South Africa. He participated in the "First International Congress" and was made lieutenant the same year (1886) by the general himself. Wiggens, pp. 13-20.

The Schoch couple had visited the Army headquarters in 1884 and 1885. They wanted to become Salvationists right away, but the general advised them to wait until a work in the Netherlands was started. Schoch was a member of the governing committee of the "Emmanual

Mission," which he together with J.J. van Heest and others had founded. The mission was related to the (Vrije) Evangelische Gemeente (Weteringskerk) at Amsterdam led by J.G. Smitt. *Maran-Atha* 6/1 (August 1915),2-4; 8/1 (April 1917),4-5.

13. Wiggens, p. 20. *100 Jaar Leger des Heils*, special edition of *Strijdkreet* (1978), 14, reported 7 corps instead of 11, and 13,000 copies of *De Heilssoldaat* in place of 14,000.

14. *100 Jaar Leger des Heils*, p. 15.

15. In 1892 15,000 people waited to welcome General Booth on the Amsterdam station square, while another 50,000 lined the streets (Wiggens, p. 154). During the five days' visit the general addressed 13,000 people in about 20 public meetings. "Jaarverslag en Staat van Inkomsten en Uitgaven van het Leger des Heils in Nederland van 1 mei 1891-1 juni 1892" (Amsterdam: Leger des Heils, 1892), p. 18.

16. Dowie was enrolled in the Faculty of Arts and studied Junior Latin, Junior Greek, Logic, and Moral Philosophy. Rolvix Harlan, *John Alexander Dowie and the Christian Catholic Apostolic Church in Zion* (Evansville, WI: Press of R.M. Antes, 1906), p. 29.

17. Harlan, pp. 30-33, contains Dowie's testimony in his tract "The Gospel of Divine Healing and How I Came to Preach It"; Anton Darms, *Life and Work of John Alexander Dowie* (Zion: Christian Catholic Church, n.d.), p. 5.

18. As to the reasons why Dowie left the Congregational Church Harlan states, "In 1878 he conceived the notion that it was wrong for a minister to take up a salary and went into evangelistic work, depending upon voluntary offerings" (p. 30). Gordon Lindsay, *John Alexander Dowie* (Dallas, Texas: Christ for the Nations, reprint 1980), p. 45, quotes Dowie saying that the Congregational Church killed initiative and individual energy and was "badly steered and terribly overladen with worldliness and apathy."

19. Philip Lee Cook, "Zion City, Illinois: Twentieth Century Utopia" (Ph.D. thesis, University of Colorado, 1965), p. 14.

20. Edith L. Blumhofer, "The Christian Catholic Church and the Apostolic Faith: A Study in the 1906 Pentecostal Revival," paper presented at the 12th annual meeting of the Society of Pentecostal Studies, Pasadena, CA, November 1982, p. 9; B. Wielenga, "De genezing op het gebed," *Schild en Pijl* 1/5 (1918),9-10.

21. According to Darms, p. 6, Dowie's address was published in the final printed report of the convention.

22. The first series started from California in 1889. Cook, p. 16.

23. Harlan, pp. 4-5, notes that publications of Zion had been printed in German, French, Danish, Norwegian, and Dutch with some little work done in Chinese and Japanese. One tract known in a Dutch translation is "Dokters, Medicijnen en Duivels," translated by a certain Van der Paardt, Apeldoorn, n.d., referred to by Wielenga, p. 9.

In the archive of the Zion Historical Society the author found the following translations of *Leaves of Healing*: in German as *Blätter der Heilung*, vols. 1-4 (15 December 1899/15 February 1904); in French as *Feuilles de Guérison*, vols. 1-2 (15 October 1904/15 January 1906); and in Dutch as *Bladen der Heeling*, vols. 1-2 (1 June 1899/July 1900).

24. Harlan, pp. 2-3. No unmarried man could hold office above that of deacon.

25. Harlan, p. 36. The same basis of fellowship applies to the Christian Catholic Church of today.

26. Harlan, p. 37.

27. Darms, p. 37. Next to the sacrament of baptism, the sacrament of the Lord's Supper was administrated. Infants were not baptized, but instead they were consecrated. *Leaves of Healing* not only printed the names of all those baptized by triune immersion, but also of all the infants consecrated.

28. Volunteer membership of the Seventies involved little obligations. For the Host, however, a solemn vow pledging absolute loyalty to Dowie as Elijah the Restorer was required. Up to this time only officers had to accept Dowie as such. Cook, pp. 266-67.

29. Cook, pp. 46-47.

30. Ibid., p. 102.

31. Ibid., p. 103.

32. Ibid.

33. Ibid., p. 74.

34. Ibid., pp. 301-11.

35. Harlan, p. 6.

36. Zion would be a semi-socialistic city with profit-sharing industries. Dowie viewed the capitalistic system as basically wrong and felt that more could be accomplished by cooperation than by competition. Under the profit-sharing system labor unions would not be necessary, for in Zion a workman was "worthy of his hire." Dowie also opposed insurance as he believed that each man was his brother's keeper. Cook, pp. 125-31, 205-06.

37. Cook, p. 3.

38. Ibid., p. 23.

39. *Leaves of Healing* 15/23 (24 September 1904),803. In 1906 an estimated 200 negroes lived in Zion and "they participated in all branches of the various institutions and industries," Cook, p. 250, quoting from *Inter-Ocean* (Chicago, 7 April 1906). When Dowie was removed from office most of the negroes remained loyal to him (Cook, p. 383), which implies that a large part of the then-no-more-than-300 loyal Dowieites were negroes.

40. Cook, p. 215.

41. Harlan, p. 15. One prayer of Dowie lasted three-quarters of an hour! Harlan found the services wearisome, but was impressed with the tremendous energy of Dowie. For long hours he would have the center of the platform (p. 102).

42. Cook, p. 19.

43. Harlan, p. 189.

44. Ibid., p. 15.

45. Cook, p. 315.

46. Harlan, p. 142. On p. 147 Harlan commented, "There is no matter to such an argument starting with the presuppositions which Mr. Dowie and his people all accept uncritically, unless we can find an array of contrary texts." Unlike most literalists Dowie did not use the King James Version of the Bible, but the Revised Version of 1881. Dowie urged his flock to use this version, because "language was always losing its force, or altering its meaning." Cook, p. 24.

47. Harlan, p. 142.

48. Beaman, p. 31.

49. Cook, p. 26.

50. Harlan, p. 140.

51. Ibid., p. 79.

52. Ibid., p. 26.

53. Dowie knew what the man was paying the girls in his store because some of them were attending the meetings. Cook, pp. 26-27.

54. "God's Way of Healing," often published in *Leaves of Healing* and reprinted in Harlan, pp. 112-13, had the following headings: God's Way of Healing Is a Person, Not a Thing; The Lord Jesus, the Christ, Is Still the Healer; Divine Healing Rests on the Christ's Atonement; Disease Can Never Be God's Will; The Gifts of Healing Are Permanent; There Are Four Modes of Divine Healing. The four modes of divine healing referred to are the direct prayer of faith; intercessory prayer of two or more; the anointing of the elders, with the prayer of faith; and the laying on of hands of those who believe, and whom God has prepared and called to that ministry. (Matthew 8:5-13; Matthew 18:19; James 5:14-15; Mark 16:18).

55. Before praying for healing Dowie always asked two questions: (1) So far as you know your own heart, have you truly repented of your sins and given yourself entirely to God in the name of Jesus for salvation? and (2) Are you determined by his grace to rest in him alone for healing? Harlan, p. 117.

56. Harlan, p. 115.

57. Harlan identified two steps: (1) fixity, or concentration of attention; and (2) submission, and stated that this method "puts the subject in a position of mental submission to the healer as a voicer of God's requirements," pp. 116-17.

58. Harlan, p. 84.

59. Ibid.

60. Harlan, p. 157. Of course the New Testament speaks of but one devil, therefore demon possession rather than devil possession should be used.

61. Harlan, pp. 150-51. Dowie saw the spirit of man as the essential difference between man and the animal, the animal having a soul but no spirit.

62. Cook, p. 35.

63. Jay Beaman, "Pacifism and the World View of Early Pentecostalism," paper presented at the 13th annual meeting of the Society for Pentecostal Studies, November 1983, p. 21.

64. Cf. Jay Beaman, "Pentecostal Pacifism: The Origin, Development, and Rejection of Pacific Belief Among Pentecostals" (M.Div. thesis, North American Baptist Seminary, Sioux Falls, 1982).
65. Blumhofer, pp. 11-13.
66. Harlan, p. 89.
67. Ibid., p. 91.
68. Ibid., p. 37.
69. Cook, pp. 109-10; Harlan, pp. 56-57.
70. Harlan, p. 37. Cook, p. 110-15.
71. Cook, pp. 276-86. Arthur Newcomb, *Dowie, Anointed of the Lord* (New York/London: The Century Co., 1930), p. 395.
72. *Leaves of Healing* 15/23 (24 September 1906). When Dowie was removed from office the word "Apostolic" was dropped by the new regime under Voliva.
73. The letter of resignation, delivered to Dowie by telegram, was signed by Voliva, Piper, Brasefield, Excell, Speicher, and Cantel. Cook, p. 373.
74. Cook, p. 413.
75. Ibid., p. 414.
76. Walter J. Hollenweger, *The Pentecostals* (London: SCM Press, 1972), p. 118.
77. *Leaves of Healing* 15 (9 July 1904),344.
78. Jaap Goudsmit, *Anderhalve eeuw doktoren aan de arts: Geschiedenis van de medische opleiding in Nederland* (Amsterdam: SUA, 1978), p. 21.
79. J.A. Verdoorn, *Het Gezondheidswezen te Amsterdam in de 19e eeuw* (Nijmegen: SUN, 1981), p. 15.
80. K.J. Kraan, *"Opdat u genezing ontvangt": Handboek voor de dienst der genezing* (Hoornaar: Gideon, 1973), pp. 481-82; W.J. Hollenweger, *Enthusiastisches Christentum* (Zurich: Zwingli Verlag, 1969), p. 48.
81. J.L. Zegers, *De Geloofsgenezing, hare leer en hare waarde* (The Hague: W.A. Beschoor, 1886), pp. 42-43.
82. Zegers, p. 42. Many believers from the "Afscheiding" left for America during the second part of the 19th century and with them several ministers including the three consecutive ministers from Hazenberg's church at Niekerk: R. Duiker, G.E. Boer, and H. van Hoogen. *Anderhalve eeuw Gereformeerden in stad en land*, vol. 3: *Groningen* (Kampen: J.H. Kok, 1984), p. 19.
83. W. Hazenberg, *Jezus de Geneesheer of De Kranken door Christus genezen* (Veendam: J. van Petegem, [1893]), pp. 9-11.
84. W. Hazenberg, "Genezen door het geloof," *Het Eeuwige Leven* 3/4 (September 1882),7-72; Idem, "Het leven door ongeloof verkort," *Het Eeuwige Leven* 3/7 (December 1882),115-17.
   Medical doctor I.C. Burkens wrote a refutation to which editor Huet replied that he did not want to take full responsibility of the content of Hazenberg's letters. *Het Eeuwige Leven* 3/8 (January 1883),135-38.
85. B. Wielenga and J.H. Gunning J.Hz. seem to be incorrect in stating that when Hazenberg was in America he was influenced by Dowie.

Dowie only came to America in 1888, while Hazenberg had left America in 1880. As Hazenberg already practiced faith healing in 1882 it is not likely that he had his message from Dowie. It of course remains possible that Hazenberg on later occasions met Dowie and agreed with him on his message. B. Wielenga "De genezing op het gebed," *Schild en Pijl* 1/5 (1918),11; J.H. Gunning J.Hz., *William Booth* (Amsterdam: H.J. Spruyt, [1936]), p. 254.

86. W. Hazenberg, *Bijbelleer der Genezing des Lichaams op het Gebed des Geloofs met Getuigenissen van Genezingen in Nederland* (Veendam: J. van Petegem, [1896]). Idem, *De Tweeërlei Rust* (Utrecht: Joh. de Liefde, n.d.).

87. Wielenga, p. 11. Dr. H.H. Kuyper wrote 4 articles against Hazenberg in the *Friesche Kerkbode* in the period December 1898 to January 1899.

88. *Goddelijk Genezingsblad* 1/1 (1899) records that W. Hazenberg had temporarily left for South Africa on 25 January 1899, but it would seem that he did not return to the Netherlands.

89. C.R. van Leeuwen, *Ziekte . . . . . en hoe te genezen: Een woord over Goddelijke genezing* (Amsterdam: J. Clausen, 1901), pp. 18-21.

90. Ibid., p. 12.

91. Ibid., p. 74.

92. Ibid., pp. 29-30.

93. The complete correspondence together with appendices was published: W.H. Lieftinck, *'Geloofsgenezing' (protest-voorlichting waarschuwing)* (Naarden: Gooische Drukkerij, 1911). According to Lieftinck whole regions in Holland were contaminated with the heresy. The back page of *Zion Boodschapper* contained a long list of fellow workers in the large cities.

Another publication propagating faith healing was: R.R. Posthuma, *De Geloofsgenezing* (Hoorn: Posthuma, 1905), to which J. Beumer wrote: *De Geloofsgenezing door R.R. Posthuma* (Utrecht: n.p., 1907).

94. Wielenga, pp. 11-13.

95. *Goddelijk Genezingsblad* 1/1-1/3 (1899) gives names and addresses of representatives and places of meetings.

An investigation in the publications of the ten-yearly census gave an interesting list of believers who according to the name of their persuasion were followers of faith healing. At the census of December 1899, 48 persons (20 males and 28 females) were counted as members of the "Geloofsvereeniging in de volheid van Christus." The same census counted another 11 members (4 males and 7 females) of the "Geloofsvereeniging van de Goddelijke Genezing." From the total of 59 all but 2 came from Amsterdam. *Uitkomsten der achtste tienjaarljksche Volkstelling*, vol. 12 (The Hague: C.B.S., 1901), pp. 134-35.

The census of December 1909 showed:

	members	males	females
Algemeene Christelijke kerk in Sion	7	2	5
Bethel genezen door gebed	21	10	11
Geloofsgenezing	9	4	5
Geloofsver. in de volheid van Christus	71	37	34

Uitkomsten der negende tienjaarlijksche Volkstelling, vol. 3 (The Hague: C.B.S., 1911), pp. 208-11.
In the publication of the census of 1920 the figures of the smaller groups were not listed. Information obtained from the archive of the Centraal Bureau voor de Statistiek in Voorburg showed 2 females had been recorded as "Vrije Evangel. Gebedsgenezing," and 1 male as "Genezing op gebed." The census of December 1930 recorded only 1 member of "Genezing door gebed."
96. Wielenga, p. 3.
97. Cf. a collection of papers in Vinson Synan, ed., *Aspects of Pentecostal-Charismatic Origins* (Plainfield, NJ: Logos International, 1975).
98. Donald W. Dayton "From Christian Perfection to the 'Baptism of the Holy Ghost,' " in *Aspects of Pentecostal-Charismatic Origins,* p. 48.
Some 30 years before, Charles Finney had already used the term baptism of the Holy Spirit to describe the experience of entire sanctification. John L. Gresham Jr., *Charles G. Finney's Doctrine of the Baptism of the Holy Spirit* (Peabody, MA: Hendrickson, 1987), p. 66.
99. J.C. Rullmann, *Abraham Kuyper: Een levensschets* (Kampen: J.H. Kok, 1928), p. 81. Cf. W.F.A. Winckel, *Leven en Arbeid van Dr. A. Kuyper* (Amsterdam: W. ten Have, 1919), pp. 64-67.
100. Rullmann, pp. 78-94.
101. J.C. Rullmann, *Kuyper-Bibliografie,* vol. 1: *(1860-1879)* (Den Haag: Js. Bootsma, 1923), pp. 189-90; Ernest R. Sandeen, *The Roots of Fundamentalism* (Grand Rapids: Baker Book House, 1978), pp. 178-79; G. Brillenburg Wurth, "De gemeenschapsbeweging en de beweging van Möttlingen," in *Beproeft de geesten,* ed. N. Buffinga, (Culemborg: De Pauw, 1934), p. 178.
102. This suggestion was made by Winckel, p. 67.
103. A. Kuyper, *Het werk van den Heiligen Geest* 3 vols. (Amsterdam: J.A. Wormser, 1888-1889). In this work Kuyper turned against Pietism and Methodism. He distinguished eight separate stages of the work of the Holy Spirit in the life of the believer: (1) rebirth (in Kuyper's terminology the implanting of the ability to believe); (2) preservation of the implanted new life; (3) calling; (4) conviction of sin and justification; (5) conversion; (6) sanctification; (7) complete deliverance from all sin at death; and (8) glorification (2:129-33).
In his discussion of the spiritual gifts Kuyper simply ascertained that the gifts of tongues and interpretation and of physical healing no longer functioned. The gift of prophecy operated in the preaching of the Word (1:244-50).
104. J. Kuiper, *Geschiedenis van het godsdienstig en kerkelijk leven in Nederland* (Utrecht: A.H. ten Bokkel Huinink, 1900), p. 486; J. Karelse, *Zijn takken over de muur* (Utrecht: Bond van Vrije Evangelische Gemeenten, 1956), p. 72.
105. Sandeen, p. 179; William M. Menzies, "The Non-Wesleyan Origins of the Pentecostal Movement," in *Aspects of Pentecostal-Charismatic Origins,* p. 86.

106. Robert Mapes Anderson, *Vision of the Disinherited* (New York/ Oxford: Oxford University Press, 1979), p. 41. Sandeen, p. 179.

107. Melvin E. Dieter "Wesleyan-Holiness Aspects of Pentecostal Origins," in *Aspects of Pentecostal-Charismatic Origins*, pp. 67-69; Donald Dayton, "The Rise of the Evangelical Healing Movement in Nineteenth Century America," *Pneuma* 4/1 (Spring 1982),1-18.

108. For a full discussion, see Paul Fleisch, *Die Moderne Gemeinschaftsbewegung in Deutschland*, vol. 1: Die Geschichte der deutschen Gemeinschaftsbewegung bis zum Auftreten des Zungenredens, 1875-1907 (Leipzig: Verlag H.G. Wallmann, 3d ed., 1912).

109. Eifion Evans, *The Welsh Revival of 1904* (Bridgend, Wales: Evangelical Press of Wales, 1969), pp. 65-68, 77-80, 190-92.

110. Ibid., p. 163.

111. Ibid.

112. Desmond Cartwright, "From the Back Streets of Brixton to the Royal Albert Hall: British Pentecostalism 1907-1926," in *Pentecostal Research in Europe: Problems, Promises and People*, ed. Walter J. Hollenweger (Frankfurt/Bern: Peter Lang, forthcoming).

113. Martin Robinson, "The Charismatic Anglican-Historical and Contemporary: A Comparison Between the Life and Work of Alexander Boddy (1854-1930) and Michael Harper" (M.Litt. thesis, University of Birmingham, 1976) p. 37.

114. Thomas Ball Barratt, *When the Fire Fell and an Outline of My Life* (Oslo: Alfons Hansen & Sonner, 1927), p. 96. Barratt wrote a letter to Evan Roberts on 2 January 1904. One of Evan Robert's co-workers replied with, "We are praying for Norway, Spain, America etc. May the Lord bless them with the Baptism of the Holy Ghost, and your folks as well." To which Barratt in his book adds, "None of us thought then how all these prayers would eventually be answered. The Pentecostal Movement is no doubt the outcome of it all, Hallelujah!" (p. 97).

115. Frank Bartleman, *Azusa Street* (Plainfield, NJ: Logos International, 1980), pp. 15-35. Originally published in 1925 as *"Pentecost" Came to Los Angeles: How It Was in the Beginning.*

116. J. Cynddylan Jones, "Introduction," in *The Awakening in Wales and Some of the Hidden Springs*, Jessie Penn Lewis (London: Marshall Brothers, 1905), p. 6. Cf. Evans, p. 195.

117. Joh. de Heer, *'K zal gedenken* (Den Haag: J.N. Voorhoeve, 1949), p. 35.

118. Ibid., pp. 34-35.

119. M. ten Broek, *De Geestelijke Opwekking in Holland* (Ermelo: Gebr. Mooij, 1905 2d printing), pp. 6-8, 46-48.

120. H.J. Couvée, *Is de Gemeenschapsbeweging nodig?* (n.p.: Ned. Chr. Gemeenschapsbond, 1927), p. 4.

121. H.J. Couvée, *De Nederlandsche Christelijke Gemeenschapsbond zijn ontstaan, zijn bedoeling en zijn beginselen* (Amerongen: Ned. Chr. Gemeenschapsbond, n.d.), p. 9-10.

122. Ibid., pp. 10, 14; Couvée, *Is Gemeenschapsbeweging nodig?*, p. 5.

123. Couvée, *De Nederlandsche Christelijke Gemeenschapsbond*, p. 5.
124. P.H. Ritter Jr., *Over Joh. de Heer* (Baarn: Hollandia Drukkerij, [1936]), p. 14.
125. Joh. de Heer, *'K zal gedenken*, pp. 19-21.
126. Joh. de Heer, "Reiservaringen," *Jeruël* no. 105 (August 1905),3.
127. Joh. de Heer, *'K zal gedenken*, p. 31. For life and work of Joh. de Heer see also articles by Henk Fonteyn who is presently writing a dissertation about him at the University of Utrecht: "Johannes de Heer: Prediker van de parousie," in *Religieuze bewegingen in Nederland* 9, ed. R. Kranenborg (Amsterdam: VU, 1984),30-39; "Johannes de Heer: Een theologisch portret," *Soteria* 3/3 (September 1985),19-22.
128. Joh. de Heer, "Op den uitkijk," *Jeruël*, April 1907 and January 1908. Quoted in *Ermelosch Zendingsblad* 48/5 (May 1907),1-4; 49/2 (February 1908),5-11.

3 ORIGIN OF PENTECOSTALISM OUTSIDE THE NETHERLANDS

Azusa Street Revival

William Joseph Seymour (1870-1922) was born in Center-ville, Louisana, the son of former slaves. Later in his life he joined the Holiness movement and became minister with the *Evening Light Saints*, at that time the most interracially advanced denomination in the U.S.A. In December 1905 he enrolled in Charles Parham's Bible school at Houston, Texas. As Parham, a sympathizer of the Ku Klux Klan, practiced strict segregation Seymour had to follow the lessons from outside the classroom beside the door left ajar.[1]

Charles Fox Parham (1873-1929) had been a Methodist minister in Kansas (1893-1895). Influenced by the Holiness movement, he had left the Methodist church to become an independent evangelist. Since he was healed by prayer from heart disease in 1897, he repudiated doctors and medicines, cancelled all his insurances and started preaching divine healing. In Bethel Healing Home at Topeka, Kansas, a combination of a healing home and a Bible school, he taught salvation, healing, sanctification, second coming, and baptism with the Holy Spirit. During 1900 he visited Frank W. Sandford's apocalyptic fortress "Shiloh" in Durham, Maine, and John Alexander Dowie's utopian Zion City.[2] Parham returned to Topeka convinced that nobody had yet found the true baptism with the Holy Spirit.[3] In October 1900 he opened a new Bible school at Topeka modelled after Sandford's "Shiloh," with the Bible being the only textbook. Parham asked his students to study Acts chapter 2 and to look for the biblical evidence of the baptism with the Holy Spirit. On 1 January 1901 Parham laid hands on one of the students,

Agnes Ozman, who started to speak in tongues.[4] Some days later other students and Parham himself had the same experience. This event became the vindication for Parham's exegesis that a true baptism with the Holy Spirit must be accompanied by glossolalia. By means of campaigns and publications he and his students propagated this message, initially with little success. In 1905 Parham made Houston his headquarters and opened a short-term Bible school in December. One of his students was William Seymour.

Seymour accepted Parham's teaching on glossolalia without receiving the experience for himself. In January 1906 he left for Los Angeles, California, where he was invited to pastor a small, black Holiness church. His sermons on the biblical evidence of the baptism with the Holy Spirit did not square with the Holiness views of his congregation and Seymour ended up directing prayer meetings in the home of Mr. and Mrs. Richard Asberry at 214 North Bonnie Brae Street. During a ten-day fast in April 1906 a number of the prayer group members received the gift of glossolalia including Seymour. After 14 April services were held at 312 Azusa Street where the revival would quickly gain world-wide attention. Walter J. Hollenweger records:

> In the revival in Los Angeles white bishops and black workers, men and women, Asians and Mexicans, white professors and black laundry women were equals (1906!). No wonder that the religious press and secular press reported the extra-ordinary events in detail. As they could not understand the revolutionary nature of this Pentecostal spirituality, they took refuge in ridicule and scoffed: "What good can come from a self-appointed negro prophet?"[5]

In September 1906 Seymour published his first issue of *The Apostolic Faith*. The paper immediately circulated around the world growing quickly from 5,000 to 50,000 copies per number. Excerpts from letters received demonstrate how soon the movement assumed an international scope. Through this paper a little band of believers in Amsterdam, led by Gerrit Polman, got acquainted with the message of the "latter rain" giving rise to the Dutch Pentecostal movement.

The old Azusa Street papers declared, "We are not fighting men or churches, but seeking to displace dead forms and creeds and wild fanaticism with living, practical Christianity."[6] Seymour summarized his message with justification (forgiveness of sins); sanctification (freedom from original sin); physical healing; Spirit baptism (with tongues) upon the sanctified life.[7] Justification and sanctification were explained in terms of the Holiness movement. As to healing, Seymour saw in every sickness a work of Satan and believed Christ would heal every disease: "Now if Jesus bore our sickness, why should we bear them?"[8] Medical help was discouraged:

> Canes, crutches, medicine bottles, and glasses are being thrown aside as God heals. That is the safe way. No need to keep an old crutch or medicine bottle of any kind around after God heals you. Some, in keeping some such appliance as a souvenir, have been tempted to use them again and have lost their healing.[9]

A later issue of *Apostolic Faith* openly taught it was wrong for believers to take medicine: "Medicine is for the unbelievers, but the remedy for the saints we find in Jas. 5:14."[10] Though sickness was regarded a work of Satan, Seymour maintained that a child of God could not be possessed by evil spirits. He distinguished between possession of the soul and oppression in the flesh: "A demon might be in the flesh as in the case of cancer. The devil may oppress the body with sickness but that is very different from possessing the soul."[11] While speaking in tongues was first emphasized as the sign of the Spirit baptism, it was later moderated to being one of the signs, but not the real evidence: "Your life must measure with the fruits of the Spirit. If you get angry, or speak evil, or backbite, I care not how many tongues you may have, you have not the baptism with the Holy Spirit. You have lost your salvation. You need the Blood in your soul."[12] The necessity of a "sanctified life" had been stressed from the start and included the restitution of sin: "The Blood of Jesus will never blot out any sin between man and man they can make right; but if we can't make wrongs right the Blood graciously covers. (Matt. 5:23, 24)."[13]

Seymour saw the Apostolic Faith Mission as "undenominational and unsectarian," and not controlled by any man: "every mission will have its own elders and teachers as the Holy Ghost shall appoint and teach the pure word of God. Every mission will be in harmony and work in unity."[14] Three ordinances were practiced: foot washing, communion, and water baptism. For the foot-washing service (only open to believers) the women and men assembled separately. The water baptism was administrated to believers by single immersion with the trinitarian formula of Matthew 28:19.[15] Women were allowed full participation in ministry: "We have no right to lay a straw in her way, but to be men of holiness, purity and virtue, to hold up the standard and encourage the woman in her work, and God will honor and bless us as never before. It is the same Holy Spirit in the woman as in the man."[16] Seymour believed in the "faith line" for Christian workers, which meant that no collections were taken: "The ones that give, give as the Lord speaks to them and do not want their names mentioned."[17]

The name Apostolic Faith referred to a restoration of primitive Christianity, in particular an orientation to the period described in the book of Acts. The new experience with the Spirit was seen in close relation with the soon return of Christ and urged the believers to proclaim the gospel to the uttermost parts of the world.

Apostolic Faith Across the Atlantic

In this section the expansion of the Pentecostal movement to Western Europe will be traced through brief descriptions of four outstanding leaders in this revival: Barratt, Pethrus, Boddy, and Paul. Special attention is given to the German situation as it strongly affected the attitude of many religious leaders in the Netherlands towards the Pentecostals.

THOMAS B. BARRATT

Thomas Barratt (1862-1940), an English-born Methodist minister from Norway, travelled to the U.S.A. in 1905 to raise funds for the building of his interdenominational city mission at Oslo (then called Christiana). During his stay of more than a year he heard of the Azusa Street events and read *The Apostolic Faith* paper of September 1906. He attended meetings in New York held by Azusa Street missionaries en route to Africa. On 7 October 1906 he was, in his own words, baptized with the Holy Spirit in his room at New York, but without glossolalia. He wrote to Azusa Street and got the reply to keep on praying for the full baptism with the Holy Spirit, that is, with the speaking in tongues. When he did receive the gift of glossolalia on 15 November 1906 he reinterpreted his earlier Spirit baptism as having been an "anointing" of the Holy Spirit, and his later experience as his baptism.[18]

Barratt returned to Norway in December 1906 to become the apostle of the Pentecostal movement to Europe. The meetings he conducted in a large gymnasium at Oslo were the first Pentecostal gatherings in Europe and drew international attention. From Oslo the message spread to at least fifty different places in Norway during 1907.[19] Lewi Pethrus from Sweden, Alexander Boddy from England, and Jonathan Paul from Germany, all came to Oslo where they were convinced of the divine nature of the movement and subsequently became leaders of the Pentecostal movement in their respective countries.

Although Barratt's connection with the annual Methodist Conference was severed in the summer of 1907, he remained a member of the Methodist church and admonished believers that entered the Pentecostal movement not to leave their church. As a good Methodist he defended infant baptism until he changed his mind on the subject in 1913. Together with his wife he was (re)baptized by immersion by Lewi Pethrus in Stockholm.[20] Finally he left the Methodists in 1916 and reorganized his congregation at Oslo as an independent Pentecostal assembly. In 1919 adult baptism became a condition for membership. The first period in which the movement was unorganized and interdenominational had passed.[21] In Norway this led to a strong expansion of the Pentecostal movement. Barratt's own church in Oslo grew from 200 members in 1916 to 1,700 in 1933.[22]

Lewi Pethrus

Lewi Pethrus (1884-1974), a Baptist minister from Sweden, was won for the Pentecostal movement through his visit to Oslo in February 1907. According to his autobiography *A Spiritual Memoir* (1973) he prayed for the Spirit baptism, but was disappointed when no remarkable outward manifestations occurred. Even when Barratt laid hands on him he did not feel anything special. Then he understood that an earlier experience during 1902 in fact had been his baptism with the Holy Spirit:

> My experience dates back to a time when hardly anybody preached the baptism in the Holy Spirit, at least not in the circles I was moving. It took place five years before the Pentecostal revival came to Sweden. It happened in such a way that it is absolutely excluded that there could be any such influence as the power of suggestion. This is particularly true when it comes to my speaking in tongues, for I was completely unprepared for this. I did not quite know what happened to me when under the influence of a mighty power which filled my entire being I began to speak words that I could not understand.[23]

However, an address given by Lewi Pethrus on 26 August 1927 at London seems to contradict his account in *A Spiritual Memoir*. In this address 1902 is only mentioned in negative terms, while his Spirit baptism is dated 1907:

> I was preaching from 1902, but I was in very dry surroundings . . . and my spiritual life went down more and more . . . and so God came in the wonderful year 1907, and praise God I was the first of the preachers in the country who received the baptism with the Holy Spirit and since then I have stayed just in the centre of the fire the whole time.[24]

In any case when Pethrus returned from Oslo he started preaching the Pentecostal message and others in his church received the Spirit baptism with the sign of tongues. Soon he moved to Stockholm. In 1913 Pethrus with the members of his Stockholm church were expelled from the Baptist Union.[25]

From the start the Swedish Pentecostals have placed a great emphasis on the importance of establishing autonomous local assemblies. Although centralization was seen as a great threat and a cause for division, Lewi Pethrus on basis of his charismatic leadership assumed apostolic authority. Remarkable is his absence from all the international conferences prior to 1921 in Amsterdam. His international contribution really commenced when he in 1939 convened the next international conference at Stockholm. At the early conferences Sweden was usually represented by A.G. Johnson who was in Los Angeles during 1906.[26]

ALEXANDER A. BODDY

Alexander Boddy (1854-1930) had read law and had worked as a solicitor before he followed the steps of his father in becoming an Anglican priest. In 1884 he was appointed to a working-class parish at Sunderland where he became vicar in 1886. He married Mary Pollock in 1891, after which three children were born: Mary (1892), Jane (1893), and James (1895). Boddy was an experienced traveller. Since 1876 he made journeys to Scandinavia, Russia, North Africa, Asia Minor, and North America. He wrote a number of extensive travel books and was member of several geographical societies. Martin Robinson in his thesis on Boddy notes, "From the accounts of his travels there emerges a man with a great strength of character, ability to communicate, great sense of humour and breadth of vision."[27]

Praying for more spiritual power Boddy experienced a baptism with the Holy Spirit in 1892.[28] Of equal importance was the healing of his wife from asthma in 1899 through prayer. Mrs. Boddy discovered that she had the gift of healing. Boddy wrote a series of twelve tracts, six of which were later republished in *Confidence*.[29] His theology was of the Holiness type. Boddy visited the Welsh Revival and saw it as a preparation for what happened in Sunderland.[30]

In March 1907 Boddy spent four days with Barratt in Oslo and concluded that the Pentecostal revival was of God. He persuaded Barratt to visit his church at Sunderland. On 31

August Barratt arrived and stayed until 18 October 1907. Every day two meetings were held in the large Parish Hall with after-meetings in the vestry of the church. In his diary Barratt described many exorcisms of a dramatic nature, emotional scenes, singing in the Spirit, prophecies, tongues and interpretation, visions, trances, and rolling over on the floor, that were taking place.[31] Boddy's wife and two daughters were baptized with the Holy Spirit and spoke in tongues, while he himself only received this gift after Barratt was gone, on 2 December 1907. He was the fiftieth person to speak in tongues in Sunderland.

In April 1908 he started the publication of *Confidence*, which soon developed into a paper of international value for the emerging Pentecostal movement. The same significance can be attributed to the Whitsuntide Conferences that were convened by Boddy between 1908 and 1914. During the first conference (6-11 June 1908) G.R. Polman received his baptism with the Holy Spirit. Boddy's visit to the Pentecostal assembly at Amsterdam during September 1908 greatly encouraged the Dutch Pentecostals. In January 1909 Boddy assisted Cecil Polhill in founding the Pentecostal Missionary Union (P.M.U.). Cecil Henry Polhill (1860-1938), the wealthy landlord of Howbury Hall, had received his baptism with the Holy Spirit in Los Angeles. As one of the Cambridge Seven he had been a missionary to China. No wonder that most of the missionaries who went out through the P.M.U. were sent to China and Tibet.

Boddy's influence upon the Pentecostal movement declined during the First World War, partly due to his pro-war stand.[32] The Sunderland conferences were no longer held and *Confidence* appeared less frequently from 1917 on. The Pentecostal movement in England developed more and more outside the established churches, with the result that Boddy, who remained in the Anglican church, became isolated. By 1926, when the P.M.U. merged into the Assemblies of God (founded in 1924), Boddy and Polhill had disappeared from the Pentecostal scene. Their special significance for the Pentecostal movement in the Netherlands will be further considered in following chapters.

JONATHAN A.B. PAUL

Jonathan Paul (1853-1931) was born in Gartz, the son of a Lutheran pastor. He was named Jonathan in the expectation that he would become a minister too.[33] After his theological studies he pastored in different Lutheran churches. In 1890 he gave up smoking and immediately received his (Holiness) baptism with the Holy Spirit.[34] He wrote several books including his systematic *Ihr werdet die Kraft des Heiligen Geistes empfangen* (1896), which was later republished by the Pentecostal movement, and *Die Gabe des Heiligen Geistes* (1896). Besides this he was active in the upcoming "Gemeinschaftsbewegung" and became secretary of the influential "Gnadauer Verband" in 1894.[35] The Gemeinschaftsbewegung was an orthodox countermovement in protest against modernism in the state church. Evangelization and the formation of "gemeinschaften" (fellowships) was energetically carried out. In October 1898 Paul started the monthly *Die Heiligung*, in which he propagated the message of sanctification. During 1899 he moved to Steglitz, Berlin, to become involved in itinerant evangelization work within the state church. In 1901 he joined Jakob Vetter in the preparation of the "Deutsche Zelt Mission." The next year the first tent meetings were held in Mülheim a.d. Ruhr. Articles in *Heiligung* during 1904 with his testimony of a new sanctification, that had released him from all inclination to sin, caused him to become suspect of teaching perfectionism.[36] In spite of criticism his evangelistic work with the tent continued to bear much fruit. Tent meetings at Mülheim during 1905 produced so many converts that a new assembly was founded under leadership of Emil Humburg who came from Velbert. The effect of the Welsh Revival and visits of American Holiness evangelists like Torrey in 1905 brought the longing for a special Spirit baptism within the Gemeinschaftsbewegung almost to a boiling point.[37] When the first reports of the Pentecostal revival at Los Angeles and Oslo arrived they were received with great enthusiasm.

In March 1907 Paul travelled to Oslo and became convinced it was a work of the Holy Spirit. He rejoiced in the manifestation of glossolalia, but did not know whether it was also intended for him personally or not.[38] E. Meyer who had also attended the Oslo meetings invited two Norwegian female missionaries to his mission at Hamburg. Evangelist Heinrich Dallmeyer met the Norwegian sisters there and asked them to come with him to Kassel. The meetings at Kassel started on 7 July and were stopped by the police on 1 August. The unfortunate events that took place at Kassel caused a lasting division between the brethren of the Gemeinschaftsbewegung and the Pentecostal movement. Ernst Giese has demonstrated conclusively that Heinrich Dallmeyer himself was most responsible for the irregularities.[39] Dallmeyer, who was in charge of the meetings, had refused to listen to the warnings of the two Norwegian missionaries that some of the manifestations were not of the Holy Spirit and had to be stopped. Also the plea of Elias Schrenk, who visited Kassel during the third week, to cancel the public meetings and to have private meetings instead was disregarded by Dallmeyer.[40] When the police intervened Dallmeyer left Kassel and declared everything as demonical. Unwilling to take the responsibility for what had happened he put all the blame on the Pentecostals and became their most hostile opponent.

When Jonathan Paul received the gift of glossolalia on 15 September 1907 and openly testified of his experience, the tension within the "Gemeinschaftsbewegung" worsened. Meetings were held to discuss the "tongues movement": 19 to 20 December 1907 in Barmen and 2 to 4 April in Eisenbach. The participants were divided into three camps: the opponents, who declared everything demonical; the neutrals, who felt that a general judgement could not be passed on; and the advocates, who held most of it to be divine.[41]

In December 1908 a Pentecostal conference was held in Hamburg with representatives from England, Norway, Sweden, Switzerland, and the Netherlands. It gave the German Pentecostals a welcome opportunity to discuss the issue with Pentecostals from abroad. During the conference it was decided to start the publication of *Pfingstgrüsse*, edited by

Jonathan Paul, beginning in February 1909. In July 1909 the first Mülheim Conference took place. Articles by Paul in *Pfingstgrüsse* were sharply attacked by Kühn in his *Allianzblatt*.[42] The opponents were no longer prepared to dialogue and called for a meeting held at Berlin on 15 September 1909, with the sole purpose to publicly repudiate the Pentecostal movement. The fact that the movement came from Los Angeles was seen as a certain proof of its diabolic nature. Los Angeles was considered a "rendez-vous of spiritistic spirits"![43] Around 60 men arrived at Berlin, which resulted in the "Berlin Declaration" signed by 56 participants. The Pentecostal movement was condemned as being "not from above, but from below" because it came from Los Angeles; had many manifestations in common with Spiritism; allowed for allegedly unscriptural female ministry; taught perfectionism; and accepted J. Paul as leader.[44]

Friends of J. Paul immediately called for another conference at Mülheim; 2,500 tickets were issued, a number that was never reached on any Gemeinschaftsbewegung or Allianz conference.[45] Local newspapers reported that 6,000 to 10,000 people attended the meetings. A counterdeclaration was issued in which the Pentecostal movement was regarded as a gift from above, not from below, although it was admitted that like in any other movement not everything that occurred was divine. The accusation of teaching perfectionism, which in fact was directed against Paul, was said to misrepresent Paul's teaching on every point.[46]

The Berlin Declaration had made Paul persona non grata so that he was forced to leave the tent mission.[47] The neutrals still tried to bring the Pentecostal brethren back into the fellowship. In January 1911, however, under pressure of their colleagues, the neutrals agreed with a definite condemnation of the Pentecostal movement.

Obviously the conflict between the Pentecostal movement and the Gemeinschaftsbewegung did a lot of harm to both sides. Thanks to the outstanding leadership of men like Jonathan Paul and to the wise counsel and encouragement from abroad, the young movement in Germany survived. The condemnation by the German Gemeinschaftsbewegung was measured out in many publications and had negative effects for the Pentecostal movement in the Netherlands, as it made many prejudiced against all Pentecostal manifestations.

Arthur S. Booth-Clibborn

Arthur Sydney Clibborn was born 12 February 1855 in Moate Contey Sealan, Ireland, in a family with a long Quaker tradition. Converted in 1875 and "baptized with the Holy Spirit" (Holiness terminology) two years later, he became minister with the Society of Friends.[48] As soon as the Salvation Army came to Ireland he joined them, but explicitly maintained his (pacifistic) Quaker views by stating he "could never forego any of the essential truths of Quakerism, and entered the work on that understanding."[49]

From 1881 Arthur Clibborn assisted Catherine Booth (Kate, 1858-1955), the eldest and most gifted daughter of the general, also known as the "Maréchale," in France and Switzerland. When the Swiss government forbade them to hold meetings, they became involved in civil disobedience: "Kate's reaction was automatic: She would test the power of the decree by disobeying it."[50] When Arthur married Catherine in 1887 he, like other sons in law of the general, took the name Booth.

In June 1896 they were placed in command over the Salvation Army in the Netherlands and Belgium.[51] During this time Booth-Clibborn became interested in John Alexander Dowie's teaching on divine healing and the imminent coming of Christ as put forward in his weekly *Leaves of Healing*. When Dowie visited Europe late in 1900 the couple met with him in London and Paris.[52] Booth-Clibborn's involvement with Dowie of course influenced the work in the Netherlands. Polman for instance discussed these thoughts with the cadets in the training school.[53] When Booth-Clibborn was refused the liberty to speak of this "full gospel" which in the eyes of the general was "false and dangerous error," he, with Catherine, left the Salvation Army in January 1902.[54] Arthur immediately joined Dowie's church in Zion, while Catherine, for a short while, followed a little later. A number of Dutch officers, including Polman, stepped out of the Army and likewise joined Dowie.

Officially the resignation of Booth-Clibborn was solely attributed to the association with Dowie, yet other reasons were involved as well. William, one of the ten children of the Booth-Clibborn family, stated his parents "had stepped out on questions of conscience and the advocacy of advanced truth such as Divine Healing, the Second Coming of Christ, and the anti-Christian character of all carnal warfare."[55] The "questions of conscience" might well have had to do with the general's autocratic rule. From time to time he regrouped all leaders in the various countries. When such happened in 1896 his son Ballington refused to leave the United States and resigned.[56] The next reshuffling in 1902 caused another son, Herbert, to resign, only three weeks after the resignation of Arthur and Catherine. Herbert was in charge over the work in Australia where he had pleaded in vain for decentralization.[57]

The "advance truth" of divine healing and the second coming referred to the association with Dowie, but the matter of pacifism was a different issue. In accordance with his Quaker background Booth-Clibborn was a convinced pacifist. During the Anglo-Boer war (October 1899-May 1902) he was stationed in the Netherlands and read the war propaganda from both sides. In response he wrote his book *Blood Against Blood* as a protest against war and the shedding of blood. While in Amsterdam he visited imprisoned conscientious objectors encouraging them to continue in the good way.[58] Implying that the general did not agree with him on the issue of pacifism, he stated that Mrs. Booth felt considerably drawn towards his views:

> It is my deep conviction that had she been alive during the last decade and face to face with its great military developments, and of threatening conscription in England, she would have agreed with the main lines of this book, and also with the definite stand taken by her eldest daughter Catherine, my dear wife, on this question at the time of the Anglo-Dutch War.[59]

In July 1902 Arthur and Catherine arrived in Zion and stayed for four months. Dowie was much pleased to have such highly respected Europeans come to his church, yet within a week Catherine withstood him in public. When the prophet asked all who accepted him as Elijah to stand, Catherine alone remained seated.[60] One day she asked Dowie why he had not ordained her husband. Dowie answered: "It is you that I want, and I will not ordain him without you."[61] At length Catherine succeeded in persuading Arthur to at least leave the city. They lived in Amsterdam and Brussels for about two years, moving to Paris in 1904. During this time Booth-Clibborn was the representative of Zion in the Netherlands and Belgium.[62] Arthur suffered from the effects of a neglected influenza settling in his knees. Initially he refused medical help, but in face of death four operations saved his life, leaving him crippled for the rest of his days. By accepting surgical aid he had violated the laws of Zion and his dismissal followed as a matter of course.[63] From Paris they went to England to settle down in Westcliff-on-Sea, some 45 miles from London. William, their son, wrote concerning this period:

> When the time came for the world-wide outpouring of God's Spirit, the Booth-Clibborn branch of the Booth Family was prepared. We were independent, free from all sectarian bias and influence, not affiliated with any particular part of organized Christianity. Mother was evangelizing in many churches, her revival work proving eminently successful. Father was devoting his time at home to Biblical research and writing. In his studies he had come to the conclusion that God would in the last days of this age, send a great revival that would restore the gifts of the Spirit in greater use in the Church, and whose main characteristic would be the Baptism of the Holy Spirit as received on the day of Pentecost, Acts 2:4. He often spoke of his expectation and watched all activities and developments in the Christian world for its appearance, praying earnestly that it might soon come.[64]

Through Mrs. Catherine Price, who probably was the first Pentecostal in England, Booth-Clibborn had come in contact with Pentecostalism. As he came over sick from Paris he had first stayed in her house.[65.]

In November 1908 Arthur took his son William to several Pentecostal meetings in London. As a result William received his Spirit baptism and spoke in tongues. Most of the other children as well as the Swiss governess Alice Moser and Adele Coulon, former Salvation Army officer who was a second mother to the children, followed in the same experience.[66] Arthur and Catherine both accepted it as from God, but although they longed for it they did not receive the experience in like manner. Catherine went on evangelizing in many churches mostly in France and England, while Arthur seems to have worked largely in Pentecostal circles in England, Germany, and to a lesser extent in the Netherlands. Arthur was a gladly received speaker on many Pentecostal conferences and wrote articles for several Pentecostal periodicals. When the American *Weekly Evangel* in 1915 recommended the American edition of *Blood Against Blood*, Booth-Clibborn was described as "an English Pentecostal brother."[67] Yet, from his own writings and those of his son William it would seem that he never spoke in tongues, which in most Pentecostal circles meant that one was not fully Spirit baptized.[68] This may account for his absence in the International Pentecostal Council that met during the years 1912 to 1914.

William, who accompanied his father on his mission in England, Germany, and the Netherlands during 1909 to 1912, later became a prominent leader in the American Pentecostal movement.[69] Several times he was to visit the Pentecostal work of Polman at Amsterdam. Eric, another son of Booth-Clibborn, lived some time with the Polmans in Amsterdam. He went to Africa as a missionary, but died soon after arrival.[70]

Arthur was not only a preacher, but also a poet. He wrote some 300 hymns in four languages. Due to his illness he had to withdraw from public speaking years before he died in 1939.[71] He influenced the early Pentecostals in Europe, Polman in particular, with his strong emphasis on pacifism, not in the least through his publication *Blood Against Blood*. At the outbreak of World War I the book had a second edition and a third one especially for America. A Dutch translation appeared in 1918.

NOTES

1. For Seymour see Douglas J. Nelson, "For Such a Time as This: The Story of Bishop William J. Seymour and the Azusa Street Revival" (Ph.D. thesis, University of Birmingham, 1981).

2. On Sandford see William Charles Hiss, "Shiloh, Frank W. Sandford and the Kingdom: 1893-1948" (Ph.D. thesis, Tufts University, 1978). Frank W. Sandford (1862-1948), a former Baptist minister, founded his own work in 1893. His Bible school gradually grew into a self-contained village of over 600 inhabitants. Situated on top of a hill, Shiloh's main buildings formed a four-sided spiritual fortress resembling the New Jerusalem. Convinced that the traditional evangelistic methods had failed he was now seeking another way of preparing the world for the last days. He came to see his primary role as the forerunner of the millennial Christ. In November 1901 he announced himself to be Elijah from Malachi 4, about the same time as Dowie did. Parham stayed at Shiloh during the summer of 1900 and was much impressed. Sandford later became disappointed in Parham concluding that he had fallen into a snare of enthusiasm (Hiss, p. 247).

3. Sarah E. Parham, comp., *The Life of Charles F. Parham: The Founder of the Apostolic Faith Movement* (Birmingham, AL: Commercial Printing Co., 1930), p. 48; Chas. F. Parham, *A Voice Crying in the Wilderness* (Baxter Springs, KS: Apostolic Faith Bible College, n.d.), pp. 30-31.

4. Parham, *Life*, pp. 65-68; Agnes N. Ozman LaBerge, *What God Hath Wrought* (Chicago: Herald Publishing Co. Press, n.d.), pp. 27-30. Reprinted in *"The Higher Christian Life": Sources of the Holiness, Pentecostal and Keswick Movements,* vol. 24 (New York: Garland Publishing, 1985).

   Robert Mapes Anderson in his *Vision of the Disinherited: The Making of American Pentecostalism* demonstrated how a Pentecostal mythology is at work in the Pentecostal descriptions of the events at Topeka (pp. 52-57).

5. W.J. Hollenweger, "After Twenty Years' Research on Pentecostalism," *International Review of Mission* 75/297 (January 1986),5-6.

6. "The Apostolic Faith Movement," *Apostolic Faith* 1/1 (September 1906),2.

7. W.J. Seymour, "The Precious Atonement," *Apostolic Faith* 1/1 (September 1906),2.

8. Seymour, "Precious Atonement."

9. *Apostolic Faith* 1/1 (September 1906),2.

10. "Questions Answered," *Apostolic Faith* 1/11 (January 1908),2.

11. Ibid.

12. *Apostolic Faith* 1/9 (June-September 1907),2.

13. "Apostolic Faith Movement," *Apostolic Faith* 1/1 (September 1906),2.

14. "Questions Answered."

15. "The Ordinances Taught by Our Lord," *Apostolic Faith* 1/10 (September 1907),2.

16. "Who May Prophesy?" *Apostolic Faith* 1/12 (January 1908),2.
17. "Pentecostal Faith Line," *Apostolic Faith* 1/1 (September 1906),3.
18. T.B. Barratt, pp. 105-32.
19. Nils Bloch-Hoell, *The Pentecostal Movement* (Oslo: Universitetsforlaget, 1964), p. 68.
20. Mrs. Barratt had already been baptized as an adult when she became Methodist, but not by immersion.
21. Ibid., p. 72.
22. Ibid., p. 73.
23. Lewi Pethrus, *A Spiritual Memoir* (Plainfield, NJ: Logos International, 1973), p. 20.
24. Lewi Pethrus, "The Revival in Sweden," *Elim Evangel* 8/18 (September 1927),281-84.
25. The reason assigned to Pethrus' expulsion from the Baptist Union was that he had allowed other Christians to partake of the Lord's Supper. Barratt notes that "behind this act there was evidently a definite feeling of ill-will towards the Pentecostal Movement." Barratt, p. 178. Pethrus noted in "The Revival in Sweden," p. 283: "the real reason was Pentecost."
26. In the early Pentecostal papers his name is spelled A.G. Johnson, but according to Bloch-Hoell his name should read A.G. Jansson and was later called Andrew Ek (Bloch-Hoell, p. 34). He partook in the Azusa Street Revival at a very early stage.
27. Martin Robinson, "The Charismatic Anglican," p. 29.
28. *Confidence* 2/1 (April 1909),98.
29. Boddy wrote twelve Roker tracts: (1) Born from above; (2) Forgiveness of sins; (3) Heaven upon earth; (4) Satan, devices and the wonder working blood; (5) The Holy Ghost for us; (6) Health in Christ; (7) Identification with Christ; (8) Spirituality denounced; (9) Christian Science, a soul danger; (10) Systematic prayer; (11) The new creation; and (12) Divine necrosis.
30. *Confidence* 3/8 (August 1910),193.
31. T.B. Barratt's Diary, "My Visit to England," p. 8.
32. Robinson, pp. 101 ff.
33. Ernst Giese, *Jonathan Paul, Ein Knecht Jesu Christi* (Altdorf: Missionsbuchhandlung und Verlag, 1965), p. 9.
34. Ibid., p. 25.
35. Ibid., p. 51.
36. Ibid., pp. 84-94.
37. Walter J. Hollenweger, *The Pentecostals* (London: SCM Press, 1972), p. 221.
38. Giese, *Jonathan Paul*, p. 116.
39. Ernst Giese, *Und flicken die Netze* (Marburg: Selbstverlag, 1976). Also: Paul Fleisch, *Die Moderne Gemeinschaftsbewegung in Deutschland,* vol. 2: Die deutsche Gemeinschaftsbewegung seit Auftreten des Zungenredens, Part 1: Die Zungenbewegung in Deutschland (Leipzig: Verlag H.G. Wallmann, 1914); Idem, *Die innere Entwicklung der deutschen*

Gemeinschaftsbewegung in den Jahren 1906 und 1907 (Leipzig: H.G. Wallmann, 1908).

40. Elias Schrenk, *Was lehrt uns die Kasseler Bewegung?* (Kassel: Ernst Röttgers Verlag, 1907).
41. Giese, *Jonathan Paul*, pp. 138-39.
42. Ibid., p. 151.
43. Ibid., p.155.
44. Paul Fleisch, *Die Pfingstbewegung in Deutschland* (Hannover: Heino. Feesche Verlag, 1957), pp. 112-15.
45. Ibid., p. 134.
46. Ibid., pp. 143-48.
47. Giese, *Jonathan Paul*, p. 171.
48. Catherine Booth-Clibborn [The Maréchale], *A Poet of Praise* (London: Marshall, Morgan & Scott, 1939), p. 13; "Eenige bijzonderheden uit het leven van Komm. Booth-Clibborn," *Oorlogskreet* 10/24 (13 June 1896),1-3.
49. Arthur Sydney Booth-Clibborn, *Blood Against Blood* 3d ed (New York: Charles Cook, n.d.), p. 175.
50. Richard Collier, *The General Next to God* (London: Collins, 1965), p. 160.
51. J.H. Gunning J.Hz., Netherlands Reformed minister, who from the start had been very sympathetic towards the Salvation Army, wrote that Catherine had become completely adapted to the grand and lighthearted France, which made the transition to the small and critical Holland difficult. Besides she felt handicapped always needing an interpreter. Gunning found her too theatrical for the Dutch character: "Often she came in a brown penitential garment girded with a rope, bare-footed with a black veil, on the platform." Arthur was "a mystic who secluded himself too much and mixed little with the Dutch." J.H. Gunning J.Hz., *William Booth*, p. 319. Cf. James Strahan, *The Maréchale* 16th ed. (London: James Clarke & Co., n.d.), p. 206.
52. *Leaves of Healing* 10 (4 January 1902),470, which also carried Booth-Clibborn's letter of application to Zion as well as the announcement that his brother Percy Clibborn was leaving the Salvation Army and joining Zion too.
53. Wumkes, p. 12.
54. "Our Loss in Holland," *War Cry*, 25 January 1902.
55. William Booth-Clibborn, *The Baptism in the Holy Spirit* 3d ed. (Portland, OR.: Booth-Clibborn Book Concern, 1944), p. 13.
56. Ballington had become an American citizen which helped the Salvation Army to become accepted in America. After his resignation he established the "Volunteers of America." Arch R. Wiggens, *The History of The Salvation Army*, vol. 4 (London: Thomas Nelson & Sons, 1964), pp. 355-60.
57. Ibid., pp. 362-65. Herbert married the Dutch Cornelia Ida Ernestine Schoch, daughter of staff-captain and Mrs. Schoch of Amsterdam.
58. *Blood Against Blood*, pp. 59-60.

59. Ibid., p. 175. P.W. Wilson, *General Evangeline Booth of the Salvation Army* (New York: Charles Scribner's Sons, 1948), pp. 138-39, combines pacifism, association with Dowie's message, and insubordination with Booth-Clibborn's departure.

60. James Strahan, *The Maréchale* (London: Hodder and Stoughton, n.d.), pp. 271-72. The chapter on Dowie is only present in the early editions.

61. Ibid., p. 275.

62. Ibid., p. 283, speaks of two dark and silent years in Brussels before moving to Paris. The *Schweizer Evangelist* of 7 February 1902, p. 44, reported that the Booth-Clibborn couple had both left the Zion church and had returned to Europe starting an independent evangelistic mission in Holland and France. This report can only be correct with reference to Catherine, but not with reference to Arthur. *Leaves of Healing* 15 (9 July 1904),344, reported the Booth-Clibborns were about to move from Brussels to France to take charge over the Zion work at Paris. In this report both Arthur and Catherine are called Elders of the Zion church, which is in clear contradiction with Catherine's report in James Strahan. In *Leaves of Healing* 15 (24 September 1904),815, Elder A.S. Booth-Clibborn is still recorded as representative of Zion living in Amsterdam. According to the registration service at Amsterdam the Booth-Clibborn family left Amsterdam on 22 December 1903 for France.

63. Strahan, pp. 284-85.

64. William Booth-Clibborn, *Baptism*, p. 13. Cf. Idem, "My Personal Testimony to Pentecost," *Redemption Tidings* 5/4 (April 1929),2-5; 5/5 (May 1929),3-4; 5/6 (June 1929),2-4.

65. William Booth-Clibborn, *Baptism*, p. 26.

66. Ibid., pp. 59-60.

67. "Pentecostal Saints Opposed to War," *Weekly Evangel*, 19 June 1915 and 10 July 1915. Quoted in Jay Beaman, "Pacifism and the World View of Early Pentecostalism," paper presented at the 13th annual meeting of the Society of Pentecostal Studies, November 1983, note 61.

68. *Confidence* 4/6 (June 1911), 128, stated, "Mr. Booth-Clibborn said he had not yet spoken in tongue, and would not be satisfied till he did."

69. William Booth-Clibborn, *Baptism*, p. 2. William was one of the leaders of the "first Southern Bible Conference" sponsored by the Pentecostal Assemblies of the World in 1922. Later he was one of the founders of the oneness Pentecostal group the Apostolic Churches of Jesus Christ, which later merged with the United Pentecostal Church.

   William E. Booth-Clibborn, *A Call to Dust and Ashes* (St. Paul: by the author, n.d.); Arthur L. Clanton, *A History of Oneness Organizations* (Hazelwood, MO: Pentecostal Publishing House, 1970), pp. 18, 30, 33; Frank Ewart, *The Phenomenon of Pentecost* (St. Louis: Pentecostal Publishing House, 1947), p. 54. Quoted in Beaman, note 60.

70. Carl Brumback, *Suddenly From Heaven* (Springfield, MO: Gospel Publishing House, 1961), pp. 46-47, 339.

71. *A Poet of Praise*, pp. 25-26, VII.

4 PREPARATION OF GERRIT ROELOF POLMAN

Gerrit R. Polman

Westenholte, the place where Gerrit Roelof Polman was born, was a "buurschap" (a hamlet with a purely agricultural character) between the Friver IJssel and the city of Zwolle in the province of Overijssel. For centuries this province (in the east of the Netherlands) had been one of the poor regions. During the 17th and 18th centuries the traditional supremacy of the nobility in Overijssel broke down in favor of a growing upper-middle class. This was not so in the agricultural areas, where the feudal structures survived much longer. A decisive position in social life was kept by the land-holder. The farms were for the most part tenant farms, but this situation turned upside down in the 19th century.

Due to a large-scale reclamation program (between 1812 and 1833 the cultivated area doubled!), many were given opportunity to start a farm of their own. A class of independent small farmers developed that bridged the social contrasts between the large farmers and the land-workers. In 1888 more than 67% of all land-users owned their land.[1] In no other province had the self-exploitation of farms grown to such an extent. In a stock-breeding area like Westenholte the situation was somewhat different. The 19th-century reclamation program was of less importance here as, for the most part, the area was already cultivated. Stock-breeding also demanded much capital which made it less accessible for peasants. Therefore the social distance between farmers and land-workers remained much larger than in the arable farming areas.[2]

Halfway through the 19th century the general situation in Overijssel in comparison with other provinces was favorable.

Poverty was low and occurred in the cities rather than in the country. With reference to their Saxon descent P.W.J. van den Berg described the people of Overijssel as religious, yet not of an individualistic, but of a community oriented nature.[3] Protestantism in Overijssel did not obtain the sharp dogmatic character of Calvinism in other parts of the Netherlands. The form and expression of church life was often determined by village tradition. Churchgoing, partaking of the Lord's Supper, and church weddings for instance could be a strict rule in one village, while in the neighboring village it could be a custom not to observe any of these rites.[4]

G.A. Wumkes in his *De Pinksterbeweging voornamelijk in Nederland* (1916) presented G.R. Polman as the son of a farmer from Westenholte, but omitted the names of the parents. Nearly seventy years later, when in the course of this study the correspondence between Wumkes and Polman was found, it became evident that the omission was not accidental. Polman explicitly requested Wumkes not to mention the names of his parents on account of a personal reason.[5] This personal reason was kept secret by Polman even to his children. Now, decades later, it can and should be disclosed as it is relevant to understanding the course of Polman's life.

In the afternoon of 2 May 1868 the 43-year-old farmer Coenraad Roelofs entered the registration service of Zwollerkerspel. He informed the officer that in his house at Westenholte no. 8 at eleven o'clock that morning his unmarried stepdaughter Hendrikje Polman, 28 years old, had given birth to a son named Gerrit Roelof.[6] Fifteen days later the child was baptized in the Netherlands Reformed Church in Zwolle. In the baptismal register the word "onecht" (illegitimate or, more literal, "not genuine") was noted. This mark was not washed away with the sacred water, but left its imprint in the life of Gerrit Roelof Polman.[7] In a hamlet such as Westenholte, with only a small number of farms along one dike, this could not be kept secret. Even more so because it was not the first blot that had stained the Polman family.

Grandfather Antonij Polman (1802-1848), himself also an illegitimate child, had come from Zwolle to Westenholte when he married the farmer's daughter Gerridina Duetman (1807-1866) in the year 1827.[8] Nine children were born including the above-mentioned Hendrikje (1839-1901). After the death of Antonij Polman, the 44-year-old widow Gerridina sinned against local customs by marrying her farm-hand Coenraad Roelofs on 12 June 1851, who in addition was Roman Catholic and 17 years younger! Coenraad Roelofs (1824-1905), born in Nijmegen, then became Netherlands Reformed and took charge of the farm. No further children were born.

When Gerridina died on 23 February 1866 Coenraad was only 42 and his stepdaughter Hendrikje 27 years old. Law did not permit them to marry, but in practice Hendrikje took over the place of her mother. Six children were born, three of which died a few months after their birth. Each time Coenraad Roelofs notified the registrar that another illegitimate child was born in his house and in his presence. The first child, also called Gerrit Roelof, was born 25 January 1867, only eleven months after Coenraad had become a widower, but the boy died in August of the same year. On 2 May 1868 the subject of this study, Gerrit Roelof Polman, arrived. As the stepfather/stepdaughter relationship was illegal, the child inherited his mother's surname. Father's surname, Roelofs, did survive in the middle name: Roelof.[9] In December 1870 Evert Derk was added to the family, followed by twins in April 1879: Gerridina and Coenradus. Gerrit Roelof was only eleven when both of the twins died in their fourth month. Gerridina Antonia completed the family in April 1881.[10]

The population of Westenholte, some stock-farmers, a market-gardener, and a clog-maker, was not poor. Most of them belonged to the orthodox wing of the Netherlands Reformed Church. No doubt the relation between Coenraad Roelofs and Hendrikje Polman was considered as incest and was the subject of much local gossip, stirred up every time a new Polman was born. Under these unfavorable circumstances Gerrit Roelof had to find his way in life.

As all farmers Coenraad was very occupied with his work and Hendrikje cared for the house. Once every Sunday they dutifully went to the Netherlands Reformed Church in Zwolle, about an hour's walk from Westenholte. It seems that the church attendance was more the effort of Hendrikje than that of Coenraad.[11]

Gerrit Roelof's formal education was limited to the elementary school. During the harvest (June till September) he most probably had to remain at home to look after the other children or to work in the fields. After reaching the age of twelve the children were usually taken from school and trained further on the farm.[12] Helping his father on the farm kept him busy most of the year. During the long winter evenings he enjoyed skittle playing, ice-skating, playing cards, and visiting the circus or fair with his friends as well as smoking cigars and drinking liquor. Once he went to the theatre, but the play "The Green Devil" made such an awful impression on him he never returned there.[13] Through the church's Sunday school and during the winter months' catechism under Jan Vermeer, he gained knowledge of the traditional Netherlands Reformed faith. In his teens he was a member of the church young men's society and as such assisted in teaching the Sunday-school classes. Besides this he participated in a Christian choral society that practiced in a home at Westenholte.[14]

At the invitation of the choir, the evangelist Linthout from Zwolle started coming to Westenholte to preach there every week. Gerrit much respected the evangelist, who spoke with great conviction about the eternal life and called for a personal decision. Inwardly Gerrit had always believed in the existence of heaven and hell. As he lacked all assurance of reaching heaven the thought of death and hell made him tremble and kept him awake many a night. No wonder that the sermons of the evangelist made him feel uneasy. The following is taken from an interview when Gerrit was an officer with the Salvation Army in 1894:

Once I had made a positive arrangement with friends and girlfriends to go to the fair together. On the evening of the appointment there was also a meeting with the evangelist. The whole day I did not know what to do! Fair or Mission? I went to the fair, but . . . felt very miserable the entire evening, and was definitely an obstacle for the others. I only came to some rest, when I made a firm decision never to do such a thing again. When I came home that night, my mother said: "The evangelist has prayed for you." I was afraid to go to him, but

I went anyway and became more and more convinced. What perhaps distinguished me from any other soul in these meetings was that I felt a certain need to express that I wanted to give myself to the Lord. Sometimes I got up halfway from my chair determined to express it this time, but . . . the presence of friends and relatives made me sit back again and decide to pray at home. However, this never brought me the full deliverance. The devil always told me, that such a thing does not go that fast. I struggled again a full month, until I at last after hearing a testimony of the evangelist (a real Salvation Army testimony, I would say now), I came to a decision for myself, although I can not claim to have been converted at that time. Converted I became. . . .

[Interviewer:] "Yes, tell us, how that happened!"

Well, I knew then for certain that I needed to become converted, but . . . the devil still tried to always make me believe, that it did not happen at once. I was busy working in the garden, suddenly I got the conviction, that the devil was lying: I threw my tools away, went inside, and locked myself up in my room. I did not want to get up, before I was convinced that I was converted. I struggled with God, . . . and I got up as a born again youngster. I was then about 20 years old.[15]

From this interview and from the description by Wumkes it becomes evident that the conversion was preceded by a time of spiritual struggle. During this time the evangelist showed special interest in Gerrit and prayed for him when he was absent. The quick way of escape he offered in the style of American and English revival evangelists was attractive, but not conforming to Polman's reformed upbringing. Polman's Calvinistic background is revealed in his prayer, noted by Wumkes, that he one day might also be converted.[16] Also the constantly reappearing thought that conversion does not come that easily is along the same lines. When he later attributes this thought to the devil, he speaks as a Salvationist.

The conversion experience, which Wumkes dated on his twentieth birthday, was a dramatic turning point in Polman's life. Finally he received the peace and rest he had longed for. Great was his deliverance. He, who was marked "illegitimate" from the day he was born, from now on knew he was a "legitimate" child of God. It also led to a more individualistic orientation of religion, that was later strengthened when he joined the Salvation Army. Immediately after his conversion he told his family and friends of the salvation he had found in Jesus Christ. Hendrikje, his mother, encouraged him to start praying aloud before dinner. That same month, May 1888, Gerrit had to join the army.

The conscription, introduced by Napoleon in 1810 and further developed by law in 1861, required registration for all the 18-year-olds, followed by drawing of lots for the 19-year-olds and finally enrolment for the conscripted 20-year-olds. Thanks to this registration the following personal description of Gerrit has been preserved. He was of average size (1.72 m.), had an oval face with a large nose and large mouth, grey eyes, and curly fair hair.[17] Later in life he grew a moustache and chin-beard. In the same register Hendrikje Polman appears as both mother and guardian of the new recruit.

On 9 May 1888 Gerrit Roelof Polman joined the fifth regiment infantry at Nijmegen. Out of his familiar environment he at first did not dare to openly testify of his faith, which in turn made him feel unhappy. Once his parents sent him a paper from the Salvation Army that had just started in the Netherlands. Out of fear of being considered a Salvationist by his comrades, he requested his parents not to do so again. Back in Westenholte for Christmas leave he made his first visit with some friends to a Salvation Army meeting in Oldenbroek. They walked five hours during the night arriving at seven o'clock in the morning. The meeting at ten-thirty meant a lot to Gerrit as he gave his first testimony in public. Released from his fear, he began to evangelize his mates in the army, who mockingly called him a tinny parson.[18]

After ten months of national service Polman returned home equipped with firmness and boldness. The Salvation Army had now come to Kampen and of course Polman went to the meetings. He remained in the rear with a cigar behind his back. The officer informed him that smoking was not allowed. Polman, much ashamed, twice assured the officer that he was not smoking, but only letting the cigar go out![19]

In the same spirit as the Salvation Army Polman evangelized in Westenholte with some friends. Next they hired a stable in Zwolle and held meetings on Saturday nights. No longer did Polman go to church on Sunday, but instead evangelized in parks and on streets in Zwolle. Some drunkards were converted and brought to the meetings. When the Salvation Army started a corps at Zwolle Polman immediately became a soldier. Although he much enjoyed the work on the farm, an inner conviction of being called for a different service matured in him. As eldest son he was supposed to take over the farm, and after initial objection, his parents in the end agreed that he should join the ranks of the Salvation Army. His brother Evert Derk took his place on the farm. Of his farewell, in November 1891, we are informed: "Never will I forget, how, when I left, my friends called after me as a farewell cry: *Be true.* I have never forgotten it and I never will."[20]

Joining the Ranks of The Salvation Army

In November 1891 Gerrit Roelof Polman left Westenholte for the Salvation Army training school at Rotterdam. The school was certainly not intended for academic education. Mrs. Booth had made clear:

> . . . that it would be just as sensible to spend the time and exhaust the energies of the apprentice intended to build houses in studying the problems of astronomy, as to teach men and women destined for spiritual warfare dead languages and a great deal of other useless lumber, commonly imposed upon students for the ministry.[21]

The main object of the Army training school was to learn how to make converts: "We say teach the builder how to build houses, the shoemaker how to make shoes, and a soul-winner HOW TO WIN SOULS."[22]

During the morning hours the cadets were taught the Bible; Doctrine of the Salvation Army; Orders and Regulations for Officers; Corps Administration; Reading; Writing; and "the further rudiments belonging to every good education."[23] The latter probably referred to scrubbing and cleaning. No doubt *Orders and Regulations for Soldiers of the Salvation Army* containing "64 pages of red-hot truth and wise counsel" by General Booth, published in May 1890, along with his *In Darkest England and the Way Out*, of which a Dutch translation became available during 1891, was closely read.[24] During the afternoons the cadets went two by two visiting slums or new converts and selling the *Oorlogskreet*. In the evenings meetings were held.

The meetings usually drew a motley crowd of young and old, serious and not-serious. The more removed from the platform, the more noise and mocking was heard. The officer in charge had the difficult task to keep the people amused and at the same time lead sinners to salvation and collect good offerings. Songs, testimonies, and prayers, interspersed with several collections and all kinds of interruptions from the audience, led to a Bible reading and a short sermon. W. van Nes stated, "Usually the captain has the common sense not to explain what he himself does not understand and not to say what he himself does not know and therefore his sermon is mostly not in the least related to what he has just read."[25] According to Van Nes' description the sermon generally came down to:

> My dear friends, that which I have just read to you is very beautiful and very true, but you cannot do anything with it, if you are not saved. Are you saved? I am saved. You can be saved. Here and now! Do you want to? If you do not want to be saved, you will go to hell and if you are saved now, you can, even if you die tonight, calmly await your death, your place is then in heaven.[26]

Circumstances for the Salvation Army officers were very poor. Each corps had to pay for its own costs. In 1892 the weekly salaries for an unmarried male lieutenant was $f7.00$ and for a captain $f8.00$. For females the figures were respectively $f5.00$ and $f6.00$. These salaries were, however, seldom reached as all other expenses, like rent, heating and light, had to be paid first. In some corps the officers could spend an average of only $f0.90$ per week for food.[27]

Furthermore the officers had to pay for the number of *Oorlogskreet* they were responsible for, whether they sold them or not.[28]

After six months of training Polman was made lieutenant and in April 1892 assigned to Arnhem. The further training he received there from Captain Jacob G. Brouwer, he described as laying the practical and spiritual foundation of all he ever had been or would be.[29] From there he went to Groningen (June 1892). A life of constantly moving, typical for the Salvation Army, commenced. After Groningen Polman was promoted to captain and sent to, consecutively, Den Helder (August 1892), Haarlem (February 1893), Amsterdam (October 1893, corps Bloemgracht), Arnhem (May 1894), The Hague (September 1894), Amsterdam (June 1895, corps Gerard Doustraat), Utrecht (February 1896), and Rotterdam (March 1897). While at The Hague, at the time the largest corps in the Netherlands, Captain Polman was interviewed for the *Oorlogskreet*. On 1 December 1894 a three-page article entitled "Onze Strijders in het Veld," including his photo, appeared with many details of his childhood, conversion, and contact with the Salvation Army.

In March 1897 Polman moved from Utrecht to Rotterdam, where he married Officer Maria Adriana Helena Brinkman on 3 June of the same year. Maria, a daughter of Johan Hendricus Brinkman and Hendrina Neeltje Everdina Helmers, was born 14 September 1859 at Amsterdam. Four Salvation Army officers witnessed the ceremony among whom were 26-year-old Melchior Diederik Voskuil and 43-year-old Gerrit de Wilde. Both of them would later leave the Salvation Army and cross the path of Polman again.[30] Maria Brinkman was a trained nurse and had been directress of a nursing home at The Hague before she joined the Army. Thus she was cut out to become matron of the new Army's nursing home at Amsterdam: "God brought her into our ranks and as to capability she is certainly equal to her task."[31] She felt that the sickbed provided excellent opportunities to lead souls to salvation. When W. van Nes in 1896 wanted to demonstrate how the Salvation Army disregarded knowledge, he quoted this same Captain Brinkman saying, "Knowledge is purposeless; the soul of professors sometimes goes lost!"[32] That a woman of her education could become such a good Salvationist surprised Van Nes and he added, "We hope for the sick, that she is not too consistent in applying her principles with nursing."[33]

In September 1897 Polman became governor over the Army's land colony at Lunteren near Ede. The land colony was founded in October 1895 as a result of a special meeting held at Amsterdam, where the general had described his plan for social reform.[34] The farm on the land colony was used as training ground for the rehabilitation of discharged prisoners and tramps from the Army's shelters. Polman's farming background served him well, but new was the extensive administration he had to manage: "Adjutant Polman, the officer in command, is in every respect equal to his task. His thorough knowledge of farming enables him to bring the colony to prosperity, while his spiritual influence is a great blessing for the men."[35]

After two years death twice visited the young Polman family. On 30 September 1899 a boy was born dead and four weeks later, on 29 October 1899, Mrs. Polman died of pneumonia. In the weeks before her death Captain Polman fervently believed in God for healing, but in the end had to resign to the inevitable.[36] The funeral on 1 November 1899 at Barneveld, attended by 200 to 300 persons, was led by commissioner A.S. Booth-Clibborn and his wife Catherine Booth.[37]

In June 1900 Polman left the land colony for Groningen (corps Poelestraat), but after eight months was transferred to Amsterdam, where he was put in charge over the male training school (February 1901). For about a year he taught in Orders and Regulations of the Army, Bible, and Geography.

G.A. Wumkes in *De Pinksterbeweging voornamelijk in Nederland* (1916) wrote: "Under all these changes he remained free of the slavish fear of superiors that the firm discipline of the Salvation Army works out in many a heart. He had always, under all chastisement, felt a strong urge for independence, and this one day led to a rupture."[38]

The immediate cause for Polman's departure was the resignation of the Booth-Clibborn couple in January 1902. The resignation of such prominent leaders brought a great tension in the Dutch Salvation Army. All officers had to renew their promise of loyalty to the Army. Polman refused and was transferred to Arnhem. After a few weeks he resigned by wire.

Wilhelmine J.M. Blekkink

Wilhelmine Johanna Marie Blekkink, hereafter called Wilhelmine, was born on 21 March 1878 at Wonosobo on Java in the Dutch Indies, where her father was a school-teacher. Hendricus Sophinus Blekkink (1848-1900), son of a tailor, was married in 1875 to Maria Henriette Wanrooy (1854-1886), daughter of house-painter Bernardus Johannes Wanrooy (1818-1885) and Wilhelmina Johanna Huetink (1832-1932).[39] Immediately after the marriage the couple had moved to the Dutch Indies where six children were born. First a son, called Gerrit, then five girls: Wilhelmine, Isabella, Louise, Marie, and Johanna.[40]

Hendricus Blekkink was head-master at the "Europeesche lagere school" at Wonosobo (Middle Java). It was a seven-year elementary school basically meant for Dutch children. For the Indonesian children the government had created the "Inlandsche scholen" with a three-year elementary program in the mother tongue. Unlike other colonial powers (Portugal, Spain, and to a lesser extent, France and England) the Dutch did not force their language and customs on the native population. In 1848 it was decided that all elementary education was to be in the mother tongue of the natives. This meant that every language area needed its own reading material. Children who could cope with the Dutch language, which in practice were only those from the upper layers of the Indonesian population, were permitted to attend "Europeesche lagere school" if they so desired. All secondary education was strictly in the Dutch language.[41]

In 1886 when the family Blekkink was on furlough in Holland the mother died. The father was remarried in 1887 to Johanna Helena Everdina Hendrika van Eysden (1858-1942), a niece of his first wife. The same year they all returned to the Dutch Indies except for Gerrit, the only son, who stayed behind for further study. From the second marriage three children were born. Blekkink was transferred to Kendal and in 1892 to Pasuruan (East Java).

In Pasuruan they lived in a huge house with a swimming pool which was known as the haunted house. It is said that this house was the model for the psychological Indian novel *De Stille Kracht* by Louis Couperus published in 1900. In this novel the leading character Otto van Oudijck does not believe the stories about the occult forces that are so widespread in the Dutch Indies. In the end, however, he has to capitulate to the silent powers present in his house.[42] Blekkink, a big and very down-to-earth man, also refused to give way to the silent forces in his home, but unlike Otto van Oudijck he resisted. After a few years the manifestations, like vases floating in the air or stones coming through the ceiling, suddenly stopped.[43] Due to a liver disease Blekkink with his family retired to Holland in May 1898 and lived at Winschoten, the place where he was born, until he died on 8 May 1900. Of his second wife it is said that she was so much of a "stepmother" to the older girls that they left the house as soon as they had the opportunity.[44]

Wilhelmine was twenty years old when the Blekkink family repatriated. Apart from being on furlough she had spent all her youth in the Dutch Indies, where her family belonged to the elite of the society. Once she was engaged, but her fiancé died of cholera before the marriage.[45] She moved with the family to Winschoten in 1898. In June 1899, before the death of her father, she went to Amsterdam where she was trained as a children's nurse in the Emma Kinder Ziekenhuis. Her idea was to go to Africa as a nurse with the Red Cross.[46]

In this period Wilhelmine's religious conversion took place. Her father was a Unitarian who did not believe in Jesus as the Christ and who gave all his children perfect liberty to think and to read whatever they liked.[47] Her stepmother was Lutheran and tried to get some religion into her, but because the God she represented to her was so cruel it created an antipathy against all religion. In Holland Wilhelmine met with a different type of Christianity that did appeal to her. For the first time she heard that Jesus died on the cross for her sake. One night in her room in the hospital she had a vision in which she saw the face of Jesus and a big cross. She was told to choose between the cross and the world. That night she decided to follow Jesus for the rest of her life. Afterwards she found the courage to write a letter of 25 pages to her father. He was not pleased with the change and urged his daughter to leave the whole thing aside. Some time later when he was dying Wilhelmine went home immediately. She testified of her faith with the result that her father in his dying hour also came to a personal faith in Jesus as Christ.[48]

After two years of training in the Amsterdam hospital Wilhelmine joined the Salvation Army. She moved to the Army's "Logement de Vrede Ark" in Amsterdam in September 1901. Her two sisters Louise and Marie, who had also joined the Army, had already been living there since June. Here Wilhelmine got to read *Leaves of Healing* and left the Army shortly after, probably around the same time as Gerrit Polman, that is, February 1902. She went to France for a period of six months and then proceeded to Belgium where she was engaged in Christian work, possibly together with her sister Marie who was in Brussels at the time. Exact dates cannot be given because Wilhelmine kept her registration in Amsterdam.[49]

Details as to how Wilhelmine met Gerrit Polman are not available, but it seems likely that they met each other during the period they both served in the Salvation Army in Amsterdam: from 1901 until February 1902. In May 1903 Wilhelmine moved from Amsterdam (at least as far as registration is concerned) to Rotterdam to marry Gerrit Roelof Polman on 2 July 1903,[50] Wilhelmine being 25 years and Gerrit 35 years old. Both were, according to the wedding certificate, without a profession, although the registration service in Rotterdam had Polman recorded as "evangelist." In October 1903 the couple travelled to America to join Alexander Dowie's church in Zion City.

Louise, Wilhelmine's sister, married a Salvation Army officer and remained in the Army until the death of her husband in 1915. Marie, the other sister, left the Army and married William Bernard from England. Later they became Pentecostal missionaries to the Dutch Indies. Of the other children Gerrit, the eldest, became a freemason and Johanna, the youngest, married someone from that circle. Wilhelmine, Louise, Marie, and Isabella kept to a rigid Christian lifestyle.

Marching to Zion

Of the period between when Gerrit Polman left the Salvation Army in February 1902 and went to America in October 1903 not many details are known except for two important facts: he became a member of the Christian Catholic Church and married Wilhelmine Johanna Marie Blekkink.

At the time small circles of people interested in Zion were emerging. Usually they were gained by reading *Leaves of Healing*. Many of the officers that had left the Salvation Army after the resignation of Booth-Clibborn were in sympathy with Dowie's church. Albert Edward Marpurg, secretary of the Army's social work, had received one volume of *Leaves of Healing* from Booth-Clibborn, while he was ill due to overwork. It brought him and his wife to leave the Army and travel to Zion City in July 1902. In November of that year he returned and held meetings in Amsterdam, where every Friday evening he read translated portions from *Leaves of Healing*.[51]

Gerrit Polman and his future wife Wilhelmine were also drawn by reading *Leaves of Healing*. Polman first received a copy of the German edition *Blätter der Heilung*, while he was still in the Salvation Army.[52] Shortly after Polman resigned from the Army he moved from Arnhem to Groningen. On 6 June 1902, at the age of 34, he became a member of the Christian Catholic Church.[53] In May 1903 he moved from Groningen to Rotterdam to marry Wilhelmine Blekkink on the next 2 July.

In August 1903 Dowie had a general letter printed in *Leaves of Healing* admonishing and ordering believers in various parts of the world to march to Zion. Evidence indicates that there was a keen desire to do so.[54] Likewise the Polman couple went to Zion by way of New York, where they arrived during Dowie's visitation to that city. The crusade, starting 18 October 1903, drew much attention. Even Dutch newspapers gave notice to it.[55] Eight trains had carried 3,000 members of

Zion Restoration Host to New York. They systematically canvassed the entire city leaving literature in every house and business place.[56] For two weeks Dowie held huge meetings in Madison Square Garden and Carnegie Hall for audiences numbering up to 14,000. The spectacular proportions of the campaign must have been overwhelming for the Polmans. Apart from the great publicity the results were meager: 80 baptisms and 125 new members. Gerrit and Wilhelmine Polman were among those baptized by triune immersion at Madison Square Garden on 1 November and Wilhelmine became a member the same day.[57]

From New York they went to Zion City where they were to live more than two years. Most of the time they stayed in Elijah Hospice, a large hotel where Albert Marpurg, back in Zion, worked as a clerk. At Zion the Polmans studied languages and theology and "by self-tuition developed themselves further for their future ministry."[58] Polman was an eager student and became "quite proficient" in Greek and Hebrew.[59] His sister Gerritdina Antonia also came to Zion and joined the church in March 1904.[60]

Not many entered Zion as first-hand converts. The vast majority came from existing religious bodies. Divine healing was Dowie's chief point in contact with the people he won.[61] This approach was quite different from that of the Salvation Army. In Zion the canes and crutches exhibited on the walls in Shiloh Tabernacle were the "trophies" captured from the devil, while in the Salvation Army the same expression applied to souls saved.[62]

On 14 July 1904 Gerrit and Wilhelmine Polman were ordained as deacon and deaconess. In Zion a deacon or deaconess was qualified to conduct a church, to preach, and to administer the ordinances. During the period the Polmans were in Zion the great events were the New York visitation (October 1903); Dowie's world tour (February-June 1904); and the "First Apostle" declaration (September 1904). Although the Polmans witnessed some of the economic recession that came to the city, they were gone before the collapse took place.

On 5 January 1906 Gerrit and Wilhelmine Polman were among those set apart and consecrated for ministry as messengers of Zion designated to various parts of the world. Overseer John G. Speicher and others laid hands upon them for a "special baptism of the Holy Spirit."[63] On the occasion Polman was ordained evangelist. There was a Zion branch in the Netherlands, started a few years before by Booth-Clibborn. Polman was to "follow up the work and to make known the glorious Everlasting Gospel of Salvation, Healing and Holy Living."[64] Dowie, although not present, was quoted, "In speaking of him once the First Apostle said, Deacon Polman was a Dutchman from top to toe, and therefore to Holland he should go."[65] The Polmans left immediately after the meeting and arrived at Rotterdam the same month. This means they never met Wilbur Glenn Voliva who arrived in Zion in February and would soon challenge the leadership of Dowie.

NOTES

1. B.H. Slicher van Bath, *Een samenleving onder spanning: Geschiedenis van het platteland in Overijssel* (Assen: Van Gorcum & Comp. N.V., 1957), p. 638.
2. Ibid., p. 471.
3. P.W.J. van den Berg, "Het Protestantisme in Overijssel," in *Overijssel*, ed. G.A.J. van Engelen van der Veen, G.J. ter Kuile, and R. Schuiling (Deventer: A.E. Kluwer, 1931), p. 891.

   J.P. Kruijt, *De onkerkelijkheid in Nederland* (Groningen/Batavia: P. Noordhoff, 1933), p. 111, characterized the religious disposition of the people of Overijssel, especially in agricultural areas, with conservatism, togetherness, and kind-heartedness.
4. Van den Berg, p. 901; cf. Kruijt, p. 113.
5. "Mag ik U beleefd verzoeken om *niet* de namen mijner ouders te vermelden, ik heb daar mijne persoonlijke reden voor en U zult mij wel niet ten kwade duiden, dat ik U dit verzoek." G.R. Polman to G.A. Wumkes, 8 February 1915.
6. Birth certificate, Zwollerkerspel: 1868, no. 61.
7. "Doopboek 1867-1884," filed in the Gemeentelijke Archiefdienst Zwolle under KA017 no. 134. On the same day, 17 May 1868, 9 children were recorded to have been baptized among whom two were"onecht." The hamlet of Westenholte where the Polman family lived formed part of the municipality of Zwollerkerspel, but for their church life they belonged to the parish Zwolle.
8. On 12 January 1802 Antonij Polman was born at Zwolle. His mother Johanna Polman was unmarried and named her child after her own father Antonij Polman. When the boy was baptized on 8 February

1802 Johanna had to mention the name of the father of her child, which was recorded as Lodewijk Ledeman, officer on the vessel "De Bruinvis" under captain Rijstenberg. "Doopregister," Gemeentelijke Archiefdienst Zwolle RBSO 071, pp. 228-29.

9. Gerrit Roelof himself never informed his children about the stepfather/stepdaughter relationship of his parents, but instead told his children that his parents married in Germany and somehow this marriage was not recognized in Holland.

10. The six children of Hendrikje Polman were all born at Westenholte no. 8: Gerrit Roelof 25 January 1867 (died 6 August 1867); Gerrit Roelof 2 May 1868; Evert Derk 21 December 1870; Gerridina 11 April 1879 (died 29 July 1879); Coenradus 11 April 1879 (died 2 August 1879); Gerridina Antonia 24 April 1881.

11. Both times Polman referred to his church attendance as a child he mentioned that he went with his mother: "Onze Strijders in het Veld," *Oorlogskreet*, 1 December 1894, p. 6; G.R. Polman to G.A. Wumkes, 27 December 1915.

12. J. Zeehuisen, "Statististieke bijdrage tot de kennis van den stoffelijken en zedelijken toestand van de landbouwende klasse in het kwartier Salland, provincie Overijssel," in *Tijdschrift voor Staathuishoudkunde en Statistiek*, vol. 6, ed. R.W.A. Sloet tot Oldhuis (Zwolle: W.E.J. Tjeenk Willink, 1851), pp. 394-96.

13. "Onze Strijders in het Veld," p. 6.

14. J. Zeehuisen (p. 393) observed the interest among land-workers for church singing already in 1851. He mentioned the formation of a choral society in Zwollerkerspel that visited the hamlets during the winter evenings.

15. "Onze Strijders," pp. 6-7.

16. G.A. Wumkes, *De Pinksterbeweging voornamelijk in Nederland* (Amsterdam: G.R. Polman, 1916), p. 9.

17. "Nationale Militie Provincie Overijssel, Gemeente Zwollerkerspel, Lotingsregister 1888," filed in the Rijksarchief at Zwolle. The complete description reads: Size: 1.724 m.; Face: oval; Forehead: ordinary; Eyes: grey; Nose: large; Mouth: idem; Chin: round; Hair: fair; Eyebrows: idem; Visible signs: left temple. His curly hair is apparent from photos. The sign on the left temple is not visible on photos nor is it remembered by his children. The average size was shorter than today. In 1865 only 24.61% of the conscripted was above 1.70 m., while in 1968 the average size was 1.78. Jan en Annie Romein, *De lage landen bij de zee* (Amsterdam: Em. Querido, 1977), p. 476.

18. Wumkes, p. 10.

19. "Onze Strijders," p. 7.

20. Ibid.

21. F. de Booth-Tucker, *The Life of Catherine Booth*, vol. 1 (London: International Headquarters, 1892), p. 225.

22. Ibid.

23. "Jaarverslag en Staat van Inkomsten en Uitgaven van het Leger des

Heils in Nederland van 1 mei 1891-1 juni 1892" (Amsterdam: Leger des Heils, 1892), p. 16. Cf. Tom le Clercq, *Een protest tegen het Leger des Heils* (Amsterdam: Jacques Dusseau & Co., 1892), pp. 9-10; and the reply by the Salvation Army: "Antwoord op 'Een protest tegen het Leger des Heils' " (Amsterdam: Leger des Heils, 1892), p. 3.

24. William Booth, *In Engelands Donkerste Wildernissen en De Weg ter Ontkoming*, translated by C.S. Adama van Scheltema (Amsterdam: S.L. van Looy, 1891). Adama van Scheltema (1815-1897) was a retired Netherlands Reformed minister. Influenced by the Réveil he became a forerunner of the temperance movement. He also translated works from Spurgeon, Bunyan, and Blumhardt, and aided by J.J. van Krieken published songs from Philips and Sankey.

25. W. van Nes, *Een Geestelijke en Maatschappelijke Woekerplant of De Stichting van Generaal Booth* (Utrecht: Kemik & Zoon, 1896), pp. 66-67. Van Nes, a former head teacher, had worked for the Salvation Army between 1892 and 1895, during which time he was responsible for all its publications. Having left the Army he refrained from writing against it until he felt the Army was becoming a threat to the social issue. Many were under the impression that the Army helped to solve the problems of society, while its main concern (also in their social welfare endeavor), according to Van Nes, was not to save society, but to save souls. Van Nes called for a social welfare program free from churchly and political influences.

26. Ibid.

27. Le Clercq, pp. 28, 41. Not disputed by "Antwoord op 'Een protest tegen het Leger des Heils.' "

28. Le Clercq, p. 44. Cf. "Antwoord," pp. 22-23. Polman apparently was quite zealous in selling War Cry's. He numbered one on the list for ordering 390 of the 1901 Christmas issue. Schuurman was second with 190 issues. *Strijdkreet*, 4 January 1902, p. 11.

29. "Strijders in het Veld," p. 7.

30. Marriage certificate, Rotterdam 1897 no. 968. Voskuil and De Wilde will reappear in the following chapters.

31. C.O., "Iets over onze Ziekenverpleging," *De Wijde Wereld* no. 10 (15 October 1895),313.

32. Van Nes, p. 57.

33. Ibid., p. 12.

34. The scheme outlined in his book *In Darkest England and the Way Out* included the formation of three colonies: the city colony, the land colony, and the overseas colony. The city colony would recruit men for the land colony and subsequently the land colony would produce emigrants for the overseas colony. The plan was never fully realized. The land colony in the Netherlands was the only one outside the United Kingdom that "was from the start run in full agreement with the plans outlined by the General." Robert Sandall, *The History of The Salvation Army*, vol. 3 (London: Thomas Nelson & Sons, 1955), p. 155.

35. A.S. Booth-Clibborn, *Broederschap met Noodlijdenden* (Amsterdam: Leger des Heils, n.d.), p. 28.

36. Lucie E. Cosandey, "Op den Oever der Doodsrivier: De laatste levensdagen van adjudante Polman," *Strijdkreet* 13/45 (11 November 1899),1-2.
37. "Dood, waar is uw prikkel? Hel, waar is uw overwinning?" *Strijdkreet* 13/45 (11-11-1889),2.
38. Wumkes, p. 12.
39. In 1971 part of the family tree of the mentioned B.J. Wanrooy and W.J. Huetink was published by Stichting Ozewold Derk. Only the male descendants were followed. In May 1982 another family tree was published, including the females, entitled: *De Parenteel Huetink-Wanrooy* (Wychen: Stichting Ozewold Derk, 1982).
40. Gerrit Jan Bernard 1876-1925 born at Tandjung Pinang; Wilhelmine Johanna Marie 1878-1961; Isabella Constance 1879-1944; Louise Marie Margaretha 1881-1964; Marie Henriette 1882-1932; and Johanna Theodora 1884-1958, all born at Wonosobo.
41. I.J. Brugmans, "Onderwijspolitiek," in *Geld en geweten: Een bundel opstellen over anderhalve eeuw Nederlands bestuur in de Indonesische archipel*, vol. 2 (Den Haag: Martinus Nijhoff, 1980), pp. 187-202.
42. Louis Couperus (1863-1923) spent part of his youth in the Dutch Indies. In 1899 he was there again, just after the Blekkinks had left Pasuruan. One year later *De Stille Kracht* was published. Many details of the house and of the occult events that took place there correspond with the experience of the Blekkink family.
43. L. de Jong-Polman, Interview, 12 August 1985. Lydia de Jong heard the story from her mother on several occasions. The story is known by all grandchildren and is a loved subject at any family reunion. The house was later demolished, but a painting of it is still in existence.
44. *Parenteel Blekkink-Wanrooy*, p. 9.
45. Ibid., p. 28.
46. "A Vision and a Life Story: An Address by Mrs. Polman of Amsterdam, at the Sunderland Convention," *Confidence* 7/10 (October 1914),186-89.
47. Ibid. Possibly Mrs. Polman was using a wrong translation in calling her father a Unitarian and it would be better to read modernist instead. G.R. Polman in "Holland: News from the Island of Terschelling," *Confidence* 9/9 (Sept. 1916), 153, divided the Christians on Terschelling in two groups: orthodox and Unitarians. In this case Polman translated the Dutch "vrijzinnig" with Unitarian, which should read modernist.
48. "A Vision and a Life Story," p. 188.
49. *Leaves of Healing*, 10 February 1906, p. 408. Louise, although remaining in the Army, left for Groningen on 1 March 1902, while Marie left for Brussels on 26 February 1902.
50. Marriage certificate Rotterdam 1903, no. 1279. The four witnesses that signed the certificate were all town clerks, which suggests that no friends or family were present.
51. *Leaves of Healing*, 10 February 1906, p. 408. In 1903 Marpurg

returned to Zion where he worked 18 months as a clerk in Elijah Hospice before he and his wife studied at Zion College. In January 1906 they went to Michigan to work under the Dutch there.

52. Ibid. The report further states that the story of Ethel Post's healing had interested Polman very much.
53. Christian Catholic Church in Zion to author, Zion, 2 March 1984.
54. Philip Lee Cook, "Zion City, Illinois: Twentieth Century Utopia" (Ph.D. thesis, University of Colorado, 1965), p. 217.
55. Also the small local newspaper *Nieuwe Harlinger Courant* reported the visit as news from abroad in nos. 127 (30 October 1903) and 139 (27 November 1903).
56. Rolvix Harlan, "John Alexander Dowie and the Christian Catholic Apostolic Church in Zion" (Ph.D. thesis, University of Chicago, Evansville, Wis., 1906), p. 104. Harlan also gives the text of the 4,200,000 little printed messages that were delivered.
57. *Leaves of Healing*, 7 November 1903, p. 94.
58. Wumkes, p. 13. It is not certain whether the Polmans studied at the Zion College or at the Ministerial Training School of Zion. Wumkes mentioned "College," but the reference to Hebrew points to the Ministerial Training School, where a Greek-Hebrew course was offered. Another indication is found in *Confidence* 2/9 (September 1909), 208, where Polman mentions a Pastor Cossam who gave him such beautiful teaching during the time in America (Cossam probably should read Cossum). W.H. Cossum was principal of the Ministerial Training School. Concerning their Greek-Hebrew course it is stated, "This course is intended to receive College graduates and perfect them in biblical exegesis in Hebrew and Greek, in the history of the Church, in prophetic studies, in the great themes of God, Man, and Sin as presented in the Scriptures, and in such supplementary studies as are calculated to make more definite the knowledge of the Bible times and peoples, and to make more firm and thorough those fundamental teachings for which the Christian Catholic Apostolic Church in Zion stands." "Zion Educational Institutions," *Leaves of Healing*, 8 July 1905, p. 407.
59. *Leaves of Healing*, 10 February 1906, p. 408.
60. Christian Catholic Church in Zion to author.
61. Harlan, pp. 71-81.
62. Harlan, p. 70; cf. F. de Booth-Tucker *The Life of Catherine Booth*, vol. 2 (London: International Headquarters, 1892), p. 226.
63. *Leaves of Healing*, 10 February 1906, p. 408.
64. Ibid.
65. Ibid.

5 INCEPTION OF PENTECOSTALISM IN THE NETHERLANDS

Latter Rain in the Low Countries

Late January 1906 two Zion messengers arrived by boat at Rotterdam: Gerrit and Wilhelmine Polman. Shortly after arrival they started meetings in Amsterdam with about 25 friends interested in John Alexander Dowie's Christian Catholic Apostolic Church in Zion. They gathered in a room on the Kloveniersburgwal, large enough to keep 60 persons. When Dowie was deposed on 2 April 1906, many rumors were brought into general circulation causing Polman and his friends to move on more independently of Zion.[1] The place of meeting was changed to 42 Prinsengracht whereby taking away the partition between two rooms a little hall for 100 persons was made.

In the afterglow of the Welsh Revival they longed for a new awakening in the Netherlands. They realized that it would have to start in their own hearts and so they were praying for a baptism with the Holy Spirit. Then they received news of the Pentecostal revival at Los Angeles and other places:

> In 1906 we heard of wonderful tidings from America. Some papers were sent to us in which we read that God had again visited His people as in the times of old. We learned that God was pouring out His Holy Spirit and people were speaking in other tongues as the Spirit gave utterance.[2]

Comparing this information with biblical data led them to anticipate the Holy Spirit in like manner. This expectation was further strengthened by correspondence with those blessed in this way and by the swift multiplication of the Pentecostal experience around the world. Mrs. Polman, however, was most cautious: "Let us be careful; we have all been once disappointed in Zion City."[3]

During the summer of 1907 the Pentecostal movement had come from Norway to Germany, England, and Switzerland. In October 1907 Melchior Diederik Voskuil, former Salvation Army officer and a friend of the Polmans, travelled to Zurich in order to learn more of the new manifestations. Mrs. Polman would during his absence look after his mission in The Hague. One Saturday night she was puzzling whether or not this Pentecostal blessing was of God. While praying she had a vision of the face of Jesus, who looked sadly at her as if asking, "Do you want to follow me?" Mrs. Polman replied, "Yes, Lord, I want to follow you." The look of Jesus changed and she bursted out in tears crying: "If it is of You, then I accept it. I confess my sins and dedicate myself to You."[4] A great joy filled her heart. The next Tuesday Voskuil returned with the glad news: the Pentecostal movement is of God. When that evening the house-mates knelt for united prayer Mrs. Polman was so moved by the Holy Spirit that she broke out in speaking and singing in tongues and prophesying. This event, on 29 October 1907, is identified by Polman as the definite break with the Zion church and the start of the Pentecostal work in the Netherlands.[5] The meetings in Amsterdam obtained a totally different character. Revelations by means of prophecy or interpretation of tongues filled the believers with a holy fear. Polman described this first period thus:

> Many who had thought that they were earnest and dedicated Christians realized that much within them still had to be broken off, before the Holy Spirit could fill them. Things that one until then had done without troubling the conscience, were now recognized as sin and were confessed and omitted. What a humiliation, a confession before God and men took place! After the Holy Spirit had first done His cleansing work and all was on the altar, the divine fire came. One after the other was baptized with the Holy Spirit and as a natural consequence of every outpouring of the Holy Spirit, many sinners were converted.[6]

The description appears to be more than just a historical narrative. It also seems to reflect the pattern of how in the eyes of the early Pentecostals the Holy Spirit was to be received. The baptism with the Holy Spirit was closely related with sanctification; therefore it was preceded by a time of cleansing and waiting. During the first months only a handful received. Later on the reception of the Spirit was facilitated by having separate meetings for seekers.

On 10 January 1908 Arie Kok was the first male at Amsterdam to speak in tongues, a few days after his marriage to Elsje Aldenberg. Since his visit to the Welsh Revival he had been searching for the baptism with the Holy Spirit. When he heard of the Pentecostal revival at Los Angeles and learned that the same phenomena were taking place at Amsterdam, he started attending the meetings. This must have been during November 1907, just after Mrs. Polman's baptism. After two months of waiting and "deep cleansing" Arie Kok received his Spirit baptism at home during a private prayer session with seven persons including the Polmans.[7] Paul Fleisch quoted the following testimony:

> While he was praying in this way, this blessing came over himself in an overwhelming manner. He was filled with the Holy Spirit and commenced to praise God with new tongues. Then he stood up and walked through the room, meanwhile still speaking in new tongues, then he was driven to take a globe from the mantelpiece. Without looking at it he placed his finger on the globe and pointed to the Himalayan Mountains on the border of Tibet, still speaking in tongues.[8]

Two years later Arie and Elsje Kok would become missionaries to exactly that area.

In April 1908 Polman started the publication of *Spade Regen* (Latter Rain), simultaneously with Boddy's *Confidence*. Of course the paper concerned the recent Pentecostal outpouring of the Holy Spirit "with signs following." The international revival was seen in eschatological perspective. James 5:7-8, associating the latter rain with the second coming of the Lord, was quoted in full as the paper's subtitle. The main article continued thus:

> Thousands and thousands thank God for giving the latter rain in these days. The first drops have fallen upon the whole

earth. The wonderful revival in Wales, the remarkable work
of the Holy Spirit in British India, a few years ago, the mighty
outpouring of the Spirit in America and in different places of
the world, paired with the revelation of all spiritual gifts (1
Cor. 12:1-11), all this indicates, that we live in the time of the
latter rain and that the Lord is ready to pour out His power on
those who are prepared to receive it. Then Jesus will come to
pick up His church. Blessed, three times blessed, are those
who discern the signs of the times, who agree with the divine
purpose and receive the best possible equipment for the last
battle.[9]

News items from other periodicals were quoted with the
name of the source. Several letters were cited, among others
from Boddy, Barratt, and Paul. In spite of all enthusiasm
Polman had not received the experience himself. When he
got Boddy's invitation card for the Sunderland conference
during Whitsuntide Mrs. Polman said: "You must go to the
conference, don't trouble yourself for the meetings, I will
preach for you. You go to Sunderland and seek your
Baptism."[10]
Accompanied by Arie Kok, Polman arrived in Sunderland
on 3 June 1908. The next day, in the afternoon, during a little
prayer meeting in the Vicarage, Mr. and Mrs. Boddy laid
hands on him. Mrs. Boddy helped Polman pass a dead point
by teaching him that the Holy Spirit had already come into
him. The moment Polman acknowledged this truth he was
ready to receive the gift. When it came, he first tried to stop
it. It was again Mrs. Boddy who helped him further by telling
him not to be ashamed, but to yield his tongue to the Holy
Spirit.[11] Finally, Polman spoke and sang in tongues:

> A great power and glory came over me and while my body was
> shaking I began to praise God. I felt lost in Him. Suddenly my
> tongue began to roll in my mouth, my jaws started moving and
> everything was working towards forming another language in
> my mouth. My face had to take an unusual pose, so that I
> automatically put my hands before the eyes.[12]

Another touching event of the conference was the testimony
of a lady, whom Polman had never met before:

She said: "There sits a brother," pointing to me, "whom I saw in a vision in the month of April, and the last fourteen days I had to pray for him when I went on my knees. His face came before me, and I felt burdened with prayers for him."[13]

After the conference Polman went to Bedford to spend a few days with Cecil Polhill. Instead of a few days, he stayed for four weeks. On his way home he visited Arthur S. Booth-Clibborn in London, who was "earnestly seeking after the Pentecostal baptism."[14]

Equipped with Pentecostal power Polman resumed his ministry in Amsterdam: "The sick were healed, demons cast out, souls saved and other manifestations of the power of God were given."[15] As many visitors from all over the country were coming, the meetings were held daily. From a letter of Mrs. Polman to Mrs. Boddy, published in *Confidence* August 1908, we learn of healings and exorcism to have taken place, next to visions, tongues, shaking of the body, and perspiration. The latter was not solely attributed to the fiery prayers, but also to the hot summer and the heat of the gas lights in the hall![16]

Up to this time only a very few had received the baptism with the signs of tongues. Some had become discouraged and had left.[17] The problem was caused by the assumption that one had to speak in tongues when baptized with the Holy Spirit. Under these circumstances it is no surprise that some methodology to facilitate the reception of the Spirit developed. It started with selecting the candidates. Admittance to the Sunderland conference had been limited to ticket-holders, who declared to be in full sympathy with those seeking Pentecost with the sign of tongues.[18] In his parish Boddy had initiated weekly meetings for "those who have received the Baptism with the sign of tongues." After his visit to Sunderland Polman at once arranged similar meetings for baptized ones in Amsterdam.[19]

When Boddy was in Amsterdam, 1 to 11 September 1908, public meetings were held as well as "mutual" meetings for ticket-holders declaring to "earnestly seek the Pentecostal baptism with the sign of tongues."[20] For the Sunday meetings Polman rented a large hall opposite the Royal Palace and

Pentecostal Conference in Amsterdam, September 1908. *Middle-front*: Arie (*fifth from left*) and Elsje Kok, Gerrit and Wilhelmine Polman, and Alexander Boddy.

placed advertisements in religious papers. Being a state church minister (he was advertised as "dominé") Boddy provided for a status that enabled careful church members to also come and learn of the revival.[21] In a sermon on "the Blood and the Fire" Boddy urged the believers to first be cleansed and purged before seeking the baptism with the Holy Spirit. Whenever Polman mentioned the blessing he received at Sunderland, he spoke with tears in his eyes.[22] In mutual meetings Boddy gave useful counsel to the baptized ones and the seekers. He suggested they have little prayer bands and asked them to also pray for their pastor in order to "help him to drive the devil back."[23] Boddy was impressed with the singing that reminded him of Wales: "Never since I was at Ton-y-pandy with Evan Roberts have I heard such grand sustained melodious chorale-like psalm-singing. Of course there was no choir."[24] Besides Amsterdam, Boddy addressed one meeting at The Hague with Arie Kok and two open-air meetings at fairs at Zaandam and Hilversum with evangelist J. Timmerman and his Bible-booth.[25] At the end of his stay Polman wrote, "We here in Holland have learned to love him very much and we look upon him as our dear spiritual father to whom we can go for help and counsel in this earnest work."[26]

Boddy's visit greatly encouraged the little flock at Amsterdam and provided a pattern of worship for the coming years. Weekly gatherings "only for those seeking the full Pentecostal baptism," were arranged on Saturday nights, and mutual meetings for "those who have received the Pentecostal blessing," on Tuesday nights.[27] Apart from the public meetings (twice on Sunday and once on Wednesday) and mutual meetings (on Tuesday and Saturday), there were also the prayer sessions in homes of believers, for instance on Sunday afternoon. The printed testimonies in *Spade Regen* bear witness that many came through in these home meetings.[28] The baptized ones assisted the seekers with advice and encouraged them to press on, just like Mrs. Boddy had done with Polman.

Concerning the rate at which believers received the baptism, there are some interesting clues. Mrs. Polman was the first on 29 October 1907. More than two months later

Arie Kok was the first male on 10 January 1908. In November 1908 the fiftieth is recorded which gives an average of one per week during the first year. Between November 1908 and the beginning of 1909 the number jumped to 100 and reached 150 in July 1909.[29]

Opening Immanuel Hall in 1912

After Boddy's visit in September 1908 the Pentecostal gathering at Amsterdam grew rapidly. The hall on the Nieuwe Prinsengracht, already extended to 140 seats by adding the corridor, was much too small. Often 160 were squeezed in leaving the speaker hardly enough room to stand on a small platform, where he was surrounded by children. No matter how choking, the meetings were "full of power and revelation of the Spirit."[30] In December 1909 a horse stable in the Huidekoperstraat 22 was rented and altered by the members into a clean hall seating 250 (including gallery). Advertisements were not needed: "Some brought their relatives, others tried to get their neighbors. The youth brought their friends or the ones with whom they worked along. God saved many of them, some the first time they were in the meeting."[31] Hostile articles made some unbelievers curious, yet "they did not meet the terrible things they had read, but the Holy Spirit, who convinced them and brought them to the feet of Jesus."[32]

During the years 1910 to 1911 the work became better organized. Besides the public meetings on Sunday and Wednesday and the mutual meetings on Tuesday and Saturday, Bible classes for young people and adults commenced with a Sunday school for the children. Mrs. Polman introduced a children's prayer meeting on Tuesday evening at six-thirty, where teenage children prayed for the baptism with the Holy Spirit. Another class was held especially for those wanting to become missionaries.

The best descriptions of the early Pentecostal meetings at Amsterdam have been given by English visitors and were published in *Confidence*.[33] Most detailed is the account given by Mr. and Mrs. Mogridge from Lytham who were in

Amsterdam from 21 July till 3 August 1910. Like Boddy, Mogridge was also stirred by the singing of the Dutch saints: "It is an inspiration to see these dear people stand and hear them sing with all their souls, 'Crown Him Lord of all,' with both hands raised high above their heads, and then to sing hymn after hymn in the Spirit, clapping their hands with joy."[34] Concerning the Sunday evening meeting he wrote:

> Mr. Polman again preached with wonderful effect; the message gripped the people and held them spell-bound. . . . Those seeking the Baptism in the Holy Ghost were asked to do so in the body of the hall, as the platform was full with those seeking salvation. . . . The Spirit of God, like a mighty rushing wind, seemed to fill the place. I saw them shaking and trembling under the power of the Spirit, and crying to God in every part of the hall . . . as they knelt or sat upon the floor, with faces upturned, streaming with tears. Here I discovered the secret of the Pentecostal success in Holland. The people are in real earnest, and in their determination they get through to God.[35]

The following Sunday evening was described thus:

> There was no time for preaching. Prayer, praise, singing in the Spirit, and Testimony from lips set on fire with the Holy Ghost, was the order of that service. God's tide of holy love was flowing down upon them. Many were seeking the Baptism in the Holy Ghost; others were crying to God for salvation. Some were prostrated upon the floor under the mighty hand of God. At intervals great waves of Heavenly power seemed to rush down upon us, when scores would burst forth together in praise and adoration.[36]

On Tuesday evening Mogridge first attended the children's prayer meeting, led by Mrs. Polman. About 40 children between ten to fourteen years were present, many of them baptized with the Spirit: "Many were shaking and bent down with their faces on the floor, others were praying with those seeking Jesus, and some laid hands upon others for the Baptism of the Holy Spirit. The girls too helped one another in the same way."[37] Hereafter followed the meeting for the baptized ones. Mogridge counted 70 to 80 adults: "Prayer and praise and overflowing heavenly joy were the leading features of the meeting, which were manifested in outbursts of holy laughter, and singing in the Spirit, and praising and exalting Jesus in new tongues."[38]

As the work progressed the need for a larger place was felt again, as well as accommodation for a missionary training school and a Christian rest home. In February 1911 a former liqueur distillery and a picture-frame factory in the center of the city, Kerkstraat 342-344, were bought. The old front premises were demolished to make room for the beautiful Immanuel building. On 30 December 1911 Mrs. Polman laid the foundation stone with the inscription "Totdat Hij Komt!" (Till He Comes!). The building was opened with a conference from 1 to 12 June 1912. From Germany were present J. Paul, E. Humburg, M. Gensichen; from England Smith Wigglesworth and Mrs. Crisp, head of the P.M.U. women's training school at London; from America J.H. King and others. Missionary to Japan, H.J. Taylor, was baptized with the Holy Spirit the evening before he left.[39] Remembering what God had done in their midst and believing He would do even more in the future, the building was named "Immanuel" (God with us).[40] For a relatively small gathering it certainly was an ambitious project that cost a fortune. The total costs amounted to at least ƒ48,000 of which ƒ40,000 had to be borrowed.[41] As it was especially designed to suit the requirements of a Pentecostal meeting place (one of the first in Europe), the plan of the house deserves a closer look.

The building did not have the appearance of a church, but rather of a solid, yet ordinary, house with some kind of meeting place downstairs. There was no tower or church bells. It was adjacent to other houses and situated in a decent residential quarter, just off a busy shopping street in the center of the city. Upstairs there were three floors containing four independent apartments, two of which were let and the other two were combined and used for the Polman family and as a guest home. In the front two identical entrances led the visitors through a porch to the hall. Between the two porches was an office. The large rectangular hall contained 300 wooden chairs. From the front to the back were three rows of chairs and one row on each side of the platform. The gallery along three sides kept another 200 chairs.

At the back of the hall was a small platform with a modest lectern attached to the balustrade. On the wall behind was a large stained glass transparency bearing the picture of one of the wise virgins carrying her burning lamp and vessel filled with oil. Underneath were the words "Ja, kom Heere Jezus" (Yes, come Lord Jesus). A small organ was placed in front of the balustrade. The walls and the six round pillars were painted white. An octagonal roof window was the sole provision for daylight. A door to the left of the platform gave access to the premises at the back, which had remained intact. Here was the "upper room" where seekers, who came forward upon the invitation at the end of the meetings, gathered for prayer. Numerous believers would receive their Spirit baptism during these after-meetings. The same building also housed the training school that commenced in October 1912. On the third floor were rooms for missionaries and students.

The way the house was built and situated demonstrates that for the Pentecostals the church stood close to daily life. For them a church was not seen as a sacred place that had to be separated from the profane world. They felt no need for a tower to point to heaven, since they saw their personal faith as their witness to the world. Most remarkable is the emphasis on hospitality. Polman wrote in *Confidence*, "We have plenty of room to lodge you if you come."[42] The largest part of the house was allocated to lodgings. No wonder it was called the pilgrim's home.

The importance of fellowship is also carried over in the meeting, always called "samenkomst" (coming together) instead of the usual Protestant term "eredienst" (worship service). The design of the hall was basically Protestant with its main focus on the preacher. However, there was no pulpit to be climbed with a stair, but a just a lectern on a low platform. The speaker was only one step away from his audience. Not only was there little distance between speaker and audience, the platform itself was accessible for members to share a testimony, which was a common feature in the meetings. The loose chairs could easily be rearranged and seated around tables used for meals during the conferences. There was no altar, no special communion table, and no baptistery. The inscription outside the building "Totdat Hij Komt!" and inside the wise virgin on the back wall with the message "Ja, kom Heere Jezus" expressed the vivid expectation of the second advent. Yet, this did not prevent them from being actively involved in the extension of God's kingdom as He tarried.

NOTES

1. Polman's last change of address reported to Zion is dated in the records of Zion 10 April 1906. His next change of address on 6 June 1907 was never reported.

2. G.R. Polman, "The Pentecostal Work in Holland," *The Pentecostal Evangel*, 29 May 1926, p. 2; Idem, "De Heere heeft groote dingen bij ons gedaan: dies zijn wij verblijd!" *Spade Regen* no. 29 (March-May 1912),1.

   Polman's letter cited in *The Apostolic Faith* no. 18 (January 1909),1, then published in Portland, reads, "the blessings of the Latter Rain came to us through your paper first."

3. G.A. Wumkes, *De Pinksterbeweging voornamelijk in Nederland* (Amsterdam: G.R. Polman, 1917), p. 14.

4. Wumkes, p. 14. Noteworthy is the parallel between the conversion of Mrs. Polman and her baptism with the Holy Spirit. In both cases she saw the face of Jesus and had a conversation that resulted in her surrender to the will of God.

5. Ibid. The formulation by Wumkes gives room for the possibility that it was the content of the prophecy that made it clear to definitely break with Zion. In May 1912, just before the opening of the new hall, Polman in his brief account of the history dated the beginning with "a good 4½ years ago." This confirms that in the eyes of Polman the movement started with the event of 29 October 1907.

   It appears that most of the Zion adherents accepted the Pentecostalism since October 1907, although there still was a Zion gathering at Haarlem in 1908. The 1909 census recorded only 7 members of the "Algemeene Christelijke Kerk in Sion." Another Zion messenger, elder William van Ballegooien, tried to pick up the work at Amsterdam again from 1932 till 1938, but without success. The little flock he left behind also turned Pentecostal. *Uitkomsten negende tienjaarlijksche volkstelling*, vol. 3 (The Hague: C.B.S., 1911), p. 208; Christian Catholic Church in Zion to author, Zion, 2 March 1984; A.B.W.M. Kok, *Verleidende Geesten* (Kampen: J.H. Kok, 1939), p. 156; M. van der Sluijs, Interview, 29 March 1983.

6. G.R. Polman, "De Heere heeft groote dingen bij ons gedaan: Dies zijn wij verblijd!" *Spade Regen* no. 29 (March-May 1912),1.
7. A. and E. Kok, "Wien zal Ik zenden?" *Spade Regen* no. 12 (November 1909),1-2; cf. Idem, "Wen soll ich senden?" *Pfingstgrüsse* 3/28 (9 April 1911),220-21.
8. Paul Fleisch, *Die Pfingstbewegung in Deutschland* (Hannover: Heino. Feesche Verlag, 1957), p. 202. The event is also recorded by evangelist J. Timmerman, who was present, in his letter to J.H. Gunning J.Hz., Amsterdam, 12 September 1911.
9. "Wat zal toch dit zijn?" *Spade Regen* no. 1 (April 1908),2.
10. G.R. Polman, "Testimony from Pastor Polman," *Confidence* no. 5 (August 1908),17.
11. G.R. Polman, "Testimony," p. 18.
12. Wumkes, p. 15; cf. G.R. Polman, "Testimony," p. 17; *Spade Regen* no. 2 (May-August 1908),4.
13 G.R. Polman, "Testimony."
14. *Spade Regen* no. 2 (May-August 1908),4.
15. G.R. Polman, "Pentecostal Work in Holland," p. 2.
16. W. Polman, "Subsequent Blessing in Holland," *Confidence* no. 5 (August 1908),18. From this letter it follows that Mrs. Polman had in the meantime also spent one week in Sunderland.
17. G.R. Polman, "Testimony," p. 16.
18. *Confidence* no. 1 (April 1908),20. In no. 2 (May 1908), 5, Boddy explained: "We do not invite hostile critics, or even waverers to this conference. Sufficient kindness has been shown to such in the past."
19. W. Polman, "Subsequent Blessing," p. 19.
20. *Spade Regen* no. 2 (May-August 1908),4. The "mutual meetings" is a literal translation of the Dutch "onderlinge samenkomsten," referring to meetings not open to the general public.
21. For example E. Scharten and F.J. Trompetter came to the meetings with Boddy and were shortly afterwards baptized with the Holy Spirit. *Confidence* no. 7 (October 1908),18.
22. A.A. Boddy, "A Visit to Amsterdam," *Confidence* no. 6 (September 1908),12.
23. G.R. Polman, "Spade Regen," *Confidence* no. 6 (September 1908),20; cf. *Spade Regen* no. 3 (September-October 1908),2.
24. Boddy, "Visit to Amsterdam," p. 9.
25. Ibid., p. 8. Boddy also recorded that Timmerman "was often at our meetings seeking the Baptism of the Holy Ghost." Timmerman in his annual report mentioned the visit of Boddy too: *Straatprediking: Jaarverslag der Bijbeltent voor straatevangelisatie en colportage in Nederland* (Amsterdam: J. Timmerman, 1909), pp. 11-13. At this time Arie Kok was chairman of the Bijbeltent. J. Timmerman in his letter to J.H. Gunning J.Hz., Amsterdam, 12 September 1911, revealed a cautious, but positive, attitude towards the Pentecostals.
26. G.R. Polman, *Confidence* no. 6 (September 1908),20.
27. *Spade Regen* no. 4 (November 1908),4; no. 8 (April 1909),2; A.A. Boddy, "Visit to Holland," p. 7.

28. One remarkable example of such a Sunday afternoon meeting is found in "The Strange Baptism of Sister Kok at Amsterdam," *Confidence* no. 9 (December 1909),22-24. Translated from *Spade Regen* no. 4 (November 1908),3-4. While a company of 14 were on their knees in prayer a large ball of fire was seen moving through the air outside. On Monday evenings little prayer bands came together in 7 places simultaneously. *Confidence* 2/1 (January 1909),7.
29. *Spade Regen* no. 4 (November 1908),4. *Pfingstgrüsse* 1/1 (February 1909),13. *Confidence* 2/2 (February 1909),33; 2/4 (April 1909),92; 2/8 (August 1909),189; 2/9 (September 1909),200. At the Sunderland Convention in 1913 Polman spoke of 300 members of which 200 were speaking in tongues: *Confidence* 6/8 (August 1913),164.

    In comparison Boddy was the fiftieth to receive the baptism in Sunderland on 2 December 1907, three months after Barratt's visit to Sunderland (or nine months after Boddy's visit to Oslo). In *Confidence* April 1908 Boddy wrote: "A year ago the writer only knew of some five or six persons in Great Britain who were in the experience. At the time of printing this there are probably more than 500." A.A. Boddy, *Confidence* no. 1 (April 1908),1.
30. G.R. Polman, "De Heere heeft groote dingen bij ons gedaan: Dies zijn wij verblijd!" *Spade Regen* no. 29 (March-May 1912),1.
31. Ibid.
32. Ibid.
33. Boddy's 10 days amidst the Dutch Pentecostal saints in September 1908 of course got a large coverage in *Confidence* as did another visit of Boddy on 22 November 1911. T.M. Jeffreys from Wales spent one day in Amsterdam on his way to the Mülheim Conference in July 1909. Niblock reported of his visit together with Polhill and Small from 4-6 December 1909 (Saturday till Monday), also en route to Germany. A.A. Boddy, "A Visit to Amsterdam," *Confidence* no. 6 (September 1908),6-17; Idem, "Amsterdam," *Confidence* 4/11 (December 1911),270-72; T.M. Jeffreys, "Conference at Mülheim," *Confidence* 2/8 (August 1909), 189; Niblock, "A Third German Conference," *Confidence* 3/1 (January 1910),19-20.
34. H. Mogridge, "Holland and Antwerp," *Confidence* 3/10 (Oct. 1910),244.
35. Ibid., pp. 243-44.
36. Ibid., p. 245.
37. Ibid.
38. Ibid.
39. *Spade Regen* no. 30 (June-July 1912), 117-18.
40. Polman, "De Heere," p. 2.
41. At least f30,000 was borrowed from Cecil Polhill and f10,000 from Elize Scharten. The stained glass was a gift from Germany. Edel's assembly at Brieg provided for the furniture in the training school at the back.
42. G.R. Polman, "Testimony by Pastor Polman," *Confidence* 5/8 (August 1912),175.

6 INTERNATIONAL RELATIONS

We Are an International People

In a Midday prayer meeting in London, February 1909, Mrs. Polman testified, "We are an International People, we who have received Pentecost."[1] The truth of this statement is readily confirmed when reading the early Pentecostal periodicals. News and letters from abroad and reports of conferences filled large parts of the leading papers. The Sunderland Conference convened by Boddy was held annually during Whitsuntide from 1908 till 1914. After 1909 it became known as the International Conference. Besides Great Britain, leaders from Germany, Holland, Switzerland, Norway, Sweden, and other countries were usually present.

The first Pentecostal Conference in Germany, convened by Emil Meyer in December 1908 at Hamburg, was also very international with Boddy, Polhill, Barratt, Polman, Kok, Johnson (Sweden), and Cooke-Collis (Switzerland) attending.[2] Boddy wrote that the Germans wished to do things in a scholarly fashion, but "we were too much in earnest to be tied down to written disquisitions."[3] The leaders discussed questions relating to tongues and prophecy. Here the Germans decided for the publication of *Pfingstgrüsse* to be edited by J. Paul. In 1909 the first and second Mülheim Conferences, convened by Emil Humburg, were held in July and August/September. The Mülheim Conference, thereafter held once a year, became the main conference in Germany. Apart from the conferences in Sunderland and Mülheim there were annual conferences in London, convened by Cecil Polhill, and in Zurich. All of them were frequented by guests from foreign countries.

At the Hamburg Conference of 1908 Polman was much pleased to meet T.B. Barratt, Jonathan Paul, and Eugen Edel from Brieg, whom he knew through correspondence and publications. Two years before Polman had read Edel's *Das Buch der Offenbarung* and had written to Edel on the subject.[4] Much to their surprise they met each other in Hamburg. Boddy recommended the Pentecostal work at Amsterdam and predicted that it would be "a centre of blessing."[5] Since then many believers from Germany, but also from other countries, travelled to Amsterdam to receive the Pentecostal experience. Polman's home was abundantly used: "Every room is always occupied and we may rejoice in deep spiritual fellowship and blessings."[6] The guest book "Aandenken aan de Pelgrims" bears further proof of how Amsterdam was becoming an international meeting place for Pentecostal saints. In February 1909 Eugen Edel (Brieg) with Emil Humburg (Mülheim), Hermann Knippel (Duisburg-Beeck), and August Rees (Velbert) were in Amsterdam seeking the Spirit baptism.[7] Polman and Humburg became good friends and they would frequently visit each other during the years to come. Edel invited Polman and his wife to Brieg, which resulted in a revival there.[8] At Velbert it was Arie Kok who during 1908 had introduced the Pentecostal experience in the free church led by August Rees, which after Rees' visit to Amsterdam developed into a Pentecostal assembly.[9]

In April 1909 Mrs. Ada Esselbach-Whiting came from Belgium to Amsterdam and was baptized with the Spirit. Before her marriage she had been a Church Army Mission worker in England. Since 1902 she had taken charge over the International Sailors' Rest at Antwerp (a mission of the Church of England) together with her German husband Frederich Esselbach.[10] As far as is known she was the first Pentecostal witness in Belgium.

Mrs. Polman passed Antwerp on her way from England to France in February 1910 and addressed a meeting in the Sailors' Rest: "There were several nationalities. I sang a solo and the Holy Spirit touched the hearts of the lost sons. 'Jesus is calling, is tenderly calling today.' "[11] Mogridge visited Antwerp in August 1910 and reported:

> At Antwerp we found a little Pentecostal Centre. Here we met dear Sister Esselbach, a woman with a saintly character,

possessing wonderful faith in God, almost standing alone for Pentecost in that great city of spiritual darkness. She received her Baptism in Holland and now has a little band around her waiting upon God for Pentecostal fire.[12]

In November 1910 Mrs. Esselbach was in Amsterdam again seeking healing from "extreme weakness." After prayer the Polman couple laid hands on her. According to her testimony she was instantly healed and returned home rejoicing.[13] In March 1911 Mrs. Polman addressed two meetings at Antwerp, again en route to France.

Mrs. Polman's earlier visit to France from 28 February till 19 March 1910 is extensively reported in her diary. In Reims Mrs. Polman was welcomed by Mr. Duntre. A meeting in a hall drew 80 to 100 people, among whom were two pastors. From Reims Mrs. Polman travelled to Rosny, near Paris, where Michel E. Mast led a small Pentecostal circle. Mrs. Polman observed: ". . . wisdom is needed here to lead the group in Bible paths. Brother Mast started about the 144,000, but I told him that I had not given it much thought. He seems to hold to certain ideas which he does not easily surrender."[14] In Colombes Mrs. Polman visited Mrs. Raynaud and Mrs. De Leroux. In a meeting for Spirit-baptized and seekers Mrs. Polman noted, "I saw also there again that someone is needed to hold the reins.[15] From Paris the journey went to Le Havre, where Miss Helene Biolley from Switzerland since 1896 was in charge of the "Ruban Bleu," a combination of a temperance hotel and a religious center. Stotts wrote of her, "Although a cultivated and refined lady of no mean ability, she desired to work among the dregs of society and to lift up the downs and outs, especially drunks."[16] Mrs. Polman addressed a number of meetings, also in Sanvic with V. Dessen, a colporteur-evangelist.[17]

Another visit to France, this time by Miss F.J. Trompetter from Haarlem, came the summer of 1910. She first went to see Mast in Rosny. Only a few had received the Spirit baptism. During the short stay of Miss Trompetter three were baptized and spoke in tongues.[18] Hereafter Miss Trompetter travelled to see Miss Biolley in Le Havre. In order to recognize each other at the station Miss Biolley carried a *Confidence* and Miss Trompetter, *The Apostolic Faith*. During a prayer meeting V. Dessen was baptized with the Holy Spirit, and his wife followed him in the experience shortly after Mrs. Trompetter had left. When Dessen started a Pentecostal gathering his Society refused to supply him with books any longer.[19] He remained in contact with the Dutch Pentecostals and was in Amsterdam in May 1911.[20] During March 1911 Mrs. Polman again spent 3 weeks in France and visited Rosny and Le Havre as well as Reims.[21] Polman's foreign ministry, however, was largely invested in England, Germany, and Switzerland. In a period of five years (1908-1912) Polman, mostly together with his wife, travelled at least sixteen times to England (including Scotland and Wales), thirteen times to Germany, and four times to Switzerland. Polman was usually one of the main speakers at the conferences in Sunderland, London, and Mülheim.

International Leaders' Meetings

During the International Conference at Sunderland the leaders held separate business meetings where matters of doctrine and pastoral concern were discussed. Issues that were repeatedly debated were the relation between sanctification and the Spirit baptism; the necessity of tongues; problems relating to personal prophecies; and the harm that had been caused by letting strangers speak at meetings. Polman's main concern was for the pastoral rather than the doctrinal side. His experience was much appreciated. Concerning the meeting in 1909 Boddy wrote:

> Special interest was taken in Thursday's discussion, to be opened by Holland, because it was known that at Amsterdam, under the leadership of Pastor and Mrs. Polman, the purest work in Europe had been progressing. . . . The work at Amsterdam is, in some senses, an object lesson to leaders in other centres.[22]

Polman said he was fortunate that his people only knew Dutch. He simply refrained from interpreting whenever a stranger preached something that seemed wrong.[23] Boddy wrote in 1911:

> Pastor Polman is a wary Pastor. He can sniff a wolf, even though he looks very lamb-like. He takes him into his study, and gives him (or her) such a searching cross-questioning as lays that one bare. Only when he is thoroughly satisfied does he permit that person to speak, or even testify or pray. So the work has been kept pure, and things some of us lament in Great Britain are unknown here, as they are in Germany also.[24]

In order to safeguard the work the leaders decided to form an International Council that would meet once or twice a year. At the first meeting in Sunderland, June 1912, those present were Boddy, Polhill, Barratt, Paul, Humburg, Schilling, Polman, and J.H. King, from the U.S.A. The second meeting was held in Amsterdam, December 1912; the third in Sunderland, June 1913. It seems that the announced session for December 1913 in Amsterdam was put off. The following and also final meeting was held in Sunderland, June 1914. Each time the Council met a declaration or report was made. The content of these can be cataloged as follows:

1. Warnings against allowing strangers to speak at meetings unless letters of recommendation are produced
2. Warnings against specific wrong teachings
3. Warnings against specific publications, such as Jessie Penn Lewis' *War on the Saints* (1912)
4. Statements of doctrinal position[25]

Mrs. Polman fully shared in the ministry of her husband. Here again it is Boddy who informs us: "Pastor Polman and his gifted wife are well mated indeed. Mrs. Polman has exceptional powers, and is not only a true wife and a deeply taught Christian, but is also highly educated and is an accomplished linguist."[26] She preached regularly at the conferences and taught at the leaders' meetings, or contributed through other spiritual gifts such as tongues and interpretation, prophecy, and visions. Born in the East Indies she felt like a cosmopolitan: "I have been studying the

characteristics of the English, the German, the French, and
the Dutch. I do not belong to any of these, I am International.
I was not born in Holland, but I feel at home anywhere."[27]
After ten years of marriage three children were born in the
Polman family: Naomi Dorothee (1913), Theophilus Conrad
(1915), and Lydia Catherine (1917).

During the First World War

The outbreak of the First World War disrupted the international meetings. The Netherlands, Switzerland, and the
Scandinavian countries remained neutral, while Germany and
England were opposing each other in war. Frank Bartleman's
Two Years Mission Work in Europe (October 1912 till October
1914) provides interesting insight in European Pentecostalism around the eruption of the war. Bartleman warned against
the war spirit he experienced among Christians in Germany
and England. In June and July 1913 he had been in
Amsterdam and gave a remarkable prophecy:

> I remember prophesying of a great war when we passed
> through Amsterdam on the way to the continent from
> England. I pictured the whole thing out, telling them just what
> part little Holland would be destined to play in it. She was to
> stand between the wild beast forces, the nations, a haven of
> refuge. At that time I was tempted over this message also, and
> wondered what made me give it. I was afraid they would lose
> faith in me altogether. But when we came through en route
> for home, after the World War had started, all that I had
> prophesied had come true.[28]

With reference to the Pentecostal scene the prophecy found
fulfillment in the ministry of Polman. Holland was flocked
with interned soldiers from England, Germany, Belgium, and
France. The Esselbach couple and another family had to flee
from Antwerp and found refuge in Immanuel, Amsterdam.[29]
Polman distributed New Testaments among the interned
soldiers and helped tracing missing relatives: "there is the
terrible suffering of so many millions, and we cannot be
indifferent about that. Our part is to do what we can to help

the needy ones, and bring the gospel of peace to them who are in unrest."[30] Polman felt a particular mission towards the Belgian soldiers:

> Who will help me to spread the Bible among 32,000 Belgian soldiers? People give plenty of money at this time for killing men in this War. Is it not our duty as Christians to give for bringing life, life eternal? If this terrible War would be a medium to get the Full Gospel into Belgium, that would be glorious. I am praying and working for that.[31]

The following excerpts from letters of Belgian soldiers demonstrate how welcome Polman's ministry was received:

> You cannot believe how glad and thankful I am for your letter, I who am far away from wife, children and country, without friend, lonely and sad. And now dear sir, you offer me your friendship and love, which I take kneeling from your hand, and I thank and praise God that He has sent me a good friend, which comforts me. Never in my life will I forget that. . . . Since I received and read your letter I am wholly changed and live as renewed. Your encouragement and beautiful words about our poor country shows your goodness towards us. . . . Your letter is for all of us the wise counsel of an intelligent and deep-feeling father. For your counsel I am so thankful. . . . We acknowledge that God has enabled you to show this love to us and our wives and children, who found a refuge in your hospitable country.[32]

The war placed a heavy burden on the "unity in the Spirit" that European Pentecostals had cherished among themselves. Especially for the German and British Pentecostals, who were liable to military service the situation demanded that a stand be taken. Both *Confidence* and *Pfingstgrüsse* sided with the national pro-war feelings. *Pfingstgrüsse* reprinted militant articles from the *Allianzblatt* and *Heilig dem Herrn* which not only justified, but even glorified the war. Letters from Christian soldiers on the battle field carried the same message: God was with Kaiser Wilhelm and the German army.[33] Many Pentecostals lost their lives on the battle field, including both sons of J. Paul.[34]

On the other side Boddy and also Polhill were convinced

that God was with the Allies and favored active participation in the conflict.[35] In his support of the war Boddy simply took the traditional stand of an Anglican clergyman. Nevertheless he maintained a loving attitude towards the German Pentecostals and believed they were "not in full possession of the facts as we hear them."[36] By this time, much to the regret of Boddy, many independent Pentecostal assemblies had emerged, outside of the Anglican Church. These non-Anglican Pentecostals predominantly refused combatant service. A number of their young leaders were imprisoned because as members of a non-registered sect, they did not qualify for recognition as conscientious objectors.[37] A.S. Booth-Clibborn, an outspoken pacifist, probably influenced many.[38] Boddy's stand the in war combined with his refusal to cooperate in the after-war developments to organize British Pentecostalism as an independent force resulted in his loss of leadership.[39] Donald Gee, a conscientious objector himself, wrote that by 1918 Boddy had "lost the Fire," and was "only a shadow of the former master of assemblies."[40]

Polman like most Pentecostals, including Boddy, saw the war as heralding Jesus' return, but as to Christian participation he took a pacifistic stand. Like A.S. Booth-Clibborn he visited imprisoned conscientious objectors in order to encourage them.[41] Realizing the different opinions on the matter, as some Dutch Pentecostals were called up for mobilization, he wrote:

> The children of God at present are not unanimous about the right to make war and whether or not the Christian should partake, be it conscripted or voluntary, as well as whether the sixth command should also be maintained in this matter. We do not want to judge each other, but surrender each other to God. It is necessary, that we let ourselves be illuminated by the Word of God and walk as Enoch with God.[42]

With a silent allusion to *Pfingstgrüsse* in which Germany had been compared with Israel, Polman continued:

> An appeal to the Old Testament wars cannot justify the waging of wars in these days. Israel was as a nation the people of God. Today there is however no nation in the world that as a nation can be called the people of God. . . . God's people,

the body of Christ, shall come forth from all race and language and people and nation. Therefore it is of minor importance for the assembly of Christ, which party in the present waging war will achieve the victory. For her the principal matter is, that Christ, also by means of all this, can purify, cleanse and whiten His assembly, and prepare her for His return.[43]

Polman found it important to regard the war as anti-Christian and brought about by the forces of darkness, for "if one does not, one is in danger of being carried away by the spirit of war."[44] Citing 1 Cor. 12:13, "For by one Spirit are we all baptized into one body, whether Jews or Gentiles, whether bond or free," Polman warned against nationalism, which was threatening the unity among the children of God of different nationalities.[45] Neither party had a divine right to fight, as war "is unchristian."[46] On this matter Polman counteracted the opposing positions *Pfingstgrüsse* and *Confidence* had taken.

Although travelling was difficult Polman managed to make several journeys to England, Germany, Belgium, and Switzerland. When in England he visited German prisoners of war and did the same to English soldiers in German prisoners' camps.[47] As Polman remained in contact with Pentecostals on both sides he had an important function as a mediator that would continue until after the war. His reconciliating role culminated in the International Conference of 1921 at Amsterdam.

When, during 1917, the German social-democrats tried to agree with the social-democrats in the hostile countries to conclude the war, one German soldier posed the significant question, "What are the children of God in Germany and in the hostile countries doing against that?"[48] The soldier called for a global day of prayer and pleaded for a conference to be held in one of the neutral countries. Polman translated the letter for *Spade Regen* and expressed how eager he was to have an international conference in Amsterdam to meet each other as before the war, but such was not possible at the moment:

> We remember our dear friends in the various countries at war and suffer with them in this world crisis, and pray . . . that if this war is not a prelude of the great tribulation, there may soon be a time in which we will again stand next to each other

on one platform to glorify Christ. What a meeting that will be![49]

In September 1917 a similar appeal to global prayer for peace was made by a so-called "Prayer Union" from Switzerland. Their "Call to the Children of God in this Difficult Time" was translated by Polman and published as a supplement to *Spade Regen* in October 1917. It contained the same thought: If socialists of all countries try to bring peace, what are the children of God doing? "Where are the Christians who, free of all patriotic egoism or political party spirit, have love for the brethren abroad?"[50]

After the War

From 9-11 August 1918, just before the end of the war, Polman was able to go to the Mülheim Conference again. Most of the German leaders were still in the military service, but had obtained permission to attend.[51] The hope was expressed that soon believers from all countries could gather as before.[52] In August 1919 Polman tried to convene such a conference in Amsterdam. Because Boddy, Polhill, and Barratt could not come it was postponed.[53]

The first post-war Mülheim Conference, 5 to 8 August 1919, inaugurated a new phase of the Pentecostal Movement in Germany. This new phase was described as a "crisis" in the sense of a judgement upon the people of God. It started among the leaders during the preliminary conference (31 July-4 August). Of course the sad events of the lost war prompted the Germans to self-examination. Another reason that had contributed to the German readiness to wear the penitential garment was the revelation of sexual sins.[54] Through visions and prophecies the leaders were brought under the judgement of God. At the actual conference Humburg, Paul, and Edel made public confessions of guilt. J. Paul denounced his own teachings on perfectionism. He blamed himself for having made a doctrine out of what was intended as a personal experience of sanctification.[55] The confessions confirmed by visions and revelations created such a deep conviction of sin and guilt upon the congregation that all had to cry out: Unclean! Unclean![56] Polman, who had also taken part in the preliminary conference, felt broken in spirit and was prayed for:

> Those, whom had prayed with me, and whom God had used by means of visions and revelations to place myself and my labour in the true light of God, laid their hands upon me, and then the Holy Spirit came with such a power, that I was completely taken in His possession. I know that nothing does more harm to the work of God, than the human spirit. It cannot produce anything but wood, hay and stubble. Much in my labour has been in this kind of spirit, which I am quite willing to admit. This has been a hindrance for the furthering of the work of God in the Pentecostal Movement. But thank God, the way is open now. A new era in the Pentecostal Movement will open up. It will indeed go through the depths, but it will lead to true life.[57]

In Amsterdam and in Haarlem Polman testified of his personal experience at Mülheim. As of September 1919 *Spade Regen* was dominated by the message to come under the judgement of God and to crucify the human spirit. The appeal it would seem was not readily accepted, but according to testimonies in *Spade Regen* some believers in Amsterdam and Haarlem went through similar "crisis" experiences.[58] The German influence was very strong in this period. Polman attended the meetings of German leaders in April and October 1919 in Berlin. *Spade Regen* published Voget's sermon in Mülheim and Paul's confession. In November 1919 Humburg and Martensen came over to Amsterdam. Most of the meetings were only open to those Pentecostals "who are completely united with us in the great purpose of this new revival."[59] Afterwards Polman wrote:

> God has done a work of creation in our assemblies at Amsterdam, Haarlem and Rotterdam, which during these days could assemble together. The crisis in these assemblies is a transitional period, which had brought us in heavenly places with Christ, the Resurrected. Where man's own spirit has gone in the death of Christ, there is a work being cut in the

inner life of the brothers and sisters and for them a new era has commenced.[60]

In January 1920 J. Paul came and stayed for two months. Polman organized meetings with clergy and other guests.[61]

Through Polman the German "crisis" was carried to Great Britain. Strengthened by a prophecy uttered in Amsterdam that the hearts in England would be open for this message, Polman travelled to the conference of the Pentecostal Missionary Union in London in May 1920: "God gave us the wisdom and the power to testify of Him, how He had revealed Himself to us, and both the leaders and the whole congregation entered into this blessing."[62] Polman sensed a general longing for a revival among the children of God in England. He remained several days for meetings with Pastor Saxby, a former Baptist, in London. In July and August Polman spent a few weeks in Ireland and Wales with George Jeffreys and on the way had meetings in Liverpool and Lytham. Letters from Booth-Clibborn, Saxby, and E.C. Boulton from Hull gave evidence to how the message was received.[63]

International Pentecostal Conference in Amsterdam, 1921

In the autumn of 1920 Polman sent out invitations to all countries for an International Pentecostal Convention in Amsterdam, the subject of the conference being "The purpose of God concerning His people in the present time." From 9 to 16 January 1921 this conference finally brought the British and German leaders together for the first time since the war. The local newspaper *De Amsterdammer* wrote:

> It was a solemn moment when Mr. G.R. Polman, leader of the Pentecostal Movement in our country, opened this meeting and reminded of the great war, that however had not been able to bring division between the Pentecostal people of the countries that opposed each other with arms and in fact still do, although the guns have been silenced.[64]

Present were leaders of Great Britain, Germany, Switzerland, Denmark, Sweden, and the U.S.A., and missionaries from China, India, Africa, and South America.[65] Polman was much pleased to meet several leaders from Denmark and Sweden, including Lewi Pethrus, for the first time. The beginning ran stiffly till one incident broke the ice. At the table one of the Englishmen sat across from a German participant, who had lost part of his ear during the war. The Englishman assured his German brother that it could not have been him, since he had refused to bear arms and had suffered in prison as a conscientious objector.[66] Max Wood Moorehead later reported that "every trace of war spirit and race prejudice was obliterated."[67] In the hall the various nationalities were so grouped, that an interpreter, sitting with his back to the platform, could raise his voice among them without disturbing the other nationalities.[68]

The main question of the conference was, "Is the great work of spiritual judgement and humiliation, which has gone over Germany, Holland and parts of England in the last two years, really of God?"[69] There was a strong difference of opinion upon this point, to which Donald Gee commented:

> The German preachers seemed determined to monopolise the Convention with a new teaching they were very much stressing at that time, of a deeper death to self that all must pass through, and their doctrine was reinforced by frequent visions of an extremely personal nature for those present, and by prophecies. The Swedish brethren became very weary of this over-balanced emphasis on a purely negative side of truth, and finally a decided clash occurred between the two parties. In many ways it repeated the old clash between "prophets" and "teachers." Nevertheless the Conference provided a shining example of the victory of Christian love rising above all differences of opinion, and it concluded with a wonderful communion service at midnight, after which all separated in unbroken love and fellowship in Christ.[70]

Polman wrote that the conference could not be compared with any conference held before because of the "differentiation in opinion that was first revealed, and afterwards the fusion of all own opinions in the melting-pot of God's love."[71]

International Pentecostal Conference in Amsterdam, January 1921. *Front row, sitting, l. to r.:* Mr. and Mrs. W. Bernard; Mr. J. Walshaw and grandchild; Pastor J. Paul; Pastor O. Witt; Mr. and Mrs. G. R. Polman and daughter; Mrs. Walshaw. *Second row, standing:* Miss A. Stopkuchen; Miss T. Bakker; Pastor Kusch; Miss E. Eichhorn; Pastor E. Edel; Pastor C. Voget; Mr. A. S. Booth-Clibborn; Pastor A. L. Fraser; Miss P. van Wieren; Pastor L. Pethrus; Mr. and Mrs. Björner; Miss E. Scharten; Miss Nelly Alsop; Miss Caffyn. *Third row:* Miss G. Roos; Miss A. Gnirrep; Mr. and Mrs. H. Steiner; Mr. A. Wieneke; Pastor E. Humburg; Pastor E. Fris; Mr. Ericson; Mr. A. Johnson; Mr. O. Nelson; Miss Davies Colley; Miss M. Achterrath; Miss L. Mackinlay; Miss E. de Vries. *Fourth row:* Misses J. and J. van Donselaar; Mr. Beruldson; Mr. J. Poppinga; Mr. D. Gee; Mr. A. Holmgren; Mr. J. Voskamp; Mr. Zimmerman; Mr. W. Scheuermeier; Mr. Max Wood Moorhead; Mr. R. Schober; Mr. D. Flood; Miss H. Hacklander; Mr. C. van Wynen.

In the reports published in the various Pentecostal periodicals Polman asked the brethren from all lands to inform him of their views concerning another International Conference to be held at Amsterdam. The plan was however not carried out. In spite of Polman's efforts the situation from before 1914 did not come back. The Sunderland Conferences had ceased. Conferences in Mülheim, Zurich, London, and other places continued, but never were such international meeting places as before. Instead the Pentecostals concentrated on organizing national denominations. In Germany this was initially exercised through the "Hauptbrüdertag" where the leaders met each other. In Great Britain three separate Pentecostal denominations emerged: the Apostolic Church, the Elim Pentecostal Church, and the Assemblies of God. The development in The Netherlands will be discussed hereafter. The heavy emphasis on death to self gradually disappeared in Holland, but remained strong in Germany.[72] Polman's foreign ministry to England, Germany, and Switzerland continued as well as to Belgium and to France.

Ministry to France and Belgium

Because the Pentecostal developments in Belgium and France from before 1930 are still obscure, even after George Raymond Stotts' "The History of the Modern Pentecostal Movement in France," further details as to Polman's ministry in these countries are given here.

Stotts' sole reference to Polman concerns a visit to Le Havre in 1920. Upon invitation of Miss Biolley, G.R. Polman together with Smith Wigglesworth gave studies on divine healing and the baptism with the Holy Spirit.[73] From 25 November till 4 December 1922 Mrs. Polman once more visited Miss Biolley at Le Havre: "It was glorious to meet all these old friends again after eleven years."[74] Sunday morning and evening the mission hall in the Rue Dauphine was filled with about 100 persons.[75] The Delanis couple was much strengthened by the visit and received a calling for the mission field in Martinique.[76] Nine months later, in August 1923, Mrs. Polman was at the farewell service and presented a gift from Amsterdam.[77] During another visit in 1925 Mrs. Polman had a conversation with a Russian Jew, who had a furrier shop at Le Havre. When two years later, in February 1927, the Polman couple was there again, the Russian Jew and his Catholic wife went to the meetings and were both converted together with seven others. Some were healed and one woman was delivered from a "drink devil."[78] In a baptismal service six were baptized, including the Russian Jew and his wife. One meeting was held with the Baptists in Sanvic. Already in May 1927 Mrs. Polman was back in Le Havre. Again healings occurred and a baptismal service was held.[79] This time 73-year-old Mrs. Biolley went along with Mrs. Polman to Amsterdam to preach at the Whitsuntide Conference.[80]

In Antwerp Mrs. Ada Esselbach was still laboring in the International Sailors' Rest. In November 1919 Boddy met her again and wrote:

> During the German occupation she had permission to travel to Brussels to the meetings held by Miss Doyle at Chaussée de Fleurgat on Thursdays, and helped much by her stirring addresses. One day she dropped a copy of *Confidence* in my friend the British Chaplain's letter box in Brussels, to his wonder and joy. Thenceforward they often had fellowship in prayer. This was a comfort in those years of trial.[81]

The chaplain was H.S.T. Gahan of Christ Church, Brussels, "a consecrated Christian minister, who is going on with God and pressing after more blessing."[82] How open the British minister was to the Pentecostal message is revealed in correspondence of G. Sandberg from Stockholm with Gahan and Mrs. Esselbach during 1920. Sandberg, who was planning to start a mission in Belgium, had first written to Polman. On 28 April 1920 Polman replied:

> We have in Antwerp some friends who hold meetings and do everything they can to spread the Pentecostal truths. Of course we are longing to bring more light in that dark country. Till now we have had no opportunity to do more for Belgium. We send Pentecostal papers and tracts to them, that is all we can do.[83]

In September 1920 Sandberg wrote to Mrs. Esselbach concerning his plans. Mrs. Esselbach replied that she would be very pleased with a Swedish missionary as so many Scandinavians came to the Sailors' Rest. She wrote, "Belgium does need earnest workers, Pentecostal workers, it is dark, very dark, but whether they will receive it is another question," and "Dear Mr. Gahan is the most spiritual man I know here in Belgium and truly believes in Pentecost."[84] Gaham himself also reacted very positively:

> If the Lord directs you or other Pentecostal workers to come and work for Him by preaching the Gospel in this country, then come; by all means. There are various workers and organizations, Belgian and American. But there is still room for more; room for all who may be sent. This country should be flooded with the Gospel in its purest form; and there is none so pure as the Pentecostal. There are wonderful openings and a wonderful readiness.[85]

Further details as to how Sandberg proceeded are not available.[86] Meanwhile Sandberg's letter had quickened Polman's burden for Belgium anew. *Spade Regen* recorded in July 1920: "We have written Sister Esselbach concerning our plan, to also begin a Pentecostal work in Belgium." Mrs. Esselbach replied with thanks for any help coming from Holland and promised her support. Polman continued, "We hope to be able to send a few sisters around Autumn to do a pioneer work there."[87] At least one female worker from Polman, Jo Schotanus, was briefly attached to the work in Antwerp, before she went to The Hague.[88] In July 1921 Polman had made a short visit to Antwerp and wrote: "In Antwerp opportunities have been presented to us to preach the Gospel of a full deliverance and we hope to have some meetings there soon. Pray for the sisters, who labour there, their work is difficult, but the Lord can do miracles."[89] In October 1923 *Spade Regen* mentioned that a hall had been rented in Antwerp for one full year to have meetings twice a month: "There are some brothers and sisters who gladly unite to form a circle, to evangelize in Antwerp under our leadership."[90] In March 1924 we are informed:

The work in Antwerp is being blessed. Twice a month we have our meetings there in a mission hall of the reformed church. From different denominations we assemble there with some brothers and sisters, to search together for a deeper spiritual life. . . . The attendance in the meetings is slowly progressing and this too gives us hope for the future. This labour is still very initial and demands a lot of patience. Because of the deep need, we will try to meet their desire to have a meeting every week if possible.[91]

Alas our information ends here. Mrs. Esselbach once more visited Amsterdam during Easter 1926.[92] Meanwhile another Dutchman had commenced spreading the Pentecostal message in Flanders.

Cornelis T. Potma (1861-1929) was born at Sneek, where his parents had a large leaded window trade.[93] In about 1881 he left for America. He was converted and for many years evangelized among the negroes in Virginia. After acquaintance with the Pentecostal Movement he was baptized with the Spirit. During 1912 he spent some time with Polman at Amsterdam, on his way to South Africa.[94] Shortly after the First World War he went to Belgium to work with the Belgian Gospel Mission, founded by Ralph C. Norton in 1918.[95] As Norton did not agree with the Pentecostal message Potma ended up as an independent itinerant evangelist. The British Elim churches supported him financially and sent him Robert Taylor and his wife to assist in the work.[96] Potma also received help from the Flemish Gabriel d'Hondt. In June 1925 Potma and Taylor settled in Deurne, Antwerp, while d'Hondt remained at Gent.[97] From 30 May till 6 June 1926 Potma organized a Pentecostal Revival Campaign with George Jeffreys "in the land of superstition and ignorance of the truth" to be held in the El Bardo Hall. At the close of the campaign 18 people were baptized by Jeffreys in the Antwerp Public Baths: "The Lord has established a work here after many years of struggle and effort in Him."[98] In July 1929 Potma died and was succeeded by the Dutch Rietdijk couple.

Johan Rietdijk (1901-1986), born at Maassluis, had enrolled at Norton's Flemish Bible School in 1922. In 1925 he married Anke van Hoften (1874-1975), born at Harlingen.

Because Anke was 27 years older than Johan, Norton disapproved of the marriage and dismissed Rietdijk from the school.[99] Rietdijk joined Potma and became an outstanding Pentecostal leader. It would seem that Potma and Polman were not on good terms, which prevented Rietdijk from getting in touch with Polman until after the death of Potma. In December 1929 *Spade Regen* published a letter from Rietdijk and recommended his work in Deurne.[100] In May 1930 Rietdijk visited Polman at Amsterdam. By Easter 1930 Rietdijk had opened a hall at Kiel, near Antwerp.[101] From Kiel and later from Hoboken Rietdijk and his gifted wife exercised a significant role in the formative years of the Flemish Pentecostal Movement. Recently David Bundy made a study of Rietdijk's many writings and concluded: "They reveal him to be one of the most thoughtful, articulate and original Pentecostal theologians."[102]

NOTES

1. *Confidence* 2/2 (February 1909),49.
2. For complete list see *Confidence* Supplement to no. 9 (December 1908),1.
3. *Confidence* 2/1 (January 1909),3.
4. *Spade Regen* no. 7 (March 1909),4.
5. Ibid.
6. *Spade Regen* no. 12 (November 1909),4. In *Confidence* 2/9 (September 1909), 208, Polman wrote, "We rent a large house so that we are able to receive them in our own home and have spiritual communion with each other and pray with them for the blessing they need."
7. *Spade Regen* no. 7 (March 1909),4.
8. G.A. Wumkes, *De Pinksterbeweging voornamelijk in Nederland* (Utrecht: G.J.A. Ruys, 1916), p. 16. In *Confidence* 2/9 (September 1909),208, Polman wrote concerning his visit to Brieg in May, "About 50 received the full Baptism, and 120 received an anointing."
9. Hans Ditthardt and Theo Koch, *Velbert 50 Jahre mit vollem Evangelium* (Erzhausen: Leuchter Verlag, 1960), p. 5.
10. *Confidence* 2/4 (April 1909),91; 2/5 (May 1909),118; 13/1 (January-March 1920),10-11; *Spade Regen* no. 8 (April 1909),3.
11. W. Polman, "Diary 1910-1912."
12. H. Mogridge, "Holland and Antwerp," p. 245.
13. *Confidence* 3/11 (November 1910),251; *Spade Regen* no. 20 (December 1910),4.
14. W. Polman, Diary.

15. Ibid.
16. George Raymond Stotts, "The History of the Modern Pentecostal Movement in France," (Ph.D. thesis, Texas Tech University, 1973), pp. 50-51. Published as: *Le Pentecôstisme au pays de Voltaire* (Craponne: Viens et Vois, 1981). Stotts failed to check *Confidence* and therefore was unaware of the interesting details in the letters by Mast (See note 18).
17. Ibid.
18. F.J. Trompetter, "Frankrijk," *Spade Regen* no. 18 (October 1910),3-4. *Confidence* 3/5 (May 1910), 113, published a letter from Michel E. Mast stating that so far only one person had the "Bible evidence," which is spoken in tongues. In a following letter, Mast obviously refers to the Dutch visitor, when he writes: "During the visit of a Sister, our dear Lord blessed us richly. He deepened His work in several, and baptized one Brother and two Sisters in His Holy Ghost and Fire. They had the sign of the overflowing love for Jesus and the sign of the Tongues." *Confidence* 3/9 (September 1910), 220-21; cf. A.A. Boddy, "Days in France," *Confidence* 2/11 (November 1909),262-64; 11/4 (October 1918),63.
19. F.J. Trompetter, "Frankrijk," including letter from Mrs. Alexandrine Dessen. *Confidence* 4/10 (October 1911),235; cf. letter Mrs. Peters in *Confidence* 4/11 (August 1911),189.
20. *Spade Regen* no. 23 (June 1911),4.
21. W. Polman, "Een bezoek aan Frankrijk," *Spade Regen* no. 22 (March-May 1911),2-3.
22. *Confidence* 2/6 (June 1909),131, 134.
23. Ibid.
24. *Confidence* 4/12 (December 1911),271. In the same article Boddy wrote, "The work at Amsterdam is one of the best commendations of the blessed Pentecostal Movement that we know of."
25. "A Consultative International Pentecostal Council," *Confidence* 5/6 (June 1912),133; "At Amsterdam: Session of the International Council," *Confidence* 5/12 (December 1912),275, 283-84; "Declaration: International Advisory Pentecostal Council," *Confidence* 6/7 (July 1913),135-36; "A Warning from the Advisory Council," *Confidence* 7/6 (June 1914),108-09. For a discussion of these meetings, see Cornelis van der Laan, "The Proceedings of the Leaders' Meetings (1908-1911) and of the International Pentecostal Council (1912-1914)," *EPTA Bulletin* 6/3 (1987),76-96.
26. *Confidence* no. 6 (September 1908),17.
27. *Confidence* 5/2 (February 1912),32.
28. Frank Bartleman, *Two Years Mission Work in Europe* (Los Angeles: by author, n.d.), p. 37. Bartleman also visited Polman in 1910, see his *Around the World by Faith* (Los Angeles: by author, n.d.), pp. 16, 20.
29. *Confidence* 7/11 (November 1914),204; cf. Polman's guestbook "Aandenken aan de Pelgrims," pp. 93-94.
30. Ibid.
31. *Confidence* 8/2 (February 1915),29.

32. *Confidence* 8/7 (July 1915),134-35. Polman received hundreds of letters from interned Belgian soldiers. G.R. Polman, "The Gospel to All Nations," *Flames of Fire* no. 30 (August 1915).

33. See *Pfingstgrüsse* 7/8 (22 November 1914),57-59; 7/9 (29 November 1914),67-68, 72. Cf. Walter J. Hollenweger, *The Pentecostals* (London: SCM, 1972), pp. 232-33.

34. Ernst Giese, *Jonathan Paul, Ein Knecht Jesu Christi* (Altdorf: Missionsbuchhandlung und Verlag, 1965), pp. 211-12; cf. *Confidence* 7/10 (October 1914),191.

35. Donald Gee, *Wind and Flame* (Croydon: Heath Press, 1967), pp. 101-02.

36. *Confidence* 8/2 (February 1915),28. Boddy corresponded with C.O. Voget and J. Paul and published their letters in *Confidence*: 7/10 (October 1914),191; 8/2 (February 1915),28-29; cf. Martin Robinson "The Charismatic Anglican—Historical and Contemporary," (M. Litt. thesis, University of Birmingham, 1976), pp. 97-101.

37. Gee, pp. 101-04.

38. Ibid., p. 102. Gee recorded that while the whole nation seemed to be singing "Tipperary" Booth-Clibborn wrote "It's a straight way that leads to glory," to the same tune.

39. For a full discussion, see Martin Robinson, "The Charismatic Anglican."

40. Donald Gee, *These Men I Knew* (Nottingham: Assemblies of God, 1980),p. 22.

41. Arthur Sydney Booth-Clibborn, *Blood Against Blood* 3d ed. (New York: Charles C. Cook, n.d.), pp. 59-60; Lydia de Jong-Polman, Interview, Boskoop, 29 December 1983.

42. *Spade Regen* no. 38 (December 1914),3.

43. Ibid.

44. Ibid., p. 4.

45. *Spade Regen* no. 39 (January 1916),4.

46. Ibid.

47. *Confidence* 7/11 (November 1914),204-05; 8/5 (May 1915),93; *Pfingstgrüsse* 7/7 (15 November 1914),54. Once in Germany Polman was thought to be a spy. He told the policemen that questioned him, "You understand more about war, than the gospel, and I understand more about the gospel, than I do about war." Then they left him and let him go. *Flames of Fire* no. 30 (August 1915).

48. *Spade Regen* 10/5 (August 1917),20.

49. Ibid.

50. *Spade Regen* 10/7 (October 1917), Supplement.

51. *Spade Regen* 11/6 (September 1918),24.

52. Ibid. Besides Polman a few ladies from Denmark were present. On the Mülheim Conference of 1919 Sweden demonstrated the unity by sending a deputation. Some English brethren had a parcel of food delivered which was gladly received as the first "peace dove." By letter the English friends explained that Christians are not allowed to take part in bloodshed. Consequently they had refused to fight in the

war and had suffered because of it. *Pfingstgrüsse*, much pleased with the sign of friendship, published part of the letter, but added that one could differ on the matter of partaking in war. Other letters of sympathy were received from the U.S.A. and Poland. *Pfingstgrüsse* 11/20 (5 October 1919),87; 11/21 (19 October 1919),91; 11/25 (14 December 1919),107; 12/6 (14 March 1920),23.

53. *Spade Regen* 12/5 (August 1919),79.

54. Paul Fleisch, *Die Pfingstbewegung in Deutschland* (Hannover: Heino. Feesche Verlag, 1957), pp. 263-64; Chr. Krust, *50 Jahre Deutsche Pfingstbewegung* (Altdorf: Missionsbuchhandlung und Verlag, 1958), pp. 135-37.

55. Ernst Giese, *Jonathan Paul, Ein Knecht Jesu Christi* (Altdorf: Missionsbuchhandlung und Verlag, 1965), pp. 217-24. Fleisch, pp. 258-64; cf. J. Paul, "Trek uw schoenen uit!" *Spade Regen* 12/9 (December 1919),136-39.

56. G.R. Polman, "De Conferentie te Mülheim-Ruhr," *Spade Regen* 12/6 (September 1919),86; cf. G.R. Polman, "De Crisis in de Pinkster-beweging," *Spade Regen* 12/8 (November 1919),115-17.

57. G.R. Polman, "Een Persoonlijk Getuigenis," *Spade Regen* 12/6 (September 1919),84.

58. *Spade Regen* 12/6 (September 1919),96, reported that the new revival was not generally "revealed" and to some it was still strange. This indicates that the Dutch Pentecostals, whose circumstances were quite different, did not readily accept the message. For testimonies of believers that did go through similar crisis experiences, see *Spade Regen* 12/7 (October 1919),104-05, 110-12; 12/9 (December 1919),141-43.

59. *Spade Regen* 12/8 (November 1919),128.

60. *Spade Regen* 12/9 (December 1919),143.

61. *Spade Regen* 12/12 (March 1920),190. J. Paul would again stay in Holland from December 1920 till January 1921 and from December 1921 till February 1922.

62. *Spade Regen* 13/3 (July 1920),48.

63. *Spade Regen* 13/4 (July 1920),61-62. Boulton wrote, "I feel that I have entered the greatest crisis of my life and ministry."

64. "Zending en Evangelisatie: Internationale Pinkster-conferentie," *De Amsterdammer* 9/2674 (10 January 1921).

65. Boddy, Polhill, and Barratt, though invited, were not present. Also Mast from France was unable to attend. *Confidence* no. 125 (April-June 1921), 20, published a photo of the attenders to the conference mentioning their country: *Germany*: Pastor J. Paul, Pastor E. Edel, Pastor Kusch, Pastor E. Humburg, Pastor C. Voget, Pastor R. Schober, Mr. A. Wieneke (missionary to China), Miss A. Stoptkuchen, Miss E. Eichhorn, Miss M. Achterrath, Miss H. Hacklander, Mr. J. Poppinga (missionary to South Africa), Mr. J. Voskamp. *England*: Mr. A.S. Booth-Clibborn, Mr. and Mrs. W. Bernard, Mr. and Mrs. J. Walshaw and grandchild, Miss Nelly Alsop, Miss Caffyn, Miss Davies Colley (missionary to India), Miss L.

Mackinlay, Mr. Zimmerman. *Scotland*: Mr. Beruldsen, Mr. D. Gee. *Sweden*: Pastor O. Witt, Pastor L. Pethrus, Pastor R. Fris, Mr. A. Johnson, Mr. J. Erikson (missionary to the Congo), Mr. O. Nelson (missionary to Argentina), Mr. A. Holmgren, Mr. D. Flood (missionary to the Congo). *Denmark*: Mr. and Mrs. Bjrner, *Switzerland*: Mr. and Mrs. H. Steiner, Mr. W. Scheuermeier. *America*: Pastor A.L. Fraser, Mr. Max Wood Moorhead. *Holland*: Mr. and Mrs. Polman and daughter, Miss P. van Wieren, Miss E. Scharten (missionary to China), Miss G. Roos, Miss T. Bakker, Miss A. Gnirrep, Miss E. de Vries, Misses J. and J. van Donselaar, Mr. C. van Wynen.

66. "Über die Internationale Pfingstkonferenz in Amsterdam," *Pfingst-grüsse* 13/4 (April 1921),26. The incident made a profound impression on eyewitness Martha Visser. Martha Marijs-Visser, Interview, The Hague, 17 August 1984.

67. Max Wood Moorhead, "Notes and Impressions of the International Convention at Amsterdam, Holland, Jan. 8-17, 1921," *Elim Evangel* 2/2 (March 1921),35-36.

68. "The International Pentecostal Convention at Amsterdam, Holland," *Trust*, April 1921, p. 9; "Pentecostal Items," *Trust*, March 1921, pp. 9-11.

69. A.S. Booth-Clibborn, "De Internationale Pinksterconferentie in Holland," *Spade Regen* 13/11 (February 1921),169-70. Translated in *Trust*, April 1921, pp. 9, 14; *Pentecostal Evangel*, 2 April 1921.

70. Donald Gee, *Wind and Flame* (Croyden: Heath Press, 1967), p. 121. The tension between the German and the Swedish brethren, noted by Gee, was also related to a strong difference of opinion about church structure and water baptism. Cf. Lewi Pethrus, "Den internationalla pingstkonferensen i Amsterdam," *Evangelii Härold*, 27 January 1921; Idem, "Amsterdam-Wien," *Evangelii Härold*, 3 February 1921; Rakel Fris and Rikard Fris, *Vaår Trosväg* (Stockholm: Forlaget Filadelfia, pp. 141-43; Rakel Fris, *Insyn i Mina Mines Värld*, pp. 153-55.

71. *Spade Regen* 13/11 (February 1921),167.

72. After the 1928 Mülheim Conference some Pentecostals from America, being disturbed, wrote: "It is as if a total different Lord is speaking here. . . . God is yet the same. Why then would He in Germany speak so totally different and reveal Himself so totally different as here in America?" The writer realized some Americans were extreme in only speaking in terms of joy and jubilation, but in Germany the other extreme was revealed: always in sackcloth and ashes. Fleisch, pp. 312-13.

73. Stotts, p. 52. Stotts is quoting from "Le Hâvre: départ du Réveil en France," *Vie et Lumière* no. 29 (October-December 1966),4. No record of this visit was found in *Spade Regen*, to which must be added that issues 12/11 and 12/12, February and March 1920, could not be located.

74. "Bezoek aan Frankrijk," *Spade Regen* 15/9 (December 1922),141-43. On the out-journey Mast had been visited in Paris and on the way

home a meeting was held in the French-Scandinavian student's home in Paris, of which a certain Neeser was director.

75. Ibid. Every day meetings and house visitations were held, also in nearby Sanvic where Miss Pedley, an English lady, labored. *Spade Regen* 15/12 (March 1923),92, recorded a visit to Paris for meetings with the scattered believers there. One young girl, who was dying of appendicitis, was healed.

76. "Zendelingen naar Martinique," *Spade Regen* 16/5 (August 1923),79-80.

77. "Zendelingen naar Martinique," *Spade Regen* 16/6 (September 1923),95-96. On the way home some time was spent with Baptist friends in Paris. *Spade Regen* 16/9 (December 1923),143-44, quotes from two letters of Delanis and bears a picture on the cover.

78. "Le Havre," *Spade Regen* 19/12 (March 1927),187-89. Miss Biolley is here described as the leader of the Pentecostal assembly at Le Havre. On the way some missionaries in Paris were visited. Mention is made of the Berntz-Lanz couple, Mrs. Berntz being a daughter of Dr. Lanz, a dentist at Neuchâtel, who worked with the Pentecostals there.

79. W. Polman, "Le Havre," *Spade Regen* 20/2 (May 1927),31-32. Four people were baptized.

80. *Spade Regen* 20/3 (June 1927),43, 45. During the Monday baptismal service one young French lady was baptized.

81. A.A. Boddy, "Winter Days in Belgium," *Confidence* 13/1 (January-March 1920),11.

82. Ibid., p. 5.

83. G.R. Polman to G. Sandberg, Amsterdam, 28 April 1920. The correspondence with Sandberg was found in the Archives of the Swedish Pentecostal Movement at Stockholm.

84. Ada Esselbach to G. Sandberg, Antwerp, 5 October 1920.

85. H.S.T. Gahan to G. Sandberg, Brussels, 24 September 1920.

86. David D. Bundy, "Pentecostalism in Belgium," *Pneuma* 8/1 (Spring 1986),41-56, mentions Leon Viquerat as the first Swedish missionary, who was active in Wallonia (the French part) from 1928.

87. *Spade Regen* 13/4 (July 1920),62.

88. Martha Visser, Interview, The Hague, 17 August 1984.

89. *Spade Regen* 14/4 (July 1921),63.

90. *Spade Regen* 16/7 (October 1923),112.

91. "België," *Spade Regen* 16/12 (March 1924),191-92.

92. *Spade Regen* 19/1 (April 1926),10. The last reference to Mrs. Esselbach in *Confidence* was found in no. 129 (April-June 1922), 18. It concerned the publication of her testimony in a tract (16 pages) entitled *My Doctor* (Brasschaet, Antwerp: International Bible Depôt). It was planned to have it also printed in French and Flemish.

93. C. van der Laan and P.N. van der Laan, *Pinksteren in Beweging* (Kampen: J.H. Kok, 1982), p. 152.

94. *Spade Regen* no. 30 (June-July 1912),4. In the guestbook of the Maranatha Home, 73 Highbury New Park, London, Potma's name was found in July, October and December 1912, with Amsterdam as

his home address. Potma's period in South Africa remains obscure. *The Elim Evangel* 1/3 (June 1920),49, mentioned Potma, with the addition "now of Belgium," among the speakers of the Swanwick Convention, 24-29 April 1920.

95. C.T. Potma, "Revival in Belgium," *The Pentecostal Evangel*, 28 May 1921. At this time Potma was still working with Norton. Potma mentioned the plan for a Flemish Bible School "of which I will, maybe, take charge." Cf. "Gospel Work in Belgium," *The Pentecostal Evangel*, 9 January 1926, p. 7, for a brief overview of the work of Norton.

96. Some of Potma's frequent travels to England to secure financial support can be dated by references in the Maranatha Home guestbook: November 1927; September 1928; January, March, and July (just before his death) 1929.

97. *Pinksteren in beweging*, pp. 152-53. Potma's break with Norton can be dated in 1922. According to *Pfingstgrüsse* 14/7 (July 1922),13, Potma had rented a ballroom at Antwerp and held Pentecostal meetings.

98. C.T. Potma, "The Foursquare Gospel in Belgium," *The Elim Evangel* 7/13 (July 1926),153. Cf. correspondence between Potma and Jeffreys kept in the Elim archives in England.

99. *Pinksteren in beweging*, pp. 153-56.

100. "België," *Spade Regen* 22/9 (December 1929),143-44.

101. Joh. Rietdijk, "België," *Spade Regen* 23/4 (July 1930),63. In his letter, dated 30 May 1930, Rietdijk mentioned that with the opening service (Easter 1930) one "brother from our sister assembly at Brussels" brought greetings.

102. David D. Bundy, "Pentecostalism in Belgium," p. 49. Cf. Bundy's "Johannes Rietdijk, Pentecostal Theologian," in *Pentecostal Research in Europe: Problems, Promises and People*, ed. W.J. Hollenweger (Frankfurt/Bern: P. Lang, forthcoming).

7 GROWTH OF PENTECOSTAL CIRCLES IN THE NETHERLANDS

From Amsterdam the Pentecostal message spread to other places throughout the country. Small circles of Pentecostal believers came and went. Some developed into independent assemblies. Others languished, often due to lack of leadership. As long as Polman was in office there was a strong unity based on his undisputed leadership. In this survey the developments outside of Amsterdam will be related. Where possible special consideration is given to ascertain the background of the people that were drawn. In her cross-section view of the Pentecostal work in Holland, "Faith, Floods and Flowers," Mrs. Polman wrote in 1929:

> Thousands have been and are being blessed through the Pentecostal Movement in Holland. It is not for us to count the number of those who have been saved, healed, and baptized with the Holy Spirit, and who have come under the influence of this blessed flood of the Latter Rain, but we will give you an inkling of the extent of the work and the character.[1]

We will follow Mrs. Polman on her journey along the "many and varied Assemblies working in the unity of the Spirit in Holland."

Haarlem

. . . Haarlem, surely you have heard of the famous city of flowers! Yes, there is a large Assembly in Haarlem and their work and hall are a replica of ours in Amsterdam. A lively band of consecrated, deeply taught people have survived many difficulties in Haarlem and are boldly proclaiming the Pentecostal message.[2]

During 1908 there still was a Dowie circle in Haarlem, that met in the Jacobijnerstraat under leadership of evangelist Hendrik Bos.[3] When Polman was asked to speak, he testified of his new experience with the Holy Spirit. Bos did not accept the message and refused to invite Polman again. Some of the women, deeply impressed with what they had heard, decided to unite in prayer to also receive this Pentecostal blessing. Prayer meetings commenced in the home of Suus and Els van Looi and Sientje Kleefman in the Van Marumstraat, where they ran a ironing business.[4]

Sientje Kleefman (1886-1986) came from the Netherlands Reformed Church, but was confirmed in the Gereformeerde Kerk. With her parents she attended the meetings of evangelist Bos. Her parents and three of the seven children were eventually to become Pentecostal.[5] Soon Riek Trompetter, a school-teacher, joined the small prayer circle in the Van Marumstraat 40. She had been warned that the Pentecostals were of the devil, but after attending the conference with Alexander Boddy in September 1908 she knew better. In a home prayer meeting in Amsterdam she received the baptism with the Holy Spirit on 30 September after Polman laid hands on her.[6] During the Easter Conference 1909 Suus and Els van Looi received their Spirit baptism in Amsterdam too. One week later Sientje Kleefman came through while she was alone in her room in Haarlem. As she did not speak in tongues, she was told by the others that it was not the real baptism, but an "anointing."[7] Sientje never accepted this explanation and although a few weeks later she did receive the tongues, she always maintained to have been baptized that first time.[8] Polman came weekly on Thursday evenings, otherwise the meetings were led by Riek Trompetter. In 1910 public meetings were held in "Jeruël," 68 Bakenessergracht.[9]

Jan Hendrik Schat (1887-1977), a telegraphist who lived in Amsterdam, had visited the Pentecostal meetings there in 1908 and became converted. When he moved to Haarlem in 1910 he joined the Pentecostals there. On 10 December 1911 he was the first male at Haarlem to be baptized with the Spirit. Riek Trompetter seemed to have been waiting for this event, for she immediately handed over leadership to him.[10]

Several other places of meeting followed until in 1916 a former pub in the Nieuwe Kruisstraat 14 was rented and redecorated. A number of people were converted and baptized with the Spirit. After two years the attendance had doubled and the hall became too small.[11] Efforts to hire or buy a larger hall failed. In 1922 the building in the Nieuwe Kruisstraat 14 was bought and rebuilt. The hall was made twice as large, with a small room and lodging upstairs. On 21 September 1922 the new "Immanuel" hall was opened.[12] Polman wrote:

> We thank God for the circle in Haarlem, that has been formed in the beginning of this Pentecostal revival and has always been characterized by faithfulness and dedication. It has slowly, but steadily extended itself and does a lot for the outer mission. It is always a pleasure for us to go to Haarlem, although God has also given there capable laborers. They are used to solid food there, and one could say are hard to satisfy, but that comes forth out of the deep longing for God and the Eternal reality.[13]

The building was bought for f5,000, of which f4,000 had to be borrowed.[14] The cost of rebuilding and decorating was covered by gifts from members of the assembly. In connection with the property the assembly was incorporated in 1926 in Stichting Gebouw Immanuel.[15]

The Pentecostal assembly at Haarlem always worked in good harmony with Amsterdam. The conferences in Amsterdam were well attended by believers from Haarlem. There was a great love for the mission work. The proceeds of the annual mission bazaars, where all kinds of donated articles and the products of the sewing circle were sold, was often around f1,000.[16] Polman and the missionaries on furlough regularly visited the assembly. Polman did not dictate the work, but encouraged or at least allowed for an independent development.

Compared with the other assemblies in the country Haarlem was privileged with capable leadership. J.H. Schat led the work after 1912. In 1920 there was a small "council of brothers" that led the work and who together with the "council of brothers" from Amsterdam formed a mission committee.[17] The six men in whose name the building was bought in 1922, and who also formed the board of Stichting Gebouw Immanuel incorporated in 1926, were probably the same persons. They were: J.H. Schat, who climbed from telegraphist to personnel manager with the Post, Telephone and Telegraph service; Dirk Peters, caretaker; Anthonie Andrea, book-keeper; Jan Thomas Erdtsieck, civil servant; Jan Berend van der Molen, book-keeper; Pieter Schornagel, cigar-maker(!).[18] Of these men Schat, Erdtsieck, and Van der Molen preached. There were no rich among the members; all came from the working class or were small tradesmen.[19]

Terschelling

Terschelling is a little isle north of the province of Friesland, about two hours by boat from Harlingen. G.A. Wumkes commenced his office as minister of the Netherlands Reformed Church in Hoorn on Terschelling and wrote down the general history of the isle in his *Tussen Flie en Borne* (Wester-Schelling: J. Oepkes, 1900). Once he considered writing a monograph about the Pentecostal assembly on Terschelling. Polman, much pleased with the idea, calling it "a divine inspiration," provided Wumkes with many details including a hand-written report by eyewitness Cil Bakker. Wumkes never finished the project, but did keep the gathered material and his rough notes in his files. This combined with data found elsewhere resulted in the most documented description of how a Pentecostal assembly outside of Amsterdam came to being.

Herre Stegenga succeeded G.A. Wumkes as minister of the Netherlands Reformed Church in Hoorn on Terschelling in 1898. Stegenga was even more orthodox than his predecessor. Therefore the tension, which had started under Wumkes between the modernist and orthodox wing in the church, increased. When at the elections the modernists won and got a majority in the church council, the position of Stegenga became very difficult. The orthodox wing fought back by founding a Christian elementary school. The situation worsened by the arrival of a stranger. Hinne Haitjema, an

American evangelist, started coming to the isle around July 1902, going from house to house with his paper *De Vrije Evangelie Trompet.*

Haitjema was of Frisian descent. His father came from the "fijne Mennisten" (precise-orthodox Mennonites), from the southwest part of Friesland. The "fijne Mennisten" were known for their refusal of arms, their practice of foot-washing and their sober and strict lifestyle. They wore old-fashioned clothing, used no silver, gold, or mirrors, and abstained from tobacco and liquor. When the government continued to refuse them exemption from military service, many left for America around 1853 and settled in Indiana and in Michigan.[20] Haitjema's parents went to Elkhart County, Indiana. Hinne, born in 1858, married and became a farmer. A serious illness around 1890 brought him to conversion.[21] He became an independent evangelist preaching salvation and sanctification along the lines of the Holiness movement. On the basis of a revelation he went to the Netherlands in early 1902.[22] He stayed with relatives at Dedemsvaart and from there he journeyed through the country, distributing his papers and preaching wherever he had opportunity. In November 1903 he knocked at the door of Herre Stegenga in Hoorn on Terschelling. The minister, who had hawkers at his door before, asked the stranger inside. Haitjema tried to convince the Reformed minister that the church had become Babel. The infant baptism was unscriptural. First one had to be converted, then baptized in water by immersion, and after that be baptized with the Holy Spirit to live a holy life. Haitjema urged Stegenga to leave the church.[23]

Stegenga, who was already heading for a crisis in his church, accepted the message and resigned on 17 December 1903.[24] From then onwards he held meetings with his orthodox following in their unfinished school building.[25] In these meetings Stegenga introduced Haitjema, but many did not appreciate Haitjema's message and manners.[26] Haitjema brought a revivalistic speech, invited the audience to make a personal decision for Christ, and held prayer sessions after the meetings. Stegenga came more and more under influence of Haitjema. When he had to deliver a sermon he was often unprepared, wanting to say only what the Lord gave him to

speak.[27] The more Stegenga sided with Haitjema, the more
he drifted away from the majority of his following.

In November 1904 J. Adolfs was appointed head of the
school and leader of the mission that continued the meetings
in the school building. Stegenga withdrew and with Haitjema
started separate meetings in the home of C.A. Bakker at Lies.
Only a small part remained loyal to him. Unlike the mission in
the school building, this little group developed into a separate
assembly outside the Reformed church. Memberships with
the church as well as with the school were denounced. The
latter estranged them even further from the orthodox party.
Herre Stegenga left in 1905 for Apeldoorn, where his father
P. Stegenga Azn. did evangelistic work and edited a paper
entitled *Het Lampje*. Herre Stegenga turned theosophist, but
was later regained for the Reformed church and became
missionary to the Dutch Indies (1913-1920).[28] Haitjema
continued leading the group at Lies. On 22 October 1905 he
baptized one lady of 24 years at sea.[29]

In November 1907 Haitjema visited the Pentecostal
gatherings at Amsterdam. He stayed three days with the
Polmans and fasted for the Pentecostal baptism, but did not
receive the experience. Polman and Haitjema did not get
along. Haitjema regarded Polman as "fleshly" for not being
vegetarian like himself. Polman, on the other hand, did not
feel "one in Spirit" with Haitjema.[30] M.D. Voskuil from The
Hague, who at this time still sympathized with the Pentecostal
movement, went with Haitjema to Terschelling in January
1908. Within a few days five were baptized with the Spirit and
spoke in tongues. Voskuil came back alone and requested
that Polman come to Terschelling as well. In February 1908
Polman made his first trip to the isle in the company of
Voskuil. In the house of C.A. Bakker Polman had a big
quarrel with Haitjema, who was becoming over-wrought and
started to call himself Elijah. Haitjema left Terschelling and
settled at Breda to work among the Catholics. In March 1908
the *Ermelosch Zendingsblad* reported:

> The American evangelist H. at Breda, known in many places
> by the distributing of "De Vrij Evangelie trompet" and later
> of "De blijde tijding," was lately full of desire to receive the

Pentecostal baptism with the sign of speaking in unknown languages. Meetings where one prayed and spoke were held in his home. But at last signs of mental derangement began to reveal themselves with Mr. H., and it became so serious, that on Saturday morning, when Mr. H. was wandering around his house, the police of Breda brought him for observation to the City Hospital.[31]

Haitjema's brother David came over from America to take him back home. He had some weeks of rest with his oldest sister and returned to his farm, never to be heard of again.[32] After the departure of Haitjema the little flock on Terschelling continued as a Pentecostal assembly. Most of the members received the Spirit baptism right at the beginning, the others much later. They were earnest believers with a simple faith, consisting of fishermen, farmers, sailors, housewives, and one shopkeeper. They met in homes and had no leader besides Polman, who came over about once a year.

In the case of Terschelling the Pentecostal experience had come to an isolated group separated from the Reformed church. The changes under Stegenga and Haitjema, and the price they had paid for their loyalty, had prepared them for "a deeper work of the Spirit," that is, the Spirit baptism. In the eyes of the other parties on Terschelling it confirmed their reputation of being sectarian. On such a small isle this implied that the Pentecostal message had little chance of winning converts.[33] Polman wrote in 1917, "Nobody dares to join them out of fear for the other Christians."[34] Nevertheless they commanded the respect of the community for their irreproachable behavior. Polman always praised their simplicity and dedication: "They are the heart of the Pentecostal Movement in Holland; they are doing the most in proportion for the kingdom of God."[35]

Several times Polman tried to rent the church building or the school at Hoorn for public meetings, but was refused and held open-air meetings instead. These open-air meetings in the dunes drew crowds of 200 people among whom were orthodox and modern church members alike. Polman sensed the same longing for God among both parties, but noted that as their teachers did not meet this need the people were kept in a drowsy condition.[36] He wrote to Boddy, "I believe that the only hope for that isle is the Pentecostal Movement, because all there is that is religious is as dead as a doornail."[37] The awakening Polman hoped for never came, but the relation to one another did improve.

When in 1921 two Pentecostal daughters from Terschelling, Trijntje Bakker and Geertje Roos, went to the mission field in China, the Reformed church allowed Polman to use their building "Ons Huis" for the farewell service free of charge.[38] The event made a deep impression upon the islanders. Never before had missionaries been sent out from Terschelling. When six years later the two Pentecostal sisters returned, the islanders prepared them a warm welcome.[39] Again the building "Ons Huis" was given without charge. The Christian school at Hoorn carefully opened its doors too. In 1925 when another missionary to China, Piet Klaver, was on Terschelling he was permitted to use the school building for a public meeting. The teacher-evangelist of the school was present and in his introductory words expressed the hope that through this evening they would draw closer to each other.[40] On 13 November 1927 the next meeting in the school building was held with Geertje Roos speaking.[41] Summarizing it can be said that although the Pentecostal assembly on Terschelling did not grow in number, it did mature in quality. The latter can be measured by the general respect for their exemplary life and the admiration for their missionary zeal.

Sneek and Harlingen

In Sneek and Harlingen, two cities in Friesland, Polman was able to introduce the Pentecostal message among the Baptists. Polman knew the Baptist pastor at Sneek, Gerrit de Wilde, from his time with the Salvation Army, when they were fellow officers. Gerrit de Wilde (1853-1914), born in Amsterdam, had been one of the three official witnesses to Polman's first marriage in 1897. In 1903 he had become Baptist and since June 1903 he was pastoring the Baptist assembly of Sneek and also assisted in the Baptist assembly of Harlingen. The Pentecostal conference with Boddy during

September 1908 in Amsterdam drew some believers from Sneek. One sister "received her Pentecost on arriving."[42] De Wilde arrived a little later having just returned from Berlin, where he had met Jonathan Paul.[43] From this time on a little nucleus within the Baptist assembly in Sneek started seeking after the Pentecostal blessing. Some of the pastoral letters Polman and his wife wrote to these followers have been kept. On 5 October 1908 Polman urged them to remain in fellowship with the other brothers and sisters and to avoid forming a separate club, but added: "Of course you must have your prayer sessions with all who search after this blessing."[44]

De Wilde welcomed Polman to visit the Baptists in Harlingen when he would be in that place en route to Terschelling. In January 1909 returning from a visit to the isle Polman attended a Monday night meeting of the Baptists in Harlingen. When the elder invited him to speak he testified of the work of God in Amsterdam and other places. Some of the brothers and sisters came to Polman in his guest house that same evening, wanting to hear more from him.[45] Polman informed De Wilde of his visit writing: "It could well be that in Harlingen the members are going ahead of the leaders, the opposite from Sneek, some, I think at least seven are going ahead and I believe even more."[46] The situation in Sneek did not permit Polman, much to his regret, to also visit the group of seekers there.[47] In Sneek pastor De Wilde had embraced the Pentecostal message, which caused a lot of tension as many members did not approve of it. Some refused to sing Psalms that mentioned the Holy Spirit.[48] In January 1909 De Wilde wrote a letter of explanation to his Baptist colleagues in order to refute rumors. Finally on 11 July 1909 De Wilde left for America, where he would pastor the Dutch Baptist congregation in Paterson, New Jersey, until his death in 1914. From his letters it is evident that he remained in full sympathy with the Pentecostal message.[49]

Immediately after De Wilde's departure the Pentecostal adherents in Sneek were excluded from the Baptist assembly. Some returned and after public confession of guilt were readmitted.[50] *Spade Regen* November 1909 reports Polman visiting Harlingen and (for the first time) Sneek. In Sneek the believers were in the midst of "resistance and misjudgement."[51] The Baptist periodical *De Christen* 2 December 1909 suggested that the situation in Sneek was calming down. The Lord's Supper could again be celebrated. Only ten members were said to continue in their withdrawal.[52] In Harlingen, where according to *De Christen* the same "contagious illness" had broken loose, six members had left, one of whom was regained in November 1909.[53]

The Pentecostal work in Harlingen never got larger than a handful of believers meeting in homes. After 1912 we lose track of it. In Sneek it was a little better. Leading persons were T. van Tuinen, a baker's roundsman, and Klaas Rusticus (1867-1944), a department head in a rope yard.[54] Meetings were held in the home of Rusticus, Prinsengracht 10, and occasionally, when Polman came over, a hall was rented for public services. During 1915 to 1920 public meetings, led by Rusticus or Van Tuinen, were conducted on a more regular basis.[55] On his visits to Sneek Polman got acquainted with G.A. Wumkes, minister of the local Reformed church. Wumkes' publication *De Pinksterbeweging voornamelijk in Nederland* (1916) lists Sneek among the existing Pentecostal circles. Another list of Pentecostal assemblies compiled by Polman in 1926 omits Sneek.[56] One young lady from Sneek went to the training school at Amsterdam from 1919 till 1921.[57] On two occasions, 1920 and 1922, Jonathan Paul addressed meetings in Sneek.[58] In 1922 a mission service with Elize Scharten drew 300 people.[59] The last reference to Sneek in *Spade Regen* is found in February 1925 when missionary Piet Klaver addressed a meeting and remarked that attendance was small.[60]

Delfzijl and Groningen

> . . . In Groningen many of the smaller Assemblies of the North meet together regular.[61]

Groningen is a province in the north of The Netherlands, east of Friesland. As the province and its capital carry the same name, it is sometimes not clear whether the province or the city is meant. More than once *Spade Regen* has used the province name to denote believers from other places like Delfzijl. Around 1909 the Pentecostal message reached Delfzijl by means of two unmarried ladies: Jantien van Driessum and Bé Zwart. The ladies had been introduced to the German Pentecostal movement while visiting relatives near Mülheim. They were baptized with the Holy Spirit there and brought the blessing to Delfzijl. The prayer sessions that would commence in their home on the Oude Schans 7 became the cradle of the present "Eben Haëzer" Pentecostal assembly.[62]

In 1917 Elle van der Molen, a carpenter from Delfzijl, was converted and baptized with the Holy Spirit, while he temporarily was working on Terschelling and stayed with a Pentecostal family. Back in Delfzijl Van der Molen soon became the leader of the meetings that were held in the home on the Oude Schans.[63] That same year, 1917, *Spade Regen* reported that the Pentecostal circle in Delfzijl was very active with open-air meetings and home visitations and was looking for a place to have public meetings: "God bless this band of heroes and help them to warm the cold North by the glow of Divine love that He, through the Holy Spirit, had poured out in our hearts." [64] On Sunday, 16 September 1917, believers from Delfzijl and Groningen were in Amsterdam in connection with the baptismal service that afternoon.[65] *Spade Regen* April 1918 recorded Polman's first visit to Delfzijl. When Polman or one of the missionaries came a hall was rented; otherwise all meetings continued in the home of Van Driessum and Zwart.[66]

Early in 1925 the circle numbered between 10 and 15 believers and included a dockyard worker, two carpenters, and the wife of a pilot.[67] Those that joined the Pentecostals were not understood by their environment and became subject to criticism. While going from house to house with *Klanken des Vredes* and *Spade Regen* the two ladies Van Driessum and Zwart met Roelof Kamp, who owned a drapery-shop in nearby Appingedam. When the Kamp family left the Netherlands Reformed Church and joined the Pentecostals during 1925, a great loss in clientele was suffered.[68]

During 1926 Elle van der Molen with his colleague Jan de

Jonge from Wagenborgen worked in Groningen, where they stayed with a Pentecostal family and attended Pentecostal meetings in the home of Carel F. Gnirrep, an engineer who had come from Amsterdam. Jan de Jonge was the only carpenter in a family of land-workers, members of the Netherlands Reformed Church. In the home of Gnirrep he was converted and became the means by which his parents, five sisters, and two brothers with their relations-in-law were all converted too. Most of them joined the Pentecostal assembly at Delfzijl, which gave it a considerable growth.[69] During the Amsterdam Whitsuntide Conference of 1929 a wedding confirmation service for two couples from Delfzijl was conducted by Polman on Sunday morning. The following day they were baptized by immersion.[70] Around this time the choir "Looft den Heere" was formed by believers of the Delfzijl area.[71]

In the city of Groningen Polman had already addressed a meeting in 1918 together with missionary J. Thiessen:

> There was an attentive audience, that was very interested. Missionary Thiessen spoke about the Russian and Finnish revolution, that he had experienced himself, and related it with the return of the Lord. They expect us to be back in Groningen soon and even requested us to come and hold a conference for several days. Perhaps there are among the workers in God's kingdom in or outside of Groningen some who would apply to co-operate with us in this matter.[72]

With his call to the "workers in God's kingdom" Polman tried to find a broader basis before proceeding further. The call, it would seem, was not answered and for several years no such conference was being held. In the meantime the couple C.F. Gnirrep and A. Gnirrep-Romberg moved from Amsterdam to Groningen and started home meetings in Koninginnelaan 27a. On 12 September 1926 the couple arranged a mutual meeting in Groningen for the Pentecostal believers in the region. About 25 believers from Groningen, Delfzijl, Appingedam, and Oude Pekela turned up. It was decided to have monthly meetings of this kind in rotating places for all Pentecostals in the area.[73] The next meeting was in Appingedam in the home of Kamp. Also believers from Veendam were present.[74]

In January 1927 Polman came over for a series of public meetings in Groningen, Delfzijl, and Veendam. In Groningen many from other circles and denominations attended.[75] The home assembly at Groningen grew and from June 1927 till March 1928 they held public meetings on Sunday evenings in the "Schortingshuis" on the Vischmarkt. Mrs. Gnirrep also organized meetings for young girls that worked in the factories.[76]

Hilversum

. . . Forty miles from Amsterdam, you can visit the work at Hilversum, a residential city of beautiful parks and villas. During the whole of the summer open air meetings are held by the consecrated believers at Hilversum. The work is large and progressive. Showers of blessings of the Latter Rain have created at Hilversum a garden of spiritual flowers.[77]

When Wumkes published his list of assemblies and circles in 1916, not Hilversum, but the neighboring Bussum was recorded. Already in 1909 four believers at Bussum had received their Spirit baptism. In *Spade Regen*, however, Bussum is only mentioned twice during 1918.[78] Hereafter we lose track of Bussum, but in Hilversum the Pentecostal flame was to be carried on. Through the testimony of a certain Tine Visser two couples, Van Ravenzwaay and De Wild, came in contact with the Pentecostal movement and were converted and baptized with the Holy Spirit.[79] In the home of Van Ravenzwaay, Larenseweg 8, house meetings commenced during 1918. Gijsbertus van Ravenzwaay (1891-1962), an engine driver, and his wife Hendrika Vijge (1892-1979) left the Netherlands Reformed Church to which they traditionally belonged.[80] Gerrit de Wild (1886-1975), a gardener, and his wife Boutertje van der Schaft (1891-1985) had no previous church connection.[81] A few times Polman came over to get the work going. Public meetings were started in the course of 1919 in a hall at Noordsche Boschje, in the center of the city. Every Sunday someone from Amsterdam came to lead the service.[82] In November 1925 the assembly was able to hire a larger hall in the same street on a long-term lease. The hall with 100 seats was redecorated and outside the sign "Immanuel Hall" was erected.[83]

There was a warm relationship between the assemblies in Amsterdam and Hilversum. The Hilversum believers were standing guests at the conferences in Amsterdam and participated in the responsibility for the mission. Often on Ascension Day a large group from Amsterdam travelled to Hilversum, some by bicycle, for a joint open-air meeting in the afternoon and a public meeting in the hall at night.[84] It must have been a zealous and steady assembly. There is no indication of difficulties anywhere in *Spade Regen*. The Sunday school and Bible classes, led by Tine Visser, were flourishing and the youth was very enthusiastic. Upon arrival for the Easter Conference in 1930 Mrs. Polman described them as "our faithful ones from Hilversum together with their fiery youngsters."[85]

The members were mainly from the working class with some small tradesmen.[86] There was no pastor among them. When no speaker from Amsterdam arrived, Van Ravenzwaay or De Wild would take the service. As of December 1930 the place of meeting was moved to Toornlaan 4.[87]

Utrecht

> . . . in Utrecht, the city of the great Cathedral and the University . . .[88]

Spade Regen's first reference to Utrecht is found in 1913 when a certain Verwaal wrote from Utrecht concerning the healing of their daughter Maria.[89] Possibly Verwaal belonged to the "similar sect" A. Manussen alluded to in his article against the "so-called Tongue movement" of Amsterdam in December 1916: "Some years ago we had a similar sect here in Utrecht; the 'teaching' and the 'tongue speaking' were exactly like the teaching and the language I heard lately from the tongue people."[90] Wumkes included Utrecht in his listing of assemblies and circles published in 1916, but *Spade Regen* was silent during this period. The second reference to Utrecht came in August 1919:

> Also the meetings in Utrecht are being held more regularly and the small circle there is slowly growing. There is a need for a hall. We pray, that God will send help, to be able to also hold meetings in Utrecht.[91]

In December 1924 more details followed when a letter from the Utrecht circle was quoted:

> In our small circle, where we have now assembled together for about two years, we experience blessed times. . . . Some of us were already converted when they came to us. Some time afterwards, however, they got into a great inner need and felt as if they were not converted. They experienced what Paul says in Romans 7: "I miserable man, who shall deliver me." This was to them an affliction of the heart, that however was wholesome. . . . Partly due to prayer and intercession they suddenly entered into the freedom of the Spirit, of which Romans 8 speaks. . . . This all is glorious and worthy to be mentioned. However, in all of us lives one great longing, that is strong and deep, namely the desire for unity of all the saints in Christ. For our gladness can only be complete when John 17:21 is fulfilled. . . . Partly as glorious proof of God's love and rich grace over us we are able to witness that one from us has received the baptism of the Holy Spirit like more among us have also experienced it.[92]

Believers from Utrecht regularly attended the conferences at Amsterdam and donated money for the mission. There is no record of Polman ever visiting the group in Utrecht. Once Klaver addressed a meeting while on furlough in 1925 and noted that attendance was very meager.[93] Utrecht was never listed among the places of public services being announced in every *Spade Regen*. No further information is known but that Polman in 1926 and Mrs. Polman in 1929 included Utrecht in their overview of the work. It may be concluded that the little assembly in Utrecht operated independently from Amsterdam.

The Hague

> . . . Our Pentecostal brothers and sisters of The Hague are very zealous; they meet in an attractive Pentecostal hall on one of the prominent streets. Their work is aggressive, they spread tracts and papers, witness fearlessly for Christ and are always eager to win sinners who surrender their lives to Christ through the influence of the sweet Gospel of joy and peace.[94]

In The Hague Mrs. Polman received her baptism with the Holy Spirit (29 October 1907) in the home of M.D. Voskuil. Voskuil, a former Salvation Army officer, had examined the Pentecostal manifestations in Zurich and at first sympathized with the movement. During 1908 he had second thoughts, but at the Hamburg Conference in December 1908 he told "how his fears had been removed and how he had been led back into full sympathy."[95] Also his second love for the Pentecostals was of short duration. *Spade Regen* never mentioned his name in connection with the work.[96] The Pentecostal message must have penetrated the house circle led by Voskuil, but further information is lacking.

During the summer of 1908 Arie and Elsje Kok, who temporarily lived in The Hague, started conducting public meetings on the Loosduinschekade 59. Alexander Boddy addressed one such meeting in September 1908 and recorded that about 20 persons were present; one young soldier was recently converted.[97] *Spade Regen* November 1908 referred to "wonderful reports" from The Hague and by December 1908 six had received the "Comforter."[98] After the Kok family had left for the mission field (August 1909), the meetings were no longer announced in *Spade Regen*, although they must have continued for some time. At least in July 1910 Polman still went to The Hague on a regular basis.[99] Hereafter the work faded away until a new start was made in March 1920.

In the course of 1916, the year when Wumkes' *De Pinksterbeweging voornamelijk in Nederland* would appear, Polman received more opportunities to introduce the Pentecostal movement among Christian circles.[100] H. Plokker, who had succeeded Johan de Heer as leader of the city mission "Jeruël" in The Hague, invited the Polman couple to his mission in the spring of 1916. Among those present was Martha Visser, who would become a key figure in the coming work. Plokker edited *De Wapendrager* and participated in *Maran-Atha* of the "Nederlandsche Tentzending." When Plokker went along with the Pentecostals for some time he ran into difficulties with his evangelical friends. During 1918 he left Jeruël and silently disappeared from *Maran-Atha*.[101]

One month before the aforesaid meeting in 1916, Martha Visser (1896-1985) had been confirmed in the Netherlands Reformed Church. Since that first Jeruël meeting she frequently returned to the mission and after some months she received the assurance of being a child of God. Late in 1917 she was baptized by immersion by Plokker.[102] After the troubles in Jeruël in 1918, she went to Baptist meetings for some time. She remained friends with the Plokker family and supported them in the struggle, but at first stayed aloof from the Pentecostal movement. In early 1919 she examined the Pentecostal message in her Bible and became convinced of the biblical nature of the claims.[103] One Wednesday evening in August she visited the Amsterdam assembly. By this time several believers from The Hague frequently went to Amsterdam and requested Polman to start meetings at The Hague.[104]

The new work was launched in March 1920 with services addressed by Jonathan Paul. Weekly public meetings followed on Friday evenings and mutual meetings on Sunday evenings.[105] Plokker was not involved in this development as his sympathy with the Pentecostal movement had cooled down. Competent male leadership was lacking. Soon Martha Visser and Johanna Schotanus (born 1894) were given charge over the meetings. They felt incapable because they were young, female, and inexperienced.[106] Jo Schotanus had for a short period assisted Mrs. Esselbach in her sailors' home at Antwerp before coming to The Hague and felt a call for the mission field.[107] Martha Visser, highly intelligent and with a respected position in society, delivered good sermons, but was not "baptized with the Spirit."[108]

That Polman accepted a young female who could not speak in tongues in leadership reveals his open attitude towards female ministry, but also towards those who did not have the gift of glossolalia. As some members of the The Hague assembly, including co-worker Jo Schotanus, did not share the same attitude, the position of Martha Visser was challenged. The work never really flourished. About 20 persons, mostly females, attended.[109] In March 1921 Jo Schotanus had left for Amsterdam and Martha Visser continued the leadership alone. When Jo Schotanus after a long stay at Amsterdam returned, the two ladies had a quarrel. The "baptized" Jo Schotanus felt that the "unbaptized" Martha Visser was not spiritual enough. Of course the conflict much harmed the work with the sad outcome that the meetings were suspended in October 1923.[110] Although Martha Visser left the Pentecostal movement out of disappointment, she kept a high respect for Polman and never denounced the Pentecostal message. Fifteen years later when Pieter van der Woude commenced another work at The Hague, she would again throw herself into a Pentecostal adventure with similar sorrowful results.[111]

According to *Spade Regen* public meetings at The Hague resumed in July 1925. During 1927 the work grew so much that H. Metz from Rotterdam, who was in charge, moved to The Hague.[112] The assembly was active in open-air evangelization and in spreading literature.[113] On Tuesday, 8 May 1928, a new hall with 200 seats on the Conradkade 61 was opened. Metz related

> . . . how God in a wonderful way had provided in everything: Everything had come by simply believing in God and trusting. . . . There had been no requests for money, etc., but all needs had been prayerfully placed in God's hands and the Lord had provided.[114]

Under Metz the assembly at The Hague worked independently of Amsterdam, but in good harmony. For the Amsterdam conferences a large group from The Hague came over and usually Metz addressed one of the meetings. When Metz died in 1939 a lady worker, Mrs. Van Geresteijn, took over leadership.[115]

Rotterdam

> . . . In Rotterdam, a city of shipbuilding, large docks and worldwide trade, there is a beautiful assembly of spiritual flowers to the glory of God and the spreading of the full truth. A substantial and progressive Assembly is Rotterdam . . .[116]

The Pentecostal work at Rotterdam only started late in 1916. In October 1916 Polman wrote to Wumkes, "Also in Rotterdam it got through in a small circle, with the speaking in tongues."[117] *Spade Regen*'s first reference we find in January 1917:

> "He has filled the hungry with good things" Luke 1:53. These words have been fulfilled in Rotterdam, where some bold and faithful believers have assembled, united in one place, waiting for the promise of the Father, the Holy Spirit, like God has poured out in the beginning. In their mutual meetings two brothers had received the Pentecostal blessing and during our first visit there a sister received this blessing too; she spoke and sang in other languages. The next Sunday two sisters received the baptism of the Spirit.[118]

The same issue of *Spade Regen* speaks of another lady from Rotterdam, who came over for the Christmas and New Year services and was baptized with the Spirit at Amsterdam. Possibly the "mutual meetings" referred to were held in the home of the Schreurs family at Adamshofstraat 175. The children of the Stokker family, whose parents joined the Pentecostals during 1917, remember the Sunday prayer sessions in the house of Schreurs as being rather noisy.[119]

Another witness to these home meetings was found when this present author in the Koninklijke Bibliotheek (Royal Library) in The Hague called for G.A. Wumkes' *De Pinkster-beweging voornamelijk in Nederland* (1916). Inside the book was a small paper with hand-written notes dated Sunday, 7 July 1918, with the address and name of Schreurs. It contained an interpretation of glossolalia through a "brother Bokhorst" and a prophecy. The two prophetic utterances carried three messages: a call to evangelize the world; Jesus is coming soon; and an appeal to receive the baptism with the

Holy Spirit, also described in terms of going a deeper way. [120]
Probably these were the principal components of the Pentecostal communication at the time.

Next to the home meetings, public meetings in a rented
hall were recorded in *Spade Regen* starting September 1917:

> We are thankful, that we have been able to meet the many
> requests to hold regular meetings in Rotterdam. The small
> circle extended so much that it was necessary to hire a hall to
> also give opportunity to those who are longing to learn more
> of this revival, to hear more about it. As from the first meeting
> there was a wonderful spirit and we felt, as before, one with
> the people of Rotterdam. [121]

The meetings were held every Monday evening at Bloemstraat 104. On Tuesday evenings the same hall was used by A.
Manussen, an independent evangelist from Utrecht. Manussen had started his evangelistic work around 1905. In 1913 he
made news when he baptized 20 believers by immersion in a
lake at Rotterdam. [122] Manussen edited *Ons Maandblaadje* in
which he wrote against the "so-called Tongue movement" in
December 1916. [123] Nevertheless some of his flock at
Rotterdam started visiting the Monday evening services in
the same building and accepted the deeper truths Polman
proclaimed. For example the Stokker family: Jacobus Alexander Stokker (1874-1940), a carpenter, and his wife Gerardina
Maria Scheffer (1871-1956). Through the ministry of Manussen and the mission "Jeruël" they had become devout
believers, but had lost connection with the Gereformeerde
Kerk to which they originally belonged. Once they attended
the meetings Polman conducted at Bloemstraat 104 they
became Pentecostals. Jacob Stokker would play the organ or
cornet at the meetings. In this period the sister of Mrs.
Stokker seemed to be in her dying hour, but was healed after
Polman had prayed with her. [124] More healings occurred
according to testimonies in *Spade Regen*. [125] Another independent evangelist by the name of Valk, a former carpenter,
accepted the Pentecostal message and with his family and
some of his following he joined the new movement. He kept

leading a small house group in his home, which later would develop into an independent Pentecostal circle.[126]

Already in October 1917 the Monday evening meetings were transferred from the Bloemstraat to the Oppert 149. This rapid changing of meeting places became a pattern throughout the period under Polman. Between 1917 and 1930 the place of worship, always a rented hall, was changed at least nine times.[127] During 1921 public Sunday meetings commenced in the Van Alkemadestraat 24b, where they would remain nearly five years. On Saturday evenings open-air evangelization was held on the Noordplein, "the focus of communism and unbelief."[128] The work grew and in December 1925 Polman expected another Immanuel Hall to be opened in the near future.[129] This never happened, but they did move to a larger hall in June 1926.

During the Easter and Whitsuntide conferences a group from Rotterdam travelled by train to Amsterdam. Halfway through the journey another group of pilgrims from The Hague assembly joined them. As Pentecostal people like to sing, the train was immediately altered into a place of worship. From the Amsterdam station they continued their song of praise while marching to the Immanuel Hall, where they would arrive just before the ten o'clock service.[130]

Most of the members came from the working class. Polman wrote in 1926, ". . . there are also here not many rich, not many noble."[131] Professions that could be ascertained were carpenter, dockyard worker, factory worker, salesman, domestic servant, chief clerk and fire-brigade director.[132] Most of them had a religious background, but were estranged from the church they belonged to through birth. Many had been converted through one of the free missions like that of "Jeruël," Manussen, or Valk, or through the Salvation Army. The Pentecostal message led them into a deeper religious experience. Yet a substantial part of the Pentecostal assembly was added through its own evangelistic efforts. A number were converted as a result of the open-air meetings. At least one was a socialist before he became a dedicated believer in Pentecostal assembly. A few tramps were converted and brought back into society.[133] Some of the factory workers were recorded to have brought in several of their colleagues by their testimonies at work.[134]

As the assembly lacked steady leadership it, in spite of Polman's efforts, foundered. The first years Polman had travelled to Rotterdam every second week to conduct the services himself. In 1921 the assembly was governed by a "council of brothers" who had appointed a certain Kuiper as their pastor.[135] Kuiper failed after which Bernard Kedde (born 1898) from Amsterdam was given charge over the work, while Schreurs and Heinen were the local elders.[136] Kedde came over weekly and was a competent leader. When Kedde withdrew from the ministry in 1927, it had its attendant problems for the Rotterdam assembly. *Spade Regen* November 1927 recorded:

> Our brothers and sisters at Rotterdam had to fight a lot of difficulties lately. The devil had not been sitting still there, but we know that he is a defeated enemy, and will always suffer defeat against the power of the blood of the Lamb. The constant changing of halls had not profited the work and now it is wonderful that one has succeeded in finding a building to assemble in regularly.[137]

Hanselman, a salesman from Rotterdam, was then ordained by Polman to pastor the flock.[138] The optimistic report by Mrs. Polman in 1929, with which this section began, was especially written for American consumption. In reality the year 1929 must have been problematic. Hanselman resigned and the meeting place after two other addresses returned to Van Alkemadestraat 24b. After 1930 the work fell apart and only a few independent house circles remained. When in 1932, after the death of Polman, Pieter van der Woude (1895-1978) started a new Pentecostal assembly at Rotterdam many of the earlier believers joined his work.

Leiden and Gouda

From Leiden little more is known but that public meetings had been held between 1920 and 1922 on the Hooglandsche Kerkgracht 40. During 1917 believers from Leiden requested

Polman to help form a Pentecostal circle there.[139] In April 1920 Polman went to Leiden and reported that Erdtsieck from Haarlem was going to lead the Wednesday evening meetings, now and then relieved by other "brothers."[140] As of October 1922 the announcements of these meetings ceased and here our information ends.[141]

During 1918 Polman twice held meetings at Gouda.[142] Slowly a circle of Pentecostal believers developed. As of February 1926 public meetings were held in the building Tot Heil des Volks. *Spade Regen* recorded that the work still had to struggle with many difficulties. Every Sunday morning someone from Rotterdam took charge over the meetings.[143] Later Gerard Boerma, a brother of one of the elders from the Amsterdam assembly, seems to have taken over responsibility.[144] It must have been a small group and after 1930 the work soon foundered.[145]

Heerlen

. . . All over Holland the Assemblies are scattered wherever one travels; in Heerlen, in the south of Holland, an industrial district filled with mines . . .[146]

In the southern provinces Noord-Brabant and Limburg, traditional strongholds of Roman Catholicism, the Pentecostal message was hardly heard. There are indications of some isolated adherents here and there, but only in the coal-mine area of Sittard, Treebeek, and Heerlen was an assembly established.[147]

During 1916 through the ministry of a certain G. van der Lip from Heerlen, some mine-workers were converted. On Christmas 1916 they attended the services at Amsterdam and gave their testimonies.[148] The work slowly grew and in 1917 Van der Lip led circles in Heerlen and Sittard. He also bought a "Bible tent" in order to sell Bibles at markets. On 28 April 1918 the "Emmanuel" Hall was opened at Heerlen. A former pub was bought by a Pentecostal believer and rebuilt after the pattern of the Amsterdam "Immanuel." The hall could seat 100 persons, while the second and third floors contained an "upper room" and ample place for lodgings. Polman and some believers from Amsterdam and Haarlem came over for the feast day. On the train they already had a time of prayer seasoned with singing in tongues, which "shortened the journey a lot."[149] In Sittard many mine-workers entered the train. The Pentecostals used the opportunity to preach to them and to invite them to the meetings at Heerlen. The following day, after the morning service, more than 10 persons came forward to surrender themselves to Christ. After the evening service some went upstairs, where one believer from Haarlem was baptized with the Spirit.[150]

After a period of apparent difficulties (presumably they had lost their building) Van der Lip in July 1920 informed the readers of *Spade Regen* that they had got hold of two building sites, one at Heerlen and one at Treebeek. God willing, two mission halls would be built.[151] At this point the name of Van der Lip disappears from *Spade Regen*. In March 1921 Polman visited Heerlen for a mutual meeting with 30 believers. Polman temporarily filled the need for leadership by sending Bernard Kedde (born 1898) with two lady workers from Amsterdam. Six months later, in his field report, Kedde did not show much enthusiasm. Limburg is called a "dark region, with little spiritual life," and "It is here like in the days of Noah."[152] When Kedde went to Limburg again in 1923 he noticed an improvement: "Some souls have been added and that says a lot in this region."[153] In 1924 Willem van Hugten, a school-teacher from the Dutch Indies on furlough in Holland, labored a few months in Limburg. Several converts were made before he returned to Java.[154] Polman, who occasionally visited Limburg, reported the need for a building and a leader. On 27 June 1926 a modest, bright hall with 85 seats could be opened:

> Over the years the work there had to fight all sorts of difficulties. But never has the ruler of darkness been able to disturb it completely. Partly because we had no co-operation from any side, we were forced to meet in homes all these years. This is not beneficial for a healthy development of the work. . . . Now it has come so far, that we have been able to hire a nice hall. It is situated in the centre of the mine district, namely Heerlen, Geerstraat 68.[155]

Especially during the past half year there had been much progress. A number had been converted, others were baptized with the Holy Spirit. Catholics were now praising God in new tongues.[156]

One interesting side of the work in Limburg is that it reveals some of the Pentecostal attitude towards Catholicism. In the reports for *Spade Regen* the image of light and darkness is frequently employed. Limburg is the dark area where the light of the Pentecostal witness is much needed. With reference to Van der Lip, whose ministry began in the coal-mines, the imagery could be elaborated with "underneath the earth the seed was sown."[157] Yet there is no sign of bitter feelings towards the Catholic Church. Not even in the lamentation that for years no cooperation was received in securing a hall, which no doubt can be attributed to the strong grip the Catholic Church had on society. Although Polman considered Limburg "full of lifeless religion as Rome in particular has," he realized, "The real battle is not between Roman or Protestant, but between born-again or not born-again."[158] When Polman opened the new hall in 1926 he explained to the audience that the purpose of the meetings was not to found a new church or circle, but to bring the old gospel for the salvation of all.[159]

In spite of the visits of Polman and the short stays of the missionaries on furlough (Klaver, Bakker, and Roos), the growth of 1926 did not carry on.[160] Here again the lack of local leadership was felt. The meetings at Geerstraat 68 did continue, but the light was not as bright. After the cessation of *Spade Regen* in 1931 we lose track of it. Possibly part of the work was carried on by the "Gemeente des Heeren." It would take another 30 years before a new Pentecostal assembly was established at Treebeek.

Apeldoorn

Between 1913 and 1921 missionary J. Thiessen stayed several years in Apeldoorn and was very active in the city mission "Maranatha." During this furlough he also entered the Pentecostal movement and came in contact with Polman.[161]

Around 1920 Polman held a meeting in the "Maranatha" hall, which at that time fell under the chairmanship of Dr. J.H. Gunning J.Hz.[162] In the summer of 1921 Polman took part in organizing open-air meetings.[163] On 11 November 1921 the Christian Healing Home Bethel, Billitonlaan 1, was opened in the presence of Polman. The two Pentecostal ladies in charge, Clinge-Doorenbos and Jonker, labored in "spiritual fellowship with Amsterdam." Polman wrote:

> This work is the result of the blessing, that God has given them during the past time in connection with our meetings in Apeldoorn. We pray, that this house may truly be a house of God, where many a tired soul will find peace, many sick healing, many bound ones deliverance.[164]

Apart from this promising start, there is no report as to how the work progressed and how the relationship with Amsterdam continued.[165] *Spade Regen* only recorded one more visit of Polman to Apeldoorn in 1922.[166]

In 1923 Aaldrik Mik (1894-1931), painter and anarchist with a Lutheran background, was converted during a Maranatha meeting. Shortly afterwards Mik came in contact with Polman and was baptized in the Spirit and in water in Amsterdam. Immediately he started with open-air evangelization in Apeldoorn and held meetings at home.[167] Sometimes he went to Twello, where a few Pentecostal believers lived. During the Easter Conference in Amsterdam 1926, Mik's wife Reiniera Christina van de Worp (1895-1935) was converted on Friday, baptized in water on Monday, while the Spirit baptism followed at home on Tuesday. Mik wrote an enthusiastic letter to Polman in which he also applied for membership.[168] When in 1927 the "Gemeente des Heeren" entered Apeldoorn, Mik and his house circle joined them, much to the regret of Polman, who cancelled Mik's membership.[169]

Zwolle and Meppel

In 1907 Harm Schuurman married Salvation Army officer Sanna Kuiper at Amsterdam. As Salvation Army officers were not allowed to marry outside their ranks, they left the Salvation Army and joined the Pentecostal movement, which had just started. On 5 July 1908 their only child Emmanuel was born. Around 1911 they moved to Zwolle, where Schuurman had found a modest job with the Dutch railways.[170] In his spare time Schuurman started to evangelize. Sometimes he was aided by Trijntje Bakker and Geertje Roos from the Amsterdam training school. Gradually a Pentecostal assembly emerged, that held meetings in the Voorstraat 17. Polman came in 1919, and in 1922 meetings with Jonathan Paul were held in the Lutheran church, Koestraat.[171] Schuurman also had work in Meppel together with a certain De Jong, a school-teacher from Staphorst. De Jong had organized meetings with Polman in 1919 and with Jonathan Paul in 1920.[172] In the building "Hulp in Lijden" weekly meetings were conducted by De Jong or Schuurman.

Schuurman's son Emmanuel was converted in 1924 and then assisted in the work. Around 1928 De Jong died of pneumonia. In his dying hour he laid hands on the 20-year-old Emmanuel and delegated the work to him.[173] Emmanuel continued the meetings in Hulp in Lijden at Meppel, while his father carried on at Zwolle. In spite of his limited education and young age, Emmanuel wrote two notable pamphlets: *Wat zegt Gods Woord?* (1928, 18 pages) and *Behoud den rechte weg* (1929, 15 pages). The first dealt with salvation and water baptism, the latter with the baptism with the Holy Spirit.

Both assemblies were small in size. The members were from the working class and were small tradesmen. For the most part they had a churchly background.[174]

Stadskanaal

In November 1917 *Spade Regen* mentioned a group of earnest believers at Stadskanaal looking for a place to have public Pentecostal meetings.[175] During 1919 and 1920 several public meetings were held by Polman.[176] Preparatory work had been done by students of the training school in spreading *Klanken des Vredes* from house to house, and by a certain Jac.

Munniksma, who lived nearby.[177] In March 1919 an anarchistic socialist was converted and one lady received healing.[178] The leader of a circle of believers opened his church building Rehoboth for meetings.[179] During the summer of 1919 the Pentecostals were very active with meetings every night and open-air on Sunday afternoons.[180] After 1920, however, we lose track of it. In the March 1923 *Spade Regen,* referring to an article in various newspapers concerning a Pentecostal baptismal service at Stadskanaal, was printed, "Readers of *Spade Regen* will have understood, that this circle does not belong to the Pentecostal movement."[181] Possibly the circle at Stadskanaal had broken with Polman and joined the "Gemeente des Heeren," which will be discussed hereafter.

Apart from the places already dealt with, there were other places with Pentecostal believers, but the lack of information prohibits a separate treatment. Most of these places are only mentioned once or twice in *Spade Regen,* often in connection with a visit to Amsterdam. It involves the following place names: Amersfoort, Bloemendaal, Boskoop, Delft, Deventer, Enschede, Geldermalsen, Groede, Heemstede, Den Helder, Leeuwarden, Loppersum, Minnertsga, Noord-Brabant (province), Nieuwe and Oude Pekela, Nieuw Weerdinge, Nijmegen, Oldenbroek, Oude Schans, Roermond, Twello, Velp, Winschoten, Wolvega, Wormerveer, Wijckel, Zaandam, Zutphen.[182]

Gemeente des Heeren

In May 1926 *The Pentecostal Evangel* published an account of the Pentecostal work in The Netherlands in which Polman wrote, "We praise God that through all the years the unity in the Spirit had been kept among us, and that throughout the country we are one."[183] Around this time, however, the national unity was to be seriously threatened by the "Gemeente des Heeren" (Assembly of the Lord) led by Johannes Orsel (1877-1949), a former peat-cutter and anarchist from Nieuwe Pekela.[184]

Orsel was converted in the Salvation Army and through

Polman he had come in contact with the Pentecostal movement. Possibly this occurred when Polman held meetings in Nieuwe Pekela and surroundings during 1921. *Spade Regen*'s description of three men from the area who were going from place to place with a Bible-wagon, holding meetings, selling Bibles, and going from door to door fits Orsel, who had such a Bible-wagon, very well.[185] Orsel, according to an interview in the secular paper *Het Leven*, had been healed by prayer in 1918 of pleurisy. In his illness he had refused medical help in obedience to a voice saying to him, "Don't do it, lest something worse will happen to you."[186] Some time after his healing he had started to evangelize in the east part of Groningen. Several barge-families became converted and placed their vessels at the disposal of Orsel. One vessel was rebuilt and named Immanuel. It contained a meeting place for 100 persons. During 1926 some healings occurred that attracted the attention of the local press. A journalist from *Het Leven*, who visited the "floating temple" in 1927, reported: "Brother Orsel appears to be a simple man, about fifty years; not the type of fanatical maniac, but a resolute personality who considers his ideal as realized and who walks his path with the firm will of conviction."[187]

On the basis of Ezekiel's prophecy, "In that day shall messengers go forth from me in ships to make the careless Ethiopians afraid," the vessels of the "Gemeente des Heeren" sailed from Groningen southward to Haarlem in the course of 1927.[188] In the places along the way stops were made. Through open-air preaching, advertisements in the newspapers, distributing pamphlets, and selling Bibles, songbooks, and wall-texts from house to house, people were drawn to the meetings in Immanuel and converts were made. From Meppel one worked in the area around Hoogeveen (Hollandscheveld and Elim). During 1928 the vessels were at Rhenen along the Rhine. Here Albert Otten (1892-1971) and his wife Sijke Slomp (1894-1945) were converted.[189] They left the alms-house of the Netherlands Reformed Church where they worked and joined the Gemeente des Heeren as the vessels sailed for Utrecht and Haarlem in 1929. At Haarlem the vessels remained until they proceeded to Halfweg in July 1935. In 1931 Otten moved to Elim in Drente and became the prophet of the Gemeente des Heeren in the east, while Orsel remained the prophet in the west.[190]

The Gemeente des Heeren brought a radical healing message that did not allow for medical aid. Not only did they turn against medical doctors and medicines, but also against all churches and their clergy. "Hervormd" (Reformed) was called "Misvormd" (Deformed) and "Gereformeerd" was "Glad verkeerd" (Completely Wrong).[191] Only the believers of the Gemeente des Heeren were regarded as children of God and only they could be baptized with the Holy Spirit.[192] Believers were urged to live a rigid Christian life. Meanwhile Orsel had left his wife and children, which he justified by categorizing the marriage as "fleshly." Mrs. Rika Homan-Reijnders (born 1891) had also left her husband for similar reasons and with some of her children lived on board one of the vessels together with Orsel and others. Rika had become the prophetess of the movement and the "spiritual wife" of Orsel. It is quite astonishing that this was tolerated. With reference to the immediate return of the Lord, young followers were admonished not to marry, but to live "clean." Orsel demanded absolute obedience from his followers.[193]

Around 1930 the Gemeente des Heeren had founded assemblies in Elim, Apeldoorn, Rhenen, Utrecht, Westbroek, Rotterdam, and Haarlem. Shortly thereafter assemblies in Heerlen and Zwaagwesteinde were added.[194] In Apeldoorn and Rotterdam and probably also in Heerlen, co-workers of Polman joined the Gemeente des Heeren.[195] Also in the north Polman must have lost members. The loss was not just in number. The exclusive and anti-church character of this radical wing of Pentecostalism left undesirable impressions that affected the attitude of the clergy towards the Pentecostals as a whole.[196] How did Polman react to this development? *Spade Regen* never mentioned the names Gemeente des Heeren or Orsel. Yet the following excerpts no doubt deal with the issue.

In March 1923 Polman wrote: "In several newspapers a baptismal service at Stadskanaal was reported under the name of 'Pentecostal faith.' Readers of *Spade Regen* will have understood, that this circle does not belong to the Pentecostal movement."[197] When membership cards were introduced in April 1925 it was stated that they also served as identification cards to gain access to mutual meetings of Pentecostal gatherings in other places:

> This way we will also be cleared from a lot of slander, for there are some, who pretend to belong to us, but in reality do not. They try to press themselves upon some of our brothers and sisters for help, or for holding meetings, while later on one has to discover one has been cheated. In future cases one can ask for an identification-card, that every true Pentecostal brother or sister can receive from us.[198]

Whereas these two admonitions could still refer to others, the following citation from August 1927 must point to the Gemeente des Heeren:

> A SERIOUS WARNING.
> We are forced to warn our brothers and sisters of some, who give the impression, that they belong to the Pentecostal movement. In particular in the North of our country, some go around, pretending to be called to proclaim the Gospel. We would advise to first check their lives, and to acquaint oneself with their teachings concerning marriage and with their deeds that relate to this. We do believe, that one will then stay aloof from these sinful people. Those that are sent from us, will gladly show you their identification-card. . . . Let us in addition to the above also say, that it is not according to the Divine order in His assembly, when some throw themselves up to preach the Gospel, without having been sent by the local assembly, and after having given proof, that they are called of God, and such a calling is also executed in fellowship with the assembly to which one belongs. We are called to advance the unity of God's children, and if that is not the result of our deeds, this all is not after the will of God.[199]

One more "serious warning" followed in July 1928:

> To our regret we must again warn our readers of a movement in our country, that evangelizes under the name "Immanuel" and, as is reported to us, sometimes pretends to belong to the Pentecostal movement. If one asks these fellows whether they belong to "Immanuel," Kerkstraat, Amsterdam, they confirm

this with "yes" and then insist on selling their literature. We again state, that there has never been any connection with this movement, and we feel we have to warn our brothers and sisters, not to have any fellowship with these people. Not only because of the above-mentioned reason, but also because of their unscriptural relations. The members of the Pentecostal movement have an identification-card, that every loyal brother or sister in fellowship with us, receives upon request.[200]

In short Polman turned against the Gemeente des Heeren because of their unscriptural teaching and behavior concerning marriage; their pretending to belong to the Pentecostal movement to find access among Pentecostal believers; their self-appointed ministers; their disturbance of the unity among the children of God. Polman did not realize, however, that some of the arguments were also applicable to the Pentecostals themselves, at least in the eyes of any church or group that felt likewise threatened by the Pentecostals. Nevertheless it must be said that Polman revealed a much more open attitude towards the churches and never claimed to be the sole agency of the Holy Spirit. The methods of the Gemeente des Heeren certainly harmed Polman's effort to win clergy for the Pentecostal experience.

Synopsis

From our excursion to the various Pentecostal gatherings it became evident how important the role of Polman has been in introducing Pentecostalism in the Netherlands. The reports of his many visits were taken from *Spade Regen*, but it is certain that not all his trips were recorded. Where *Spade Regen* was the only source of information the picture remained unsatisfactory (Utrecht, Leiden, Gouda, Heerlen, and Stadskanaal). Other places could be threshed out into detail (Terschelling!).

Polman certainly was an evangelist to the bone, yet not like George or Stephen Jeffreys, whose large campaigns produced so many converts that wherever they preached new assemblies came in to being. Usually Polman preached in small accommodations and started with already-believers. If given the opportunity he introduced the Pentecostal message in existing circles. When interest was woken mutual meetings were launched. After Polman initiated the work it was delegated to local leadership if available. Otherwise temporary leaders were sent from Amsterdam, which often proved unsuccessful. It was mainly due to lack of capable leadership that some gatherings did not grow and languished. Females could be in charge when men were wanting, like in The Hague. The circles were usually very active in evangelization (open-air meetings and hawking papers from house to house). Baptismal services were held collectively at Amsterdam during the conferences. These conferences, the joint mission enterprise, the literature, the letters and visitations of Polman, kept the work together. Polman's leadership was undisputed, except among the Gemeente des Heeren.

Most of the Pentecostals had a churchly background. Often they were already estranged from their church or were earnest seekers; in both cases they were not satisfied with the state of the church and yielded to the Pentecostal movement. Nearly all members came from the working class or lower middle class. Of 43 adult believers from Amsterdam the profession and churchly background could be ascertained. When whole families became Pentecostal only the parents were counted. This revealed that 11 came from among the unchurched, another 14 were only nominally attached to a church, while 18 already had a more or less active church life before joining the Pentecostal movement.[201] Nearly two-thirds (28) were converted after their contact with the Pentecostals. Since a large number of the converts had long before accepted the essential truth of Christianity, the term "conversion" must be qualified. With exception of the unchurched, it often did not involve a change from a secular to a Christian ideology. Yet, it did always involve a spiritual experience by which one's faith became a personal faith.

During the years 1920 to 1930 the total number of Pentecostals in the Netherlands, estimated on the basis of this research, reached about 2,000, including children.[202] A quarter of this figure is formed by the Pentecostal assembly in Amsterdam. The figures recorded at the national census were much lower: none in December 1909; 272 in December

1920; and 508 in December 1930.[203] The absence of
Pentecostals at the census of 1909 and the low number in
1920 can be explained by the initial character of the
movement: an ecumenical renewal movement and not a
separate denomination. During 1920 to 1930 definite steps
towards denominationalism were taken, including the introduction of membership in 1925. This should have resulted in
a more reliable figure in the census of 1930. However, just a
few months before the census the Dutch Pentecostal movement suffered a dramatic downfall in connection with the
deposal of Polman. The event discouraged many from
identifying with the movement at the moment of the census.

NOTES

1. W. Polman, "Faith, Floods and Flowers," *The Latter Rain Evangel*,
   July 1929, p. 5.
2. Ibid.
3. Gezina van de Berg-Kleefman, Interview, Haarlem, 12 July 1986.
   Sientje Kleefman, (her official first name was Gezina) married Jan
   van de Berg in 1942.
4. Ibid. Apart from Suus and Els van Looi and Sientje Kleefman two
   other young ladies were involved: Pie Schmallegange and Mien
   Horeman.
5. Ibid.
6. *Spade Regen* no. 6 (November 1908),1; *Confidence* no. 7 (October
   1908),18; *Kracht van Omhoog* 8/2 (August 1944). Riek Trompetter's
   first names were in full: Frederika Johanna.
7. Van de Berg-Kleefman, Interview.
8. Ibid.
9. *Spade Regen* no. 16 (June-July 1910),4.
10. *Spade Regen* no. 29 (January 1912),3; *65 Jaar Pinkstergemeente
    Immanuel*, (Haarlem: Pinkstergemeente Immanuel, [1973]). The
    latter dated J.H. Schat's baptism on 11 November 1911, but in his
    testimony in *Spade Regen*, immediately after the event, it is dated 10
    December 1911.
11. *Spade Regen* 11/3 (June 1918),12.
12. *Spade Regen* 15/3 (June 1922),47-48 and 15/7 (October 1922),110-
    12.
13. *Spade Regen* 15/3 (June 1922),48.
14. "Schuldbekentenis," Haarlem, 27 September 1922.
15. "Oprichtingsacte," Haarlem, 7 July 1926.
16. Usually a larger hall, like "Zang en Vriendschap" in the Jansstraat,
    was rented. Net proceeds mentioned in *Spade Regen* are: ƒ900 in

1923; ƒ1,000 in 1924; ƒ1,139 in 1925; ƒ1,019 in 1926; ƒ800 in 1927; ƒ931.30 in 1928; ƒ677.50 in 1929; ƒ350 in 1930. In all these years the mortgage on the building was not redeemed. Donating money to missionaries was considered more important than clearing the building.

17. *Spade Regen* 13/8 (November 1920),122-23.
18. "Schuldbekentenis," and "Oprichtingsacte." Jan Berend van der Molen (born 1890) came from Harlingen and had stayed with Polman in Amsterdam from 13 January 1911 till 20 January 1914. *65 Jaar Pinkstergemeente Immanuel* also mentioned Haverkamp as belonging to the "council of brothers," but he came a little later.
19. Kleefman, Interview; J. Verwoert (born 1909), Interview, 22 August 86; A.M.C. van de Mije-ter Haak (born 1919), Interview, 22 August 1986. Professions that were ascertained: washwoman, bakery servant, shop employee, caretaker, book-keeper, cigar-maker (servant), milkman, fish roundsman, nurse, telegraphist, branch manager of sewing-machine shop, railway servant, school-teacher.
20. W. "Tusschen Flie en Lauwers," *Leeuwarder Courant* (22 December 1928),5; "Laatste der 'fijne Mennisten' overleden," *Algemeen Handelsblad* [1938],10.
21. *De Vrije Evangelie Trompet* no. 1, undated.
22. In a vision Haitjema saw the map of The Netherlands and a finger pointing to Terschelling. C. Bakker, Interview, 19 December 1981; Trijntje Bakker, Interview, Zeist, 29 October 1979.
23. G.A. Wumkes, *Nei Sawntich Jier* (Boalsert: A.J. Osinga, 1949), pp. 431-32; and rough notes from Wumkes' archive. Wumkes mistakenly recorded that Haitjema's grandfather left for America; in fact, it was his father.
24. In the minutes of the diocese meeting of 29 June 1904 at Alkmaar it reads that Stegenga resigned because "his conception of the nature of the church forbade him to remain working in the church any longer." "Notulen der Vergaderingen van de Classis Alkmaar aangelegd in 1891." Present in Rijksarchief Noord Holland in Haarlem under inventory number 414.
25. In many Netherlands Reformed churches there were quarrels between modern and orthodox parties. When a modern minister was appointed the church attendance often dropped to such an extent that financial problems arose. For purely practical reasons therefore, some church councils with a modern majority appointed orthodox ministers. As a modern church council and an orthodox minister went together like water and fire, it is no surprise that conflicts were the results as was the case on Terschelling. Stegenga found sympathy among orthodox colleagues, although they questioned his resignation. During this time Stegenga also kept in touch with free evangelists, Baptists, Seventh-Day Baptists, and with the mission "Jeruël" of Rotterdam.
   Heraut no. 1365 (28 February 1904),2.

[Cil Bakker] to G.R. Polman, Lies, 15 April 1917. A 19-page report of the history of the Pentecostals on Terschelling by an eyewitness. J.C. Bruggink, "Hoorn op Terschelling," *Maandbode* no. 4 (21 December 1916),12-14; and no. 5 (January 1917),1-15. [Jan Ruyge] to G.A. Wumkes, [January-March 1917]. A 20-page report with comments on the description given in the above-mentioned *Maandbode* by J.C. Bruggink. Ruyge belonged to the orthodox party that remained in the Reformed church and collected money for the school.

26. Bakker; Ruyge.
27. Ruyge.
28. Wumkes, *Nei Sawntich Jier*, p. 432; G.R. Polman to G.A. Wumkes, Amsterdam, 6 March 1917 and 27 March 1917.
29. [H. Haitjema], "Tijdens de 'Opwekking' in Wales: Een Doopsbediening in de rivier De Dee," n.p., [1905].
30. G.A. Wumkes, Rough Notes on Terschelling, [1917].
31. "Droevig einde," *Ermelosch Zendingsblad* 49/3 (March 1908),10.
32. In the Netherlands H. Haitjema had stayed with his nephew Martin Haitjema at Dedemsvaart. On inquiry with the descendants some interesting pieces of correspondence were found including fragments of letters from Haitjema both before and after his coming to the Netherlands. Hinne, also called Herre or Henry, was the eldest son of Romke Hinne Haitjema (1827-1875) from Balk, Friesland, and his wife Yitske Baukes Rijstra (1830-1874). On board the sailing vessel "Glasgow" they had left for America in 1853. Nine children were born. The youngest was only two when both parents had died. Romke had died in October 1875, ten days after returning from a visit to the Netherlands. According to a letter from 1893 all children were converted. Four brothers of Hinne became ministers in Mennonite and Free Methodist churches. One sister also preached the gospel. Hinne was married to a certain Sibbeltje and had at least one daughter. In the undated fragment of his letter written after his return to America he mentioned about his stay in the Netherlands that he had gone down somewhat, but he had no regrets. His health was restored again. In a letter dated 21 May 1908 Siebrig Belt-Smid from Plymouth, Indiana, a niece of Martin Haitjema from Dedemsvaart, inquired with her nephew after Hinne as she heard that he had become insane. Siebrig informs Martin that Hinne had been mentally ill before and was brought to a lunatic asylum. Since that time he had become very religious.
33. On a picture taken in 1916, printed on the front cover of *Confidence* 9/9 (Septembèr 1916), there are apart from the Polman family 5 men, 21 women, and 12 children. Polman noted that many men were not present because they were mostly sailors and often at sea. Some of the sailors had once visited Boddy's church in Sunderland: *Confidence* no. 6 (September 1908),17.
34. *Spade Regen* 10/6 (September 1917),24. Added was the news that someone from the province Groningen who temporary worked on

Terschelling had visited the meetings and was converted. In *Confidence* 9/9 (September 1916),153, Polman wrote that the people of the isle believed in the Pentecostals, but did not come to the meetings because the way was too narrow to them.

35. G.R. Polman, "Holland: News from the Island of Terschelling," *Confidence* 9/9 (September 1916),153; cf. G.R. Polman, "Amongst the Ice-floes of the Zuyder Zee," *Confidence* 2/2 (February 1909),51-52.

36. *Spade Regen* 15/3 (June 1922),48.

37. G.R. Polman, "News from the Island of Terschelling," pp. 153-54.

38. *Spade Regen* 14/7 (October 1921),111. Concerning the kind gesture of the Reformed church to let the building free of charge, Polman noted: "We were very thankful for this, more so because this act of kindness bears witness to some kind of rapprochement."

39. Ida van Marle, *Zij volgde haar roeping* (The Hague: Gazon, 1976), p. 69; Trijntje Bakker, Interview, Zeist: 29 October 1979.

40. *Spade Regen* 17/11 (February 1925),172-73.

41. *Spade Regen* 20/8 (November 1927),121-22.

42. A.A. Boddy, "A Visit to Holland," *Confidence* no. 6 (September 1908),17.

43. Ibid.

44. G.R. Polman to believers at Sneek, Amsterdam, 5 October 1908.

45. G.R. Polman to G. de Wilde, Zwolle, 15 January 1909; *Spade Regen* no. 6 (January-March 1909),3; *Confidence* 2/2 (February 1909),52.

46. G.R. Polman to G. de Wilde, Zwolle, 15 January 1909.

47. G.R. Polman to believers at Sneek, Amsterdam, 19 January 1909.

48. G. de Wilde to colleague [Roeles at Deventer], Sneek, 5 January 1909. Present in the archives of the Unie van Baptisten, Rijksarchief Utrecht.

49. G. de Wilde to Roeles, Paterson: 15 August 1911 and 24 November 1911, Archives Unie van Baptisten, Rijksarchief Utrecht.

50. "Uit de gemeenten," *De Christen* 28 (11 November 1909),359.

51. *Spade Regen* no. 12 (November 1909),3.

52. *De Christen* 28 (2 December 1909),380.

53. *De Christen* 28 (18 November 1909),366.

54. Ibe Sjoerd Rusticus, Interview, 12 October 1987. Ibe Sjoerd Rusticus, born 26 January 1905, remembers visiting the Pentecostal assembly in Amsterdam in 1909! Ibe was baptized in water by Polman in 1920.

55. Rusticus, Interview. During 1915 to 1917 there was a period of disagreement between Rusticus and Van Tuinen, at which time separate meetings were held. In 1924 Rusticus withdrew from the Pentecostal assembly and joined the Reformed church.

56. G.A. Wumkes, *De Pinksterbeweging voornamelijk in Nederland* (Utrecht: G.J.A. Ruys, 1916), p. 19, lists Amsterdam, Haarlem, Terschelling, Sneek, Delfzijl, Utrecht, and Bussum. G.R. Polman, "The Pentecostal Work in Holland," *The Pentecostal Evangel*, 29 May 1926, p. 2, lists Amsterdam, Haarlem, Rotterdam, Hilversum, Utrecht,

Terschelling, Heerlen, and "different little groups in other places." W. Polman, "Faith, Floods and Flowers: Cross Section View of the Pentecostal Work in Holland," *The Latter Rain Evangel*, July 1929, pp. 3-5, lists Amsterdam, Rotterdam, The Hague, Haarlem, Hilversum, Heerlen, Utrecht, Terschelling, and Groningen.

57. Maria Petra Bosma (born 1897) came from Sneek to Amsterdam in May 1919 and stayed with the Polmans until, according to the registration service, she left for Utrecht in November 1921. Cf. *Spade Regen* 12/4 (July 1919),64.

58. *Spade Regen* 12/2 (March 1920),190; 13/1 (April 1920),8; 14/12 (March 1922),199.

59. *Spade Regen* 14/7 (October 1921),111-12.

60. *Spade Regen* 17/11 (February 1925),173.

61. W. Polman, "Faith, Floods and Flowers," p. 5.

62. Jantje Schipper-Kamp, Interview, 14 August 1986; Harmina Kuiper-De Jonge, Interview, 14 August 1986. Jantje Kamp, born 1901, joined the Pentecostal assembly in May 1925. Harmina de Jonge, born in 1906, joined early 1927. The precise year the two ladies Van Driessum and Zwart got acquainted with the German Pentecostal movement is uncertain, but 1909 seems likely. The Mülheim Conferences commenced in that year. In 1910 when Piet Klaver was stationed at Delfzijl as Salvation Army officer, he came in contact with a Pentecostal believer who had visited the Mülheim Conference. P. Klaver, "Herinneringen van een Pinksterpionier," *Kracht van Omhoog* 28/16 (12 February 1965),9. Cf. M. de Boer-Wildeboer, "Verslag van het ontstaan en groei van de 'Pinkstergemeente' te Delfzijl," Delfzijl, 1981; J.A. Pronk to author, October 1981, with testimony from Hendrik de Jonge and "Geschiedenis in telegramstijl," a short historical overview, 1906 to 1969.

63. *Spade Regen* 10/6 (September 1917),24.

64. Ibid.

65. *Spade Regen* 10/7 (October 1917),28.

66. Polman came twice in 1918, and further in 1924 and 1927. Klaver came in 1925 and 1929. Bakker and Roos came in 1918 and 1928. *Spade Regen* 11/1 (April 1918),4; 11/7 (October 1918),28; 17/8 (November 1914),125; 17/11 (February 1925),173; 19/11 (February 1927),173-75; 21/8 (November 1928),128-29; 22/1 (April 1929),14.

67. Schipper-Kamp, Interview.

68. Ibid.

69. Ibid. Kuiper-De Jonge, Interview. *Spade Regen* 19/8 (November 1926),127-28, quotes a letter from Gnirrep dated 25 October in which a young man is said to have been converted in their home a few months before.

70. *Spade Regen* 22/3 (June 1929),46, refers to two couples from Groningen. They were Jan de Jonge with Jantiena Helmantel and Hermiena de Jonge (Jan's sister) with Hendrik Kuiper (1905-1982).

71. Kuiper-De Jonge and Schipper-Kamp, Interviews. The cover of

Spade Regen 23/2 (May 1930), shows a picture of the choir with 7 males and 6 females. The same issue recorded that during the Whitsuntide Conference of 1930 one male and one female from Groningen were baptized with the Holy Spirit.

72. Spade Regen 11/7 (October 1918),28. During 1917 believers from Groningen twice visited the Pentecostal assembly at Amsterdam. On Sunday 16 September in connection with the baptismal service that afternoon and in December for the Christmas Conference. Spade Regen 10/7 (October 1917)28; 10/10 (January 1918),38.

73. Spade Regen 19/8 (November 1926),127-28.

74. Spade Regen 19/11 (February 1927),173-75. The first reference to Veendam is found in Spade Regen no. 35 (November 1913),3, where a certain C.F. Striezenou from Veendam testified of salvation, Spirit baptism and healing. In September 1921 Polman held a meeting in Nieuwe Pekela and a baptismal service at Veendam. Spade Regen 14/7 (October 1921),119-20. Spade Regen 19/7 (October 1926),109, recorded that a small circle at Veendam had been formed.

75. Ibid.

76. Spade Regen 21/8 (November 1928),126-27.

77. W. Polman, "Faith, Floods and Flowers," p. 5. Hilversum is only about 30 km. from Amsterdam.

78. Polman's letter, dated 7 April 1909, in Confidence 2/4 (April 1909),92, read: "In Bussum, near Amsterdam, four have received their baptism, and they need leading, of course. But God is making everything well." Spade Regen 11/4 (July 1918),16, recorded alternate meetings at Bussum and Naarden. Spade Regen 11/8 (November 1918),32, mentioned meetings at Bussum and Hilversum. Hereafter only Hilversum carried on.

79. Hendrika van Strijland-van Ravenzwaay, Interview, 16 August 1986. Hendrika (born 1912) is the oldest child of the Van Ravenzwaay family. She remembers the house meetings very well. When she was six years old she was dedicated by Polman together with her younger brother and sister in their parents' home. Later 5 more children were born.

Gerrit de Wild, Interview, 15 August 1986. Gerrit (born 1929) is one of the 9 children in the De Wild family.

F. v.d. Burg, Speech during opening new hall Pinkstergemeente 'Elim,' Hilversum, 14 December 1985.

80. Van Strijland, Interview.

81. De Wild, Interview.

82. Spade Regen 11/8 (November 1918),32, recorded Polman's first visit to Hilversum. Spade Regen 12/5 (August 1919),79, reported that every Sunday a brother from Amsterdam went to Hilversum. According to Spade Regen 15/8 (November 1922),127, F.A. Tienpont belonged to the brethren that regularly went to Hilversum. Hendrika van Strijland-van Ravenzwaay remembered that Nico Vetter also came regularly before he went to Venezuela in 1925.

83. Spade Regen 18/9 (December 1925),143-44.

84. *Spade Regen* 12/3 (June 1919),46, and 19/2 (May 1926),30.
85. *Spade Regen* 23/2 (May 1930)28.
86. Professions ascertained are engine driver, gardener, policeman, plumber, cycle dealer.
87. In *Spade Regen* 23/9 (December 1930) the address is changed from Noordsche Boschje 56 to Toornlaan 4 without comment.
88. W. Polman, "Faith, Floods and Flowers," p. 5.
89. *Spade Regen* no. 35 (November 1913),4. The healing occurred at home on 24 August 1913. According to the Amsterdam registration service a certain Jannigje Ina Verwaal (born 1891) stayed with the Polmans from June till August 1912 after which she moved to Utrecht.
90. A. Manussen, "De zogenaamde Tongenbeweging," *Ons Maandblaadje* 3/35 (December 1916),3.
91. *Spade Regen* 12/5 (August 1919),79.
92. *Spade Regen* 17/9 (December 1924),142-43.
93. *Spade Regen* 17/11 (February 1925),174.
94. W. Polman, "Faith, Floods and Flowers," p. 5.
95. *Confidence* 2/1 (January 1909),7.
96. Voskuil later worked as an evangelist at Edam and Utrecht. *Maran-Atha* 9/12 (March 1919),92; *Het Zoeklicht* 4 (1922-23),237.
97. A.A. Boddy, "A Visit to Holland," *Confidence* no. 6 (September 1908),7-8.
98. *Spade Regen* no. 5 (December 1908),4, recorded 6 baptized ones at The Hague. *Spade Regen* carried the following testimonies of Spirit baptized ones from The Hague concerning this period: Lampje Kok, no. 3 (September-October 1908),2; IJnsche Kok, Spirit baptism dated 4 January 1908, no. 5 (December 1908),2; C. Klein, Spirit baptism dated 12 November 1908, no. 6 (January-February 1909),2-3; and Tjeerd de Vries, Spirit baptism dated 26 December 1908, no. 7 (March 1909),4. Tjeerd de Vries who received his Spirit baptism at Amsterdam, mentioned that his sister received the Spirit during May 1908.

    Spade Regen no. 12 (November 1909),4, reported, "souls are being converted and baptized with the Holy Spirit," and "One sister who was converted and baptized with the Holy Spirit, is testifying with gladness, how God used the tongues as the means to lead her unbelieving husband to Jesus." *Spade Regen* no. 13 (December 1909),4, contained a letter from Z. Aandewiel from The Hague with her testimony of salvation, Spirit baptism, and healing.
99. H. Mogridge visited Amsterdam in July 1910 and wrote that Polman "goes to The Hague regularly once a week to hold Pentecostal meetings." *Confidence* 3/10 (October 1910),243. In April 1910 missionary D. Awrey from China among other places also preached in The Hague: *Spade Regen* no. 15 (April-May 1910),4. Around July/August 1910 Frank Bartleman once preached in The Hague: *Around the World by Faith* (Los Angeles: by author, n.d.), p. 20.
100. G.R. Polman to G.A. Wumkes, 29 August 1916.

101. Visser to Polman, 27 January 1921. H. Plokker wrote in *Maran-Atha* until 8/9 (December 1917).
102. M. Visser to G.R. Polman, 27 January 1921; Idem, Interview, The Hague, 17 August 1984. Martha Visser was a school-teacher during 1914 to 1917. Hereafter she started administrative work for the Koninklijk Instituut van Ingenieurs. She became their book-keeper and remained there 50 years.
103. Visser to Polman, 27 January 1921; cf. *Spade Regen* 13/7 (October 1920), 107; "Verlaten," 13/9 (December 1920),133-34.
104. *Spade Regen* 12/5 (August 1919),79.
105. *Spade Regen* 12/12 (March 1920),190; Idem 13/1 (April 1920) 8,15; M. Visser to Polman, 27 January 1921.
106. M. Visser to G.R. Polman, 3 January 1921. During the first period the meetings were led by a certain "brother Reijnders." M. Visser to G.R. Polman, [February 1921].
107. Visser, Interview.
108. In her letters of that period Martha Visser described herself as "unbaptized." The reason for this was her not speaking in tongues. Much later in life she felt that her experience with the Holy Spirit in "Jeruël" was her baptism with the Holy Spirit, although it was not accompanied with speaking in tongues. In 1939 in England she at last did receive the gift of glossolalia. Visser, Interview.
109. Visser, Interview.
110. M. Visser to G.R. Polman, 2 October 1923; Idem to K. Andrea, 30 November 1923 and 4 December 1923.
111. Martha Visser visited Polman at his sick-bed shortly before his death and attended the funeral. During 1939 to 1947 she again had a position of leadership in a Pentecostal assembly at The Hague under supervision of Pieter van der Woude from Rotterdam. She was the only female in the "council of brothers" that led the assembly. She also participated in the national council of leaders of that time, in which Mrs. Polman was the second woman. At the time she married C.A. Marijs in October 1947 her position had become so difficult that she felt forced to resign and left the Pentecostal movement altogether. She returned to the Netherlands Reformed Church and wrote several mildly critical articles about the Pentecostal movement for church periodicals. In 1962 her novel *De Zwarte* (Kampen: Kok) appeared, which in fact concerned her second period with the Pentecostals: 1939 to 1947. She also wrote poems and 40 children books.
112. *Spade Regen* 20/8 (November 1927),122.
113. When permission was requested to preach and sing in the Metropool on Sunday afternoons, it was granted on probation for one time. It became such a success that the local newspaper reported, "The Supervisory Council readily granted permission to the Pentecostal assembly to continue their undogmatic and soul-searching work on a regular basis." *Spade Regen* 20/11 (February 1928),173-74.
114. *Spade Regen* 21/2 (May 1928),30.

115. The funeral of Metz was led by P. Klaver. The sole reference to the death of Metz was found in P. Klaver, "Geliefde Zendingsvrienden," *De Vereenigde Zendingsvrienden* 3/1 (May 1939),2. Cf. *Gouden Schoven* 10/12 (1937),19, for a letter from Mrs. Van Geresteijn.
116. W. Polman, "Faith, Flood and Flowers," p. 4.
117. G.R. Polman to G.A. Wumkes, 10 October 1916.
118. *Spade Regen* no. 41 (January 1917),4.
119. Stokker family, Interview, Rotterdam: 4 July 1986. Four children of the Stokker family were simultaneously interviewed: Jacoba Alexandra Stokker (born 1901), one son (born 1903) who preferred to remain unnamed, Adriana Hendrika Stokker (born 1904), and Maria Gerardina Rieke-Stokker (born 1914). They frequently went along with their parents to the meetings. The memory of the eldest three went back as far as 1917.
120. Albert Bokhorst was a factory worker and member of the Pentecostal assembly at Rotterdam. Schreurs was an engine driver and became an elder in the assembly.
121. *Spade Regen* 10/6 (September 1917),4.
122. "Een eigenaardige doopplechtigheid," *Wereldkroniek*, 4 October 1913, p. 439 (with photos).
123. "De z.g. 'Tongenbeweging' II," *Ons Maandblaadje* 3/35 (December 1916),1-5. Apparently there had been an earlier article on the same issue. At this time Manussen is not aware of a Pentecostal group in Rotterdam.
124. Stokker, Interview.
125. Janna Boelhouwer in *Spade Regen* 1/6 (September 1917),4; Margaretha Schareman in *Spade Regen* 11/5 (August 1918),4.
126. C.L.M. Neumeier, Interview, Rotterdam, 27 February 1986. Carl Ludwig Mozes Neumeier (born 18 February 1908) joined the Pentecostal assembly in 1926. His father, a former hair-dresser and wig-maker, had a Lutheran background. Through the evangelization work of Valk he was converted. Together with Valk he became Pentecostal, somewhere around 1920. The son C.L.M. Neumeier would later become pastor of another Pentecostal assembly until 1971.

Through *Het Zoeklicht* we learn of another free evangelist, who in the early twenties also went along with the Pentecostals. Korver was leader of the "Nederlandsche Maranatha-Zending," founded in 1921 with their paper *Maranatha-Boodschap.* They distributed bread, coffee, and tracts among the poor. According to Johan de Heer Korver belonged to the Pentecostals, but did not propagate it in his work. *Het Zoeklicht* 4 (1922-23),221-22, 254.
127. From the *Spade Regen* references the following list of meeting places could be drawn:

1. Bloemstraat 104	September 1917
2. Oppert 149	November 1917
3. Hovenierstraat 41b	December 1919

4. Van Alkemadestraat 24b,	July 1921
5. "Maranatha" Hovenierstraat 43	June 1926
6. "Het Blauwe Kruis" Oppert 67	May 1927
7. Erasmusstraat 34	October 1927
8. "De Eendracht" Goudscheweg 132	April 1929
9. Botersloot 88a	July 1929
10. Van Alkemadestraat 24b	November 1929
	(until January 1931)

128. *Spade Regen* 18/11 (February 1926),173.
129. *Spade Regen* 18/9 (December 1925),144.
130. *Spade Regen* 19/1 (April 1926),11; and 19/3 (June 1926),43-46.
131. *Spade Regen* 18/11 (February 1926),174; cf. 1 Cor. 1:26.
132. Neumeier, Interview; Stokker, Interview.
133. Neumeier.
134. *Spade Regen* 18/11 (February 1926),173.
135. A.K. Evers to Martha Visser, Rotterdam, 16 November 1921. Evers was a bachelor with a Roman Catholic background. For years he had been atheist, but was converted by reading the Bible. He joined the Pentecostal assembly at Rotterdam. At the time he wrote the above-mentioned letter he had left the movement out of disappointment in the operating of the spiritual gifts. He felt cheated when some of the prophecies and visions proved false. One example of his disappointment was the ordination of Kuiper as pastor by the "council of brothers" with the formulation, "It seemed good to the Holy Spirit and to us" from Acts 15:28. Evers felt that when the Holy Spirit appoints a person, he cannot fail. Yet, Kuiper failed. Apart from this letter no evidence of this "council of brothers" and of Kuiper has been found.
136. Neumeier.
137. *Spade Regen* 20/8 (November 1927),123.
138. Ibid.; Neumeier, Interview.
139. *Spade Regen* 1/6 (September 1917),24. Already in *Spade Regen* no. 5 (December 1908),4, believers at Leiden were greeted.
140. *Spade Regen* 13/2 (May 1920),32. Here the hall Patrimonium is mentioned. As of 13/5 (August 1920), the announcements of public meetings included Leiden. Meetings were held on Wednesday evenings in the hall "Verhuurdersbond," Hooglandsche Kerkgracht 40.
141. The last reference to Leiden is that they were present when the new hall Immanuel in Haarlem was opened in September 1922. *Spade Regen* 17/7 (October 1922),111.
142. *Spade Regen* 11/4 (July 1918),16.
143. *Spade Regen* 18/11 (February 1926),174. On Monday, 2 February 1925, Klaver had addressed a meeting in the same building for an attentive audience: 17/11 (February 1925),174. As of December 1929 the name of the street was added: Peperstraat.
144. In *Spade Regen* 21/4 (July 1928),61, Boerma is speaking on behalf on Gouda on the silver wedding feast of Polman.

145. Carl Neumeier remembers that he once visited the assembly at Gouda around 1930. Only two believers were present. C.L.M. Neumeier, Interview, Rotterdam, 27 February 1986.
146. W. Polman, "Faith, Floods and Flowers," p. 5.
147. In the Baptist periodical *De Christen* 31/1326 (27 September 1912),309-10, Jan R. Fijn, Scharnderweg 15 in Maastricht reacted by letter against the rejection of the Pentecostal movement by the Baptist Union. In the next issue the editor answered the letter and called Fijn an apparent adherent of the Pentecostal movement. The same J.R. Fijn also corresponded with the Reformed minister J.H. Gunning J.Hz. during 1911 to 1913 about the Pentecostal movement. Although Fijn strongly defended the Pentecostals and read *Spade Regen*, his name has not been found in the Pentecostal sources.
148. *Spade Regen* no. 41 (January 1917),4.
149. *Spade Regen* 11/2 (May 1918),4.
150. Ibid. Address for Emmanuel Hall not given. Van der Lip's address was Klompstraat 2a. Possibly he lived above the hall. In July 1920 Van der Lip lived at Geerstraat 66.
151. *Spade Regen* 13/4 (July 1920),63.
152. *Spade Regen* 14/9 (December 1921),151-52.
153. *Spade Regen* 16/1 (April 1923),16.
154. *Spade Regen* 17/4 (July 1924),64.
155. *Spade Regen* 19/3 (June 1926),4
156. Ibid.
157. *Spade Regen* 11/3 (June 1918),4.
158. *Spade Regen* 19/11 (February 1927),175-76.
159. *Spade Regen* 19/4 (July 1926),62-63.
160. Klaver remained in Heerlen for several weeks during February 1928. In August 1928 the missionaries Bakker and Roos stayed for 17 days in the house of the Lips family. It is not known whether the name was misspelled and Van der Lip was meant here. Bakker reported, "The brothers and sisters in dark Limburg have so little spiritual help, that they appreciate it very much when someone visits them," and "In spite of all struggle and hardship they have gone through and are still going through, there still are some faithful ones who courageously go forward." *Spade Regen* 21/8 (November 1928),126. After another visit in February 1929 Klaver remarked, "The work in Limburg is not easy." *Spade Regen* 21/12 (February 1929),191.
161. J.E. van den Brink, "De Pinksterbeweging in Indonesië," *Kracht van Omhoog* 27/19 (April 1964),11.
162. This visit is not recorded in *Spade Regen*, but is mentioned in a personal letter from Martha Visser from The Hague to Miss Jonker at Apeldoorn. According to this letter it must have been during the time that Dr. Gunning was chairman of the mission Maranatha. This means it must have been before Gunning left in April 1920. J.H. Gunningh J.Hz., *Herinneringen uit mijn leven* (Amsterdam: H.J. Spruyt, 1941), pp. 232-240.

163. *Spade Regen* 14/4 (July 1921),63.

164. *Spade Regen* 14/7 (October 1921),120; 14/9 (December 1921),150-151.

165. In *Spade Regen* 15/4 (July 1922),64, "Bethel" is once more mentioned and recommended for rest or holiday.

166. *Spade Regen* 15/9 (December 1922), 122, refers to a small conference, 10 to 12 November, with believers from Twello and Deventer also present. Twice in 1922 and twice in 1926 *Spade Regen* mentioned, that believers from Apeldoorn visited the Amsterdam assembly. In 1926 and 1929 believers from Twello attended the Easter Conferences at Amsterdam.

167. G.R. Mik, Interview, 22 August 1986.

168. *Spade Regen* 19/1 (April 1926),15.

169. Mik, Interview.

170. Emmanuel Schuurman, Interview, 16 August 1986.

171. Ibid.; *Spade Regen* 11/11 (February 1919),44; 14/12 (March 1922),199.

172. *Spade Regen* 12/2 (May 1919),31; 12/12 (March 1920),190. The same De Jong also arranged for Polman to come to Staphorst on Monday 10 May 1920, *Spade Regen* 13/2 (May 1920),32.

173. Schuurman, Interview. Much later Emmanuel Schuurman, after the death of his first wife, would marry Roelie, the daughter of De Jong.

174. Professions that were ascertained: school-teacher, brick-layer, bargeman/hotel-keeper (in his hotel, Voorstraat 17 at Zwolle, the meetings were held), printer's assistant, cycle dealer, railway servant, 2 ladies ran a Christian book-shop in the Kerkstraat at Meppel. Schuurman, Interview.

Schuurman's name and the meetings held by him in Zwolle and Meppel were never mentioned in *Spade Regen*. Yet Emmanuel is certain that there was a good relationship between his father and Polman. Polman was esteemed as the national leader. The Classis Meppel of the Gereformeerde Kerken published a report concerning the Pentecostals in which reference is made to the pamphlets of E. Schuurman: J.C. Borgdorff, M. van Dijk and H. Fokkens, *De Pinkstergemeente en hare dwalingen getoetst aan Gods Woord*. Rapport van de commissie inzake de "Pinksterbeweging" aan de Classis Meppel der Gereformeerde Kerken (Hoogeveen: R. Slingenberg, 1932). Cf. H. Fokkens, "De Pinksterbeweging," *Gereformeerd Theologisch Tijdschrift* 32 (1932),520-540.

175. *Spade Regen* 10/8 (November 1917),32.

176. *Spade Regen* 11/11 (February 1919),44; 11/12 (March 1919),48; 12/1 (April 1919),15; 12/2 (May 1919),31; 12/12 (March 1920),190 (with Jonathan Paul).

177. *Spade Regen* 11/12 (March 1919),48.

178. *Spade Regen* 12/1 (April 1919),15.

179. Ibid.

180. *Spade Regen* 12/4 (July 1919),63-64.

181. *Spade Regen* 15/12 (March 1923),192. The last reference to Stadskanaal is the dedication of a child from Stadskanaal on Sunday, 2 August 1925, at Amsterdam. *Spade Regen* 18/5 (August 1925),78.

182. Believers from Den Helder attended meetings in Amsterdam during September and Christmas 1917, while Polman led one meeting in Den Helder in April 1918. *Spade Regen* 10/7 (October 1917),20; 10/10 (January 1918),38; 11/2 (May 1918),8. From other sources a little more is known relating to Den Helder. Cornelis Staalman (1889-1956) from Den Helder moved to Amsterdam around 1907, where he found work as a bench-hand in a dockyard. He rebelled against his former Brethren background and wanted to live without religion. To please his land-lady he visited the Pentecostal assembly resulting in his conversion and Spirit baptism. By 1911 Staalman had returned to Den Helder and had married Neeltje Stijl. He became a cycle-dealer and kept in contact with Polman. After some time Staalman commenced meetings in his house, but without success. The references in *Spade Regen* most likely concern Staalman. IJs Staalman, Interview, 11 March 1987; Wim Koelewijn, Interview, 11 March 1987.

183. G.R. Polman, "The Pentecostal Work in Holland," *Pentecostal Evangel*, 29 May 1926, pp. 2-3. Also published in Stanley H. Frodsman, *"With Signs Following"* (Springfield, MO: Gospel Publishing House, 1926), pp. 96-101 (only in first printing).

184. Information concerning the "Gemeente des Heeren" is hard to obtain. The group still exists, but keeps to itself. Only one issue of their paper *De Blijde Boodschapper* was obtained. Most of the information came from reports from outsiders and from interviews with ex-followers. As far as possible these data were checked with present followers.

185. *Spade Regen* 13/12 (March 1921),187, and 14/7 (October 1921),119-120 referred to meetings held in Nieuwe and Oude Pekela and Veendam. *Spade Regen* 16/7 (October 1923),112 referred to a baptismal service at Nieuwe Pekela. Other occasions for Orsel to have met Polman had been in Stadskanaal where Polman came during 1919, or in Delfzijl where Polman came in 1918.

186. "Genezingen aan boord van een bijbelschip: Bij Gemeente des Heeren," *Het Leven* 22 (1927),1178-79.

187. Ibid.

188. Ezekiel 30:9. J.C. Borgdorff, M. van Dijk and H. Fokkens, *De Pinkstergemeente en hare dwalingen getoetst aan Gods Woord*, p. 18.

    H. Fokkens, "De Pinksterbeweging," *Gereformeerd Theologisch Tijdschrift* 32 (1931-32),540. The year 1927 has been ascertained by this present author.

189. Jan Verwoert from Rhenen was also converted during this time and joined the Gemeente des Heeren. Jan Verwoert, Interview, 22 August 1986.

190. Elim and Hollandscheveld formed a much distressed area. The

population for a large part still consisted of peat-laborers or former peat-laborers, which was a population group that lived in very poor social and economic conditions and was held in low esteem far and wide. Otten, who was a former peat-laborer born in the area, obtained a large following among the laborers. He addressed their miserable situation and their dissatisfaction with the church, which did nothing on their behalf. The area has been the subject of extensive sociological research by A.J. Wichers, P.E. Kraemer, and J.W. de Koning. In their publication *Leven en werken te Elim-Hollandscheveld* (Assen: Van Gorcum & Comp., 1959), the Gemeente des Heeren is described as a protesting group (along with communism and an agricultural freedom movement): "a subjective religious movement that started chiefly among laborers shortly after the depression (unemployment!). Their protest is mainly against the formal churches" (p. 129).

P.E. Kraemer in "Enig materiaal over sectarisme in een achter-gebleven gebied," *Sociologisch Bulletin* 13/3 (1959),98-108, provided material that was not included in the above-mentioned publication, like an interesting interview with Otten. As the other work was not yet in print Kraemer used feigned names.

In 1981 anthropology student W.T.M. van Haaren, built further on the sociological research of 1959 in his " 'Jezus alleen': Een religieus-antropologisch onderzoek naar de 'Gemeente des Heeren' te Elim," (Kandidaats thesis, University of Leiden, 1981). Van Haaren writes that the first followers of the Gemeente des Heeren were largely or solely unskilled laborers: peat-laborers, land-workers and factory-workers. More or less this was also the situation in 1981. The Gemeente des Heeren had remained a workers' religion, which is expressed by two large pictures of land-workers in the meeting hall. No matter how interesting all this material is, it does only deal with the Gemeente des Heeren in Elim after 1930 and therefore largely falls outside the scope of this present study.

191. Van Haaren, p. 17 (see above).
192. Emmanuel Schuurman in a conversation with Orsel was denied being a child of God and denied having been baptized with the Spirit just because he did not belong to the Gemeente des Heeren. Interview, 21 August 1986.
193. Information from five interviews with ex-followers (all Pentecostal pastors) and confirmed during interviews with four present followers (one pastor's wife and three pastors).
194. Steven Troost started a Gemeente des Heeren at Zwaagwesteinde around 1933. Cf. K. Sikkens Sr. and K. Sikkens Jr., *Zwaagwesteinde: Het vissersdorp op de Friese heide* (Franeker: T. Wever, 1954), pp. 234-35; H.A. Veenstra, *1926-1976 50 jaar Hindurk 'Hierbaas'* (Dantumadeel: Oudheidkamer Dantumadeel, [1984]), p. 32.
195. In one *De Blijde Boodschapper* from around 1930 the following places of meetings were announced: Utrecht, Haarlem, Rotterdam, Apel-

doorn, Rhenen, Amsterdam, Westbroek. At Rotterdam meetings were held at Erasmusstraat 34. One article was written by R.C. Schreurs from Rotterdam, who first was with Polman.

196. For example the report of the Classis Meppel (1932) and the article by H. Fokkens, who stood in the Gereformeerde Kerk at Hollandscheveld (see above), treat the Gemeente des Heeren as identical with the Pentecostal movement, in spite of a letter from the Pentecostal assembly at Amsterdam stating that "they did not want to be counted among this kind of people."

197. *Spade Regen* 15/12 (March 1923),192.

198. *Spade Regen* 18/1 (April 1925),14-15.

199. *Spade Regen* 20/5 (August 1927),80.

200. *Spade Regen* 21/4 (July 1928),64.

The Gemeente des Heeren too showed preference for the name Immanuel. Not only was their vessel named thus, but so were several of their meeting places in the cities.

201. Information gathered during interviews with eyewitnesses or relatives of eyewitnesses. The survey concerns the period from 1907 to 1930. The churchly background of the 43 members specified were 12 Netherlands Reformed Church; 6 Gereformeerde Kerk; 2 Mennonite; 1 Lutheran; 1 Brethren; 1 Roman Catholic; 8 Salvation Army; 11 unchurched. The 43 members consisted of 7 singles and 20 couples; of 4 couples only 1 partner was a member. Some had large families; 1 couple had 12 children, all Pentecostals. In view of the purpose of this analysis, namely to assess the churchly background and professions, only the parents were counted in cases where whole families were Pentecostals. The professions of the 43 were: 3 shop-owners, 3 dockyard workers; 2 office clerks; 2 tailors; 2 engine drivers; 1 warehouse man; 1 plasterer; 1 cooper; 1 gardener; 1 house-painter; 1 coal transport worker; 2 nurses; 1 hair-dresser; 2 evangelists; 1 domestic servant.

202. See Appendix 2 for specification.

203. The figure of 1920 was not available in the publication of the census, but was obtained from the archive of the Centraal Bureau voor de Statistiek in Voorburg. This further revealed that of the 272 Pentecostals (133 males and 139 females), 61 kept a membership with another church: 42 Netherlands Reformed; 5 Gereformeerd; 1 Remonstrant; 6 Lutheran; 7 Salvation Army. Of the 508 Pentecostals recorded in 1930 (232 males and 276 females), 99 belonged to the Gemeente des Heeren. Again some kept a membership with another church: 29 Netherlands Reformed and 1 Baptist. Of the 99 Gemeente des Heeren another 11 were Netherlands Reformed. *Volkstelling 31 December 1930*, vol. 3: *Kerkelijke Gezindte* (The Hague: C.B.S., 1933), pp. 184-85, 188-91, 193-94.

8   MISSION WORK

To the Uttermost Parts of the Earth

At the Hamburg Conference, December 1908, Cecil Polhill addressed the issue of foreign mission. Polhill saw the Pentecostal experience as a gift for service and for missionary service in particular: "This Pentecostal Blessing which has come to us must go right through the world."[1] He felt that the Welsh Revival had been quenched through lack of missionary spirit. Polhill had been a missionary to China from 1885 to 1900 through the "China Inland Mission" and still was a member of their council. Upon his initiative the "Pentecostal Missionary Union" (P.M.U.) was founded on 9 January 1909. Candidates had to be baptized with the Holy Spirit with "the Signs and Gifts" and to believe in the infallibility of the Holy Scriptures. The educational standard required a fair knowledge of every book in the Bible and an "accurate knowledge of the Doctrine of Salvation and Sanctification."[2] No salaries were guaranteed. All candidates went through a training school which was soon established in London. The magazine *Fragments of Fire*, which after October 1911 continued as *Flames of Fire*, was edited by Polhill. Until Polman founded the Dutch Pentecostal Missionary Society in 1920 all Dutch missionaries were sent by the P.M.U.

CHINA

Arie Kok (1883-1951) and his wife Elsje Roelofje Aldenberg (born 1887 at Deventer) were the first fruits "given to the Lord for the Foreign Mission Field."[3] Arie Kok, a clerk of the Post Office, had been active in evangelistic circles since his visit to the Welsh Revival in 1905.[4] When he joined the Pentecostal movement his evangelical friends turned away from him.[5] His remarkable baptism with the Holy Spirit and calling for Tibet has already been mentioned. Arie and Elsje Kok had been important co-workers of Polman; their departure was certainly a loss for the work at home. In August 1909 the couple left for the P.M.U. training school in London. During the farewell meeting the whole assembly was praying for them amidst sobs and tears. With the laying on of hands they were consecrated for the mission field, after which the assembly sang, "Dat 's Heeren zegen op u daal" (May the blessing of the Lord descend upon you).[6] The Dutch Pentecostals were caught by a spirit of mission. Teenage children formed praying bands for the mission in heathen countries. Offering boxes were placed in the houses. A Bible class of about 20 young men and women was established as training for evangelists and missionaries.[7] After several months of preparation in London the Kok family left for China in early 1910. On the way they stopped in Russia to work some time in Dorpat and Reval.[8] In concert with the China Inland Mission they would, after a thorough language study, pioneer in Likiang in the northwest of the province Yunnan, on the border of Tibet. By the time they settled there they received help from Elize Scharten.

Cornelia Elisabeth Scharten (1876-1965) was a daughter of Lutheran minister Karel Scharten (1836-1909) and his wife Johanna Stumphius (1840-1908). Two of her brothers and one brother-in-law were Lutheran ministers, too, while her sister Jenneke was married to missionary Johannes Pik.[9] Elize had been trained as handicraft instructor in Sweden. In 1903 she was co-founder of the Christian home "Welkom" that practiced inner mission in the red-light district of Amsterdam.[10] During 1907 Elize and some of her colleagues from "Welkom" visited a Pentecostal meeting:

> There was speaking with other tongues, and interpretation was given. What I had read so often in the Bible and had wondered: why are these gifts of the Holy Spirit no longer seen and heard in the church; that I was seeing and hearing now. I could not help saying a thanksgiving, because God's grace was still the same.[11]

One of the elders of the Lutheran church warned father Scharten that his daughter had attended a "spiritistic meeting" and had even prayed! For some time Elize refrained from going there again, but kept informed about the developments. In September 1908, shortly after the death of her mother, Elize had a conversation with Alexander Boddy in Amsterdam. The Anglican minister advised her to search for the baptism with the Holy Spirit. She visited the public and mutual meetings. On 28 September 1908 she received her Spirit baptism at home: "My mouth was filled with laughing. O grace of God, so great and rich. I was allowed to praise and glorify my Lord in foreign languages."[12] Again father Scharten was warned, but he replied, "I have received a better daughter, so it is all right."[13] Elize became a zealous co-worker in the Pentecostal assembly and had her testimony printed in a pamphlet entitled *Tot eer van God* (To the glory of God). In February 1911 Elize Scharten and Trijntje Baas were sent from Amsterdam to the P.M.U. women's training home at London. Trijntje Baas remained in London, but Elize left for China in April 1912 to assist the Kok family in opening a mission post in Likiang.

The Immanuel Hall, Amsterdam, was opened in June 1912. The building behind the hall housed the missionary training school that commenced in October 1912.[14] From the first class three students—Piet Klaver, Trijntje Bakker, and Geertje Roos—would all go to China. Instruction was given in Bible study; Religions of heathendom; Geography; English; French; and German (optional).[15] The many activities of the Pentecostal assembly provided for abundant practical exercise of all kinds. Klaver wrote concerning this time:

> The Bible school in Amsterdam was very primitive. When brother and sister Polman were present, we were instructed by them. Because one was of the opinion that the Dutch Indies would become my field of work, I was also instructed by a sister from Java. This did not take long. Yet it was a blessed time. We were mainly instructed from the Bible. In the morning before breakfast there was always a prayer meeting and after the lessons there was again a time for kneeling. Different petitions were made. The Spirit of God

often worked in a mighty way. There were messages in
strange languages with interpretation and lots of prophecies.
I remember there was also prophesied that the coming war
would not pass our borders. In those days of course nobody
thought of a world war. There were about six or seven persons
in training, but I was the only male student. I had the task to
clean the upper room. In everything there was a cheerful and
merry spirit.[16]

Piet Klaver (1890-1970) was the youngest of six children in
a Christian family. His father, Jan Klaver, had a baker's shop
in Amsterdam. In May 1907 Piet Klaver was converted in a
Salvation Army meeting. During 1909 he went to the
Salvation Army training school and became an Army officer
until in 1911 he joined the Pentecostal movement. His first
acquaintance with Pentecostalism occurred just before he
finished the training school. He visited one meeting at 42
Nieuwe Prinsengracht. Arie Kok preached on Hebrews 11.
In the middle of his sermon he gave a message in tongues.[17]
During 1911 Klaver again attended a Pentecostal meeting.
Polman's sermon on the second coming of Christ and the
rapture of the Church, based on 1 Thess. 4:16-17, was
completely new to him. He started reading *Spade Regen* and
prayed for the baptism with the Holy Spirit. He was
disappointed when this did not happen immediately. After
the Wednesday evening service on 31 May 1911 his friend
insisted that he remain for prayer. Klaver was tired, but to do
his friend a favor he knelt thinking, You can pray a long time,
before I will be baptized with the Spirit. Suddenly the Spirit
came over him and he fluently spoke in tongues.[18] As Klaver
had a call for the mission field he followed the training school
and proceeded to London in March 1914 for further studies.
Idigje de Vries, who had been in the P.M.U. women's
training home since September 1911, sailed for China in
April 1914. Due to illness she had to resign in February
1916.[19] In December 1915 Klaver was able to leave for China
to assist Kok and Scharten at Likiang.[20] In China he married
Rose Waters from Liverpool, also a P.M.U. missionary.
   During 1918 Annie Kok, a sister of Arie Kok, came from
America to Likiang to teach the children of her brother. She

had received her Spirit baptism in Amsterdam in 1911 and with her parents and two sisters she had moved to Grand Rapids.[21] When in 1919 Arie Kok got over-tired and had to leave Likiang, Klaver took over leadership of the mission. The Kok family went to Peking for rest, but in the end never returned to the mission field. Annie Kok remained at Likiang until 1925. Because of his proficiency in the Chinese language Arie Kok became chancellor of the Dutch legation at Peking and as such he sometimes could be a help for missionaries.[22]

Trijntje Bakker (1891-1980) and Geertje Roos (born 1879) from Terschelling went to the missionary training school in Amsterdam in October 1912. Because of the World War their departure for China was postponed. In the meantime they and other students from the school (all women) canvassed parts of the country with tracts and papers. For this purpose Polman started the publication of *Klanken des Vredes* an illustrated periodical for non-Christians, which was sold for three cents. Finally in October 1921 the ladies Bakker and Roos were able to travel to China together with Elize Scharten, who had been on furlough.

Likiang was along a trade route to Tibet. The tribes that lived there had Tibetan blood and were, like the Tibetans, despised by the Chinese. The area had never been reached with the gospel. It took quite some time to win the trust of the people and to see the first converts. The latter was also due to the heavy demands of the missionaries, who insisted that converts forsook all use of opium and alcohol. In dress, food, and housing the missionaries accommodated to the local way of living. Soon after some converts were gained Kok established a Bible school and trained capable men as evangelists.[23] His strategy to train inland evangelists proved successful. From Likiang a number of out-stations were founded where inland evangelists led the work. Several journeys were made into Tibet. Elize Scharten studied some of the important oral tribal languages. When she had developed a written form she prepared a dictionary and translated the gospel of Mark, a catechism, and a songbook.[24] The Dutch missionaries cooperated with other P.M.U. missionaries and later with missionaries from America and

Germany.[25] Due to a civil war all missionaries had to leave the area during 1927. Elize Scharten returned to China in 1929 followed by Trijntje Bakker in 1931, while Piet Klaver went to the Dutch Indies in 1929.[26]

BELGIAN CONGO

The Dutch missionary effort was not limited to China. In spite of the world war Anna Meester (born 1887) from Wolvega was able to leave for Belgian Congo in December 1914. She had been a nurse in a deaconesses' nursing home at Haarlem and had followed the missionary training school at Amsterdam. It was the fulfillment of a prophecy concerning Africa, printed in *Spade Regen* one year before.[27] She was sent by the P.M.U., but worked with the Congo Inland Mission.[28] When she had mastered the language she not only nursed the sick, but also taught children to read and write in their native tongue.[29] During her furlough (1918 to 1920) she passed the midwifery exam in England. In 1924 she got over-tired and had to resign from the mission field.[30]

DUTCH PENTECOSTAL MISSIONARY SOCIETY

In the meantime an important development had taken place at home. During 1920 the "council of brothers" from the Pentecostal assemblies at Amsterdam and Haarlem decided to form a Dutch Pentecostal Missionary Society. On 28 October 1920 "Het Pinksterzendingsgenootschap" designed to "train, send out and sustain missionaries to spread the gospel of Jesus Christ to all nations, especially those who have not yet been reached," was founded.[31] It became incorporated as "Vereeniging" in January 1923. Membership was open to those who "acknowledge the true, eternal Divinity of Christ and who by their way of living testify to be redeemed by the blood of Jesus Christ, believing in the second coming of Christ for His church and the baptism with the Holy Spirit, as is written in the Holy Scriptures."[32] The mission work was financed by free gifts from members and sympathizers and by the proceeds of annual bazaars. Upon request offering boxes were supplied to place in the houses. All Pentecostal assemblies shared in the missionary effort. The following missionaries were sent by the Dutch Society: Anna Meester for her second term in Congo in 1920; Trijntje Bakker and Geertje Roos to China in 1921; Anna Gnirrep to Java in 1921; William Bernard from Liverpool, England, with his Dutch wife Marie Henriette Blekkink (sister of Mrs. Polman) to Java in 1923; Adolf Wieneke from Velbert, Germany, to China in 1923; Nico and Maartje Vetter to Venezuela in 1925; Piet Klaver and family for their second term to China in 1925.[33]

VENEZUELA

Nicolaas Vetter (1899-1945), son of a blacksmith, was born in Amsterdam and had joined the Pentecostal assembly in his Sunday-school years. His parents were Netherlands Reformed, but came in touch with Pentecostalism in 1910. Nico welcomed the change because it brought him the gospel in a way he could understand. About 1916 he was baptized with the Spirit, while he was alone in his room.[34] He married Maartje van de Goor in February 1919. They were active in the children's work of the assembly. Both felt a call for the mission field. At first they thought of Congo, but Venezuela was the country they were to go to. After a period of training they left in December 1924. The first two years they worked in a neglected mission post at Los Teques and then moved to El Tocuyo in consent with P.G. Bender, an American Pentecostal missionary.[35]

Vetter was an effective church planter. Within three years eight out-stations were opened, where trained inland evangelists were given charge. Vetter saw the need to have a home for repudiated women and disowned children: "In the whole of Venezuela the. Mission has not been able to do anything along this line."[36] The Vetter family started such a home in their own house and soon they cared for ten children, some being orphans.[37] There was no hospital in the area. The two medical doctors were very expensive. Vetter and his fellow workers prayed for the sick and cared for them as far as they could. Some were healed in answer to prayer.[38] Although the people were very poor, they brought their tithes (*in natura*) without being asked to.[39] The climate and the hard labor took a heavy toll on the Vetters' physical constitution. Often they were attacked by fever. At the end of 1935 Vetter was dying of malaria and was carried to a hospital in England. Upon prayer he was miraculously healed.[40] The situation of the Pentecostal movement at home required that he continue his ministry in the Netherlands.

DUTCH INDIES

The last area to consider in connection with the foreign mission is that of the Dutch Indies. Since 1909 Polman had been mailing *Spade Regen* to this archipelago and in 1920 he published a cry of distress from believers there to send Pentecostal missionaries to Java.[41] Thiessen was the first to respond. Johann Thiessen (1869-1953) was born in Russia. His ancestors were Mennonites who had fled from Friesland to Russia three centuries before and had never mixed with the population there. The descendants spoke a German-Dutch dialect. After a theological study in Switzerland and a short medical training in the Netherlands, Thiessen went to the Dutch Indies as missionary of the Doopsgezinde Kerk from 1901 till 1912. During his furlough he attended Pentecostal meetings at Basel, Switzerland, and was baptized with the Holy Spirit.[42] The German Pentecostal leader Jonathan Paul had a great influence upon his life. For several years he lived at Apeldoorn where he was active in the city mission "Evangelisatie Maranatha" together with a certain Smit.[43] Between 1916 and 1918 (at the time of the revolution!) Thiessen was in Russia.[44] During the summer of 1918 Thiessen returned to Apeldoorn and from there worked together with Polman and made journeys to Eastern Europe. His Dutch wife Anna Maria Vink, a niece of professor A.H. den Hartog, received her Spirit baptism in Amsterdam in 1920.[45] The same year Thiessen participated in the founding of the Dutch Pentecostal Missionary Society and became its vice-president.

In 1921 Thiessen returned to the Dutch Indies, where he became an important pioneer of the Pentecostal movement.

His attempts to integrate the Pentecostal message in existing evangelical circles on Java were not welcomed. In 1923 the "Bond voor Evangelisatie in Nederlandsch Oost-Indië" expelled from its board the members in sympathy with the Pentecostals.[46] The same year Thiessen founded "De Pinksterbeweging" (Geraja Gerakan Pentekosta) in Bandung, Java, and started publication of *Dit is het.*[47] Polman and Thiessen kept in touch with each other. The Dutch missionaries to China usually visited Java on their way. Two sons of Thiessen, John and Henk, went to the Elim Bible College in London and spent considerable time in Holland during 1926.[48] When in 1929 J. Thiessen visited Polman "old ties of friendship were renewed."[49] The same year Piet Klaver became attached to Thiessen's mission at Java. The other Dutch missionaries that went to the Dutch Indies occasionally cooperated with Thiessen. Anna Gnirrep worked on Java in a home for neglected children from 1921 till 1927.[50] William Bernard (1866-1945) and Marie Henriette Blekkink (1882-1932) left for Java in August 1922 together with Miss Mina Hansen (1893-1939) from Denmark, who had stayed about a year with the Polmans in Amsterdam. They settled at Temanggung, where they worked with H.E. Horstman.[51] In 1924 they were involved in the foundation of "De Pinkstergemeente in Nederlandsch-Indië" at Bandung with the paper *De Pinksterbode.*[52] Due to the illness of William Bernard the family had to resign from the mission field in 1925, while Mina Hansen remained to carry on the work.[53]

Through contacts with Elize Scharten, Thiessen, Gnirrep, and Bernard the Dutch female evangelist Margaretha A. Alt (1883-1962) was won for the Pentecostal movement. She had been a Seventh-Day Baptist, but with an independent evangelistic work at Gambang Waluh, near Temanggung. She had planted a church, and opened a home for mentally defective children (later it became an orphanage) and a school.[54] When she was baptized with the Holy Spirit in 1926 it brought a revival in her church.[55] In 1929 she started publication of the *Gouden Schoven* and in 1935 she founded the "Pinksterzending."[56] To the Dutch Pentecostals she is most known through her songbook *Glorieklokken.*[57]

SUMMARY

Compared with the small size of the Dutch Pentecostal movement, the missionary endeavors are very impressive. The missionary zeal was embedded in an eschatological scheme. Bringing the gospel to all nations was regarded as a prerequisite for the second coming of Christ. As Tibet had the reputation of being the most closed area for the gospel, it became a special target for the early Pentecostal mission. The missionaries worked along the lines of the China Inland Mission. They went inland, lived among the people and had no guarantee of salary. Donald Gee believed that the foreign missionary zeal hindered the expansion of the British Pentecostal assemblies at home: "Giving was disproportionate. Young men with gifts for ministry were encouraged to believe that the only Field on which they could show forth a genuine consecration was somewhere in distant lands."[58] The same could be said of the Dutch situation. Capable men and women went to the mission field, while at home the growth stagnated by lack of leadership. On the other hand the foreign mission had a stimulating effect. It confirmed the Pentecostals as being loyal to the great commission of Christ. In providing a joint effort it strengthened the unity among the Pentecostals. It gave the Pentecostals a status that commanded respect from outsiders.

Inland Mission: Propagating the Message at Home

LITERATURE

The immediate availability of Pentecostal periodicals and tracts contributed much to the swift spreading of Pentecostalism around the world. Polman had learned the strategic value of the printed message during his period with the Salvation Army and Dowie. In April 1908 Polman started publication of *Spade Regen*. It had four pages (27.5 × 40 cm.) and was sent to anyone interested, free of charge. Voluntary donations were not sufficient for a monthly appearance. From April

1908 until January 1917 41 numbers were published at irregular times. The circulation grew from 3,000 to 6,000.[59] As of April 1917 (volume 10, number 1) it became a monthly paper with an annual subscription charge of 65 cents. With April 1919 (volume 12, number 1) it was changed to a 16-page brochure format (26.5 × 19 cm.), subscription being raised to ƒ1.00. The photo on the front cover was usually dedicated to foreign mission. Publication ceased in March 1931, one year before the death of Polman. Of the 208 issues, all but 9 were found.[60] As of June 1915 *Klanken des Vredes* was published monthly as an evangelization paper. It was an attractive illustrated paper with 8 pages (27.5 × 40 cm.) and was sold for 3 cents per issue. Every month 10,000 to 12,000 copies were printed and of the two-color Christmas issue even 20,000.[61] Each number contained a song with music, often translated from German (Pfingstjubel) or English. Many issues of *Spade Regen* and *Klanken des Vredes* were sent to Dutch-speaking people in South Africa, Dutch Indies, and Belgium. But also to Germany, Switzerland, England, East Africa, Egypt, Canada, U.S.A., South America, and China.[62]

The only tract Polman published was T.B. Barratt's *Een Pinksterdoop met tongen, NIET van den duivel* in 1908 (issued by Boddy as *Pentecost with tongues, not of the devil*). As the title suggests it sought to refute allegations that the Pentecostal experience was from the devil. The tract was written for orthodox Christians, among whom Pentecostalism was recruiting its members. Along this line is the following statement Barratt made in 1909:

> A minister, not in favour of this revival, said to me personally: "I must acknowledge that it is generally the most devoted and Christ-like of God's people in the various churches, who are drawn into this revival." And he was right. But why is this? Because they find the nourishment their souls are seeking for in it and feel that this is God's voice to them and His Church in these days.[63]

The above also explains why their evangelical colleagues, who were depending on the same category of people, felt threatened and denounced the Pentecostals as diabolic.

In a series "Pinksteruitgaven" (Pentecostal Publications) Polman had the following brochures published:

1. Dr. G.A. Wumkes, *De Pinksterbeweging voornamelijk in Nederland* (Amsterdam: G.R. Polman, 1917, 23 pages);
2. T.B. Barratt, *De waarheid inzake de Pinksteropwekking* (Amsterdam: G.R. Polman, 1917, 32 pages);
3. Pastor J. Paul, *De oplossing van het wereldraadsel* (Amsterdam: G.R. Polman, 1920, 36 pages);
4. Elize Scharten, *Uit het binnenland van China* (Amsterdam: G.R. Polman, 1922, 30 pages).

Wumkes' writing was a sympathetic historical description of the Dutch Pentecostal movement from a Netherlands Reformed minister. Before Polman started the series "Pinksteruitgaven" he had it published through G.J.A. Ruys, Utrecht, in 1916. Wumkes' study received a lot of attention in Christian circles. Time was ripe for more Pentecostal publications. Polman translated Barratt's lecture "The Truth About the Pentecostal Revival" delivered at London and Zurich in 1909.[64] It contained Barratt's personal experience and an interesting discussion on the movement in the light of scripture, church history, and contemporary criticism. One of the reasons Polman selected this 8-year-old lecture must have been its emphasis on the ecumenical aspect as one of the miracles in this revival:

> Even Catholics have through this revival been converted and brought into brotherhood with the Protestants. But this proves more clearly her pure character. A revival that is able to unite around Christ the hearts that have been long divided, must exactly be the revival meant by Christ when he prayed, that all his disciples would be one.[65]

J. Paul's eschatological work, translated from *Die Lösung des Rätsels der Gegenwart*, was written after the turbulent years of war and revolution. It is interlarded with the speculative and far-fetched use of the Bible, which is common in the writings of evangelical end time prophets. In the rise of Bolshevism and Zionism Paul saw the fulfillment of Daniel 2 and 7.[66]

The last publication in the series "Pinksteruitgaven" concerned an illustrated description of the foreign mission work in China and Tibet by Elize Scharten and a recommendation to support the Dutch Pentecostal Missionary Society. Besides a publication of Pentecostal hymns with notes, a booklet with poems and Bible verses to comfort the sick was published: W.J.M. Polman-Blekkink, *Dauwdruppels* (Amsterdam: G.R. Polman, 1927, 64 pages).

Pentecostal literature not published by Polman includes the already mentioned *Tot eer van God* by Elize Scharten (1908); *Wat zegt Gods woord* (1928) and *Behoud den rechten weg* (1929) by E. Schuurman; and the paper *De Blijde Boodschapper* edited by J. Orsel of the Gemeente des Heeren.[67] To this list may be added A. Zijp, *Om het behoud van den zegen: Een woord aan geloovigen* (Amsterdam: by author, 1926, 11 pages). It was recommended by Polman as "a help to spread the baptism with the Holy Spirit."[68] The baptism with the Holy Spirit was put forth as an experience subsequent to conversion and evidenced by cheerfulness and power to witness. Tongues were not mentioned by Zijp, who had just received this experience without tongues himself. Albert Zijp (1890-1977), a merchant in eggs and cheese, had gone through a spiritual awakening since attending the Pentecostal meetings at Amsterdam. In 1926 he was not only baptized with the Holy Spirit, but also in water.[69] His petition to the Gereformeerde Kerk, to which he originally belonged, to abolish the infant baptism as unscriptural and to introduce the baptism for believers, was repudiated and his membership cancelled.[70] Zijp's publication of the petition with an answer from the synod was never mentioned in *Spade Regen*. One other publication recommended by Polman was A.S. Booth-Clibborn's pacifistic *Bloed tegen Bloed* (Blood Against Blood).[71]

EVANGELIZATION

Except for *Klanken des Vredes* all the above-mentioned publications were written for believers. When Pentecostals went out to reach unbelievers, by means of open-air meetings or going from house to house, they probably made use of evangelistic tracts obtained from non-Pentecostal organizations. In 1910 *Spade Regen* referred to a group of 20 members that distributed tracts every Sunday afternoon.[72] As of 1915 students from the training school canvassed parts of the country with *Klanken des Vredes*, Bibles, and tracts.[73] In November 1917 the interdenominational "Bond voor Evangelisatie Huis aan Huis" (Union for Evangelization House to House) was founded at Amsterdam. Of the 70 members more than 30 were Pentecostals.[74] For two hours per week they went from house to house. By 1920 the Pentecostals had their own tracts union called "Immanuel." The 34 members visited ships in the harbor, worked on markets, and held open-air meetings.[75] In May 1926 *Spade Regen* referred to a group of 70 that went out two by two, house to house, "proclaiming the message of salvation by means of literature and testimony":

> One represents no sect that places a special emphasis on one truth, but they may go and preach only Christ as the Saviour of sinners and His fullness. One does not try to make proselytes of the Pentecostal assembly, but to be a blessing for everyone.[76]

Open-air meetings were usually held on Saturday evening and during the summer also on Sunday afternoon. The singing was accompanied by mandolin and guitar.[77] According to eyewitnesses many unchurched were gained by these evangelistic efforts. In 1923 the "Evangelie en Verbandboot 't Anker" (Gospel and Charity Boat "The Anchor") started to bring the gospel among the barge-men. The work was non-denominational, but was mainly done by Pentecostals. They carried Bibles and tracts, rendered first-aid and free clothing.[78]

SOCIAL WORK

Besides Sunday school and Bible classes for young people, there were other activities with a more or less social emphasis that attracted outsiders or commanded their respect. Neighbors who never came to the meetings expressed their appreciation that the Immanuel building was not only used for services but also for charity.[79] Immediately after World War I Mrs. Polman played a part in a relief program for underfed Austrian children, for which she was awarded by the Austrian government with the *Patriae A.C. Humanitatie*.[80] From Immanuel parcels with food and clothing as well as money were sent to the poor in Bulgaria and Germany.[81] Female workers in uniform (former students of the training school), who went from house to house with *Klanken des Vredes*, often helped the sick and lonely with small domestic duties.[82] For young girls there was a sewing school.[83] At Christmas, special evenings for factory girls were organized.[84] Since 1915 a "mothers circle" operated, which kept a relief fund and provided domestic help for mothers with newly born children.[85] The Immanuel home was always open for those who needed spiritual help or physical rest. In 1919 Polman bought another house at Zandvoort, which was used during the summer partly as a rest home and was called "Lydia."[86] The healing home "Bethel" at Apeldoorn has already been mentioned as well as Polman's visitations to conscientious objectors in prison and his help in tracing missing relatives of interned soldiers during the world war.[87]

The social concern of Dutch Pentecostalism, which has also been detected in the area of foreign mission, is significant, no matter how modest it may have been. Robert Mapes Anderson in his sociological study of North American Pentecostalism, *Vision of the Disinherited*, noticed the absence of any social welfare work among the first-generation American Pentecostals.[88] Possibly the Salvation Army background of Polman and other Dutch Pentecostals was one reason why they showed more social involvement than their American co-religionists.

NOTES

1. "The Pentecostal Movement and the Foreign Mission Field," *Confidence* 2/1 (January 1909),15-16.
2. "The Pentecostal Missionary Union," *Confidence* 2/1 (January 1909),13-14. The first issue of *Flames of Fire* (October 1911) contained the following statement of faith:

The Doctrines We Hold
1. Atonement through the Blood
2. Sanctification through the Spirit
3. The Baptism of the Holy Spirit and fire with signs, as power for service
4. The ordinances of Water Baptism and of the Lord's Supper
5. The plenary inspiration of Old and New Testaments (entire)
6. The pre-millennial Advent of our Lord
7. The Eternity of bliss, or of punishment.

The statement of faith was never repeated in following issues of *Flames of Fire*. As of January 1917 the following statement appeared on the back page:

> We pray for Holiness and Divine Power; for our Nation that it may refuse the evil and choose the good, part with sin and turn to God, and thus deserve victory; for Foreign Missions throughout the wide world, and a gracious spiritual revival.
>
> We teach that all men are by nature in sin, but all can be saved through faith in Christ crucified; that men can live holy lives through Christ living within; and that there is a baptism in the Holy Spirit (Acts 2), equipping workers with power for service. We offer to pray with those seeking this promised power, that they may receive forthwith; we also lay hands on the sick for their recovery.
>
> Christians of all denominations are cordially invited, also the unsaved, that they may be reconciled to God.

3. G.R. Polman, "Farewell Meetings with Mr. and Mrs. Kok at Amsterdam," *Confidence* 2/9 (September 1909),208a-208b.
4. Joh. de Heer, "Reiservaringen," *Jeruël* no. 105 (August 1905) recorded that Arie Kok testified of his experience in Wales during one meeting at Enkhuizen in June 1905. From *Straatprediking: Jaarverslag der Bijbeltent voor straatevangelisatie en colportage in Nederland* (Amsterdam: J. Timmerman, 1909), it appears that A. Kok was chairman of the Bijbeltent council.
5. A. Kok, "Wien zal Ik zenden?" *Spade Regen* no. 12 (November 1909),1-2.
6. "Eerste uitzending naar de heidenwereld," *Spade Regen* no. 11 (August-October 1909),4; cf. Polman "Farewell Meetings with Mr. and Mrs. Kok."
7. Polman, "Farewell Meetings with Mr. and Mrs. Kok."
8. *Spade Regen* no. 14 (January-March 1910),4.
9. K. Scharten, "Genealogie van de familie Scharten," *Gens Nostra* 34 (1979),49-60.
10. "Welkom" was first situated on the Zeedijk and in 1908 moved to the 15 Warmoesstraat. The work was interdenominational. Their bimonthly paper was called *Welkom*.
11. E. Scharten, "Gaat heen in de gehele wereld en predikt het evangelie

aan alle schepselen," *Volle Evangelie Koerier* 10/9 (March 1948). A series of articles appeared under this name from February 1948 till July 1950.

12. Ibid., 10/10 (April 1948).

13. Ibid., 10/12 (June 1948).

14. W. Polman, "De Opening der Zendingsschool," *Spade Regen* no. 31 (August-November 1912),4; P.N. Corry, "Holland: Dedication of Missionary Home," *Confidence* 5/11 (November 1912),259-60.

    The building of the training home is supposed to have been used by Napoleon, when he visited Amsterdam to discuss the method of drying up the Zuider Zee. Edel's assembly at Brieg had supplied the furniture. One of the first students came from Germany. Upon request from German mission friends Polman had a German prospectus of the training school printed in September 1913. *Spade Regen* no. 34 (September 1913),136.

15. "The Pentecostal Bible School in Holland," *Confidence* 7/4 (April 1914),78.

16. P. Klaver, "Herinneringen van een Pinksterpionier," *Kracht van Omhoog* 28/19 (26 March 1965),8.

17. Ibid., 28/16 (12 February 1965),8.

18. Ibid.

19. *Spade Regen* no. 36 (March 1914),4, recorded that Ida de Vries' farewell from Amsterdam had been on 11 January 1914. Other references to her were found in the P.M.U. Minute Book, present in the Assemblies of God Headquarters in Nottingham, England.

20. "Holland: News from Pastor Polman," *Confidence* 8/12 (December 1915),235-36, gives a description of the farewell service at Amsterdam, about 400 persons were present; cf. *Spade Regen* no. 39 (January 1916),4.

21. *Spade Regen* 10/11 (February 1918),207-08; cf. Anna C.A. Kok, "How God Protected Christian Chinese from Bandits," *The Latter Rain Evangel* (June 1925),18-19.

22. After World War II Kok left China. In the meantime he had disassociated himself from the Pentecostal movement. In 1948 he participated in the founding of the militant "International Council of Christian Churches" and became their General Secretary. In January 1951 he died in the U.S.A.

23. A. and E. Kok "Een Bijbelschool op het Zendingsveld," *Spade Regen* no. 40 (July 1916),4. The Bible school was started by Kok in 1914. Three male students were taken in. They moved into the home of the missionaries. After two years Kok decided to add a third year to the course. Students were taught in Biblical History; Dogmatics; Church History; Prayer; Singing; Bible Study; Biblical Geography; General Geography; General Knowledge. Besides the fulltime students there were other helpers, who went through a one-month course. They were instructed in singing and in the basic principles of the Christian truth.

24. Concerning Elize Scharten a wealth of material is available from the family archive, including 7 diaries. Her newsletters were printed in

Spade Regen, Confidence, Flames of Fire, but also in the non-Pentecostal paper *Welkom,* and occasionally in such Lutheran papers as *Een vaste burg is onze God!, Opwaarts,* and *De Wartburg.* Between February 1948 and July 1950 she had a series of articles published in the *Volle Evangelie Koerier.*

Ida van Marle, *Zij volgde haar roeping* (The Hague: Gazon, 1976), contains a biography of Trijntje Bakker.

25. Cf. Donald Gee, "The Challenge of Yunnan," *The Pentecostal Evangel* (5 March 1938),4-5; Robert Bolton, "South of the Clouds: Church Planting in Yünnan Province Through Lisu People Movements (1906-1949)" (term paper, Fuller Theological Seminary, Los Angeles, 1974); Hans Ditthardt and Theo Koch, *Velbert 50 Jahre mit Vollem Evangelium* (Erzhausen: Leuchter Verlag, 1960).

26. Trijntje Bakker stayed until 1938. Afterwards she was not able to return to China because of the war. Apart from a furlough between 1934 and 1936 Elize Scharten remained in Likiang until 1947.

27. *Spade Regen* no. 33 (May 1913),4, recorded a prophecy that was uttered sometime before. God was to give a great revival to Africa. Because of Simon from Cyrene, who had carried the cross for Jesus, the people of Africa would not be forgotten. The curse would turn into a blessing. Every tribe would get its messenger, some were to come from Holland.

28. "Oorlog en Zending," *Spade Regen* no. 38 (December 1914),3-4; Alma E. Doering, "The Kongo Inland Mission," *Confidence* 7/11 (November 1914),216-18.

29. *Spade Regen* no. 39 (January 1916),4.

30. *Spade Regen* 17/2 (May 1924),30, 32.

31. *Spade Regen* 13/8 (November 1920),122-23. The first board consisted of Mr. and Mrs. Polman, J. Thiessen, W. Heuvelink, J. Th. Erdtsieck Jr., L. Oltmann, and Miss F.J. Trompetter. In 1923 when J. Thiessen had returned to the Dutch Indies, he was replaced in the board by F.A. Tienpont and J.H. Schat Jr. In 1928 W. Heuvelink was replaced by A.C. van Ingen, at which time Otto Karrenberg from Velbert, who represented the Dutch Mission in Germany, was added to the board. *Spade Regen* 16/8 (November 1923),125-26; 21/3 (June 1928),48.

32. *Nederlandsche Staatscourant,* Supplement, 17 April 1923, no. 74. Filed under "Statuten Vereenigingen 1923 no. 452"; cf. "Het Pinksterzend-ingsgenootschap," *Spade Regen* 16/8 (November 1923),125-26.

33. Elize Scharten remained with the P.M.U. until 1926, when the P.M.U. was merged with the British Assemblies of God. Since 1931 both Elize Scharten and Trijntje Bakker were associated with the German "Vereinigte Missionsfreunde e.V., Velbert," which was founded in that same year. At that time the Dutch Mission Society was at loose ends due to the resignation of Polman. For a good communication with the Dutch sponsors Klaver started publication of *De Vereenigde Zendingsvrienden* in May 1937.

34. N. Vetter, *Gouden Schoven* 9 (October-November 1936); Idem, "Amsterdam," *Het Middernachtelijk Geroep* 2/7 (1939),57.

35. *Spade Regen* 20/1 (April 1927),15-16; 20/9 (December 1927),143.

36. *Spade Regen* 20/12 (March 1928),192. Vetter had already taken a sick young woman into his home in July 1927. *Spade Regen* 20/6 (September 1927),95-96.

37. *Spade Regen* 21/4 (July 1928)62-63; 21/10 (January 1929),159-60; 23/3 (June 1930),44-45.

38. *Spade Regen* 20/6 (September 1927),95-96; 21/10 (January 1929),159-60.

39. *Spade Regen* 21/10 (January 1929),159-60; 23/3 (June 1930),44.

40. Br., "Bij het heengaan van br. Vetter." Loose leaf found in *Kracht van Omhoog* 9/2 (August 1945).

41. *Spade Regen* no. 6 (January-February 1909),4; 13/6 (September 1920),90.

42. J.E. van den Brink, "De Pinksterbeweging in Indonesië," *Kracht van Omhoog* 27/19 (April 1964),11; *The Mennonite Encyclopedia*, vol. 4 (Scottdale, PA: Mennonite Publishing House, 1959), p. 712. The exact year of his connection with the Pentecostal movement is uncertain.

43. J.H. Gunning J.Hz., *Herinneringen uit mijn leven* (Amsterdam: H.J. Spruyt, 1941), pp. 232-240. In August 1918 when Gunning opened the hall "Maranatha" at Apeldoorn, J. Thiessen participated in the service.

44. When G.A. Wumkes visited Polman in June 1917 he met J. Thiessen there. G.A. Wumkes, *Nei Sawntich Jier* (Boalsert: A.J. Osinga, 1949), p. 434. This date falls in the period that Thiessen is supposed to be in Russia.

   In 1918 Thiessen wanted to bring the Pentecostal gospel to the Ukraine and the Balkans in cooperation with Polman and issue a Pentecostal paper in the Dutch and German languages. In the Ukraine lived 80,000 people of Dutch descent. *Spade Regen* 11/7 (October 1918),28.

45. "Ter nagedachtenis van 'Onze lieve Ma,' " *Dit is het* 8/11 (May 1931),180-184.

46. Cf. the following articles from *Ons Orgaan:* "Br. Hoekendijk," 17/271 (November),192-91; "Bond voor Evangelisatie in Ned. O.-Indië," 18/280 (August 1923),268-89; "De Pinksterbeweging," 18/282 (October 1923),282-83; 18/283 (November 1923),290-91; 19/285 (January 1924),308-09; 19/286 (February 1924),315-16.

47. *Spade Regen* 14/7 (October 1921),119, quotes from Thiessen's first letter from Bandung, Java; cf. H. Thiessen, *Het Gouden Jubileum van de Pinksterbeweging* (The Hague: by author, 1973).

48. *Spade Regen* 19/4 (July 1926),62; cf. John and Henk Thiessen "An Aggressive Work in Java," *The Elim Evangel* 8/22 (November 1927),339-40.

49. *Spade Regen* 22/7 (October 1929),107-08.

50. *Spade Regen* 20/7 (October 1927),112. The home for neglected children was led by Mrs. Middelberg and was not connected to the Pentecostal movement.

51. Bernard, an English businessman, had lost his first wife in 1912. *Confidence* 5/2 (February 1912),43. On 20 June 1914 he married Marie Blekkink, sister of Mrs. Polman, who had been raised in the Dutch Indies. *Spade Regen* 15/3 (June 1922),46.

52. "Java," *Spade Regen* 17/8 (November 1924),125-26.

The founding of "De Pinkstergemeente in Nederlandsch-Indië" in Bandung, domicile of Thiessen, suggests dissatisfaction with Thiessen's "De Pinksterbeweging." In 1921 the "Bethel Temple" church at Seattle, Washington, founded by W.H. Offiler, had sent two Pentecostal missionaries to the Dutch Indies. C. Groesbeek and D. van Klaveren were from Dutch descent and started to work on Bali. They had little success until they moved to Java in 1922 or 1923. According to several publications they were the first Pentecostal missionaries to the Dutch Indies. This present survey however establishes that J. Thiessen arrived on Java in 1921. This means that Thiessen introduced Pentecostalism on Java before Van Klaveren and Groesbeek. At first they all worked together. One year after Thiessen had founded "De Pinksterbeweging," Groesbeek, Van Klaveren, Bernard, F.G. van Gessel and others founded "De Pinkstergemeente in Nederlandsch-Indië," which was incorporated in June 1924. Today the church is known as "Geredja Pentekosta di Indonesia."

The paper *Pinksterbode* was edited by Mrs. Bernard-Blekkink. In January 1925 it was continued by F. van Abcoude under the name *Pinksterkracht*. At the end of 1927 *Pinksterkracht* was edited by Miss M.A. Alt and renamed into *Gouden Schoven* in 1929. In July 1934 *Gouden Schoven* ceased to be the organ of "De Pinkstergemeente in Nederlandsch-Indië." Subsequently it became the organ of "De Pinksterzending" founded by M.A. Alt in 1935.

H. Thiessen, Interview, 8 June 1981; Idem, *Het gouden jubileum van de Pinkster-Beweging*; M.A. Alt, "Wat doet de pinkstergemeente voor haar Officieel orgaan *Gouden Schoven?*" *Gouden Schoven* 10/5 (1 March 1934),20-21; Idem, "Kennisgeving," *Gouden Schoven* 10/14 (15 July 1934),14; C. van der Laan and P.N. van der Laan, *Pinksteren in beweging* (Kampen: J.H. Kok, 1982), pp. 47-51; H.D.J. Boissevain, *De zending in oost en west*, vol. 2 (Hoenderloo: Zendingsstudie-Raad, 1945), p. 252; A.H. Mandey, "50 Years of Indonesia," *World Pentecost* no. 1 (1973),26-27; Karl Roebling, *Pentecostals Around the World* (Hicksville, NY: Exposition Press, 1978), p. 65.

53. *Spade Regen* 17/12 (March 1925),192; 18/8 (November 1925),127-28. Mina Hanssen later married F.A. Abell and cooperated with M.A. Alt. During 1936 and 1937 the couple twice visited Holland. Mina Abell-Hansen died in 1939. *Kracht van Omhoog* 2/11 (May 1939),4.

54. M.A. Alt, *Herinneringen uit mijn leven* (Velp: Pinksterzending, 1971), p. 44.

55. Ibid., pp. 60-64; M.A. Alt, "Van het oogstveld: Gambang Waloh," *Pinksterkracht* 3/2 (February 1927),15-16; Idem, 3/8 (August 1927),15-16. *Spade Regen* 20/2 (May 1927),30-31; 20/4 (July 1927),63-64.

In her autobiography M.A. Alt chose to omit the influence of Thiessen as well as of Gnirrep and Bernard. Thiessen's important role is however obvious from letters printed in *Spade Regen*. In a letter to Polman (dated 1 November 1922) Thiessen referred to Miss Alt as a tired slave of legalistic Sabbatarianism, who had been set free by the Pentecostal Spirit proclaimed to her by Thiessen and Gnirrep. *Spade Regen* 15/10 (January 1923),159-60; cf. 15/9 (December 1922), 144.

56. The "Pinksterzending" was a secession from "De Pinkstergemeente in Nederlandsch-Indië," like the latter was probably a secession from Thiessen's "De Pinksterbeweging."

57. After World War II the *Glorieklokken* songbook became most popular in the Pentecostal assemblies in the Netherlands and is still in use today.

58. Donald Gee, *Wind and Flame*, p. 90.

59. *Spade Regen* no. 6 (January-February 1909),24; no. 8 (April 1909),4; no. 30 (June-July 1912),4; no. 37 (July 1914),4; 10/1 (April 1917),4.

60. The 9 missing issues of *Spade Regen* are: of vol. 12 the nos. 11 and 12 (January and February 1920); of vol. 14 the nos. 1, 2, 3, 5, 6, 8, and 11 (April, May, June, August, September, November 1921, and January 1922).

61. *Confidence* 8/12 (December 1915),235; *Spade Regen* no. 39 (January 1916),4.

62. *Spade Regen* no. 6 (January-February 1909),4; 20/1 (April 1927),12.

63. T.B. Barratt, *De waarheid inzake de Pinksteropwekking* (Amsterdam: G.R. Polman, 1917), p. 16.

64. First published as a separate pamphlet and subsequently included in T.B. Barratt, *In the Days of the Latter Rain* (London: Simpkin, Marshall, Hamilton, Kent & Co., 1909).

65. Barratt, *De waarheid*, p. 8. Not included in the rev. ed. of *In the Days of the Latter Rain*, published by Elim Publishing House in 1928.

66. J. Paul's brochure was reviewed by Joh. de Heer in *Zoeklicht* 2 (1920-1921),394, who called the explanation of Daniel 2 and 7 deviating.

67. One other title only known through a book review in *Zoeklicht* 2 (1920-21),394, is *Een Goddelijke waarschuwing aan Predikanten, Bestuur en Gemeenteleden* (A Divine warning to Ministers, Council and Church members) written by a certain B. and available through B. Kedde, Davostraat 24 at Deventer. Perhaps it was a translation of T.B. Barratt's *A Friendly Talk with Ministers and Christian Workers* issued by Boddy in 1909, although according to the review the content was much sharper than Barratt's friendly talk. It is described as a penitential sermon. All those not converted, born again and filled with the Spirit must resign. All who receive a salary are outside the will of God! The apparent publisher B. Kedde became a co-worker of Polman during 1921.

68. *Spade Regen* 19/6 (September 1926),96.

69. A. Zijp to M.A. Alt, 3 August 1961. This and other interesting

correspondence and publications from Zijp was found with his daughter Mrs. J.M. Burgers-Zijp in Amsterdam.

70. A. Zijp, *Moeten of mogen wij onze kindertjes laten doopen?*, Bezwaarschrift ingezonden aan de Generale Synode der Gereformeerde Kerken, met het antwoord der Synode (Amsterdam: by author, 1926).

71. *Spade Regen* 12/1 (April 1919),16.

72. *Spade Regen* no. 20 (December 1910),4.

73. *Spade Regen* 10/5 (August 1917),184, reported that in a few days 3,000 issues of *Klanken des Vredes* were sold in Enschede. In many places it was distributed from house to house.

74. *Spade Regen* 10/11 (February 1918),76. Founded by C. Ingwersen C.Mzn., editor of *De Amsterdammer*.

75. *Spade Regen* 13/5 (August 1920),76. In 1922 a similar tracts union was founded by the Pentecostals at Haarlem with 19 members. *Spade Regen* 15/2 (May 1922),32.

76. *Spade Regen* 19/2 (May 1926),29.

77. *Spade Regen* 15/1 (April 1922),15.

78. "Vereeniging 't Anker," *Spade Regen* 17/1 (April 1924),15-16; 17/12 (March 1925),192; 19/5 (August 1926),80; 21/6 (September 1928),96. *Klanken des Vredes* regularly published their newsletter as of 9/11 (April 1924). Cf. *Zoeklicht* (1921-1922),245.

79. *Spade Regen* 14/10 (January 1922),166-67.

80. The award is kept with the children of Polman. No reference to the Austrian award was ever found in any of the publications or correspondence from Polman. Investigation with the Austrian embassy confirmed that the Red Cross award *Patriae A.C. Humanitatie* was presented to Mrs. Polman by the embassy in 1924: "Ehrenzeichen II Klasse mit Kriegsdekoration, Kinderaktion des Protestantischen Komites." The award dated from the time of the monarchy. Cf. Vaclav Mericka, *Orden und Ehrenzeichen der Österreichisch-Ungarischen Monarchie* (Wien/München, 1974), pp. 252-55.

81. *Spade Regen* 15/9 (December 1922),143-44, reported from a letter J. Thiessen received from J.E. Varonaeff, which told of a famine in Bulgaria. Polman opened an account for food relief. *Spade Regen* 15/11 (February 1923),175, reported that boxes with clothing had been brought to the poor in Germany and 500,000 German marks had been paid into the general poor fund of the German Pentecostal movement. *Spade Regen* 21/3 (June 1928),46, quoted from a letter of Mrs. Manuloff asking for help for homeless Pentecostal believers in Bulgaria.

82. *Spade Regen* 22/2 (May 1929),31-32.

83. *Spade Regen* 15/10 (January 1923),153.

84. *Spade Regen* 18/10 (January 1926), 157, reported that more than 100 factory girls attended the evening, of whom 12 since came to the young people's Bible classes.

85. *Spade Regen* 17/11 (March 1925),172.

86. *Spade Regen* 20/3 (June 1927),46. In *Pfingstgrüsse* 17/8 (August 1925),

128, the home "Lydia" was advertised as a Christian hotel for DM 6.00 per day.

87. *Spade Regen* 14/7 (October 1921),120; 14/9 (December 1921),150-51; Lydia de Jong-Polman, Interview, Boskoop, 29 December 1983.

88. Robert Mapes Anderson, *Vision of the Disinherited* (New York/ Oxford: Oxford University Press, 1979), pp. 199-201.

9 INSTITUTIONALIZATION AND DECLINE

From a Movement Towards a Church

A number of the first Pentecostal leaders in Europe were ministers of existing denominations. Initially they tried to spread the Pentecostal experience in their own church. Only when such failed, they, often under compulsion, severed their church connection. Boddy, never hindered by the Church of England, remained Anglican, but in the end was disappointed in his hopes.[1] When Polman entered the Pentecostal movement he was not tied to any denomination. He had been in the Netherlands Reformed Church, the Salvation Army, and had just loosened his relation with the Christian Catholic Apostolic Church in Zion.

For Polman the outpouring of the Holy Spirit with the speaking of tongues was the sign that Jesus would soon return. It was the latter rain that would precede the final great harvest (James 5:7-8). Therefore he called his paper *Spade Regen* (Latter Rain). As time was short Polman did not seek to establish a new church, but rather to revive the existing churches by the power of the Holy Spirit. He found it "glorious to see that children of God from different denominations or associations and of the Salvation Army gather together to pray for the baptism of the Holy Spirit."[2] In March 1909 Polman recorded, "Amongst those who have received the Pentecostal blessing or are seeking it, we know Reformed, Gereformeerd, Lutheran, Baptists, Evangelicals, Salvationists and others."[3] To Gunning (Netherlands Reformed minister) Polman wrote in 1910:

> We have not adopted a name and do not make members, everyone is free to go where they belong. . . . We do not have offices of apostles or prophets, but we do have the gift of

202

prophecy in our midst, speaking in unknown languages and interpretation, as well as revelation.[4]

Loyal to his vision of an interdenominational revival Polman put all the emphasis on the baptism with the Holy Spirit and was initially, at least in his publications, silent about water baptism, as this would imply a direct confrontation with the existing churches. This accounts for the remarkable absence of a baptistery in the Immanuel Hall when it was built in 1912. Nevertheless there was a strong opposition against the Pentecostals among orthodox and Evangelical circles, much inspired by the "Berlin Declaration" of 1909. Polman did not write against his opponents, but did express his sorrow that fellow brothers and sisters judged the movement without investigating themselves.[5]

During 1916 and 1917 Wumkes' publication *De Pinkster-beweging voornamelijk in Nederland* brought the Pentecostals a lot of publicity. Polman extended his contacts with clergy from different churches, but in the end did not achieve what he aimed for. In general the churches rejected the Pente-costals as a sect. In the face of blunt disapproval Polman gradually shifted his position. In November 1917, after ten years in the Pentecostal movement, Mrs. Polman uttered her disappointment in other Christians and ministers:

> One has tried to stigmatize us as devil's children, as necro-mancers, fanatics, spiritists, immorals, seducers, lunatics, neurotics, gluttons, wine boozers, swindlers, loveless, yet, shall I repeat the several epithets with which one has labeled us, who believe in the Pentecostal miracle and long for it?[6]

In the same year (1917) *Spade Regen* recorded the first references to the celebrating of the Lord's Supper and to baptismal services in a hired swimming pool.[7] Gradually the water baptism would gain more importance simultaneously with a growing emphasis on organization.

Concerning the organization Wumkes had stated that every Pentecostal circle was independent and self-governing. He also noted the great need for experienced leaders. Discipline (in the case of public sin) was carried out by the believers among themselves.[8] The members were united by spiritual unity, mutual trust and agreement in the main thoughts.[9] Wumkes concluded:

> What course the Pentecostal movement will take and which influence she will have upon the Christian churches cannot be said beforehand. For that the event is too young. But that it has to come to an organization in order to reach something positive and lasting, is certain. The leaders shrank from it out of fear, that the human element would then dominate too much. For them the Holy Spirit is the great organizer. The spiritual life must spontaneously create its own forms. Only then is there power, truth and freedom. Their wavering to appoint elders and deacons flows forth from the same fear. They say: the office must not be searched, but the Holy Spirit has to move and to equip the personalities sanctified for this purpose (1 Cor. 12:28). All system in organization means death. They never go further than the need itself points out.[10]

In a personal conversation Wumkes once questioned Polman's reluctance to appoint offices.[11] Wumkes might have been right when he in his memoirs judged that Polman wanted to maintain his official lead at the time. However, unknown to Wumkes, Polman did eventually install offices in his assembly at Amsterdam.

In November 1920 *Spade Regen* suddenly refers to a "council of brothers" at Amsterdam, consisting of 20 males "of whom most have been with us from the beginning and have been with us in all storms and difficulties and in whom God has done a great work."[12] The "council of brothers" met once a month to discuss the affairs of the assembly. Polman found it a "privilege for a pastor, who has such a circle of loyal brothers around him."[13] At Haarlem a similar, but smaller, council was formed. It was hoped that in all Pentecostal circles in the country "councils of brothers" would emerge and would be united to one council. In the memory of eyewitnesses these "brothers" functioned as elders. They had separate seats on one side of the platform.[14] The same issue of *Spade Regen* (November 1920) informed about the formation of the Dutch Pentecostal Missionary Society.

During the International Conference in January 1921

Polman was impressed by the Swedish leaders, who much stressed the necessity to get organized into independent local assemblies. Lewi Pethrus' evaluation of the movement was translated in *Spade Regen*:

> We have noticed how important it is, that souls that are baptized with the Spirit are brought into freedom. In the countries where this has happened the revival continued, but this has not been the case, where one worked in opposite direction. Our English friends shared with us, that one can hardly speak of a revival in England. The most prominent preachers of the Pentecostal movement remained in their respective churches. One has sacrificed freedom to forbearance and the revival has slowly come to an end.[15]

The Swedish concern for independent Pentecostal assemblies and a similar development in Germany influenced Polman to proceed in this way. During this period the Germans decided to concentrate more on building up local assemblies and to have regional conferences instead of one large annual conference at Mülheim, while Voget and Paul were acknowledged as national leaders.[16] About 1924 the messages in *Spade Regen* adopted a different tone. Gone was the heavy emphasis on death to self. A number of articles dealt with church structure and offices, but at the same time the unity among God's children was stressed.

During 1924 Polman made two journeys to England, where he witnessed how the British Assemblies of God was established on basis of a "Statement of Fundamental Truths."[17] It is not without pain when Polman finally introduced church membership in April 1925. The same month, with Easter, the first baptismal service was held in Immanuel in the newly built-in baptistery. Polman admitted he had not expected the Lord to tarry this long when he started his *Spade Regen* publications.[18] Rethinking the course of history he wrote:

> In the beginning it seemed to us, and we had hoped, that the fruit of this revival had spread itself in the different existing denominations and we, who externally stood outside, had been allowed to be a blessing for the different denominations. We

often expressed, as we had wished, that our small hall at the Nieuwe Prinsengracht would always be large enough, to thus further the unity among the different denominations, and to lose ourselves as the Pentecostal movement into the larger body of Christianity. That we also in this way were allowed to see the fulfillment of Joel's prophecy. His Spirit upon all flesh, upon all children of God, no matter from which name.[19]

Being frustrated in his vision of an interdenominational revival, Polman complied with requests from members of the Amsterdam assembly and from other assemblies in the country, to provide for more organization: "God wants to have assemblies, who love the full truth, who unite, not to separate themselves from others, but to advance the Kingdom of God."[20] In the background there was the conflict with the emerging "Gemeente des Heeren." The membership cards would also solve the problem of intruders coming to the meetings "who pretend to belong to us, while in fact they do not."[21] The application for membership contained an interesting statement of faith, which will be further discussed in the following chapter. Members were supposed to believe in the baptism with the Holy Spirit, but the experience itself was no prerequisite.[22] Neither was water baptism a condition for membership. According to some eyewitnesses the membership card included a statement regarding the paying of tithes, which was one reason why a number of the regular visitors refused to apply for membership.[23] Polman wrote that the majority became official members, but the others were not excluded. The sacraments (water baptism and the Lord's Supper) remained open to anyone who loved the Lord.[24]

In this time Percy Corry, from England, and Bernard Kedde were prominent co-workers of Polman.[25] Percy N. Corry had already visited Amsterdam during the opening of the training school in October 1912, just before he went to India as a missionary.[26] With Christmas 1923 Corry was in Amsterdam again and stayed until Easter 1924. He took charge over the meetings when the Polmans were away and introduced midday prayer sessions.[27]

As of Christmas 1925 Corry once more stayed a prolonged period in Amsterdam, probably until August 1926. It was a time of great revival. From January to August 1926 not less than 152 believers were baptized in water, "most of them new converts," while more than 200 were baptized with the Holy Spirit.[28] Children under 9 years old were speaking and singing in tongues. "Whole households came into the blessing. Demons were cast out and many were healed."[29] Out of the new converts an evangelistic band of seventy was formed, who went out two by two. In this atmosphere of revival, which seemed to vindicate the earlier move towards institutionalization, the official installation of elders in July 1926 was only a small pace further.

During the preceding months the issue of church government had received much attention, also by means of articles in *Spade Regen*: "Where the Holy Spirit is acknowledged in the assembly as Lord, there an organized assembly is shaped by the Spirit and by biblical names."[30] The "council of brothers" was now regarded a temporary solution, that would have to be replaced by elders. In a mutual meeting with 120 members present, twelve of the "eldest brothers" (probably a reference to the council of brothers) were presented, from whom the members had to elect seven elders. The seven elected aged between 48 and 72 years, with one exception of 35. They were manual workers and one shop owner.[31] On Monday, 5 July 1926, in a following mutual meeting with the members, the seven elders were ordained in an unusual manner. Those at the rear laid their hands on the row in front of them and so onwards to the front, where Polman, Corry, and Kedde laid hands on the seven. This way every member had part in the ordination.[32] A remarkable vision of a straight hand that drew a crooked line was seen. The straight hand was interpreted as the Spirit of God and the crooked line as the assembly. The Spirit identified with the assembly and used it in spite of its imperfectness.[33] The elders had regular meetings with Polman and their names and addresses were twice printed in *Spade Regen* in case someone wanted to call an elder to pray for healing (James 5:14).[34]

More articles on church structure appeared in *Spade Regen*, many by Donald Gee translated from *Redemption Tidings*. The word organization was usually avoided and preference was given to the word organism: "Organization is not a nice word; one feels that it speaks of something spirit-killing. . . .

The assembly of Christ is therefore an organism."[35] In one article Gee criticized the teaching of some early Pentecostal leaders to receive the baptism with storing the Holy Spirit and to remain in your church. Gee compared this with storing new wine in old wineskins, with the result that both were lost. He felt that every revival sooner or later is forced to form new wineskins, that is, new denominations.[36] Of course Gee was right at the time, but he spoke after the event. The ideal of reviving the churches had already proven unattainable. In March 1930 Polman had not quite lost his original vision, when he wrote:

> We belong to all, we are no sect and avoid every sectarian spirit. We want to be a blessing to all and do not try to become big ourselves, but to help the whole. May the Pentecostal spirit be poured out in every church, no matter under which name, that is our prayer.[37]

Yet, the Pentecostal movement had become a Pentecostal church, which was not what Polman had in mind when he started.

In between his many journeys, abroad and at home, and besides his responsibility as pastor of the Amsterdam assembly, Polman managed to find some time for his hobbies. In his house he raised pedigree chickens and occasionally took part in contests. He liked to make photos and films of his children and developed them himself. Every year the whole family went to the farm of his brother Derk in Westenholte. Polman remained good friends with his brother and was ever pleased to help him with the harvest. At home, in Immanuel, there were always house-mates and guests staying. All meals were taken together. Breakfast started at eight o'clock. Standing behind the chairs a chorus was sung, after which Polman prayed for the meal. After breakfast there was a prayer meeting for the family, house-mates, and guests. The house-mates fulfilled domestic duties, secretarial work, and looked after the children. Polman did a lot of home visitation and could get on well with most people, no matter the background.[38]

Resignation and Death of Gerrit R. Polman

The year 1926 had brought further structure in the Pentecostal assembly by the ordination of elders, but had also been a year of revival. Many converts were added to the assembly. The sermons in *Spade Regen* carried a more optimistic view of life in victory, much different from a few years before. It might not be accidental that this development runs parallel with the economical growth in Dutch social life. The spiritual fight, which always is an important theme in Pentecostal sermons, became more a battle with victory against evil spirits than a call of death to self. The influence from Germany was very limited in this period. After 1926 the revival quenched and a more regular church life commenced. Important events were the sudden evacuation of the missionaries from China in 1927 and the silver wedding anniversary of the Polmans on 2 July 1928. A large feast was prepared by the assembly with guests from all over the country and Humburg coming from Germany.[39] Naomi, the eldest daughter of Polman, had meanwhile been baptized in water and to some extent she cooperated in the work.

During 1928 the tie with the German Pentecostals was strengthened again by the visit of Paul, Voget, Humburg, and Schober in December. Polman expressed his gratitude that the unity with the German brethren was restored.[40] Shortly thereafter the Pentecostal assembly at Amsterdam started to decline, which led Albert Zijp to write his open letter to G.R. Polman entitled *De dwaling der Pinkstergemeente te Amsterdam* (The error of the Pentecostal assembly at Amsterdam). When the letter was published (June 1929) the assembly had just had a short uprising due to the visit of William E. Booth-Clibborn at Easter and Whitsuntide, which may account for the little attention the letter seems to have gotten among the members of the assembly.[41] Zijp had attended the Pentecostal meetings for about ten years. The letter contained a strong condemnation of the teaching that the speaking in tongues was the evidence of the baptism with the Holy Spirit. Zijp saw this error as the basic cause for the decline. In private conversations Polman agreed with Zijp, but once on the platform Polman continued to preach his "error." In his description of the deplorable situation Zijp stated that literally everything went wrong:

1. The evangelization stood still for nearly two years.
2. More and more empty chairs were in the meetings.
3. Sister assemblies in other places separated themselves.
4. Ties with foreign countries had suffered much.
5. Young converts in heathen countries were left behind.
6. Hundreds were scattered everywhere and never visited.
7. Many of the so-called baptized ones were never seen again.
8. The "Gospel and Charity Boat" had to be disposed of.
9. Visiting the sick was done irregularly.
10. The seventy no longer went out.
11. There was no caring for the poor.
12. Finances were not sufficient.[42]

Allegations that Polman had enriched himself with church money were investigated by Zijp, but were proven false. Zijp was convinced that Polman acted in good faith, but seriously erred. The members were taught to look for external signs. This had made them proud and loveless with the aforesaid results.[43]

Zijp's remarkable publication was not a hostile condemnation of the movement, but revealed the attitude of a concerned friend. Was Polman, equipped with the gift of discernment, able to discern the voice of the Spirit in this admonitory letter? Zijp was right that something serious was wrong in the assembly, but was mistaken by attributing this solely to erroneous teaching concerning glossolalia. By doing so he provided opportunity for Polman to simply dismiss the letter on the basis of deviating teaching, which is what likely happened.

Another way by which the assembly was warned were prophetic utterances during the meetings speaking of a "curse in the army" (referring to a grave sin in the assembly). Instead of finding and abolishing the curse, the prophets were silenced. Finally in the autumn of 1930 it was revealed that Polman himself was guilty of adultery. During an emotional meeting in October 1930 Polman was removed from office by the members.[44] The dramatic outcome nearly ended the movement. A great number including most of the elders left the movement altogether. Others joined the "Gemeente des Heeren," the radical wing of Pentecostalism. One group started meetings in a hall in the Wijde Steeg as of January 1931, while a very small band continued meeting in Immanuel. Polman was no longer allowed to take part in any of these meetings, although he confessed and repented of his sins. The low number of Pentecostals recorded at the national census of 31 December 1930 of only 508 is indicative of the collapse that had taken place.[45]

At the end of 1930 Polman became sick and moved to Zandvoort where he lived with his family in their home "Lydia." His illness started with an inflammation of the bladder, but ended up with nephritis. He was treated in a Roman Catholic hospital at Haarlem, but without success and suffering much pain. His witness was such that nurses and fellow patients called him an angel.[46] To his friend Humburg, Polman's last words were:

> Only love has full value and I regret that only now I understand that only the power of God's love brings our spirit to a complete rest. How different it could all have been! Now, while everything has become new in me, I should actually commence to witness, but I completely rest in God and in His doing.[47]

A letter of a friend who visited Polman the day before his death reads: "This short visit remains unforgettable and has strengthened me beyond measure. What a wonderful power is flowing from brother Polman, also in this dying. A hero of God who lays down his life and brings it at the feet of Jesus."[48] That afternoon Polman at parting said to his children, "I feel so happy."[49] At seven-thirty in the morning of 1 March 1932 he passed away.[50] The next day Mrs. Polman wrote to friends:

> My dear husband has gone to Jesus yesterday. Softly and lovely he slept and awoke with Him, who soon will bring him

along with Himself. I can not make myself believe that he is gone from us. We still needed him so much. But God knows what is better for him.[51]

The funeral on 5 March in Haarlem was attended by a few hundred people and was led by William Bernard and Emil Humburg. Speaker on behalf of the family was the brother-in-law P.A.W. Elbers, while G. Boerma, the only elder who had remained loyal to Polman, acted on behalf of the Dutch Pentecostals. At the grave Humburg read, "So faith, hope, love abide, these three; but the greatest of these is love" (1 Cor. 13:13).[52]

Although Polman had asked forgiveness of individual members of the Amsterdam Pentecostal assembly who came to him at his sickbed, the relation with the assembly was never restored. Even after his death the assembly remained estranged from Mrs. Polman. The fact that the Immanuel building officially belonged to Polman and not to the assembly certainly was a stumbling block. When in 1933 Piet Klaver was asked to return from the Dutch Indies in order to pastor over the remaining flock, the small band in Immanuel eventually united with the larger group that met in the Wijde Steeg. The year before (1932) Pieter van der Woude (1895-1978) had come back from England and had started Pentecostal meetings in Rotterdam. In 1935 Nico Vetter resigned from the mission field in Venezuela and became pastor of the Pentecostal assembly in Haarlem. Klaver, Van der Woude, and Vetter would become the prime leaders of the Dutch Pentecostal movement during the following period of gradual recovery. The era under Polman had come to a sad end, but the way the movement continued basically followed the pattern set out by Polman. On a modest scale Mrs. Polman did proceed in the ministry by helping in Pentecostal assemblies in Rotterdam and The Hague. Her last years were spent in Baarn where she died on 17 April 1961.[53]

Some Observations

The resignation of Polman is of course a painful page in the history of the Dutch Pentecostal movement. The subject is usually avoided in publications by Pentecostals. This is understandable, but prevents a constructive handling of the affair. In their untiring zeal to realize their call the Polman couple neglected the value of a balanced family life. There were always guests in the house and at the table. Ever ready to support the needy ones, both spiritually and materially, they forgot to sufficiently support each other. The marital relationship and the relationship with the children, who hardly saw their parents in private, must have suffered.

Another area to consider is how to handle criticism? If Polman had given heed to the several warnings the events could have been turned. These warnings were never mentioned in *Spade Regen*. As is common among religious leaders in similar situations, Polman preached against "a spirit of criticism." His message was even confirmed by prophecies and visions from docile members. One such vision with interpretation, published in *Spade Regen*, instructed the believers to quit judging each other and stop looking at the imperfectness and sin of God's people.[54] In September 1930, at the height of the crisis, Polman employed an article from *Redemption Tidings* entitled "The use and misuse of the tongue," to get the message across: "Touch not my anointed ones, and do my prophets no harm" (1 Chr. 16:22). The members were summoned to obey the pastor, not for the sake of himself, but for the sake of the office he held as representative of God on earth.[55] Two months later another article, again translated from the English, called "Some things, that a pastor cannot do," stated that the pastor was often the subject of unjustified criticism as soon as things were not as they should have been. The time spent to criticize the pastor was to be used to pray for him.[56] Polman was not the first, nor the last, to respond in this manner to critique. Citing "Touch not my anointed ones" is still popular among Pentecostal and other religious leaders, when their authority is threatened. But authority that is based on misusing scripture and does not allow for critique is bound to fall. Pentecostals, like so many people, have generally great difficulty in dealing with critique. Instead of appreciating critique as a gift of healing to the body, it is either ignored or eliminated by counterstatements. The manifestation of conflicting prophecies and visions is a special Pentecostal problem and leads to the following question: How does the Spirit of God relate to the human being?

The failure of Polman is indicative of a basic problem in Pentecostalism, namely the struggle between the divine and the human element, that is, the Spirit and the flesh. The baptism with the Holy Spirit is esteemed so high that having received the experience one is no longer led by the flesh, but by the Spirit. Speaking in tongues, prophecies, and visions is clothed with divine authority: "Thus speaketh the Lord." The presence and approval of God is further demonstrated by healings, exorcisms, and (during the first period) by physical manifestations like shaking and trembling. Whenever a "thus speaketh the Lord" has proven false, or a spiritual leader fails in his conduct, the Pentecostal understanding of the Spirit runs aground. On the night he was removed from office, Polman was asked to explain how he could have continued to speak in tongues, while living in sin. His answer, "Out of habit," was shocking to his audience, but calls for a revision of the Pentecostal pneumatology and practice. Such a revision cannot be elaborated within the scope of this research, but to some extent the issue will return in the following chapter.

NOTES

1. Cf. Martin Robinson, "The Charismatic Anglican-Historical and Contemporary: A comparison of the life and work of Alexander Boddy (1854-1930) and Michael Harper" (M.Lit. thesis, University of Birmingham, 1976), p. 122.
2. *Spade Regen* no. 1 (April 1908),4.
3. *Spade Regen* no. 7 (March 1909),4.
4. G.R. Polman to J.H. Gunning J.Hz., Amsterdam, 12 March 1910.
5. *Spade Regen* no. 29 (March-May 1912),2.
6. W. Polman, "Een Tienjarige ervaring in de Pinksterbeweging," *Spade Regen* 10/8 (November 1917),31.
7. *Spade Regen* 10/6 (September 1917),24, contains the first reference to water baptism; and 10/3 (June 1917),12, the first reference to the Lord's Supper. The Lord's Supper had long been celebrated every first Sunday of the month at the close of the evening service, but was never before reported in *Spade Regen*.
8. G.A. Wumkes, *De Pinksterbeweging voornamelijk in Nederland* (Utrecht: G.J.A. Ruys, 1916), p. 19.
9. Ibid.

10. Ibid., p. 22.

11. G.A. Wumkes, *Nei Sawntich Jier* (Bolsaert: A.J. Osinga, 1947),p. 437.

12. *Spade Regen* 13/8 (November 1920),122.

13. Ibid.

14. Among others: Martha Marijs-Visser, Interview, The Hague, 17 August 1984. Martha Visser's testimony is important because she had left the Pentecostal movement before the official elders were appointed in 1926 and therefore can not have mixed the council of brothers with the later elders. Nevertheless in her memory the council of brothers functioned as elders. She also recalled that the council made a strong impression upon her at the time and commanded her respect.

15. L. Pethrus, "De Internationale Pinksterconferentie te Amsterdam," *Spade Regen* 13/12 (March 1921),180.

16. *Spade Regen* 15/5 (August 1922),80; 15/8 (November 1922),123-24; Paul Fleisch, *Die Pfingstbewegung in Deutschland* (Hannover: Heino. Feesche Verlag, 1957),pp. 277-78; Ernst Giese, *Jonathan Paul* (Altdorf: Missionsbuchhandlung und Verlag, 1965), p. 236.

    Polman remarked that the majority of the Pentecostal circles in Germany first had belonged to the "Gemeinschaftsbewegung" and had basically remained the same in organization. But that in the Netherlands the Pentecostal circles were not formed from existing missions, but from believers belonging to several churches and circles. *Spade Regen* 15/8 (November 1922),123.

17. Around February 1924 Polman spoke at meetings with Mogridge in Lytham, with Myerscough in Preston, and next in London and in Dover. *Spade Regen* 16/12 (March 1924),190-91. During the first part of August 1924 Polman attended conventions in Hull and London. The convention in London was held by the Assemblies of God and chaired by Myerscough. *Spade Regen* 17/6 (September 1924),95-96.

18. *Spade Regen* 18/1 (April 1925),16.

19. Ibid., p. 14.

20. Ibid.

21. Ibid.

22. Hendrik Jacobus van den Berg (born 1899) is one such example. He became a member in 1925 without having the experience of the baptism with the Holy Spirit. One year later he was baptized in water. H.J. van den Berg, Interview, Zandvoort, 12 July 1984.

23. Unfortunately no membership cards have been found. Simon Schaap (born 1900), whose father was the treasurer of the assembly, refused membership because of the tithes. S. Schaap, Interview, Amsterdam, 5 March 1985; H.J. van den Berg, Interview; C.L.M. Neuemeier, Interview, Rotterdam, 27 February 1986. Some other eyewitnesses, however, did not recall that tithes were ever mentioned.

24. *Spade Regen* 18/1 (April 1925),14.

25. Bernard Kedde (born 1898) moved from Deventer to Amsterdam in May 1922. He stayed in Immanuel and worked throughout the country, leading meetings in Heerlen, Rotterdam, The Hague, and

Sneek. From January 1923 until April 1927 *Spade Regen* published 25 articles from his hand. After April 1927 he suddenly withdrew from the ministry.

26. *Confidence* 5/11 (November 1912),265; 5/12 (December 1912),285; 7/6 (June 1914),117; Guestbook "Aandenken aan de Pelgrims."

27. *Spade Regen* 16/10 (January 1924),159; 16/11 (February 1924),176; 16/12 (March 1924),192; 18/10 (January 1926),157-58.

28. G.R. Polman, "Mighty Movings in Holland," *The Pentecostal Evangel* (4 December 1926). Numbers correspond with the figures mentioned in *Spade Regen* over this period. Cf. P.N. Corry in *Redemption Tidings* 2/1 (January 1926),11; 2/2 (February 1926),9; 2/5 (May 1926),9; 2/6 (June 1926),11.

29. Polman, "Mighty Movings."

30. B. Kedde, *Spade Regen* 19/4 (July 1926),60.

31. Names were printed in *Spade Regen*. Ages and professions were collected from the Registration Service Registers present in the Amsterdam City Archives and from interviewing children of the elders. They all remained elders as long as Polman was in office. The complete list of elders:

> Geert Boerma (1890-1974), cooper.
> Laurens Schaap (born 1878), shop-owner, church treasurer.
> Josephus Franciscus Wilhelm Helgering (born 1878), coal transport worker.
> Gerardus Hermanus van der Veen (born 1876), diamond cutter?, church organist.
> Martinus Johannes van Gennep (born 1874), dockyard worker.
> Jan Bakkenist (born 1854).
> Klaas Verwaal (1862-1941).

It seems certain that they all first belonged to the "council of brothers." The elders took places on the platform, except for Van der Veen, who played the organ. Some time before the elders were chosen, part of the "council of brothers" were already seated on the platform, namely Schaap, Helgering, Bakkenist, and a certain Ludwig Oltmann (1864-1926). Oltmann, a plasterer, died in March 1926, just before the election of elders. Of these men at least Van der Veen, Schaap, Van Gennep, and Oltmann had been with Polman from the beginning in the hall on the Nieuwe Prinsengracht. Oltmann, born in Germany, knew Polman from the time they both were in the Salvation Army. Oltmann had also joined the Dowie movement and had lost all his savings by investing in Zion. Van der Veen (often called Veen) had been with Polman from the very start. Schaap had no previous church connection when he was converted and radically delivered from alcohol in the Pentecostal assembly. His wife was a believer, but never joined the Pentecostal assembly.

> "In memoriam Br. Verwaal," *Kracht van Omhoog* 4/10 (April 1941); "Ontbonden en met Christus," *Spade Regen* 18/12 (March 1926),189; *Spade Regen* 21/4 (July 1928),62.

32. *Spade Regen* 19/4 (July 1926),61.

33. Ibid., p. 31.

34. *Spade Regen* 19/6 (September 1926),96; 19/12 (March 1927),189.

35. G.R. Polman, "De ideale gemeente," *Spade Regen* 21/8 (November 1928),115.

36. Donald Gee, "Over herders en schaapskooien," *Spade Regen* 22/1 (April 1929),5-9.

37. *Spade Regen* 22/12 (March 1930),190-91.

381. Most details about the family life were taken from an interview with Lydia de Jong-Polman, Boskoop, 29 December 1983.

39. *Spade Regen* 21/4 (July 1928),60-62.

40. *Spade Regen* 21/10 (January 1929),153.

41. Nearly all interviewed eyewitnesses had never heard of the open letter by Zijp. One exception was Simon Schaap, whose father was an elder.

42. A. Zijp, *De dwaling der Pinkstergemeente te Amsterdam* (Amsterdam: by author, 1929), pp. 16-17.

43. Ibid., pp. 17-18. Albert Zijp (1890-1977) saw his membership with the Gereformeerde Kerk cancelled in 1926, because of his repudiation of infant baptism. Upon the advice of Polman he did not become a member of the Pentecostal assembly (p. 7). In August 1928 he was healed in a Sunday meeting after the laying on of hands by Polman and the elders. In 1929 he left the Pentecostal assembly and started independent evangelistic activities. In 1945 he founded the "Stichting der Internationale Gemeenschap van Christusbelijders," later renamed "Internationale Gemeenschap van Christenen" (International Communion of Christians). As such he issued the paper *Oorspronkelijk Christendom* (Original Christianity) since April 1949 and besides wrote a number of brochures. The work was extended with an American division (1958) and a mission post in Austria (Mission Home "Rehoboth" near Villach). In 1946 Zijp was involved in introducing "Youth for Christ" in the Netherlands.

44. Information on this delicate matter was derived from eye witnesses and from letters of this period. Upon request of the informants, further details of the sources are omitted.

Donald Gee's discussion of the International Pentecostal Conference at Amsterdam, January 1921, in *Wind and Flame* (1967, p. 122), contains a remarkable prophecy that was uttered on the closing Sunday. According to J.E. van den Brink, a present Dutch Pentecostal leader, the prophecy referred to Polman. Van den Brink has his information from Piet Klaver. Klaver, however, was in China at the time of the Conference. Gee recorded:

All were startled when the leading German "prophet" suddenly said that he saw as in a vision one of the most outstanding leaders present "smoking five pipes at once." This he declared, represented uncleanness in his soul. By that time the Conference was getting tired of these personal visions, and upon the interpretation being submitted to the judgement of all present they unanimously rejected it, even though given through a prophet held in high esteem in the churches. The tragic sequel was that only a few years later the brother was proven to be guilty of grave uncleanness, to which he personally confessed. The prophet was vindicated, and a fresh example given of the purity of spirit needed in those who would judge spiritual things. It is with thankfulness we can record that the guilty brother became deeply repentant, and although stricken of a sickness whereof he died, his closing months were spent in a victorious witness to the power of the blood of Christ.

Cf. Donald Gee, *Spiritual Gifts in the Work of the Ministry Today* (Springfield, MO: Gospel Publishing House, 1963), pp. 59-60. J.E. van den Brink, *De eerste brief aan de Corinthiërs* (Gorinchem: Kracht van Omhoog, 1985), pp. 428-29.

45. *Volkstelling 31 December 1930*, vol. 3 (The Hague: C.B.S., 1933), pp. 184-85, 188-91, 193-94.
46. Lydia de Jong-Polman, Interview, Boskoop, 29 December 1983.
47. "Nachruf," *Heilszeugnisse* 24/7 (1 April 1932),99.
48. Ko Andrea to Martha Visser, 29 February 1932. Andrea had been in the Pentecostal assembly at The Hague in the early twenties until the meetings were stopped about 1923. Although he did not return to the movement he kept good memories about it and remained friends with Martha Visser. When they learned that Polman was ill, they visited him in the hospital, which was much appreciated by Polman.
49. Lydia de Jong-Polman, Interview.
50. "Register Akten van Overlijden, Haarlem, 1932," no. 263.
51. W. Polman, Letter to the couple Andrea and Martha Visser, 2 March 1932.
52. "Nachruf," *Heilszeugnisse*; Donald Gee, "Mr. G.R. Polman (Holland) with the Lord," *Redemption Tidings* 8/4 (April 1932),20; "Begrafenis G.R. Polman," "G.R. Polman," "Teraardebestelling Polman," unidentified and undated press cuttings. Elbers (1885-1957) was married to Mrs. Polman's sister Johanna Theodora Blekkink.
53. *Pinksterboodschap* 2/5 (May 1961).
54. *Spade Regen* 22/12 (March 1930),159-60.
55. "Het gebruik en misbruik van de tong," *Spade Regen* 23/6 (September 1930),91-94.
56. "Enkele dingen die een voorganger niet kan doen," *Spade Regen* 23/8 (November 1930),122-24.

10 THEOLOGY

Introduction

This chapter on theology and worship is, far from being comprehensive, just a brief introduction to some major elements of the early Pentecostal, largely oral, theology. A thorough discussion of the theological and socio-psychological questions falls beyond the scope of this study. The topics Scripture, Salvation, Sanctification, Spirit baptism, Spiritual gifts, and Eschatology are only treated insofar as they relate to the Dutch Pentecostals. Ecclesiology, Liturgy, Water baptism, and Communion will be discussed in the following chapter.

The early Pentecostals did not leave us with a developed theology. Being a revival movement, experience rather than dogma was stressed. This certainly holds true for the Dutch situation. Whereas Barratt, Boddy, and Paul did come to some kind of theological reflection (they had to defend their position as ministers in existing denominations), Polman (not attached to any denomination) never came to write a theological treatise, not even an apologetic. The only statement of faith that was once published in *Spade Regen* concerned the application form for membership introduced in 1925:

To the Council of the Pentecostal assembly at Amsterdam.
Impelled by an inner conviction and by a real longing to the communion of the saints, I inform you, that I would like to be accepted in the communion of the Pentecostal assembly.
By grace do I have the witness in my heart to be child of God, and to know the Lord Jesus as my personal Saviour and Redeemer.
I believe in the Holy Scripture as the infallible word of God

219

and in the all-sufficiency of Scripture as rule for faith and conduct. And in the full deliverance by the precious blood of Christ, that is shown to us in Scripture, and in the baptism with the Holy Spirit with Scriptural signs and gifts, and in the work of God, that He by that Spirit has done in the Pentecostal assembly and is still doing, and I stretch out to the full blessing of the Spirit, that God wants to give to us before Christ's return.

It is my wish to completely belong to God, to live dedicated to Him to the glorification of His name. Therefore I shall also subject myself willingly to the spiritual discipline, that is exercised in the assembly according to the Word of God, to in this way be jointly built up to a dwelling place of God in the Spirit, and to share with all His in the full blessing of the Gospel, and to await together the return of our Lord and Saviour.[1]

The statement has the form of a testimony, so typical of Pentecostals. It demonstrates that even a declaration of faith was primarily a matter of the heart. Most expressions are on the experiential level: impelled by an inner conviction, a real longing, the witness in my heart, personal Saviour, stretch out, my wish, live dedicated, subject myself willingly, jointly built up, share with all His, to await together. The declaration starts with a testimony of individual salvation and then moves to a collective sphere in which further growth and the return of the Lord is anticipated. The doctrinal part in the middle concerns Scripture, Salvation, Spirit baptism, Second coming, and Church discipline. In comparison with other Pentecostal declarations of faith some striking elements are missing: Trinity, Deity of Christ, Sanctification, Initial evidence, Water baptism, Lord's Supper, Healing, and Eternal punishment, while there is no explicit statement about the verbal inspiration of the Bible.[2]

One even earlier declaration that comes close to a statement of faith was found in the constitution of the mission society incorporated in 1923, but was never published in *Spade Regen*. Membership was open to those who "acknowledge the true, eternal Divinity of Christ and who by their way of living testify to be redeemed by the blood of Jesus Christ, believing in the second coming of Christ for His church and the baptism with the Holy Spirit, as is written in the Holy Scriptures."[3] Compared with the declaration on the form for church membership it lacks statements about Scripture and Church discipline, but adds the Deity of Christ.

The early Pentecostal theology was not a conceptual, but rather a narrative theology, transmitted by means of sermons, stories, testimonies, form of worship, and lifestyle. These types of communication carried a theological message, closely related to the Pentecostal self-understanding. By looking at the main elements of the Pentecostal preaching, testimonies, devotional writings, and form of worship, the core of this message will be unfolded. To a large extent it was a combination of ecclesiology and eschatology. The Pentecostal understanding of the church was not tied to church membership or to a confession of faith, but to an experience, a personal encounter with the living God, called the rebirth (being born from above). This in turn was related to their eschatology. The outpouring of the Holy Spirit with the speaking in tongues was a sign that Jesus was coming soon. In this period of the latter rain the gifts were restored in order to prepare the church as the bride for the eschatological wedding feast. Preparatory to second advent the bride needed to be purified (sanctification of the believers); and the gospel needed to be preached to all nations (foreign mission). In both of these areas, ecclesiology and eschatology, the expectation of the Pentecostals would eventually suffer disappointment, which would lead to a modification of their original position.

Scripture: A Rule for Faith and Conduct

With some reservation Pentecostalism can be seen as a moderate form of the fundamentalism that is rooted in British and North American millenarianism.[4] Major features they have in common are the centrality of the Bible, faith in Christ, personal salvation, emphasis on prayer, and premillennialism. If we follow James Barr's rigid interpretation of fundamentalism as a religious stream, whose overriding and only constant concern is to guard the inerrancy of the Bible, then the Dutch Pentecostals would not fall under this category. Barr started his discussion of fundamentalism by stating as its most pronounced characteristics:

1. a very strong emphasis on the inerrancy of the Bible, the absence from it of any sort of error;
2. a strong hostility to modern theology and to the methods, results, and implications of modern critical study of the Bible;
3. an assurance that those who do not share their religious viewpoint are not really "true Christians" at all.[5]

While the Pentecostals would agree with the distinction made between nominal and true Christians, they would not attach the same to maintaining a right doctrine, but to having the right experience. Although the Dutch Pentecostals held aloof from modernistic theology and kept to a simple use of Scripture, they lacked the militant dogmatic attitude generally held by fundamentalists.[6] The Dutch Pentecostals most likely accepted the inerrancy of the Bible, but never made it a cornerstone of theology. Their understanding of the Bible "as rule for faith and conduct" was more functional than dogmatic.

Nils Bloch-Hoell in his still-valuable description of Pentecostal theology distinguished two basic principles: biblicism and empiricism.[7] In the eyes of the Pentecostals the truth of biblical Christianity in general and that of Pentecostalism in particular, was empirically demonstrated by spiritual manifestations as miracles of healing and glossolalia. Likewise was the validity of salvation, sanctification and Spirit baptism usually made dependent on a personal experience. As to the Bible Pentecostals will be careful not to go against what is written, that is, as far as it is understood. In theory the Pentecostal understanding of the Bible will agree with major tenets of fundamentalism, but in practice a free exegesis of the text "as the Spirit leads" will be fully acceptable. An intuitive preference for a free exegesis prevented the early Pentecostals from getting imprisoned by "dispensationalism," the hermeneutical system embraced by most fundamentalists.[8]

An abundant use of typology and allegory provided the Pentecostals with the desired freedom to develop the favorite "spiritual meaning" of the text, always in combination with a practical application. The Old Testament in particular was treated typologically: "most of the Old Testament is image and shadow of things, that had to be fulfilled. . . . As often as we find an image or shadow in the Old Testament, we must diligently search for its counter-image in the New Testament."[9] As far as it related to the church, the New Testament served to explain the spiritual meaning of the Old Testament.[10] The church was often addressed as "spiritual Israel," but without ruling out the Israel of old: "for the election and the gifts of God are without repentance."[11]

Salvation: Redeemed by the Blood

> Dear reader, if you are not saved, then you are lost. . . . You are in acute danger and therefore you need immediate help. . . . Let me tell you simply how you can be immediately saved.[12]

The Pentecostal message of salvation was identical to that of the Salvation Army (based on Methodist theology). It was a simple and straightforward message: because Jesus died on the cross for the sins of all people, salvation is available for all who believe in His name. God is the originator and man responds. The human part concerned repenting of committed sins, and accepting in faith that Jesus died for these sins. In the sermons the human will, but more particularly the human emotion was addressed:

> Do you want to believe with your heart? Do you want to come as a broken one, a not-knowing one, a poor sinner to the Christ of Scripture? To the despised one, the bleeding one, who carried your guilt, your sin, your punishment and darkness on Calvary? Then you will find the wonderful life that fills the heart.[13]

In emphasizing the universality of salvation and in stressing man's free will to either accept or reject the offer of salvation, the message conflicted with the Calvinistic understanding of election and of the human will. For the Pentecostals anyone who truly repented of his sins and turned to God was elected.[14]

In one of the rare moments that a Dutch Pentecostal tried to reflect on the relationship between the divine and human parts in salvation, he acknowledged the human side, but added: " . . . yet it is God, Who converts man. This is a mystery. To understand the human free will and God's ordinances in mutual relation is an impossibility."[15] The universal effect of the fall of Adam was accepted. Rather than speaking of "original sin," the sinful nature (after conversion called "the old nature") of all men since Adam was stressed.[16] On the one hand humankind was not held responsible for the sin of Adam: "No one goes lost, because Adam has sinned," but on the other hand it was asserted that "all are sinners by nature."[17]

Salvation was regarded the most fundamental stage. By means of salvation one became part of the universal body of Christ and a candidate for further blessing of the Holy Spirit. Salvation included instant regeneration and justification. It was not just an improvement of the old man, but a new creation, a new heart, and a new spirit. In this new state good deeds were expected, for one knows the tree by its fruit: "One is not justified by good works, but he who is justified, does good works."[18]

In the Pentecostal message of salvation, an unusual stress is laid on the function of the blood in the atonement. In the blood is forgiveness of sins and sanctification and also protection against the forces of darkness: "Those living under the blood, are living under the loving protection of the Father, Son and Holy Spirit."[19] Many are the references to the blood in choruses, like, "There is power, power, wonder-working power in the precious blood of the Lamb," and in prayers, such as "We thank you Lord Jesus for the blood."[20] The emphasis on the blood corresponds with the pre-eminence giving to the second person of the God-head. This pre-eminence is evident in the sermons, testimonies, prayers (directly addressed to Christ), and choruses.

Sanctification: Cleansed from All Sin

The Pentecostal message from the Azusa Street Revival simply followed the (Wesleyan) Holiness teaching on salvation and sanctification, viewing it as two distinct works of grace, to which was added the baptism with the Holy Spirit. The understanding of sanctification would soon become a matter of great controversy in the North American Pentecostal movement. Against the concept of an instantaneous and entire sanctification subsequent to conversion and preceding the Spirit baptism, the view developed that held sanctification as process started with conversion and continuing throughout life. In the latter view sanctification was no longer a distinct experience.[21] In Europe it was not such a controversial issue, which is one reason why the concept of sanctification remained somewhat fluid.

The early Pentecostals in western Europe discerned three major steps in the Christian experience: salvation (or regeneration), sanctification, and Spirit baptism.[22] All three were regarded a work of the Holy Spirit. Barratt, Boddy, Polman, and the German leaders basically agreed that sanctification served as a spring-board to come to the Spirit baptism. But, the German leaders (Jonathan Paul in particular) seem to have placed most emphasis on sanctification, with at times a strong tendency towards perfectionism. At the Hamburg Conference (December 1908) Boddy, when asked by a German pastor whether "entire sanctification" had been a condition for "receiving Pentecost" at Sunderland, affirmed: "Yes, most emphatically. The teaching of a Clean Heart has always been on the lines of Rom. 6:6 and 11."[23] Polman added that prior to laying on hands for receiving the Spirit baptism, he first dealt personally with the seekers about sanctification. For instance: "A brother and a sister said, that they had faith in the cleansing blood of Jesus. When I then informed them that they by faith could be cleansed in the blood of Jesus, they accepted it and then they immediately received the Holy Spirit."[24]

In the example given it would seem that sanctification and Spirit baptism were received simultaneously, but this was certainly not a general pattern. It often involved a long time of praying and waiting before one received the Spirit baptism with the sign of tongues. Sanctification lacked such an external sign. It would seem that among the Dutch Pentecostals sanctification was simply accepted by faith and one was held sanctified unless the contrary was proven. The absence of accounts of sanctification in the many testimonies printed in *Spade Regen* suggests that it was not a typical emotional experience. Sanctification did include avoidance of what was regarded "worldly," such as alcohol, tobacco, cinema, and theatre.[25]

The inherent difficulty in the doctrine of sanctification if taken as a distinct work of grace, namely, that it undermines the sufficiency of salvation, was not taken seriously, probably due to ignorance. For the Pentecostals sanctification was more understood in relation with Spirit baptism than with salvation. Sanctification was usually described with terms as cleansing, emptying yourself and uniting with God, but not much with eradicating sin.[26] During the first decade it was a transition towards the Spirit baptism. Wumkes observed in 1916: "The sanctification, which is an emptying of oneself and a uniting with God, is crowned with the Spirit baptism: the gift of Power on the sanctified soul. The divine order is: cleansing, then fulfilling."[27] Hereafter the concept of sanctification in its relation with Spirit baptism gradually changed. Rather than being the crown on the "sanctified soul," the Spirit baptism would become the starting point in achieving a sanctified life. Already in 1917 Mrs. Polman emphasized a gradual successive sanctification: "It is a process, that should continue from day to day, until He comes and life in all its fullness will be revealed."[28] But first another wave of sanctification would roll in from the east border.

During 1919 to 1922 the Dutch Pentecostal movement was flooded with the German message of "death to self," or "full deliverance." It called for an emotional crisis experience in which the human spirit, understood as the human ego or personality, had to die. Polman, a little bit more sober, added: "The human spirit remains, one does not lose one's personality, but one is broken, and while one's power is gone, Christ lives in us and He has become the power whereby one lives."[29] It was a full-fledged message of sanctification, only no longer as transition to receive the Spirit baptism, but standing on its own. Mrs. Polman explained the work of purification as the baptism with fire.[30] Jonathan Paul came over three times and every time stayed for several months. Although in 1919 he had denounced his earlier teaching that tended towards perfectionism, his sermons and articles in *Spade Regen* still carried the old tendencies.[31] During this period the Dutch movement got somewhat entangled in perfectionism, but after a few years slowly regained its balance.[32]

In 1923 Bernard Kedde rejected the teaching that viewed sanctification as a prerequisite to Spirit baptism. It was just the other way around: the Spirit baptism was the means to sanctification.[33] Several months later Percy Corry argued exactly along the same line.[34] This way Kedde and Corry solved the Pentecostal embarrassment with people who had been baptized in the Spirit, but were living "after the flesh." Sanctification remained highly esteemed and to be sought but its meaning and purpose had definitely altered.

Spirit Baptism: You Shall Receive Power

SIGNIFICANCE OF THE SPIRIT BAPTISM

Most Pentecostals regard the baptism with (or in) the Holy Spirit, shortened to Spirit baptism, to be a distinct experience subsequent to conversion, accompanied by glossolalia and available for all the reborn. This specific Pentecostal understanding seems to be without precedent in church history. Nils Bloch-Hoell stated that "no previous movement claimed that Spirit baptism, evidenced by glossolalia, is a normal experience for all Christians."[35] Since Polman and other European leaders first learned the Pentecostal message through the Azusa Street revival, our discussion of its content and application must start at Los Angeles. The *Apostolic Faith* paper gave the following definition:

> The Baptism with the Holy Ghost is a gift of power upon the sanctified life; so when we get it we have the same evidence as the Disciples received on the Day of Pentecost (Acts 2:3-4) in speaking in new tongues.

To which was added:

> Too many have confused the grace of Sanctification with the enduement of Power, or the Baptism with the Holy Ghost;

> others have taken the anointing that abideth for the Baptism, and failed to reach the glory and power of a true Pentecost.[36]

The understanding of the Spirit baptism was based on the assumption that the accounts in Acts (chapters 2, 8, 10, and 19) are to be normative for 20th-century Christian experience. While sanctification referred to cleansing, the Spirit baptism referred to an enduement of power. Tongues served as the outward sign to distinguish sanctification from Spirit baptism. The "anointing" (1 John 2:27) was sort of a Spirit baptism without tongues and therefore not a "true Pentecost."[37] The atmosphere of the revival was loaded with an eschatological tension and missionary zeal: "Many are the prophecies spoken in unknown tongues and many the visions that God is giving concerning His soon coming. The heathen must first receive the gospel."[38] In fact the gift of glossolalia was seen as supernatural means to preach the gospel to the heathen without having to learn the language.[39] To describe the Spirit baptism as an enduement of power upon the sanctified life would still have been an acceptable variation within the Holiness tradition. Yet, the unconditional link with glossolalia proved to be an inadmissible innovation, which would give rise to a separate Pentecostal movement. Under the surface, however, there was still another reason why the Pentecostal message was unacceptable.

A great stumbling stone was the black origins of the revival and its interracial fellowship. For this "indecent" origin and behavior the Pentecostals were despised, for "what good can come from a self-appointed negro-prophet?"[40] Alma White, founder of the Pillar of Fire (Holiness) mission, spoke denigratingly of the "Azusa Street Slum Mission," and regarded the familiarity between the races the climax of demon worship.[41] The first argument of the notorious Berlin Declaration to repudiate the Pentecostals, because they originated from Los Angeles, was probably an allusion to these very black roots. Already in the letter of invitation to the Berlin conference, where the declaration would be made, it was written:

> The Tongue movement of 1907 has come to us by way of Christiana-Hamburg from Los Angeles. Los Angeles has,

> however, in an article brought by the movement's own organ
> . . . , been drawn as a rendez-vous of spiritistic Spirits and as
> an area, that has become fatal for the movement. This origin
> also explains the mournful character the movement with us
> wore.[42]

It is not clear to which paper the "movement's own organ" referred, but it could well have been Charles Parham's paper, also called *Apostolic Faith*, since Parham presented himself as the founder of the movement. The description of the revival as becoming overpowered by spiritistic spirits is typical for whites like Parham, who condemned the revival because of its interracial character. In a clear attempt to refute the repudiation based on the Los Angeles origin, Eugen Edel wrote:

> Often one finds the view represented as if the origin of the Pentecostal movement lies in Los Angeles in America. From this has the rumour about the "Los Angeles spirit" been constructed. But the earthly origin of the Pentecostal movement was actually in Topeka, Kansas.[43]

When Wumkes in his first draft on the Pentecostal movement on the basis of Edel's description introduced Parham as the founder of the movement, Polman corrected him:

> Parham has indeed said, that he was the founder of the movement, but that was a political move of his and later it has become apparent, that his motives were not sound. . . . The Pentecostal movement has her origin in Los Angeles (1906), in a circle of converted coloreds, who came together and prayed for the baptism with the Holy Spirit, like the first disciples received it in the beginning. Their prayer was answered and from there it has spread itself.[44]

Douglas J. Nelson in his dissertation on William J. Seymour, *For Such a Time as This*, has demonstrated how for Seymour and his black friends the interracial aspect was an even more important work of the Holy Spirit than the speaking in tongues. For most of the whites this was too revolutionary. While the blacks emphasized the equality in Christ, the whites emphasized the glossolalia. The *Apostolic*

Faith reported: "No instrument that God can use is rejected on account of color or dress or lack of education. This is why God has so built up the work."[45] During 1908 Seymour's co-worker Clara Lum stole the vital mailing lists of the *Apostolic Faith* and proceeded to issue the paper from Portland, Oregon.[46] Robbed of his paper Seymour lost his influence on the movement, but, much worse, the movement lost a major prophet, who pointed at the social relevance of Pentecost. Within a decade the North American Pentecostal movement was just as segregated as all other denominations. Seymour's later criticism against overestimating the significance of glossolalia was not heard:

> Some people today cannot believe, that they have the Holy Ghost without some outward sign; that is Heathenism. . . . We must not teach any more than the apostles. . . . When we set up tongues to be the only Bible evidence of Baptism in the Holy Ghost and Fire, we have left the divine word of God and have instituted our own teaching.[47]

The Pentecostal message came to the Netherlands by means of the *Apostolic Faith* papers and other reports from abroad. In the first issue of *Spade Regen* (April 1908) the new work of the Spirit was seen as the latter rain, God adorning the bride with costly ornaments (that is, spiritual gifts) in preparation for the eschatological wedding feast. The universal significance and the equality and unity in Christ were stressed. The revival touched "blacks and whites; old experienced preachers as well as children, pastors and members of all kinds of churches and organizations."[48] And, "Where God's Spirit is poured out, all separations fall away and one unites at the feet of the Cross and one just looks at the Saviour of all men."[49] The Spirit baptism itself was called a baptism of praise, love, and power. Praise, because it "elicits from us beauteous choruses of praise, existence of which we had never dreamed and which can only find expression in the languages descending from the areas of heavenly glory."[50] Next it enabled them to love God and Jesus more than ever before; and "we learn to appreciate our neighbor, view him amiable in Christ, like He once taught us."[51] Lastly it gave them power to be a witness wherever Jesus called. Evidently the personal experience of the Spirit baptism was not confined to the individual, but also had a collective significance of equality and unity in Christ. The renewed vertical relation with God had horizontal effects in producing a fresh appreciation of one's neighbor. This was not just wishful thinking, but basically remained the understanding throughout the period under discussion.

One important alteration would be its relation to sanctification. From being the crown upon the sanctified life, the Spirit baptism rather became the means towards a sanctified life. In line with this is the later emphasis on being continually (re)filled with the Spirit.[52] Likewise would the great eschatological purpose of the Spirit baptism to prepare the church for the second advent be moderated.[53] Rebirth was acknowledged as a work of the Holy Spirit and all the reborn were part of the body of Christ. But through the Spirit baptism the believer was equipped with the power for service (necessary in the end time) and deepened in his or her Christian experience. Next it opened the way to the spiritual gifts. The consequence that Christians were divided into two classes was in tension with the concept of equality and unity in Christ. This inherent difficulty was recognized by the leaders, who warned against forming a little band of "overcomers" at the expense of the unity with all the reborn.[54]

RECEPTION OF THE SPIRIT BAPTISM

Besides the significance, the Azusa Street revival also transmitted a pattern of how the Spirit baptism was to be received. Most detailed is the first letter Barratt got from Los Angeles, dated 28 September 1906 and signed by Mrs. I. May Throop:

> After you have fully consecrated, and know God has cleansed your heart, then fast, and wait upon God. Keep yourself in a receptive attitude—and no matter what workings go on in your body, continually let and ask God to have His own way with you. You need have no fear while you keep under the blood—"Perfect love casts out all fear." Sometimes a wonderful shaking takes place, and some times the language comes at

first, as a baby learning to talk. But let God have all—tongue, hands, feet—the whole body presented to him, as your reasonable service! When the Holy Ghost comes in, you will know it, for He will be in your very flesh. Be obedient on every line. Be nothing—that He may be all in all.[55]

Barratt's account of his own Spirit baptism would soon become a model for others. Remarkable is the attention given to expected physical manifestations. While opponents saw in these manifestations a work of Satan, the adherents on the contrary encouraged them. Compared with the puritanism of the Holiness tradition it implied an innovation in anthropology. The human body was revaluated and instead of being denied became a means of worship. There is an overall appeal to let God have His way, no matter what goes on in the body, which reveals an optimistic view of a giving, loving, and trustworthy God. The same view is found among the early Pentecostals in Europe. Fear for bodily manifestations was seen as distrusting God.[56] At the Hamburg Conference (December 1908) Boddy started his address on the Spirit baptism by emphasizing the bodily aspect and read, "Know you not that your body is the temple of the Holy Ghost which is in you" (1 Cor. 6:19 and 3:16).[57] *Spade Regen* reported after the conference:

> Paul points at the perfect sanctification of spirit, soul and *body* (1 Thess. 5:23). We tend to give more attention to the first two. In these days also the body obtains its right place. God is being trusted for bodily healing more than ever. The Spirit in us makes our mortal (not deceased) bodies alive (Romans 8:11). No wonder something extraordinary happens when the God of heaven and earth enters and makes a dwelling there. A great joy, gladness and thankfulness fills the bodily temple. The Spirit gives utterance through miraculous tongues (Acts 2:4).[58]

Physical manifestations recorded among the early Dutch Pentecostals include shaking and trembling, falling on the ground, perspiration, crying, laughing, and singing in the Spirit (besides exorcism, healing, prophecy, visions, tongues, and interpretation).[59] Mary Boddy was more cautious: "these manifestations, either in speech, or physical, always are in keeping with the Spirit of the Word, and are therefore sober, decent, orderly, temperate, self-controlled."[60] The notable positive approach to the human body was later tempered. In the end the physical manifestations like shaking and falling on the ground were discouraged, probably under pressure of the sharp criticism it provoked. Mrs. Polman, looking back after 10 years' experience in the movement, admitted they had been drunk of the new wine and had forgotten to be moderate minded in order not to offend others.[61]

The many testimonies and accounts of people receiving their Spirit baptism reveal that it is preceded by a time of preparation. The preparatory stage is divided into a learning phase and a waiting phase.[62] During the learning phase the candidate comes in contact with the Pentecostal movement and is informed about its message and methodology. Much of this information is transmitted by means of oral forms of communication. During the waiting phase the candidate consciously seeks his own experience of the Spirit baptism. The mutual and after-meetings with intercessory prayers and encouragements from the "already baptized" as well as the laying on of hands were powerful means to facilitate the reception of the Spirit.

TONGUES AS THE SEAL OF THE SPIRIT BAPTISM

Boddy in his first issue of *Confidence* wrote, "I cannot judge another, but for me, Pentecost means the Baptism of the Holy Ghost with the evidence of the Tongues."[63] Already at the first conferences, Sunderland (June 1908) and Hamburg (December 1908), the question whether tongues was the seal of the Spirit baptism was addressed and it remained the subject of extensive discussion in the years to follow.[64] Barratt, Boddy, and Polman stressed the significance of tongues as being the regular sign of the Spirit baptism, but allowed room for exceptions. Polman said in Hamburg: "In Holland none are satisfied unless they have the Sign of Tongues. They all go for the full Pentecostal baptism."[65] Jonathan Paul in the first issue of *Pfingstgrüsse* propagated a different emphasis, if not a different position:

Nobody should think, that speaking in tongues is a shibboleth for us, and that we would depreciate any child of God, who does not receive this gift. This is certainly not the case. We are not of the opinion, that only those speaking in tongues, have received the Holy Spirit. Likewise is for us the speaking in tongues in itself no evidence, that someone has been filled with the Holy Spirit. We know, that by the fruit we can see whom we deal with (Matt. 7:16). Therefore is the fruit of the Spirit (Gal. 5:22) the main issue for us. Wherever these are found, there does the Spirit dwell in the heart. We should not in any way value speaking in tongues higher, than the Bible does.[66]

In December 1910 the German leaders went even further by declaring, "According to 1 Cor. 12:13 are to be reckoned Spirit baptized, all true children of God, who have gone into the death of Jesus and have commenced His life through the Holy Spirit (Rom. 6 and 8)."[67] Meanwhile Boddy had moderated his view. First Mary Boddy ascertained, "to speak in Tongues only is not, I can see, a sufficient sign of the Baptism."[68] Then Boddy himself admitted that at first tongues had received a too-prominent place in Sunderland.[69] It brought him to deny any Spirit baptism if the tongues were not accompanied by divine love.[70] At the Sunderland conference in 1911 the place of tongues was again discussed among the leaders. Boddy observed the differences of opinion: "not all insist upon the Tongues as exclusively the sign."[71] The Polman couple admitted some had received the Spirit baptism without tongues, while some spoke in tongues without having been Spirit baptized.[72] The International Pentecostal Council (with Barratt, Boddy, Paul, and Polman) agreed to the following statement in May 1912:

> The Baptism of the Holy Ghost and Fire is the coming upon and within of the Holy Spirit to indwell the believer in His fullness, and is always borne witness to by the fruit of the Spirit and the outward manifestation, so that we may receive the same gift as the Disciples on the Day of Pentecost (Matt. 3:11; Acts 1:5-8; 2:1-4, 38-39; 1 Cor. 12:7-13; Acts 11:15-18).[73]

In the following session at Amsterdam, December 1912, the statement was repeated·and extended with exhortations to develop the fruit of the Spirit and warnings against "merely seeking soulish experiences or fleshly demonstrations, which not a few have mistaken for the work of the Spirit."[74]

Polman maintained his strong emphasis on tongues as the regular sign of the Spirit baptism, though he did view it in combination with the fruit and admitted exceptions to the rule. From testimonies in *Spade Regen* and interviews with eyewitnesses it is evident that the general assumption among the Dutch Pentecostals required the Spirit baptism to be evidenced by tongues. Tongues made the difference between an "anointing" and the "full baptism." *Spade Regen* regularly translated American and English (by Donald Gee) articles, which forwarded tongues as the sign. The obvious implication of 1 Cor. 12:30 that not all speak in tongues was overcome by introducing a distinction between tongues as a sign (Acts) and tongues as a gift (1 Cor.). Polman's position was, "*All* may receive the *sign* of tongues . . . whereas *some* receive the tongues as a *gift*."[75] Albert Zijp after 10 years attending the Pentecostal meetings wrote the following critique in his open letter:

> This is an error brother Polman, which the assembly has learned from you. I know, that it is difficult to admit this. You are yourself being swung to and fro between the opinion that you should not pose tongues as a sign, and your understanding of Scriptures according to which all Christians, that were baptized with the Holy Spirit also spoke in tongues. Hence that you every time, especially in personal conversation (for this there are several witnesses), admit, that tongues should not be posed as a sign, and yet a few days later in public you bring your old opinion again. I do not believe that you do this on purpose. I rather believe that it is a consequence of your speaking extempore, whereby probably the influence of your hearing is strongly felt. Here your aforesaid understanding of Scripture, which you have never really abandoned, plays an important role. You have taught this audience for years, that the Baptism with the Holy Spirit is known by the speaking in tongues, and now this same audience inspires you, to maintain this teaching tooth and nail. Perhaps also that part of the

audience, that knows better and discerns this error, exercises such an influence upon you, that just because they disagree with you, you resist them with all force and might of words. Because you have a warrior's nature. I am firmly convinced, that this warrior nature plays you false in this matter. As soon as you see this yourself, you will realize, that the Gerrit Roelof Polman nature must die here. I believe of you, that you would also wish that, as soon as you would be wholly convinced that your opinion is contrary to the Word of God.[76]

This sketch portrays Polman as a captive of his own message insofar as it relates to the issue of tongues. It could well be that he lacked the humility of Boddy, who admitted that tongues had been too prominent at first. Perhaps he was afraid that abandoning tongues as evidence would deny the very right of existence of a separate Pentecostal movement. In any case it appears there was some ambiguity between his private and public opinion in this matter. Yet, the declaration of faith Polman printed on the application form for membership did not mention tongues. Although he had witnessed the founding of the British Assemblies of God the year before, where speaking in tongues as "initial evidence" of the Spirit baptism became part of the Statement of Fundamental Truths, Polman refrained from laying down his personal conviction as a rule for others to endorse.

Spiritual Gifts 1: Tongues, Interpretation, Prophecy

With reference to the Spirit baptism experience had followed theology. First one became convinced of the biblical basis and then the experience was anticipated. Thereafter theology to a great extent followed the experience, in particular with reference to the exercise of spiritual gifts. In our discussion of the Spirit baptism it appeared how the Pentecostals made a distinction between tongues as a seal of the Spirit baptism and tongues as a gift. This distinction was not only introduced to comply with 1 Cor. 12:30, implying that not all speak in tongues, but also because in practice not all who received tongues continued to speak in tongues. Mrs. Polman wrote to Mrs. Boddy in August 1908 concerning this issue:

> One brother, who is also baptized, spoke in a beautiful, clear tongue, when the Spirit came upon him, but since he has not spoken any more in tongues. What do you think is the reason of it? For every meeting the fire of God comes mighty upon him, but still he does not speak in tongues any more. He was a little discouraged about it, but I told him that he probably did not get the gift of tongues, only the Bible evidence, and that God would give him perhaps another gift. Well, that was a great consolation for him, and he is now full of fire; the perspiration comes often from his face in great drops when he is praying and rejoicing.[77]

A few months later at the Hamburg conference the consensus was that the gift referred to the continuance of speaking in tongues. J. Paul affirmed: "Many of the Corinthians did not continue in speaking in Tongues. They had the 'Seal' but not the Gift."[78] Throughout the period under Polman this remained the understanding of the Dutch Pentecostals. To belong to the category of the Spirit-baptized it was enough to just once speak in tongues. Thereafter it was a matter of having the gift of tongues. Today the Dutch Pentecostals usually expect all to continue and explain 1 Cor. 12:30 by distinguishing between its usage: in private (by all) and in public (not by all).

The assumption among early American Pentecostals that tongues were a supernaturally given language for use on the mission field was soon abandoned when experience proved different. By the time missionaries left from Europe this error was not repeated and all went through a long language study program on the field. Arie Kok upon leaving for China explicitly stated: "We do not feel to have biblical ground to believe, that the gift of tongues is given by God to preach the Gospel to the heathens in their own language, without having learned it."[79] Accordingly the emphasis in early (American) Pentecostal periodicals on tongues being recognized as actual languages by foreigners or missionaries present was not vindicated by daily practice. *Spade Regen* recorded some cases in which tongues were said to have been an actual language, but these were exceptions.[80] In general Polman came to view tongues as an unintelligible speech.[81] Following H. Bavinck's explanation of glossolalia in *Magnalia Dei* Polman felt that except for Acts 2 tongues in the New Testament always were unintelligible.[82]

Another example of how theology followed experience concerns the interpretation of tongues. The New Testament data suggests that speaking in tongues is speaking unto God in contrast to prophecy which is speaking unto men (1 Cor. 14:2-3). Yet, in Pentecostal practice there was no difference between interpretation of tongues and prophecy. Both were mainly addressed to men, often starting with some standard formula like, "Thus speaketh the Lord" and continuing in the first person singular, that is, God directly speaking to men through the prophet or interpreter. One reason why Elias Schrenk repudiated the manifestation of tongues during the notorious Kassel meetings in July 1907 as unbiblical was because the interpretations he heard had been addressed to men and not, in accord with 1 Cor. 14, to God.[83] K. Lettau in his paper on tongues presented during the Hamburg conference (December 1908) concluded from the Bible, "Tongues are mainly God-ward, but other workings are not excluded."[84] In the discussion following the paper J. Paul stated, "In Germany it was chiefly said that one who speaks in Tongues speaks only to God. 1 Cor. 14:2."[85] This particular aspect was not further deepened and the discussion went into another direction. In Amsterdam as in all other Pentecostal circles the interpretation was nearly always addressed to men. Mrs. Polman stated as to the use of tongues:

> The first time I spoke in tongues it brought the whole congregation to the dust, for sin was revealed. Men and women, whom we had held in highest esteem, were found out to be abominable sinners. Interpretation often is given to help sinners to fear God, and so to cry out for salvation. Many have been saved, cleansed, and sanctified in this way. Shall we prescribe to God how He shall work?[86]

Other than revealing sin tongues along with prophecy often carried messages concerning the soon coming of Christ. The practice of tongues being addressed to men rather than to God led to introducing a distinction between use in private (to God) and in public (to men).[87] Polman stated, "The tongues are not in the first place for public services, but for personal edification, because through that gift one speaks to God and has communion with God."[88] In this respect tongues differed from the other gifts, unless it was interpreted: "The gifts are not for the inner room, nor is the speaking in the tongues when it is accompanied by interpretation, because tongues with interpretation is equal to prophecy."[89]

Numerous psycholinguists and anthropologists have investigated the speaking in tongues and found no evidence of xenoglossia (speaking in known languages), although elements of languages were present.[90] H. Newton Malony and A. Adams Lovekin in their profound study of the behavioral science perspectives on speaking in tongues suggest that glossolalia is a language in a different sense of the word. Although not in traditional semantic sentences, something meaningful is communicated.[91] Walter J. Hollenweger stressed that glossolalia is a natural human ability also occurring outside Christianity: "Just as music, normal speech, and the bread in the eucharist are common gifts of creation and may be used for religious purposes, so speaking in tongues is a natural gift which many human beings possess."[92] Taking glossolalia as primarily a religious language, a language of faith that conveys symbolic meanings understood by the emotion, would give credit to the above findings as well as with Pentecostal practice. The only correction needed would be that the interpretations given are not translations, but are, like already suggested by Pentecostal experience, prophecies.[93]

Interpretations, prophecies, and visions generally carried messages, often by means of images or figurative speech, in which God directly (first person singular) addressed an individual or the assembly. After obvious failures in the divine communication the trustworthiness of these prophetic messages was extensively discussed by the leaders during the early international conferences. The initial tests of "pleading the blood" (that is, calling upon the blood of Jesus for protection) or quickly asking those "under the power" to affirm whether Jesus Christ had come in the flesh (after 1 John 4:1-3) had proven to be unreliable.[94] In these discussions about "trying the spirits" it is interesting to note how common sense played a dominant role: "Great caution is needed where messages have to do with persons. They should not run contrary to common sense."[95] The leaders agreed that personal messages were to be discouraged, because of the problems they had caused. In short prophetic messages had to be grounded in scripture, aimed at edification, exhortation, or comfort and to bring honor to Jesus. Next they had to be spoken by "sanctified souls" and to be affirmed in the hearts of the Spirit-filled listeners.[96] In Amsterdam strangers attempting to prophesy were silenced and personal messages not allowed. Mrs. Polman said: "If we had accepted every prophecy that has been sent to us, we should all have been dead, but such are all put in the waste-paper basket."[97] Evidently Polman's authority to judge prophecies had been questioned as he himself did at first not prophesy, to which Mrs. Polman responded, "My husband has not the Gift of Prophecy, but, as God-sent leader he believes he has the right to judge because he is a prophet of God—because he is preaching the Word of God for the edifying of the Church."[98]

The difficulties encountered brought the Pentecostals to face the human elements operating in the gifts. At the Hamburg conference Barratt warned against the danger of treating anyone who had given a prophetic message as an infallible oracle: "We must remember that the oracle is a frail human being and liable to make mistakes."[99] To which J. Paul added:

> The sub-conscious mind of a man may resign itself unto God or unto self. . . . A Gift is deposited in the sub-conscious mind. Who is it that works? . . . We must distinguish clearly how a Gift is given and how it is used. . . . There would be no need to judge if there were no danger.[100]

Soon three possible sources were discerned: the divine, the human, and the demonic. At the following Sunderland conference (June 1909) the discussion was carried further by Paul:

> A man may be sincerely convinced that it is of God, and all the time unconsciously it is his own [thought]. We must in this

Pentecostal Movement, have proper leadership in the meetings, a leadership which is able to distinguish between the human and that which is of God, and also between that which is from below and that which is from above. We should not associate with Pentecostal work where there is no true leadership.[101]

J. Paul's emphasis on the authority of leadership, much endorsed by Boddy and Barratt, denotes the way the matter became regulated by Polman in Amsterdam. Polman saw it his duty to correct "soulish manifestations" in public if necessary and expected the members to accept his judgement even if he was mistaken![102] By claiming supreme authority in judging prophetic utterances Polman in fact returned towards the traditional hierarchical model, which in the end is bound to discourage spontaneity and the free operating of the spiritual gifts.

Much of the problem in handling prophecies was caused by the rather artificial distinction between the "supernatural" and the "natural." The nine gifts of the Spirit (according to 1 Cor. 12:8-10) were all by definition taken as "supernatural." That Paul used various lists and elsewhere (Romans 12:6-8) included very "natural" gifts, like serving or showing mercy, was not taken into account. In spite of the recognition of divine and human elements being at work it remained an either/or argument. The leader had to discern whether God or man was speaking, without giving proper consideration that both could be true. If man is not ruled out, as seems to have been accepted by Barratt and Paul, it would be more appropriate to view the state of inspiration as existing along a continuum rather than in a strict dichotomy (divine/human). This would possibly have given the Pentecostals a better way of handling difficulties. But, to some extent it would also have lessened the authority of prophetic messages and subsequently have called for a lower-keyed formulation.

Spiritual Gifts 2: Healing, Exorcism

Right from the start healing and exorcism have been an integral part of the Pentecostal practice. The announcements of meetings in *Spade Regen* promised: "A full deliverance for spirit, soul and body is being preached." In August 1908 Mrs. Polman reported to Mrs. Boddy: "Our hall is just packed every Sunday and Wednesday. A great many are saved; backsliders have been saved over; many are sanctified. Demons have been cast out of several and the sick have been healed."[103] Special divine healing meetings had been arranged on Monday afternoons: "We have prayed for many sick people, but, of course, I do not know if they are all healed. The Devil is loose also, but we keep victory through the Blood."[104] Evidently some questioned female ministry: "Remarks are being made, of course, of me having the gift of healing. I am a woman, and a woman cannot have it. Still I keep to the Lord. I cannot do anything, Jesus does the whole thing."[105] The message of healing primarily dealt with physical trouble, while exorcism (casting out of demons, also called deliverance) mostly dealt with afflictions in spirit or mind.[106] Presumably Boddy referred to exorcism when writing after his visit to The Hague: "We dealt specially with one or two, and the Lord gave deliverance to an oppressed one."[107]

At first exorcisms were carried out during the public meetings, but later on they were done separately.[108] In particular during 1917 Polman was much involved in a battle against spiritism. Some spiritistic mediums were visiting the meetings. Several got converted and demons were cast out.[109] Polman wrote to Wumkes that before his Spirit baptism he had always remained aloof, but since then he had received the gift of discernment and the inward spiritual power to fight the enemy.[110] As spiritism (or spiritualism) had attained some popularity, several Reformed ministers openly practiced it, and because speaking in tongues also occurred in their midst, Polman felt it necessary to emphasize the difference:

> Today one holds "seances on biblical basis." One is orthodox in faith, so-called, but at the same time one can sit at the table of devils. Where does one not find spiritists in our time? One meets them nearly everywhere, where the spiritual power of discernment cannot be revealed. It is remarkable, that some consider the Pentecostal movement as spiritistic, while it is

exactly there that spiritism cannot dwell without being
discovered. In our meetings spiritists are frequently coming,
but it does not take long before they are discovered as such
and they do not stay unless they want to become delivered.
The miracle of Pentecost is imitated by the Devil. One has
been able to prevent these imitations in Christianity, because
the power to cast out these spirits was not present. Searching
for physical healing one went to mesmerists, somnambulists,
spiritists, etc., because the Church did no longer have the
power and the faith to heal the sick. The apostasy of the
Biblical stand is the cause of such a chaos.[111]

Physical healing was a regular feature of the meetings,
whether by actually taking place, by testimonies, or by
illustrations in the sermon. It strengthened the faith of the
members and confirmed God was on their side. Early in 1910
medical student Pieter Pilon, who for several years attended
the Pentecostal meetings in Amsterdam, tried to collect
written testimonies of healings in order to ascertain the
reliability and to publish them to the glory of God.[112] Polman
warmly recommended his request to the readers of *Spade
Regen*: "The compiling and distributing of such a writing, as
aforesaid, can be a great blessing for the people of God in
connection with divine healing, and perhaps even more for
the compiler himself, who in the course of this year hopes to
finish his study for medical doctor."[113] Unfortunately the
effort failed and Pilon left for Java the next year.[114]

Judging the credibility of the testimonies it must be taken
into account that many testified "in faith," which often meant
that healing was anticipated but not yet realized. More
caution was exercised with regard to printed testimonies in
Spade Regen. Polman did not "advertise" examples of healing
in the way faith healers were doing. From interviewing
eyewitnesses it became evident that many healings were
never mentioned in *Spade Regen*. Over a period of 23 years
(1908-1931) only 21 testimonies, often with name, date, and
place-name, were found in *Spade Regen*. With one or two
exceptions they all testified of realized healings including
cases of cancer (twice), tuberculosis (twice), appendicitis
(twice), paresis, eye disease, gallstones, fever, and stomach-
ache.[115] Many of these were said to have been verified by

doctors. The sole case of someone being raised from the dead, referred to by Wielenga, came from Germany.[116] It may well be that part of the healings were only a temporal improvement, or could have been explained in some other way, yet it seems certain that actual healings in answer to prayer have occurred. Wumkes gave the following example in his memoirs (writing 30 years after the event!):

> Polman had a strong faith in healing upon prayer. One day the wife of Ds. T. v.d. Burg at Haskerhorne (1911-1920), who had friendship with my wife, was sick to death. Her mother-in-law informed us, while Polman was present. Suddenly he said: Let us pray for her! The three of them went upstairs and kneeled. From that moment life won from the death.[117]

Although ministries of healing and exorcism were being exercised, little attention was given to formulating the message in writing.[118] The articles dedicated to healing (nearly always translations) stressed that healing was part of the atonement accomplished by Christ and available for all believers.[119] During 1910 *Spade Regen* published "Gods Weg ter Genezing," a translation from Dowie's tract "God's Way of Healing," without mentioning the source. It contained no reference to medical help, but did state:

> Disease can never be God's will. It is the Devil's work, consequent upon sin, and it is impossible for the work of the Devil ever to be the will of God. Christ came to "destroy the works of the Devil," and when He was here on earth He healed "all manner of disease and all manner of sickness," and all these sufferers are expressly declared to have been "oppressed of the Devil." (1 John 3:8; Matt. 4:23; Acts 10:38).[120]

Following Dowie, Polman believed in four modes of divine healing:

> The first is the direct prayer of faith; the second, intercessory prayer of two or more; the third, the anointing of the elders, with the prayer of faith; and the fourth, the laying on of hands of those who believe, and whom God has prepared and called

to that ministry. (Matt. 8:5-13; Matt. 18:19; James 5:14-15; Mark 16:18).[121]

Contrary to Dowie, Polman did not condemn medical help, though the way of faith without the use of medical science was to be preferred.[122] B. Wielenga's (Gereformeerd) study of healing by prayer in 1918 stated: "In the Pentecostal assembly faith healing is not of primary importance. The Christian is not strictly condemned if he seeks medical help. The personal faith decides. Is the faith strong enough, let the Christian then expect healing only from God, if not, let him call the doctor."[123] A testimony of healing from appendicitis by Engeline B. Burghoorn confirms the above. Consulting the doctor was explained with "not going deep enough in prayer." In the hospital she felt tortured by the thought of "not acting after God's will." Finally, just before the operation, she left the hospital with the consent of her mother and Mrs. Polman. According to her testimony one year after the event the pain left her the same day never to return.[124] In a letter to a couple in Sneek, whose son was dying of a brain disease and who apparently had not called a doctor as yet, Mrs. Polman counseled them to have a doctor diagnose the illness, just to be safe with regard to the law. This did not imply they had to give their son medicines: " . . . you and your dear wife indeed trust and believe firmly in God's help, you do not lean upon human arm, thus you will not grieve God with this. It is only to obey the government."[125]

Without openly repudiating medical help, the pressure to walk the deeper way of faith seems to have been quite strong during the first decade. This must have lessened during the twenties since nearly all eyewitnesses of this period stated that medical help was acceptable. Even Polman called a doctor for his children in time of illness. In December 1922, in his only article on the subject, Polman wrote that much damage had been done in connection with the message on physical healing: "One has made a doctrine out of it, formed a sect from it, and has condemned others who do not believe the same."[126] Polman urged the believers not to fight against doctors and medicines, but to show their faith by works: "Who thinks to have something better, let him generate that and the upright will believe."[127] The conviction that sickness does not come from God and had to be opposed remained. Percy Corry was more militant when he wrote in 1926:

> The enemy has also succeeded in convincing the people, that he himself is not the author of illness, disease and death (Heb. 2), but God! Therefore instead of standing with God against illness and possession in the name of Jesus, the church has come to apologize for a state of affairs that continually hinders her, but of which she cannot give account without doing injustice to the Love and tenderness of God and the redemption through the Lord Jesus Christ.[128]

Here again the Pentecostals protested against fatalistic tendencies in traditional Christianity, Dutch Calvinism in particular, that had come to accept illness as sent by God. According to Sunday 10 of the Heidelberg catechism health and sickness, wealth and poverty, and all things do not come by any chance, but by the providence of God.[129] In later years K.J. Kraan (Gereformeerd) could call this article a "theological industrial accident," but this was inconceivable during the period under discussion. B. Wielenga in his aforecited study of healing by prayer (1918) defended this very article against the claims made by the faith healers. Wielenga accused the faith healers of taking illness in a very one-sided manner: "If sickness is a distortion of life, then there is also sickness in society, that is poverty; in politics, that is war; in the unanimated creation, that is crop failure."[130] Far from being socially engaged he added the bewildered statement: "When Scripture says, that God sends poverty, that is the sickness of society, and that the poverty will remain here below, so it follows that also the physical sickness is a providence of God and that this enemy of creation is a servant of God, who does what He desires."[131] Wielenga was quite right that the faith healers were only touching one side of the issues of life, but his solution to resign to the status quo was much worse. Touching one side of the point is far better than being beside the point!

In spite of their underestimation of medical science it is significant that the Pentecostals did not take the extreme position of Dowie, Hazenberg, and Van Leeuwen to forbid the usage thereof. In our discussion of the rise of faith healing during the latter part of the 19th century this extreme position could partly be explained as a (unconscious) protest against the scanty availability of medical science due to practical, economical, social, and cultural barriers. While this no longer held true for the period 1907 to 1930 the few remaining faith healers kept to their strict refusal of medical aid, often paired with an anti-church attitude. The Pentecostals, with the exception of the Gemeente des Heeren, were able to come to a more moderate position, because their message was not limited to faith healing. The Spirit baptism, opening the door to a variety of spiritual gifts, prevented a one-sided emphasis on physical healing and automatically generated a relatively more balanced attitude.[132] The Pentecostal understanding and practice of healing by prayer contained a call to the churches to rethink their theology and world-view. Alas, it needed several decades and another world war before this call was to be heard and to some extent the ministry of healing was recognized by the church.[133]

Eschatology: The Spirit and the Bride Say, "Come"

The general longing for a deeper work of the Holy Spirit among evangelical and holiness circles at the beginning of this century had created an air of expectancy for a great revival preceding Jesus' return. When the Pentecostal revival started many soon equated it with the latter rain heralding the second advent. They saw in the restoration of the spiritual gifts a reviving of authentic Christianity. The work of the Holy Spirit in the previous centuries was, however, not quite denied. A particular view on church history developed in which the Pentecostals associated themselves with revivalistic movements throughout the centuries where similar spiritual gifts had been manifested.[134] It was a popular theme to present the history of the church as one of increasing downfall since Constantine and of progressive restoration since the Reformation. While Luther had restored the message of justification by faith and Wesley that of sanctification, the Pentecostal revival had restored the manifestation of spiritual gifts.[135] From this perspective the Pentecostal revival was the climax: the latter rain. Yet, the Pentecostals acknowledged that the latter rain could have been given much earlier if only the children of God had been more receptive:

> In the Pentecostal assemblies and also elsewhere there is a mighty longing, that God by means of great revivals will bring the end of the church history back till the beginning. And it leaves for them no doubt, that the revival commenced in the days of Luther could have brought the end, if there had not been a petrifaction, that brought the initial glory to a dead point, and caused that the Holy Spirit with his gifts and powers remained concealed.[136]

This reveals that in the eyes of the Pentecostals the Christians had an active part in God's plan of salvation on earth and they could by their conduct hasten or slow down the actual fulfillment thereof. When the first optimism about an interdenominational revival became tempered and Jesus' coming still awaited, the concept about the latter rain called for modification. Instead of being the latter rain itself, the Pentecostals came to regard their own movement as a revival preparatory to the latter rain![137] Wumkes wrote in 1916:

> One does not have a set eschatology, but quite generally the expectation about the future runs around these links: Christ descends to pick up his bridal church, the dead are raised, the remaining living believers are changed and together they are picked up into the clouds to execute the judgement on the living and to bind Satan; Christ then rules for thousand years with his bride on earth; thereafter Satan is being loosened for a short while; the resurrection of the unjust takes place, the last judgement is being executed, the new heaven and the new earth are being prepared; God is all and in all.[138]

Spade Regen April 1909 gave a little more detailed overview of the events "without claiming to be perfect or comprehensive." The premillennial coming of Christ was after John Nelson Darby anticipated in two stages. Christ would first come on the clouds to pick up his church into the air (the rapture). As the wedding of the lamb would be celebrated in heaven, so the great tribulation would take place on earth and

Israel would be restored to its own land. At the end of the great tribulation Christ would return to earth with his bride, whereby his feet were to land on the Mount of Olives, to inaugurate the millennium.[139] Unbelief, apostasy, false religions, earthquakes, Jews preparing to return to the holy land, and news of revivals around the world were explained as signs of the time and fulfillments of prophecy.[140] Pointing to the literal fulfillment of Old Testament prophecies concerning the incarnation, life, and death of Jesus, Polman argued for a literal fulfillment of prophecies about the second coming. He regarded having little interest in the Parousia a sign of not being filled with the Holy Spirit: "John, full of the Holy Spirit, cried out: Come quickly, Lord Jesus!"[141] For the awakened part of the church, the wise virgins, that day would not come as a thief in the night, though the hour remained unknown: "Some have gone too far by fixing dates, which is not after the Scripture and therefore wrong, but is ignorance and indifference in connection with Jesus' return not equally unscriptural and therefore wrong?"[142]

It is no surprise that the world war intensified the existing eschatological expectations, in particular, after Turkey's dominion over Jerusalem ceased in December 1917, which was taken as the fulfillment of Luke 21:24.[143] Prophecies were given during the meetings confirming the soon coming of Christ.[144] In this eschatological atmosphere one of the members had a dream (May 1918) in which Jesus said to her: "Tell the assembly that I will come soon. But when I come there will be three persons in the assembly who will be found not prepared for My coming."[145] Upon her question whether she was one of the three it was answered: "Yes, you are one of the three. You have given much, yes you have given very much already, but you have not given yourself yet and that is just what I desire." When she brought this message to the assembly the meeting took an unusual course:

> There was no preacher anymore on the platform, no organist behind the organ, no usher at the door, all of them were lying before God in the midst of the largest part of the assembly. Nobody could speak but to God alone, nobody could be occupied with anything else but with his own soul. . . . At

quarter past twelve we closed the meeting; all went home deeply impressed with the seriousness of what had happened.[146]

The political events aroused a wide interest among Christians for the endtime prophecies. During the war evangelist Johan de Heer commenced his lectures and articles about the signs of the time which gave rise to the (interdenominational) Maranatha movement. He drew much attention with his Maranatha message, and his bi-weekly *Het Zoeklicht*, started in 1919, was also widely read by Pentecostals. Polman felt this interest for the end time was not enough in itself; the power of the Holy Spirit was needed to be prepared for His coming.[147] The turbulent closing months of the war, when monarchies were being replaced by democracies, were immediately perceived as pieces fitting the eschatological jig-saw.[148] Political and social unrest in the Netherlands strengthened the longing for a heavenly intervention. For the year 1919 the motto "Behold, I come quickly," was chosen. The thought to secure the peace by forming a league of nations was dismissed:

> The nations of the world are working to enchant humanity with a false peace, upon which an Armageddon battle will follow. The Jews are preparing themselves to return to their land, to build their temple and to practice their religion as in the old days. The church of God prepares itself for meeting Christ in the air. 1919 appears to become a special year in which these three classes will become more revealed.[149]

During 1920 Polman published J. Paul's *De oplossing van het wereldraadsel* (The solution to the world riddle). In a speculative manner Paul interpreted the rise of Bolshevism and Zionism as fulfilling Daniel 2 and 7.[150] Polman agreed with the general thought:

> The present movement, called Bolshevism, is the beginning of the tribulation that will come upon the so-called Christian countries; the kingdoms of the world are doomed to make room for the unmovable Kingdom of Jesus Christ. . . . Besides the present Bolshevistic movement there is the Zionistic

movement aiming at the restoration of Israel in Palestine, by which they unconsciously prepare for the great tribulation.[151]

Paul's conviction that the church was called to be a place of justice, peace, and true communism, virtues the world was longing for, was shared by Polman: "The true communism is revealed in the church, not in the world. There one plays with these words out of self-interest, but the true Christians are one heart and one soul."[152] The "true communism" referred to was however strictly understood in a spiritual sense and not in a material sense. In practice the Pentecostal eschatology amounted to withdrawal from the social struggle.

With the commencement of the 18th volume of *Spade Regen* (April 1925) Polman acknowledged not to have expected the Lord to tarry this long when he started the publication, but quickly added, "Now, when we look back, these eighteen years are in fact only a moment and the expectation of His coming has become stronger."[153] It remained popular to interpret contemporary events, in particular, relating to communism or Israel, as signs of the time.[154] Polman distinguished between Israel as the nation of God preparatory to the coming of Christ and the church in the dispensation of the Spirit as the mystical body of Christ. When the church would be united with Christ, God would rebuild the fallen dwelling of David and all remaining people, whether heathen or Jew, calling upon the name of the Lord would be saved (Acts 15:14-17).[155]

The influence of Darbyism is present, yet Pentecostals used the term dispensation in a different manner than dispensationalists, who taught that the spiritual gifts did not belong to the present dispensation, but to the future. In *Spade Regen* A.S. Booth-Clibborn commented on this "dispensation theory": "Satan himself has always advocated the pure, original Christianity, provided it is placed in the way past or in the far future."[156] In 1929 *Spade Regen* translated an article by Donald Gee stating:

> The most doctrinal opposition against the message of the Pentecostal movement is based on explanations of Scripture according to which there would be various "dispensations."

Some of these explanations are terribly inconsistent, looking at the assertion that the present dispensation continues until the "rapture" of the Church. The creation of the dispensation-compartments in the New Testament is, following the day of Pentecost, clearly artificial. We state boldly, that some doctrines about the Holy Spirit seem to us more like efforts to explain Scripture in accommodation to general human experience, than a courageous pronunciation of that which the Church should rightly expect until the return of the Lord.[157]

Booth-Clibborn and Gee correctly perceived some of the dangers inherent to dispensationalism. Because Pentecostals failed in formulating a distinctive eschatology, the numerous writings of dispensationalists would increasingly infiltrate Pentecostal circles.[158]

NOTES

1. *Spade Regen* 18/1 (April 1925),15.
2. For examples of Pentecostal statements of faith see Walter J. Hollenweger, *The Pentecostals* (London: SCM Press, 1972), pp. 513-22.
3. *Nederlandsche Staatscourant*, Supplement, 17 April 1923, no. 74. Filed under "Statuten Vereenigingen 1923 no. 452."
4. For an excellent treatment of the roots of fundamentalism see Ernest R. Sandeen, *The Roots of Fundamentalism: British and American Millenarianism, 1800-1930* (Grand Rapids: Baker Book House, 1978). Sandeen stated that by 1919 the millenarian movement had changed its name: "the millenarians had become Fundamentalists" (p. 246).
5. James Barr, *Fundamentalism* 2d ed. (London: SCM Press, 1981), p. 1.
6. The two articles found in *Spade Regen*, that by way of exception contained an attack on modernistic theology, were both translations: "De doop des Heiligen Geestes," 19/1 (April 1926),6-10 (from: *Bridal Call*); "Dit (of 1930 na Chr.) is het (of 30 na Chr.)," 23/3 (June 1930),35-39 (from *Redemption Tidings*).
7. Nils Bloch-Hoell, *The Pentecostal Movement* (Oslo: Universitetsforlaget, 1964).
8. Dispensationalism is the hermeneutical system that finds origin in the prophetic studies of J.N. Darby and was further developed and popularized by C.I. Scofield. The essence of this approach comes down to an advocacy of the "literal interpretation" as well as a strict separation of biblical texts relating to the church from those applicable to Israel. It leads to a compartmentalizing of Scripture in which all of the Old Testament and much of the New Testament (for

instance the Sermon on the Mount and the Lord's Prayer) lack a literal significance to the church. The church-Israel distinction determines the ecclesiology and eschatology and consequently the relationship with society. The pessimistic endtime scenario encourages a hostile attitude towards the world.

Gerald T. Sheppard, "Pentecostals and the Hermeneutics of Dispensationalism: The Anatomy of an Uneasy Relationship," *Pneuma* 6/2 (Fall 1984),5-33; cf. G.C. Officer, "Het Dispensationalisme," *Bulletin voor Charismatische Theologie* no. 17 (1986),24-29.

9. "Schaduwen en beelden," *Spade Regen* 15/8 (November 1922),121-22.

In *Spade Regen* Amalek (Ex. 17) was a type of the "flesh"; the virgins of Solomon's Song 1:3 referred to the reborn and of course the oil to the Holy Spirit. G.R. Polman, "Het Lam is waardig," 16/7 (October 1923),99-101; W. Polman, "Gij zult zijnen naam heeten Jezus," 19/9 (December 1926),132-134.

Likewise the New Testament could be used typologically. From John 11 Polman argued that Mary was a type of the human spirit, Martha of the human soul and Lazarus of the human body! G.R. Polman, "De kracht zijner opstanding," *Spade Regen* 15/7 (October 1922),99-102.

10. "De Spade Regen," *Spade Regen* 20/2 (May 1927),21-23 (from *Redemption Tidings*). In this article many portions of the Old Testament are said to have a threefold meaning: a literal (with reference to Palestine), a pardoning (with reference to Israel), and a spiritual meaning (with reference to the church). Concerning the spiritual meaning the New Testament was to be the interpreter of the Old Testament.

11. Ibid.; and V. d. K., "Wettische gebondenheid geestelijke vrijheid," *Spade Regen* 17/2 (May 1924),26-27. Elsewhere it was said the fig tree always refers to Israel: "Let op de profetieën," *Spade Regen* 20/9 (December 1927)134-36, from *Triumphs of Faith*.

12. "Onmiddellijke Redding voor U," *Klanken des Vredes* 1/3 (August 1915),7.

13. B. Kedde, "Geloof," *Klanken des Vredes* 9/12 (May 1924),93-94.

14. "Ben ik uitverkoren?" *Klanken des Vredes* 5/5 (October 1919),35.

15. V. d. K., "Ter overdenking," *Klanken des Vredes* 10/5 (October 1924),39.

16. G. R. Polman, "Wedergeboorte," 21/7 (October 1928),99-101; B. Kedde, "Opstanding," *Spade Regen* 20/1 (April 1927),3-5.

17. G.R. Polman, "De verantwoordelijkheid der gemeente Gods," *Spade Regen* 17/7 (October 1924),100; Idem, "Wedergeboorte," p. 99.

18. Idem, "Wedergeboorte," p. 100.

19. "Het geloof in Zijn Bloed," *Spade Regen* no. 25 (September-October 1911),3 (translated from *Confidence*); cf. A.A. Boddy, *Pleading the Blood* (Sunderland: by the author, n.d.).

20. Recorded by A.A. Boddy in "A Visit to Holland," *Confidence* no. 6 (September 1908),8. At the Sunderland conference 1909, Polman

stated that every meeting in Amsterdam was put "under the precious blood." The accent on the blood easily led to an undesirable usage thereof. Polman commented that they did not support the reiteration of a formula or the mechanical repetition of the word "blood." *Confidence* 2/6 (June 1909),131.

21. Cf. W.J. Hollenweger, *The Pentecostals*, p. 25.
22. "Die Hamburger Dezember-Konferenz," *Pfingstgrüsse* 1/1 (February 1909),5; "Het bezoek van Ds. Boddy," *Spade Regen* no. 3 (September-October 1908),1; "Drie stappen in het geestelijk leven," *Spade Regen* no. 7 (March 1909),1; T.B. Barratt *De waarheid inzake de Pinksteropwekking* (Amsterdam: G.R. Polman, 1917), p. 9.
23. A.A. Boddy, "The Conference in Germany," *Confidence* 2/1 (January 1909),5.
24. "Die Hamburger Dezember-Konferenz," p. 6.
25. En route to Sunderland in 1909 the couples Polman and Kok were asked in the custom-house whether they had liquor or tobacco. They replied, "We are Christians, sir, we do not drink or smoke." *Spade Regen* no. 10 (June-July 1909),1. One young man was reported to have thrown his "pernicious cigarettes" through the hall during a prayer session in 1926. Some others were "delivered from smoking cigarettes and cigars." *Spade Regen* 18/11 (February 1926),172; 19/1 (April 1926),12.

    Cinema and theatre were mentioned a few times in *Klanken des Vredes*, always in disapproving terms: "Machten des verderfs," 1/2 (July 1915),1-2; W. Polman, "Zaaien en maaien," 3/5 (October 1917),32-33.
26. M. Collin Jones, "Heiligmaking," *Spade Regen* no. 22 (March-May 1911),2 (translated from *Triumphs of Faith*). Cf. "Het groote geheim van een heilig leven," *Spade Regen* no. 10 (June-July 1909),4 (translated from *Triumphs of Faith*); "Drie stappen in het geestelijk leven," *Spade Regen* no. 7 (March 1909),1. Contrary to this an article by Jonathan Paul, "De Grondbeginselen der heiligmaking," *Spade Regen* 11/3 (July 1918), 11-12, more concerned the eradication of sin.
27. G.A. Wumkes, *De Pinksterbeweging voornamelijk in Nederland* (Utrecht: G.J.A. Ruys, 1916), pp. 19-20.
28. W. Polman, "De Heiligmaking des Geestes," *Spade Regen* 10/3 (June 1917),10.
29. G.R. Polman, "Des Menschen Geest," *Spade Regen* 12/6 (September 1919),88.
30. W. Polman, "Het Louterende Vuur," *Spade Regen* 12/7 (October 1919),102-04.
31. Also the following articles by Jonathan Paul in *Spade Regen*: "Viervoudige onttroning," 12/8 (November 1919),119-26; "Trek uw Schoenen uit!" 12/9 (December 1919),136-39; "Volkomen verlossing," 12/12 (March 1920),179-84; "Driemaal vrijgesproken," 13/2 (May 1920),26-30, and 13/3 (June 1920),40-42; "Predikende

vaten," 13/4 (July 1920),55-59; "Het verlaten watervat," 13/7 (October 1920),100-04; "Het geheim van de volkomen verlossing," 13/8 (November 1920),115-20; "Toespraak Pastor Paul," 14/4 (July 1921),53-56; "Het Hooglied van den waren Salomo," 14/9 (December 1921),157-61; "De Zoon des Menschen," 14/12-15/3 (March 1922-June 1922),189-192; 4-8; 21-25; 37-39.

32. M. Marijs-Visser, "De Pinksterbeweging (II)," *Witte Velden* 20 (October 1950),11.

33. B. Kedde, "In de opperzaal," *Spade Regen* 16/1 (May 1923),21-25; Idem, "Het doel van den doop des Geestes," *Spade Regen* 16/7 (October 1923),103-06.

34. Percy N. Corry, "De Doop des Heiligen Geestes en daarna," *Spade Regen* 16/10 (January 1924),154.

35. Nils Bloch-Hoell, *The Pentecostal Movement*, p. 141.

36. "The Apostolic Faith Movement," *Apostolic Faith* 1/1 (September 1906),2.

37. After his first Spirit baptism experience of 7 October 1906 without the sign of tongues, Barratt wrote to Los Angeles, asking why the manifestation of tongues had not come. He was answered by Seymour's co-worker G.A. Cook:

> The speaking in tongues should follow the baptism. If you had remained under the power, until the Lord had finished, you undoubtedly would have spoken in tongues, not necessarily for use in foreign field, but as a sign to you of Pentecost, the same as at the house of Cornelius and at Ephesus.

Thomas Ball Barratt, *When the Fire Fell, and an Outline of My Life* (Oslo: Alfons Hansen & Soner, 1927), p. 123.

When Barratt a few weeks later received the gift of tongues, he reformulated his earlier experience as having been an "anointing." Barratt's testimony was published in *The Apostolic Faith* 1/4 (December 1906),3.

38. *Apostolic Faith* 1/1 (September 1906),1.

39. D. William Faupel, "Glossolalia as Foreign Language: An Historical Survey of the Twentieth Century Claim," paper presented at the 12th annual meeting of the Society for Pentecostal Studies, 19 November 1982.

40. Walter J. Hollenweger, "After Twenty Years' Research on Pentecostalism," *International Review of Mission* 75/297 (January 1986), p. 6.

41. Alma White further wrote that Satan had chosen Seymour to lead this movement of fleshly lust because he was black, a descendant of Ham, cursed by Noah. Alma White, *Demons and Tongues* (Zarephath, NJ: Pillar of Fire Publisher, 1936; originally published in 1910), pp. 70, 82, 103-04. Quoted in Douglas J. Nelson, "For Such a Time as This: The Story of Bishop William J. Seymour and the Azusa Street Revival" (Ph.D. thesis, University of Birmingham, 1981), pp. 83-85. Nelson added that Alma White became a prominent ideologist for

the Ku Klux Klan in the 1920s. In spite of her obvious bias against blacks, her work belonged to the most widely quoted primary sources for information on Seymour.

42. Ernst Giese, *Jonathan Paul, Ein Knecht Jesu Christi*, 2d ed. (Altdorf: Missionsbuchhandlung un Verlag, 1965), p. 155.

43. Eugen Edel, *Die Pfingstbewegung im Lichte der Kirchengeschichte* (Brieg: by the author, 1910), pp. 66-67.

44. G.R. Polman to G.A. Wumkes, Amsterdam, 27 February 1915. As a true historian Wumkes, in his final draft, presented both versions side by side: G.A. Wumkes, *De Pinksterbeweging voornamelijk in Nederland* (Utrecht: G.J.A. Ruys, 1916), p. 4.

45. "Bible Pentecost," *The Apostolic Faith* 1/3 (November 1906),1.

46. Nelson, pp. 39, 78-80. Seymour refused his legal right to seek redress in court.

47. William J. Seymour, "Doctrines and Discipline of the Azusa Street Apostolic Faith Mission" (1915), pp. 8, 91. Quoted in Nelson, p. 289.

48. "Wat zal dit toch zijn?" *Spade Regen* no. 1 (April 1908),1. Also in R. van Oosbree, *Valiants for Truth We Have Known: Eighty Years of Holy Ghost Revival* (Pasadena, CA: RavanO, 1986), pp. 1-6.

49. Ibid., *Spade Regen*, p 4.

50. Ibid., p 1.

51. Ibid.

52. See the following articles by G.R. Polman in *Spade Regen*: "Vervuld worden met den Heiligen Geest," *Spade Regen* 18/5 (August 1925),67-69; "Kracht en volheid," 18/11 (February 1926),163-65; "De betekenis van Pinksteren," 19/3 (June 1926),35-37.

53. The parable of the wise and foolish virgins (Matthew 25) was used to illustrate that in the endtime rebirth (having a burning lamp) was not sufficient. One needed the additional Spirit baptism (the vessel with oil) to keep the lamp burning and be prepared for the bridal call. In 1912 Polman emphasized that the wise (that is, the Pentecostals) were awake and alert, but in 1929 he noticed that they all slept, the wise as well as the foolish. G.R. Polman, "Gaat uit, Hem tegemoet!" *Spade Regen* no. 28 (January-February 1912),1; Idem, "Ontwaakt!" *Spade Regen* 21/11 (February 1929),163-64.

54. T.M. Jeffreys, "De Heiliging van het Lichaam, de Gemeente, van Christus, den Heer," *Spade Regen* no. 34 (September 1913),3-4.

55. Thomas Ball Barratt, *When the Fire Fell, and an Outline of My Life*, p. 109.

56. "De Sunderland Conferentie," *Spade Regen* no. 2 (May-August 1908),2.

57. A.A. Boddy, "The Pentecostal Conference in Germany," *Confidence* 2/2 (February 1909),33.

58. "De conferentie te Hamburg," *Spade Regen* no. 5 (December 1908),4.

59. See the following reports in *Confidence*: W.P. Polman, "Subsequent Blessing in Holland," no. 5 (August 1908),18-19; G.R. and W.

Polman, "Holland," 2/4 (April 1909),91-92; Mr. and Mrs. Mogridge, "Holland and Antwerp," 3/10 (October 1910),243-45. A.E. Street in "Wat is Pinksteren?" *Spade Regen* no. 9 (May 1909),1, claimed, "A Pentecostal baptism without bodily, outward manifestations is not biblical."

60. M. Boddy, "Messages and Manifestations," *Confidence* no. 9 (December 1908),14.
61. W. Polman, "Een Tienjarige Ervaring in de Pinksterbeweging," *Spade Regen* 10/8 (November 1917),30.
62. Nils G. Holm in his religio-psychological study of glossolalia among Swedish-speaking Pentecostals in Finland observed the same pattern in 1976 as was present in the early days. Nils G. Holm, *Tungotal och andedop*, Acta Universitas Uppsaliensis: Psychologia Religionum 5 (Uppsala, Sweden: University of Uppsala, 1976).
63. A.A. Boddy, "Tongues as a Seal of Pentecost," *Confidence* no. 1 (April 1908),18.
64. [A. Kok], "Van Pinkster-Conferentiën en Samenkomsten," *Spade Regen* no. 10 (June-July 1908),1. A.A. Boddy, "The Pentecostal Conference in Germany," *Confidence* 1/2 (February 1909),33.
65. A.A. Boddy, "The Conference in Germany," *Confidence* 2/1 (January 1909),7. On the Mülheim conference the following year, Polman again strongly emphasized tongues. T.M. Jeffreys, "The Recent Conference at Mulheim," *Confidence* 2/9 (September 1909),200-200a.
66. [J. Paul], "Was sollen und wollen die Pfingstgrüsse?" *Pfingstgrüsse* 1/1 (February 1909),2.
67. "Erklärung," *Pfingstgrüsse* 3/12 (18 December 1910),89-91. The declaration was made after meetings with the neutrals in Patmos and Vandsburg and was partly repeated in *Pfingstgrüsse* 5/15 (12 January 1913),115.
68. Mary Boddy, "The Real Baptism of the Holy Ghost," *Confidence* 2/11 (November 1909),260.
69. A.A. Boddy, "Speaking in Tongues: What Is It?" *Confidence* 3/5 (May 1910),104.
70. A.A. Boddy, "Tongues: the Pentecostal Sign: Love, the Evidence of Continuance," *Confidence* 3/11 (November 1910),261.
71. "The Place of Tongues in the Pentecostal Movement," *Confidence* 4/8 (August 1911),176.
72. The Polman couple did not try to find answers as to why some did not speak in tongues, but left it to the Lord. Ibid., pp. 177-78.
73. "A Consultative International Pentecostal Council," *Confidence* 5/6 (June 1912),133.
74. "Declaration," *Confidence* 5/12 (December 1912),277. In the German translation "the outward manifestation" read "eine entsprechende Kundgebung oder Offenbarung des Geistes." "Erklärung," *Pfingstgrüsse* 5/15 (12 January 1913),114-15.
75. G.R. Polman, "Zooals de Geest hun gaf uit te spreken," *Spade Regen*

no. 41 (January 1917),1-2. Translated as "As the Spirit Gave Them Utterance," *Weekly Evangel*, (24 February 1917),5-6. Repeated in *Spade Regen* 17/3 (June 1924),38-41.

76. A. Zijp, *De dwaling der Pinkstergemeente te Amsterdam* (Amsterdam: by author, 1929), pp. 6-7.

77. W. Polman, "Subsequent Blessing in Holland," *Confidence* no. 5 (August 1908),18.

78. *Confidence* 2/2 (February 1909),34. Boddy and Polman spoke in similar terms.

79. A. and E. Kok, "Wien zal ik zenden?" *Spade Regen* no. 12 (November 1909),2. The failure of using the gift of tongues for mission by American missionaries had also reached the Dutch press: Winckel, "Gemengd Nieuws," *De Heraut* no. 1624 (14 February 1909),3.

80. During a prayer meeting on 7 November 1908 one girl spoke in tongues. Someone present who had lived in South Africa for some years recognized it as Swazi and translated the message as follows: "Jesus, Jesus Your name be praised. Great, good and lovely You are, slain for all. Your name I know; unto Your name be honour. Jesus, Shepherd, You give peace by Your blood!" Thereafter she sang in Swazi: "Hallelujah, Hallelujah, Your sacrifice and Your Name be more honour, more honour, Amen." "Talen van Menschen," *Spade Regen* no. 4 (November 1908),3.
    Two other examples were reported by Percy Corry. During the dedication of the Amsterdam missionary training home in 1912 Corry witnessed one of the lady students from Terschelling speaking in pure English, though she did not know the language: "Oh, Lord Jesus, I do love Thee." Corry added that the words "love" and "thee" are hard to pronounce for a Dutch person, but they were spoken without any trace of a Dutch accent. In 1926 Corry recalled how Polman once in Wales admonished a believer for his unbelief while speaking in perfect Welsh through the gift of tongues. P.N. Corry, "Holland," *Confidence* 5/11 (November 1912),260; Idem, "1 Korinthe 14," *Spade Regen* 18/12 (March 1926),184.

81. G.R. Polman, "Zooals de Geest hun gaf uit te spreken," *Spade Regen* no. 41 (January 1917),1-2.

82. Ibid. H. Bavinck, "De glossolalie of gave der vreemde talen," *Spade Regen* no. 29 (March-May 1912),2-3. Quoted from H. Bavinck, *Magnalia Dei* (Kampen: J.H. Kok). G.R. Polman "Wat Pinksteren voor ons moet zijn," *Spade Regen* 22/11 (February 1930),165.

83. The other reason why Schrenk felt the tongues were not biblical was because they did not sound like a foreign language. Not being a foreign language according to Acts 2 nor being a prayer according to 1 Cor. 14, the manifestations at Kassel were repudiated as unbiblical. E. Schrenk, *Die Kasseler Bewegung* (Kassel: Ernst Rötgers Verlag, 1907), pp. 5-6.

84. K. Lettau, "The Pentecostal Movement in the Light of Scripture," *Confidence* 2/1 (January 1909),10.

85. "Discussion on 'Tongues,'" *Confidence* 1/2 (February 1909),35.

86. "Testimony by Mrs. Polman," *Confidence* 2/9 (September 1909),200a.

87. Polman, "Zoals de Geest."

88. G.R. Polman, "Met nieuwe tongen," *Spade Regen* 18/4 (July 1925),51.

89. G.R. Polman, "Gij zult Mijn getuigen zijn," *Spade Regen* 13/8 (November 1920), 115. Percy Corry's teaching reached the same conclusions. He saw a fivefold usage of tongues in private: to speak to God; to pray; to praise; to thank; and to edify the believer. In public it functioned as a sign to the unbeliever and as prophecy to the believers. Percy Corry "1 Korinthe 14," *Spade Regen* 18/10-12 (January-March 1926),150-52; 166-69; 183-88.

90. For a thorough discussion of glossolalia see William J. Samarin in *Tongues of Men and Angels: The Religious Language of Pentecostalism* (New York: Macmillan, 1972); Cyril, G. Williams, *Tongues of the Spirit: A Study of Pentecostal Glossolalia and Related Phenomena* (Cardiff: University of Wales, 1981); H. Newton Malony and A. Adams Lovekin, *Glossolalia: Behavioral Science Perspectives on Speaking in Tongues* (New York/Oxford: Oxford University Press, 1985).

For a collection of research papers from exegetical, historical, theological, psychological, and socio-cultural perspectives see Watson E. Mills, *Speaking in Tongues: A Guide to Research on Glossolalia* (Grand Rapids: William B. Eerdmans, 1986).

Recent psychopathological research found none of the glossolalic groups more abnormal or hysteric than the general population, while in some cases they were even found to be more mentally healthy. Malony and Lovekin, p. 257.

91. Malony and Lovekin, p. 38. William J. Samarin in *Tongues of Men and Angels* detected that albeit no cognitive content was transmitted, a definite sense of emotional meaning was understood.

92. Walter J. Hollenweger, "After Twenty Years' Research on Pentecostalism," p. 7.

93. Significantly the later Dutch Pentecostal leader J.E. van den Brink, taking tongues as being directed to God, after more than 50 years of experience in Pentecostal meetings all over the country, concluded that tongues were generally followed by a prophecy, a revelation, or a word of knowledge, but hardly ever by an actual interpretation. Having witnessed thousands of alleged "interpretations" he noticed "that an interpretation of the tongue itself hardly occurs among us. We have not experienced this and if we ever heard it, it did not satisfy us." J.E. van den Brink, *De eerste brief aan de Corinthiërs* (Gorichem: Kracht van Omhoog, 1985), p. 409.

94. "Prophetic Messages and Their Trustworthiness," *Confidence* 2/2 (February 1909),42-44.

95. Ibid.

96. Ibid. *Confidence* 2/7 (July 1909),160-61; 5/2 (February 1912),30-33.

97. "Personal Messages: Their Dangers," *Confidence* 5/2 (February 1912),31.

98. Ibid. In the same article Mrs. Polman stated about the gift of

prophecy, "It does not only mean speaking in messages, but I believe it is to preach the Word, to edify and build up the Church." In later years Polman did prophesy in meetings, according to many eyewitnesses.

99. "Discussion on Tongues," *Confidence* 2/2 (February 1909),36-37.
100. Ibid., p. 37.
101. "The Leaders' Special Conference," *Confidence* 2/7 (July 1909),160-61.
102. G.R. Polman, "Soulish Not Spiritual," *Confidence* 7/7 (July 1914),136.
103. W. Polman, "Subsequent Blessing in Holland," *Confidence* no. 5 (August 1908),18-19.
104. Ibid.
105. Ibid.
106. The practice of healing and exorcism is only briefly described in relation to early Dutch Pentecostalism. For a theological discussion on both physical healing and exorcism: K.J. Kraan, *Genezing en bevrijding* 3 vols. (Kampen: J.H. Kok, 1983-86). On exorcism: W.C. van Dam, *Dämonen und besessene* (Aschaffenburg: Paul Pattloch Verlag, 1970); Idem, *Demonen eruit, in Jezus' naam!* (Kampen: J.H. Kok, 1973); Idem, "Dogmatici over de duivel," *Bulletin voor Charismatische Theologie* 3/1 (1980),2-10; W.W. Verhoef, "Exorcisme," *Bulletin voor Charismatische Theologie* no. 7 (Easter 1981),27-33.

    For a discussion of the para-medical and para-psychological side: W.H.C. Tenhaeff, *Magnetiseurs, Somnambules en Gebedsgenezers*, 3d rev. ed. (The Hague: Leopold, 1980); Morton T. Kelsey, *The Christian & the Supernatural* (London: Search Press, 1977).

    For a comprehensive and critical discussion on healing: Colin Brown, *Miracles and the Critical Mind* (Grand Rapids: William B. Eerdmans, 1984); Morton T. Kelsey, *Healing and Christianity* (New York: Harper & Row, 1973).

107. A.A. Boddy, "A Visit to Holland," *Confidence* no. 6 (September 1908),8.
108. H. Meijer, who attended some public meetings as an observer, reported that during a time of prayer suddenly two men came forward to the platform. Polman informed the public that they came for deliverance and asked the members to join in prayer. The singing and praying continued. After about 3 minutes Polman said: "One of them is delivered. Praise the Lord!" Meijer added that more attention was not given. H. Meijer to J.H. Gunning J.Hz., Amsterdam, 30 August 1911.

    In *Spade Regen* no. 4 (November 1908),4, Polman reported in some cases demons had to be cast out before the Holy Spirit could take full possession of spirit, soul and body. According to eyewitnesses exorcisms did not occur in the meetings, but separately, which most likely was the case during the later years.

109. G.R. Polman to G.A. Wumkes, 27 March 1917; 25 June 1917; 10 July 1917; 16 July 1917; *Spade Regen* 10 (1917),4, 8, 27-28.
110. Polman to Wumkes, 25 June 1917. With his letter of 22 July 1917 Polman enclosed a report of his experiences with spiritism and urged Wumkes to write a study on the subject. Unfortunately Polman's report was not found.
111. G.R. Polman, "Teekenen en Wonderen," *Spade Regen* 11/8 (November 1918),29.

    For more information on Spiritism: M. Beversluis, "Spiritualisme en Spiritisme," *Kerk en Secte* 3/5 no. 56 (Baarn: Hollandia, 1909). Beversluis, a Netherlands reformed minister, mentioned prophecy, speaking in tongues, healing, and other manifestations as occurring in their midst. He also named several ministers who practiced spiritism, including himself. Beversluis saw spiritism, or rather called spiritualism, as a new revelation of the glorious kingdom of God. He also edited the periodical *Geest en Leven* and had written an extensive study on the Holy Spirit: *De Heilige Geest* (Utrecht: C.H.E. Breijer, 1896). In this remarkable study, thus far ignored by theologians, he had explained the speaking in tongues as speaking in actual languages not learned by the speaker, which exegesis he saw vindicated by spiritistic manifestations.

    Cf. concerning the influence of spiritualism in the Netherlands: Emma Hardinge Britten, *Nineteenth Century Miracles; or, Spirits and Their Work in Every Country of the Earth* (New York: William Britten, 1884), pp. 326-41; Nicolette A. Bruining, *Geestelijke Stroomingen*, Religieuze Inwijding, no. 6 (Amsterdam: Maatschappij voor goedkope lectuur, n.d.).

    Cf. concerning the relationship between spiritualism and glossolalia: T. Flournoy, *From India to the Planet Mars: A Study of a Case of Somnambulism with Glossolalia* (New Hyde Park: New York University, 1963, first published 1900); E. Lombard, *De la glossolalie chez les premiers Chrétiens et des phénomènes similaires* (Lausanne: Bridel, 1910); Idem, "Essai d'une classification des phénomènes glossolalies," *Archives de Psychologie* 7 (1907),1-51.

112. His full name was Pieter Jansen Jakob Reinder Tonke Pilon, born at Heemse. His thesis for the degree of medical doctor was entitled, "Over de bacteriologische cholera-diagnostiek," (University of Amsterdam, April 1911). Once he had visited Boddy, who called him "a dear Pentecostal brother," at Sunderland: A.A. Boddy "Holland," *Confidence* 3/10 (October 1910),242. His testimony of his Spirit baptism was published as "A Dutch University Student's Pentecost," *Cloud of Witnesses to Pentecost in India* no. 8 (August 1909),25-265. After three years in the Pentecostal assembly he left for Tübingen in April 1911, and finally left for Java in September 1911 to work in the mission hospital of the Salatiga Mission at Purwodadi Grobogan. Presumably there he became estranged from the Pentecostals.
113. "Vriendelijk Verzoek," *Spade Regen* no. 14 (January-March 1910),3.

Pilon asked 8 very detailed questions, which was perhaps one reason why he received little or no response.

114. A. Winckel, "De Pinksterbeweging," *Ons Orgaan* 12/165 (26 January 1917),11, mentioned that Pilon received no response at all. Winckel errs by stating that the old issues of *Spade Regen* contained many testimonies of healing. During the first 4 years only 2 testimonies were printed. When Pilon placed his request in 1910 just one testimony had been published.

115. The one clear example of testifying "in faith" was by a former Baptist lady J.E. van der Steur from Haarlem: *Spade Regen* no. 30 (June-July 1912),3. Four months later she was regained by the Baptists and denounced her earlier testimony complaining it had been changed by the editor: *De Christen* 31/1333 (15 November 1912),365. Evidently the anticipated healing was not received.

116. B. Wielenga in "De genezing op het gebed," *Schild en Pijl* 1/5 (1918),25, stated that recently someone had been raised from the dead in a Pentecostal meeting. J.H. Gunning J.Hz. reviewing Wielenga's publication asked for full details concerning the "Lazarus-redivivus" in "Onze Leestafel," *Pniël* 27/1397 (5 October 1918). A. d'Ablaing from Velp, who sympathized with the Pentecostals, responded with information received from Mrs. Polman. The miracle had happened 8 years earlier to a young woman personally known to Mrs. Polman. A. d'Ablaing to Gunning, Velp, 30 November 1918.

The remarkable event had occurred in Mülheim shortly after Easter 1910. The woman had been dead for two and one-half hours. Emil Humburg reported: "I felt for the pulse and there was none. There was also no breath, the lower jaw hung down, and the body was cold." The body came back to life by the fervent prayers of the assembly led by Humburg. The report made no mention of a doctor having been present to confirm the death. See "Raised from the Dead," *Confidence* 3/7 (July 1910),158-60; "Opgestaan uit de dooden," *Spade Regen* no. 17 (August-September 1910),2-3; cf. Walter J. Hollenweger, *Enthusiastisches Christentum* (Zurich: Zwingli Verlag, 1969), p. 406.

117. G.A. Wumkes, *Nei Sawntich Jier* (Boalsert: A.J. Osinga, 1949), p. 437. Another example of a healing reported by a non-Pentecostal and never mentioned in *Spade Regen* is given by C.P. Siebeles in her letter of 20 March 1911 to J.H. Gunning J.Hz. It concerned a foster child staying in her home who had suffered of a longstanding eye infection and had been treated in hospital without success. After a Pentecostal lady had prayed for her she recovered within one day. Six months later the eyes were still perfect.

118. There were no special articles about exorcism found in *Spade Regen* and not many about healing.

119. John A. Harris, "Genezing door Verlossing," *Spade Regen* no. 11 (August-October 1909),1-2; D. Bryant, "Verlossing en Goddelijke Genezing," no. 14 (January-March 1910),2-3; A.B. Simpson, "Goddelijke Genezing door den Heiligen Geest," no. 20 (December

1910),2-3; "Geen enkel Zwakke onder al hun Stammen," no. 41 (January 1917),3 (taken over from unknown source).

120. "Gods Weg tot Genezing," *Spade Regen* no. 17 (August-September 1910),3; John A. Dowie "God's Way of Healing," *Leaves of Healing* 15/23 (24 September 1904),790.

121. Ibid. Wumkes, p. 21.

122. Boddy took a similar stand in "Health in Christ," *Confidence* 3/8 (August 1910),175-70.

123. Wielenga, p. 11. W.J.J. Velders, "Gebedsgenezing," in *Christelijke Encyclopedie*, vol. 6, ed. F.W. Grosheide et al. (Kampen: J.H. Kok, 1931), pp. 183-84.

    Contrary to this *De Pinkstergemeente en hare dwalingen getoetst aan Gods Woord*, Rapport van de commissie inzake de "Pinkster-beweging" aan de classis Meppel der Gereformeerde Kerken (Hoogeveen, 1932), p. 12, reported that the Pentecostals rejected the use of medicines and doctors. This report however dealt with the Gemeente des Heeren, an independent branch of the Pentecostal movement, that indeed repudiated all medical help.

124. Engeline B. Burghoorn, "Die al uw krankheden geneest," *Spade Regen* 10/9 (December 1917),36.

125. W. Polman to T. van Tuinen, Amsterdam, 18 July 1917. From this letter it appears that in a similar case at Amsterdam where the parents had not called a doctor and their daughter died, the body had been taken away by the authorities "only because the parents had not just called the doctor."

126. G.R. Polman, "Goddelijke genezing naar de Schrift," *Spade Regen* 15/9 (December 1922),139-41.

127. Ibid.

128. P.N. Corry, "Goddelijke genezing door de verzoening," *Spade Regen* 19/5 (August 1926),69-70.

129. The Dutch edition of the Heidelberg catechism is subdivided in 52 Sundays. Sunday 10 contains the question (What do you understand by the providence of God?) and the answer number 27. J.N. Bakhuizen van den Brink, ed., *De Nederlandsche Belijdenisgeschriften* (Amsterdam: Holland, 1940), p. 161.

    Cf. K.J. Kraan, *Opdat u genezing ontvangt* (Hoornaar: Gideon, 1973), pp. 194-201. Kraan demonstrated how the text and the scriptural references of the catechism are in flat contradiction.

130. Wielenga, p. 24.

131. Ibid.

132. H. Meijer in his letter to J.H. Gunning J.Hz., Amsterdam, 30 August 1911, reported his visits to meetings of the Pentecostal assembly and of faith healer Van Leeuwen. Meijer noticed the clear difference between Van Leeuwen, who violently opposed medical aid and openly attacked the churches, and the Pentecostals, who did none of these and left a rather positive impression.

133. In the 1950s the ministry of healing was extensively discussed in the Netherlands Reformed Church resulting in their pastoral letter:

Vragen rondom de gebedsgenezing (The Hague: Lectuurbureau der Ned. Hervormde Kerk, 1959).

134. Already at the Hamburg Conference in December 1908 pastor K. Littau (Lic.) presented a paper on this topic: *Confidence* 2/1 (January 1909),11, 16; E. Edel, *Die Pfingstbewegung im Lichte der Kirchengeschichte* (Brieg: by the author, 1910).

135. Cf. A.S. Booth-Clibborn, "De laatste Heils-Conferenties te Londen en Sunderland," *Spade Regen* no. 16 (June-July 1910),2-4. Cf. E. Edel, "Gottes Liebesgedanken mit dem Mensch: oder wie das Himmelreich auf Erden kommt," *Pfingstgrüsse* 5 (1912),9-12; 17-19; 26-30; 34-37; 42-44; 50-54; 59-60; 67-69; 74-75; 81-84. Also published as brochure by Emil Humburg, Mülheim, 1912.

136. V. S., "Luther," *Spade Regen* 10/7 (October 1917),26. The revival movement under the Silesian Caspar Schwenckfeld, repudiated by Luther, was a particular case in point.

137. *Spade Regen* 15/1 (March 1922),15; 15/3 (June 1922),36; 15/5 (August 1922),67-68.

138. Wumkes, p. 22.

139. "Ziet, Hij komt!" *Spade Regen* no. 8 (April 1909),1-2.

140. "De laatste dagen," *Spade Regen* no. 6 (Janaury-February 1909),3.

141. G.R. Polman, "Gekomen . . . komende naar de Schriften," *Spade Regen* no. 32 (January 1913),1; cf. Idem, "Gaat uit, Hem tegemoet!" no. 28 (January-February 1912),1-2; Idem, "De eerste en de tweede Advent," no. 27 (December 1911),1.

142. G.R. Polman, "Jezus' Wederkomst," *Spade Regen* no. 40 (July 1916),1.

143. Luke 21:24 speaks of Jerusalem being trodden by gentiles until the time of the gentiles is fulfilled. The time of the gentiles was reported to have commenced with the fall of Jerusalem and captivity to Babylon, which was dated 604 B.C., and was said to last seven times. The seven times were explained as $7 \times 360 = 2,520$ years, which ended in 1917 with the Turks leaving Jerusalem. *Spade Regen* 10/10 (January 1918),38-39. In the following issue it was stated that the year 1917 was equal to 1335 on the Islamic calendar, which was brought in relation with Daniel 12:12 where reference is made to a waiting period of 1335 days. *Spade Regen* 10/11 (February 1918),43.

144. *Spade Regen* 10/10 (January 1918),38.

145. G.R. Polman, "Ontwaakt!" *Spade Regen* 11/3 (June 1918),9.

146. Ibid.

147. G.R. Polman, "Die Dag en die Ure," *Spade Regen* 11/5 (August 1918),17.

148. *Spade Regen* 11/8 (November 1918),32; 11/9 (December 1918),36.

149. *Spade Regen* 11/10 (January 1919),40.

150. J. Paul, *De oplossing van het wereldraadsel* (Amsterdam: G.R. Polman, 1920).

151. G.R. Polman, "Ontwaakt," *Spade Regen* 13/6 (September 1920),79.

152. Idem, "Het einde aller dingen," *Spade Regen* 13/10 (January 1921),145.

153. *Spade Regen* 18/1 (April 1925),16.
154. Usually these articles were copied from other sources. One such article went so far as to suggest 1934 as a possible date for Christ's return. "Zijn wederkomst nadert . . . tekenen van het einde," *Spade Regen* 18/9 (December 1925),138-41.
155. G.R. Polman, "De roeping der gemeente als het lichaam van Christus," *Spade Regen* 17/12 (March 1925),179.
      B. Kedde in "Uw Koninkrijk kome," 17/12 (March 1925),190, explained the rapture as being part of God's plan to save the whole world:

> The teaching of Jesus' return can be made so terribly egoistic. Often one leaves the nations nothing but judgement after the rapture, while oneself thinks to "escape it." God wants to reach the nations and also the judgement will work wholesomely. We have to understand, that exactly through the rapture of the church, the peace on earth is brought closer.

156. A.S. Booth-Clibborn, "De laatste Heils-Conferenties," *Spade Regen* no. 16 (June-July 1910),4.
157. Donald Gee, "Waarom wordt Pinksteren tegengestaan?" *Spade Regen* 22/5 (August 1929),70. Translated from *Redemption Tidings*.
158. See for an interesting discussion Gerald T. Sheppard, "Pentecostals and the Hermeneutics of Dispensationalism: The Anatomy of an Uneasy Relationship," *Pneuma* 6/2 (Fall 1984),5-33.

11 ECCLESIOLOGY

A Universal Message for a Universal Church

Initially the Pentecostals considered themselves as a religious revival movement that transcended barriers of denomination, culture, class, or race. More than anything else they seemed to belong to a universal body of believers. The context in which the movement came into being defined which of these barriers were most relevant. In the multi-racial Los Angeles the crossing of the race barrier was in the fore. Frank Bartleman witnessed, "The color line was washed away in the blood."[1] In the ecclesiastically fragmented Amsterdam the interdenominational aspect assumed prime importance. Theologically Bartleman related the miracle of "color line" being washed away to the redemptive act of Christ at the cross ("washed away in the blood"), implying that the basis of fellowship was the rebirth, not the Spirit baptism. For the Pentecostals the universal body of Christ (Polman often called it the mystical body of Christ) comprised all born-again Christians, no matter the church affiliation. Yet, it was the Spirit baptism that had made them aware of this relation and had endued them with the power to transcend the differences. In time this significant ecumenical strength was choked and finally sacrificed to denominationalism. While the concept of the church as a body of born-again believers corresponded with the Darbyist view, there was a significant distinction. Polman did not turn against the churches and did not call the born-again to leave their church. Besides, Polman did not make that sharp distinction between Israel and the church with its attendant implication of dividing the Bible into separate dispensations.

Polman's perception of the Pentecostal movement as an interdenominational revival is even more remarkable if seen with reference to his former connection with Dowie's church at Zion, whose purpose it was to "smash every other church in existence."[2] Quoting from a letter of T.B. Barratt, the first issue of *Spade Regen* (April 1908) reported:

> We love everyone and do not try to divide the churches or to separate the people of God from each other. We wish that they all receive the blessing. Christ did not die for a church or sect, but for all; and all, what His death has assured, is meant for all. Hallelujah.[3]

A little later Polman wrote:

> In connection with letters received, we gladly communicate, that this paper does not represent any church or sect. We thank God, that we may believe in the unity God wants (John 17:21-23) and that we may experience, that the cross of Christ and the Holy Spirit truly makes us one.[4]

Polman explicitly related his burden to revive the churches with his Spirit baptism:

> This blessing of God has filled my heart with overflowing love for my fellow-Christians and I cannot, but love them all, although I suffer under the spiritual opposition of the churches in general, who reject this blessing, either out of ignorance or out of bitterness.[5]

The unity among the children of God is a prevailing theme in nearly all writings of Polman. He considered any fight for the existence of a church or movement, or for a certain dogma, as "fleshly."[6] The unity Polman had in mind was a relational, not a conceptual, unity:

> The centre of Divine unity is not the unity of thoughts concerning one or the other doctrine, or a certain issue of theology. A great truth of Scripture can give occasion to an outward unity, but this is not the unity meant by Christ, when He prayed: "Till they all may be one" (John 17:21). The true unity reveals itself in diversity of form, thought and being, because the fullness of God, as it dwelled in Christ, cannot dwell in one single being.[7]

Polman saw his own position as one of edifying the whole: "The purpose of the Pentecostal revival is not to build up a church, but to build up all churches."[8] Nico Vetter later confirmed this with, "It has not been the intent of Mr. G.R. Polman to found an assembly, because one felt that this experience did not belong to the members of one or the other assembly, but to the church of Jesus Christ in general."[9] Of course one can doubt the attainability of Polman's vision and question his methodology. Naive as it may have been, it certainly was a genuine and a remarkable longing.

The separate Pentecostal meetings were justified by Polman with, "As long the church doors remain closed for this revelation of God, we are automatically forced to assemble together separate from other denominations."[10] And in 1913:

> That we are still outside the churches is not our fault. More than anything else we would love to see, that the church doors would be opened to this blessing, which God is giving, to prepare the assembly for the coming of her Lord and Saviour, but up to now is every door closed out of fear, while it in fact is the only divine way to get out the spiritual deadness.[11]

With "this revelation from God" and "this blessing" Polman referred to the Pentecostal message of unity among all believers, the manifestation of spiritual gifts and the preparation for the second coming of Christ. The mission of the Pentecostal movement was not only to evangelize the world, but also to convince a skeptical Christianity of the relevance of Pentecost.[12]

In spite of the separate meetings the Pentecostals did not consider themselves as a separate denomination. Therefore they are not found in the 10-yearly census of 1909 and hardly found in 1920. Only in 1930, after the introduction of church membership by Polman in 1925, are the Pentecostals somewhat more substantially recorded in the census. For the same reason the issue of water baptism was not emphasized, although it was practiced upon request. The Lord's Supper was celebrated quite early, perhaps even from the start, but it was an open table. Unlike the Baptists the Pentecostals did not consider water baptism a prerequisite for participation. It was open to all children of God no matter the church affiliation. The following correspondence from 1937 between two people, who bring up their memory of the Pentecostal meetings they attended during 1919 to 1923, enables us to grasp some of the open atmosphere:

> There I always had the impression of belonging to the great universal Christian church, much more than I do now. If I recall how brother Polman gave the benediction, then I felt absorbed in the whole universe in which I saw no horizon. Today when I sit in the church on Sundays, then it is as if that same benediction strikes back again from all walls and belongs to our heart like the cargo to a vessel. The prayer is for our sick, for our elderly, for our schools, for our men seated in high positions, for our sins of the past week. Oh Mart, then I say to myself: for the maids on the street, for those with scabies, for all those whom never are prayed for. Then I have the greatest trouble to attain the silence in which one hears God.[13]

Martha Visser replied with:

> What you write to me about your memories and your homesickness in connection with our "good old days" I endorse completely. Especially the peculiarity, that you also bring forward, namely that in the institutionalized and not so small church you feel yourself a kind of sectarian. While in the tiny circle, cast away by official Christianity, you experienced something of the great universal Christian church. The same I have so often ascertained myself. Logic stops here and I have often wondered: was it perhaps a matter of feelings, or was it our youth? And yet, I do not believe that; it was real and I would feel it exactly the same, supposing that I could now go through it all once more.[14]

These astonishing statements from two people, whose memories dated from before the move to denominationalism, reveal something of an overwhelming ecumenical spirit in the Pentecostal meetings, not found in the traditional church.

During the period of transition (1924-1926) Bernard Kedde, co-worker of Polman, developed some interesting thoughts. Kedde used the parable of the Good Samaritan to illustrate the miserable position of the church: wounded, robbed, and lying half-dead along the road. The many wounds denoted the many schisms and divisions. Instead of just noticing the poverty of the church and then passing by, the Pentecostals were to get off their beast (referring to their own movement!) and to identify with the universal Christian church by means of daily prayer and compassion.[15] Another time Kedde discussed the divine purpose of the revivals in the course of history. It was a call to awaken a sleeping church. The call came from the head to all the members of the body, but only a few responded. In order to preserve and deepen the blessing received, the awakened assembled together. This way they kept the light of the candlestick burning. However, in the course of history, so Kedde continued, these separated circles turned sectarian the moment they considered themselves as *the* body of Christ. The external separation was carried forward to an inward separation. As long as they were a channel between the head and the body, the Holy Spirit could use them, but as soon as they became a harbor and considered their own circle as a goal rather than as a means, the Holy Spirit withdrew. Kedde prayed: "May God deliver us from the terrible sectarian spirit, that still reigns unchallenged in various circles and groups, also in our country."[16]

Once more Kedde employed church history to clarify the purpose of the Pentecostal movement. This time he compared the various revivals with the mission of John the Baptist, that is, to be a witness of the truth. He reminded the Pentecostals to be just a witness of the truth, and not the truth itself:

> Likewise also the Pentecostal movement. What is she in this age? Is she THE truth, THE Church of Jesus Christ, THE bride? No! That everyone hears this "no" well and keeps it in mind. What then is she? A HUMAN (John 1:6). A movement, a spiritual stream up to now, in the middle of the Church of Christ.[17]

Kedde then proceeded to emphasize the humanity of the Pentecostal movement: "As a movement it is a 'human' in his weakness, short-sightedness and narrow-mindedness. Yet,

God be praised, a human 'sent by God' to the whole human race."[1] And then addressing the Christians:

> Brothers and Sisters, listen to the Divine message, that is coming to you, also by means of the Pentecostal movement in all her weakness and incompleteness. Make straight the paths in your heart, in your assembly, circle and church for the Lord, Who by His Spirit wants to revive us all to a living Christianity. The Spirit of the Lord wants to clothe the Church of Christ with great power and might, bringing her in thorough sanctification and in the possession of gifts and offices according to the Word.[19]

Summarizing it can be said that the Pentecostal ecclesiology formed an integral part of their self-understanding and of their prime message to church and world. They understood the church to be an invisible body of believers (the mystical body of Christ). The particular ministry of the Pentecostals to the body was to be of an exemplary, complementary, and temporary nature. However, Polman's hope "to lose ourselves as the Pentecostal movement into the larger body of Christianity" became frustrated.[20] Much to his regret he eventually organized the movement into a Pentecostal church and introduced church membership. Hereafter the idealistic ambition to revive Christianity gradually diminished. But, although the Pentecostal ecclesiology developed towards the free church type, the idea to be part of a universal body of believers was never quite lost.

Everyone Contributes Something

> The meetings in Pentecostal circles are organized on old-Christian lines, 1 Cor. 14:26, "When you come together every one of you has a psalm, a doctrine, a tongue, a revelation, an interpretation." On Sunday mornings one is especially focused to subjects leading to a deeper spiritual life. On Sunday evenings there is a meeting to win "souls" with an after-meeting for those who long to surrender themselves to God. Everyone who feels impelled to do so, takes part. As much as possible the spontaneous character of the meeting is maintained.[21]

The above description by Wumkes brings out some of the
main characteristics of Pentecostal meetings: spontaneity,
exercise of spiritual gifts, maximum participation. Polman
wrote to Gunning (March 1910): "In our meetings there is
much spiritual freedom and therefore the character is varied.
Sometimes there is a spirit of praise and preaching of the
Word, while another time all testify of what God is doing for
them."[22] There was a clear difference between the "mutual"
meetings and the public meetings. The first concerned prayer
sessions not open for the general public. Examining the
Pentecostal liturgy we will concentrate on the public meetings. After the pattern of the Salvation Army the evening
meetings were even less formal than the morning meetings
and carried a more evangelistic character. Visitor H. Mogridge noted in 1910: "There is no set form of worship, the
Holy Spirit is the recognized Leader and Guide, and all are
there to worship and praise God in His Holy Temple."[23]
Nevertheless most meetings did follow a general pattern.

The public meetings on Sunday morning, Sunday evening,
and Wednesday evening usually lasted two to two and
one-half hours, but sometimes the after-meetings prolonged
it to 4 hours! Except for more emotion and physical
manifestations during the first years, the order of service
remained basically the same throughout the period. One of
the members stood at the door to welcome the people, in
particular, the visitors, and to hand out songbooks if necessary. Every meeting was first put "under the precious blood"
in prayer and commenced with singing a hymn standing (on
Sunday morning always a psalm). From beginning to end the
meetings were led by Polman. More hymns and choruses
followed, mainly from the Johan de Heer songbook, then the
meeting was thrown open for prayer. H. Meijer, our valuable
observer, noted in 1911:

> Prayer takes a large part of the time. After one or more
> persons have prayed one after the other, someone starts to
> sing and immediately all join and sing along. Then again
> another starts to pray. Once I counted 13 different persons
> who prayed, every time the prayer being alternated by songs.
> Even a girl of 13 or 14 years prayed aloud. Some, like Polman

and his wife and a few others, kneel before chairs on the
platform, in prayer. The breathing of sighs and exclamations
such as: Amèn, Hallelujah! Come Lord Jesus! Praise the Lord!
Jesus, Jesus! etc. etc. are very general. Sometimes one cannot
hear the prayers because of it. Such praying, nearly always
thanksgiving for received grace and prayer for more blessing;
these sighs during the praying; and repeating the choruses of
the songs over and over again is to my opinion, for those who
take part, very exciting.[24]

During this time of open prayer gifts of prophecy, tongues,
and interpretation operated. When Polman discerned that
one was not directed by the Holy Spirit he corrected such a
person publicly. He did not allow for glossolalia without
interpretation: "the Bible says when there is no interpretation
we are to keep silent in the meeting."[25] One exemption was
when the whole assembly sang in tongues, which often was
the case. Niblock wrote: "I have never before heard such
singing in the Spirit."[26] On a sign of Polman the praying
stopped and the assembly prepared itself for the sermon. In
the evening meetings the sermon was preceded by a time of
testimonies from the public. Whenever a reference to
scripture was given you could hear the rustle of leaves all
around.[27] The message was often closed with an invitation to
come forward for salvation or baptism with the Holy Spirit.
After another season of prayer, singing, and messages in the
Spirit confirming the word preached, the meeting was ended
with the apostolic blessing for the assembly. Money offerings
were given at the exit since no collections were taken during
the meetings.

T.M. Jeffreys noticed in July 1909: "Everything was done
decently and in order, and beautiful harmony prevailed."[28]
The after-meetings (as of 1912 held in the upper room) were
for those seeking·salvation, the Spirit baptism or further
blessing, joined by those already baptized in the Spirit. In
these prayer sessions all kneeled and cried out to God, many
prayed in tongues, the already-baptized encouraged the
non-baptized in their search for the Spirit baptism.[29]

The usage of the term "samenkomst" (coming together)
instead of the more regular "eredienst" (worship service) is

indicative of the Pentecostal emphasis on fellowship and equality. One Lutheran visitor remarked in 1911, "In our opinion the mutual love and fellowship is much more practiced there, than in any other church."[30] Every member had a voice irrespective of age, sex, race, education, or wealth. This was probably the most important contribution of the Pentecostal movement to society and church. The same could be said of the Salvation Army, but by means of the Spirit baptism this element was even heightened. The simplest member could be transformed into the very voice of God through the exercise of the gifts. Children prophesied and took part in the communion. Females exercised the full range of spiritual gifts in the public meetings and participated in laying hands upon seekers for salvation, healing, or Spirit baptism, while Mrs. Polman regularly preached in the assembly.[31] The open liturgy, the free participation, the joyful atmosphere, and simple language were much more inviting to members of the working class than the traditional church services. Others, like H. Meijer, found these grass-roots elements annoying:

> I cannot understand how they can be so plain and profane. One leader for instance said at the beginning of a meeting while he was knocking on his trouser-pockets, that whosoever wanted could return home tonight with his pockets full of blessing. . . . Also he felt it better to be a boiling-over Christian than a lukewarm one: "I hope therefore, that we will all boil over tonight." . . . That someone can express himself this plain can to a certain extent be understood, but how every time a whole hall full of people can laugh about it, I cannot understand, especially not during a religious meeting. Once the singing of a song went wrong, one could not find the right tune, or two tunes were sang indifferently or something like it, in any case it sounded very strange. When it was finished Polman said smiling: "Praise the Lord, also for the mistake. Hallelujah!"[32]

The singing was accompanied by an organ, actually a large harmonium, later added to by a small string-band.[33] Around 1920 a mandolin club had been formed, also including guitars and violins, that occasionally played in the meetings.[34] During

the 1920s a choir was established. Polman, who usually led
the singing, had a good voice and formed an excellent team
with the organist G. van der Veen. The Johan de Heer
songbook contained more than 700 songs. A collection of
churchly hymns and psalms included many popular Evangelical songs from the Salvation Army, Sankey, Alexander, and
others. Later Polman had a thin songbook published to be
used in addition to the Johan de Heer songbook: *Liederen met
muziek voor bijzondere samenkomsten*. The first edition (undated) contained 11 songs, a second edition (1922) had 19
songs. Nine of these were written by W. Heuvelink, a
member of the Pentecostal assembly in Haarlem, including
three to which Mrs. Polman had written the words. Like the
songs in the Johan de Heer book the central themes were the
redemptive work of Jesus; a call to the believers to consecrate
their life in His service; the prospect of heaven and of a
speedy return of Christ compensating for the suffering of
indignity on earth. Most remarkable of this Pentecostal
songbook is the absence of songs about the Holy Spirit and
the Spirit baptism. The only song mentioning the spiritual
gifts, "Als ik de liefde niet had" (If I had not love), makes
them subordinate to love.

Special meetings were held during the annual conferences
at Easter, Whitsuntide, and Christmas, opening Friday or
Saturday and closing on Monday night. Many guests from
other parts of the country came and collective meals were
held in the hall. The overall emphasis on fellowship is also
evident in the dedication of children:

> It was a solemn moment, when these little ones, amidst the
> family that ranged themselves around them, were dedicated
> to the Lord. The Saviour has said: "Let the children come to
> Me, and do not hinder them; for to such belongs the kingdom
> of heaven." As one family the assembly arose and sang: "May
> the Lord's blessing descend upon them!" with the feeling:
> They are our children, for whom we all share responsibility,
> that they grow up in the fear of the Lord.[35]

The only record in *Spade Regen* of a wedding confirmation
concerned two couples from Delfzijl and took place during

the Monday morning meeting of the Whitsuntide conference, 1929. Little detail is given: "After a short, earnest sermon the couples were confirmed. To each was presented a Bible as a guide on their path in life. . . . After the assembly had sung them a song, the ceremony was finished."[36] Other special services concerned the celebrating of the communion and water baptism.

Water Baptism and Communion

In February 1911 *Confidence* published "An Urgent Plea for Charity and Unity" by Barratt, in which he pleaded for some form of union or alliance. He noticed the same diversity of opinions among the Pentecostals that had for centuries divided the children of God:

> At the commencement of the Revival this was scarcely noticed, but many who formerly were Lutherans, Methodists, Baptists, Quakers, and so on, still retain their old views regarding various important questions. The Revival has not changed this. The object, value, time, and method of observing water baptism is still a matter of discussion, likewise the necessity, meaning, and importance of the Lord's Supper, and the proper method for conducting it. Besides this, there are other questions on which many do not agree. Even in the matter that interests us all so greatly: the Tongues.[37]

In particular the water baptism had been controversial:

> Although, as we have seen, our opinions may vary concerning the meaning and importance of the Lord's Supper, or Breaking of Bread, there seems to be no barrier, on that account, preventing us from meeting together in social communion on such occasions. Neither do the different opinions concerning tongues need to cause any ill-feeling amongst us, or any other question; but it does seem that when we come to the subject of water baptism the case is different. This ought not to be so, but the opinions are so decided and the methods so different, that nothing but the grace of God and brotherly love will be able to keep us together as ONE BODY.[38]

As Barratt perceived water baptism as being the greatest threat to the unity, he proposed that everyone should be at liberty to act in accordance with his personal view of the matter, without being criticized, judged, or condemned by the others. The subject was not to be discussed during the meetings, conferences, and conventions. Baptismal services were suggested to be held apart from the regular Pentecostal meetings. The dedication of children by the laying on of hands as well as infant baptism (if so desired by the parents) and adult baptism should all be possible "in the spirit of love, respect, and mutual forbearance." In case the leader of the assembly was unable to perform the baptism, for conscience' sake, Barratt proposed one of the elders or deacons or someone else be allowed to do so. This way Barratt felt the wants of all were satisfied and division was avoided.[39]

Though it did not come to a union or alliance as Barratt intended, it would seem that J. Paul, Boddy, Polhill, and Niblock endorsed Barratt's proposal on water baptism. Polhill wrote, "I think we are entitled to hold our views as firmly as we like, be they sprinkling or immersion, but have no right to force them upon our brother, or insist that he is wrong and we are right."[40] While Paul (Lutheran), Boddy (Anglican), and Barratt (Methodist) advocated infant baptism, Polman (former disciple of Dowie) supported believers' baptism by threefold immersion. Under influence of Pethrus (former Baptist) Barratt would later change to the Baptist understanding. Since Polman from the start stood for believers' baptism, his flexible attitude on the issue became more significant.

In line with his vision for an interdenominational revival Polman in his publications was initially silent about water baptism, though it was practiced upon request.[41] As mentioned before, the Immanuel Hall was built in 1912 without a baptistery. Wumkes' observation in 1916 that "the water baptism is considered of minor importance, but is administered by immersion upon request" was no doubt correct for the early period. When Polman had the article reprinted as a brochure the statement was altered thus: "As water baptism applies in general the believers baptize by immersion."[42]

The first reference in *Spade Regen* to a water baptism service is dated September 1917. Thereafter such baptismal services are reported about once a year. They were always held in a hired swimming pool during a Sunday afternoon in August or September. Pentecostal believers from the other circles and assemblies in the country came and joined the feast. The time in between the three meetings (morning, afternoon, and evening) was used for meals and fellowship in Immanuel. The evening meeting was filled with testimonies from those baptized and closed with the celebrating of the Lord's Supper. As of Easter 1925 the baptismal ceremonies could be held inside Immanuel. It became a pattern to keep them on the Monday afternoon of each Easter and Whitsuntide conference, followed by testimonies on the "crown-evening" (i.e., the last evening) of the conference.[43] The baptistery had been built in underneath the floor right in front of the platform. After removing the first rows of chairs, the baptistery became visible by rolling away the cover, which by an ingenious system disappeared below the platform.

The act of water baptism, sometimes called a "holy sacrament," was usually explained in terms of a burial with Christ in order to be resurrected with Him in newness of life (Romans 6:4). This meaning was accurately portrayed by the mode of immersion. The close connection between water baptism and Spirit baptism was stressed too; the first being an outward image of the latter (though the one was never made a prerequisite to the other).[44] Even children nine years old were baptized. On several occasions German visitors were baptized, who during the conference had become convinced of its necessity. The candidates wore long white robes, while Polman was dressed in a special waterproof suit of black color.[45] Baptism was conducted by threefold immersion with the trinitarian formula of Matthew 28:19.[46] The decisive distinction with infant baptism was not the immersion, but the confession. Water baptism was only practiced by believers who could testify of their faith, no matter whether they had already been baptized as an infant. Unlike the Baptists, and many Pentecostals today, a baptism by sprinkling was acceptable when it had been received upon confession. Even one of the elders, who had been sprinkled as Doopsgezind (Mennonite) believer, was never baptized by immersion.[47] Accordingly water baptism was not a condition for membership or for partaking of the Lord's Supper.

The Lord's Supper was after Protestant fashion called "Avondmaal" or "Heilig Avondmaal" (Holy Supper). The first reference in *Spade Regen* to the actual celebrating (June 1917) stated: "The first Sunday of every month we celebrate the Lord's Supper after the evening meeting. These are always times of deepest earnestness and mighty workings of the Spirit."[48] From other sources we learn that it was already celebrated in the early years. Pastor Niblock reported of his visit in December 1909:

> Sunday being the first Sunday in the month, the communion service was held after the evening service. It was a very simple service. A message on the Death of Christ was given, a short season of prayer, then the Pastor, after giving thanks, handed the Bread and Wine to the congregation. In Amsterdam no one is allowed to partake of the Bread and Wine unless they first sign a paper saying they are right with God and man and have perfect love towards all. The service was impressive because of its simplicity, and a most restful, quiet spirit was there. We were children in the Father's presence, worshipping Him for what He is, not for what He has given alone. Before the communion service one or two came forward to get right with God before partaking of the bread and wine. After this service we again went to prayer, when several were prayed with for the Baptism. The meetings at Amsterdam are ideal, nearer to Pentecost than any I have previously seen.[49]

The solemn and earnest atmosphere seems to have been a main characteristic. One Lutheran informant wrote in 1911: "One of us partook of the Lord's Supper, which is going on there very solemnly. There is as much oversight as possible by pointing out in all earnestness that nobody should use it in an unworthy manner."[50] The practice of signing a paper before partaking is, apart from the account by Niblock, unknown and certainly was not a custom during later years. The personal conviction of being right with God was the prime condition. From later years it is remembered that children of about 15 years old did partake. The celebration was regarded as a proclamation of the death of Christ; as an identification of the believer with His death and resurrection and consequently with His body; and as a proclamation of the imminent second coming.[51] The Lord's Supper was not limited to the first Sunday of the month, but was also celebrated on other occasions such as during the conferences, on the evening following a baptismal service, on Good Friday, and on the watch-night service.[52]

The table was only present in the hall on the days the communion was served. The elements, ordinary bread and wine, were administered by Polman and distributed among the members in the hall by the elders. Though the form of the communion was rather traditional with Polman acting as the priest or "dominé," the members were deeply involved. The partaking of the bread and of the traditional cup strengthened their fellowship with Christ and with each other. Sometimes people received healing or the Spirit baptism while partaking.[53] Communion and water baptism were visible celebrations of spiritual identification with Christ anticipating the heavenly wedding feast.

NOTES

1. Frank Bartleman, *Azusa Street* (Plainfield, NJ: Logos International, 1980), p. 54.
2. Rolvix Harlan, *John Alexander Dowie and the Christian Catholic Apostolic Church in Zion* (Ph.D. thesis, University of Chicago. Evansville, WI: Press of R.M. Antes, 1906), p. 91.
3. *Spade Regen* no. 1 (April 1908),1.
4. *Spade Regen* no. 7 (March 1909),4.
5. Polman to Gunning, 12 March 1910.
6. *Spade Regen* 14/10 (January 1922),52.
7. G.R. Polman, "De Goddelijke Eenheid," *Spade Regen* 10/6 (September 1917),22.
8. *Spade Regen* 12/3 (June 1919),37.
9. Nico Vetter to A.B.W.M. Kok. Quoted by A.B.W.M. Kok, "De Heilige Geest en de latere geestdrijvers," in *De Heilige Geest*, ed. J.H. Bavinck, P. Prins and G. Brillenburg Wurth (Kampen: J.H. Kok, 1949), p. 289.
10. G.R. Polman to J.H. Gunning J.Hz., Amsterdam, 12 March 1910.
11. Polman to Gunning, Amsterdam, 7 January 1913. In a letter to G.A. Wumkes dated 27 February 1915, Polman brought up the question of how to reach the believers in various churches, as there pastors in general were prejudiced against the Pentecostal movement: ". . . is it good to found a Pentecostal assembly? If so, what are those, who still are members of the different existing churches, to do?" It would seem that Wumkes encouraged Polman to get organized into a free church.

12. As the cross was the point of intersection in human history, so Pentecost was the point of intersection between the wise and foolish virgins in the eschatological parable of Jesus. G.R. Polman, "De Verborgenheid Gods," *Spade Regen* 11/10 (January 1919),38.
13. Joko Andrea to Martha Visser, The Hague, 11 March 1937.
14. Martha Visser to Joko Andrea, The Hague, March 1937.
15. B. Kedde, "De gewonde en de beroofde kerk," *Spade Regen* 17/5 (August 1924),77-79. In a previous article Kedde had similarly compared Christianity in general with the lukewarm Laodicean church (Revelation 3), while the time had come for the real church, the Philadelphian church, to be revealed. This Philadelphian church was not a particular group, circle or movement, but a collection of true believers, who would be used as a blessing to the whole. B. Kedde, "De woonplaats Gods in de gemeente," *Spade Regen* 16/12 (March 1924),181-85.
16. B. Kedde, "Wat zijn de verschillende opwekkingen in der loop der tijden," *Spade Regen* 17/7 (October 1924),107-09.
17. B. Kedde, "De stem des roependen," *Spade Regen* 18/4 (August 1925),71-74.
18. Ibid.
19. Ibid.
20. *Spade Regen* 18/1 (April 1925),16.
21. Wumkes, p. 19.
22. G.R. Polman to J.H. Gunning J.Hz., Amsterdam, 12 March 1910.
23. H. Mogridge, "Holland and Antwerp," *Confidence* 3/10 (October 1910),243.
24. H. Meijer to J.H. Gunning J.Hz., Amsterdam, 30 August 1911.
25. G.R. Polman, "Soulish Not Spiritual," *Confidence* 7/7 (July 1914),136.
26. Niblock, "A Third German Conference," *Confidence* 3/1 (January 1910),19.
27. Ibid.
28. T.M. Jeffreys, "Conference at Mülheim," *Confidence* 2/8 (August 1909),189.
29. H. Meijer to J.H. Gunning J.Hz., 30 August 1911; C.P. Siebeles to J.H. Gunning J.Hz., Amsterdam, 20 March 1911.
30. Siebeles.
31. Cor. 14:34 about women keeping silent during the church meetings was explained by referring to the oriental situation whereby the women were seated apart from the men and conversations between wives and husbands were disruptive. Therefore the apostle had required married women, who were used to asking questions of their husbands, to keep silent. Consequently the text did not deal with female ministry.

    On the Sunderland conference in 1914 the place of women in the church was discussed among the leaders. While female ministry was fully endorsed the general opinion seems to have been against women ruling over the assembly, unless men were not available. Mrs. Polman described her position as the helpmate of her husband. Whenever she

felt impelled to give a message she always asked the pastor for
permission to speak.

Percy Corry, "1 Korinthe 14," *Spade Regen* 18/12 (March 1926),187;
"Woman's Place in the Church," *Confidence* 7/11 (November
1914),208-09, 212-14; W. Polman, "Zij zullen tot één vleesch
wezen," *Spade Regen* no. 41 (January 1917),3-4.

32. Meijer to J.H. Gunning J.Hz., 30 August 1911.
33. Novel writer Jan de Hartog, son of Dr. A.H. den Hartog, in his youth
    attended the same school as Theo Polman (born 1915). In his
    Herinneringen aan Amsterdam (Amsterdam/Brussels: Elsevier, 1981),
    pp. 48-49, Jan de Hartog relates the following (invented) story:

    Theo invited us to target-practice with a catapult on the roof of the
    Pentecostal assembly on what you could call "living bait." The
    assembly was not rich enough for an organ, thus their singing was
    accompanied by a string-trio. The cellist was a fat lazy man who
    every time when he finished scratching immediately fell asleep
    with that big brown case between his thighs. We were invited to
    aim pebbles through the flap-window at the violoncello; whoever
    scored a direct hit was rewarded with a loud "pong" and an
    unintelligible shout by the big fellow, whereupon we fled from the
    roof on hands and feet.

34. A photo of the mandolin club from this period shows 16 members (12
    female and 4 male), mainly youngsters.
35. *Spade Regen* 18/5 (August 1925),78. Sometimes the dedication of
    children took place at home. Hendrika van Ravenzwaay, born 1912,
    remembered that Polman came to their home to consecrate the three
    children. She was 6 years old and sat on Polman's knee. She has never
    forgotten how Polman urged her to be an example for her smaller
    brother and sister. Hendrika van Strijland-van Ravenzwaay, Inter-
    view, 16 August 1986.
36. *Spade Regen* 22/3 (June 1929),46. In the Netherlands weddings can
    only be solemnized in a registry office. Afterwards the wedding may
    be confirmed by the church.
37. T.B. Barratt, "An Urgent Plea for Charity and Unity," *Confidence* 4/2
    (February 1911),31.
38. Ibid., *Confidence* 4/3 (March 1911),63.
39. Ibid.
40. Ibid.
41. When a believer from Sneek, where the Pentecostal circle largely
    consisted of former Baptists, requested of Polman to be baptized,
    Polman was not unwilling to do so, but wrote discreetly:

    It should for us not just be a matter of being baptized, what there
    ought to be is the experience of Rom. 6. The old life must have
    died and have become alive to God. How many boast on the
    water baptism, while they are still in the old man. First there must
    be a life that has gone through the death and brings forth fruits
    worthy of the conversion. Then the water baptism is a public
    testimony that one has become one plant with Jesus in His death

and, as natural consequence thereof, in His resurrection. I will be thankful to God, when this is your testimony and others can confirm it. Then we will gladly baptize you in the name of the Father, and the Son and the Holy Spirit. G.R. Polman to a "dear brother" at Sneek, Amsterdam, 17 July 1912.

42. G.A. Wumkes, "De Pinksterbeweging voornamelijk in Nederland," *Stemmen des Tijds* 5/11 (September 1916),267. Ibid., (Utrecht: G.J.A. Ruys, 1916), p. 19. This was the only substantial alteration made, next to a few corrections of minor errors. Polman obtained permission from Wumkes to do so.

43. Occasionally baptismal services were held on other days as well, like in August 1925, January 1926, and August 1926. When a baptism service was held on the Monday after Easter, there was probably no communion in the evening, since this was already celebrated on the Good Friday evening. Likewise with the Whitsuntide conference when the communion was celebrated on the Sunday evening.

44. Scripture verses used to stress the connection between water baptism and Spirit baptism are John 3:5; Titus 3:5; Acts 2, 8, 10, and 19. *Spade Regen* 11/6 (September 1918),24; 16/24 (February 1924),166.

45. Possibly Polman was assisted by an elder.

46. *Spade Regen* 18/2 (May 1925),26-27 gave the translation of the comment on Matthew 28:19 in J. Paul, ed. *Das Neue Testament in der Sprache der Gegenwart* (Mülheim). In this comment the baptism in the name of Jesus as reported in Acts is explained as just an abbreviation and not a different formula as had been propagated by many Pentecostals in America.

The threefold immersion practiced by Polman was changed to a single immersion by his successors Klaver, Van der Woude, and Vetter.

47. The elder was J.F.W. Helgering, according to his daughter: Truus Klerk-Helgering, Interview, 11 October 1986.

48. *Spade Regen* 10/3 (June 1917),12.

49. Niblock, "The German Conference," *Confidence* 3/1 (January 1910),20.

50. C.P. Siebeles to J.H. Gunning J.Hz., Amsterdam, 20 March 1911. Another early reference to the Lord's Supper being celebrated at Amsterdam is provided by H. Mogridge in "Holland and Antwerp," *Confidence* 3/10 (October 1910),244. Mogridge reported a communion during a Tuesday evening meeting for Spirit baptized ones.

51. *Spade Regen* 13/10 (January 1921),155-56.

52. After the watch-night service there was a time of prayer until midnight and then the New Year commenced with the celebration of the Lord's Supper.

53. During the Sunderland conference of 1911 Polman reported that many at Amsterdam received their Spirit baptism during the monthly celebration of the Lord's Supper. "The Place of Tongues in the Pentecostal Movement," *Confidence* 4/8 (August 1911),177; cf. *Spade Regen* 10/3 (June 1917),12.

12 REACTION FROM THE CHURCHES

From Caution to Condemnation

Among the first references to the Pentecostal revival found in the Dutch press was one by the free evangelist Johan de Heer and dated April 1907. In the paper *Jeruël* he gave an enthusiastic report of the revival that from Los Angeles quickly spread throughout the world.[1] On a journey to Germany his Evangelical colleagues there quickly informed him of the irregularities that meanwhile had taken place at Kassel. In January 1908 De Heer felt obliged to denounce his initial positive response:

> How we longed that the spiritual revelation of Los Angeles would draw closer; what lovely confirmations of known women and men and yet . . . Under the banner of the cross, with the battle-cry: Jesus is coming! has Satan brought in his angels and as A. Dallmeyer says in his brochure: Satan has come among the saints.[2]

De Heer extensively quoted from the readily available German condemnations of the movement, but for the moment still refrained from judging the Dutch branch of the revival.[3]

The Gereformeerd weekly *De Heraut* contained a column "Buitenland" (Abroad), which often mentioned deviating religious movements. Already in March 1907 brief reference was made to Barratt's meetings in Christiana, followed by a repudiation of the manifestations in May.[4] During 1907 and 1908 not less than 25 articles or paragraphs (always quotations from foreign papers) were devoted to Pentecostalism. Mostly they dealt with the German situation. The Kassel episode was extensively reported. Winckel, the responsible editor of these reports, saw it all as fanaticism and heresy. The notorious Berlin Declaration from September 1909 was completely translated into Dutch and warmly recommended.[5] Hereafter the interest in the matter declined and within a few years the reports from abroad had ceased. Although Winckel was aware of the Dutch Pentecostals he deliberately never discussed the Dutch situation.[6]

M.J. Beukenhorst in his article on the contemporary manifestations of glossolalia in 1908, appearing in the orthodox-Reformed periodical *Stemmen voor Waarheid en Vrede*, seemed even unaware of the existence of a Dutch Pentecostal movement.[7] It became a pattern among orthodox-Reformed and Evangelicals to condemn the Dutch Pentecostals on the basis of one-sided information from Germany. The "Vrije Evangelische" monthly *Ermelosch Zendingsblad* regularly printed warnings against the Pentecostals, including a translation of the Berlin Declaration.[8]

On 9 June 1910 a certain J.D. Root Jr. organized a public meeting at Amsterdam aimed to unmask the "lying, deceitful and blasphemous" proceedings of Polman. He called Polman a deceiver, who was only after the money of his followers. His criticism largely consisted of ridiculing the mutual meetings, which he named "porch of hell" or "chamber of horrors," and where Polman was said to hypnotize the people.[9] Polman did not react publicly, but from then onwards no longer allowed opponents to attend the mutual meetings.

At an early stage the Baptists were confronted with the Pentecostal movement through the problems that arose in their assemblies in Harlingen and Sneek. After the departure of pastor Gerrit de Wilde in July 1909 the situation was "settled" by excluding the Pentecostal adherents from the fellowship.[10] The Baptist periodical *De Christen* also published the translation of the Berlin Declaration together with a "brotherly warning" from the editor: "With deep regret we have taken cognizance of the initial devastation that the present 'Spirit' or 'Pentecostal movement' in some of our Assemblies (Sneek and Harlingen) already has caused."[11] At the annual general council of the Baptist Union in 1911 the following motion was carried:

> Having heard the explanations concerning the character and
> revelation of the so-called tongue or spirit movement, the
> council considers, that we completely and resolutely should
> keep far aloof from all intercourse with that persuasion.[12]

The statement was the first official denunciation of the
Pentecostals from any denomination in the Netherlands.
A request for further investigation was put aside. Nevertheless at the next council on 11 July 1912 at Amsterdam, F.J.
van Meerloo gave report of his personal examination concerning the Pentecostals. Van Meerloo, who lived in Amsterdam and had been pastor of the Baptist assembly that also
assembled in the Kerkstraat, had attended a number of public
Pentecostal meetings. Being an opponent he was refused
admittance to the mutual meetings by Polman, who wrote
him:

> When you have changed your opinion and are convinced that
> God had really poured out his Holy Spirit in our midst and
> you can unite in one spirit with us, like the 120 on the feast of
> Pentecost, then we will be glad when you visit our mutual
> meetings. I would like to first receive an answer from you.[13]

Van Meerloo replied by letter that the whole matter was
against Scriptures and dangerous for those following it. His
lecture before the Union drew the same conclusion. Most of
the content was dealing with the speaking in tongues, which
Van Meerloo considered "the core of the movement." He
rejected the phenomena ascribing it to overexertion and
nervous excitement worked up during the mutual meetings.
The arguments Van Meerloo used to prove the unbiblical
nature of the manifestations were weak and demonstrated a
remarkable unawareness of the article on glossolalia by
professor H. Bavinck published in *De Christen* six weeks
before Van Meerloo delivered his address.[14]
Van Meerloo argued that the tongues he had heard during
the public meetings were unscriptural because they seemed
like sounds rather than languages. The fact that missionary
Arie Kok had to learn Chinese was to Van Meerloo a
confirmation that the strange sounds were made by oneself
and were not the gift of tongues.[15] Bavinck, however, made
clear distinction between the glossolalia on the day of

Pentecost and all subsequent occurrences. On the day of Pentecost it was a prophetic speaking in other languages understood by the audience—a unique event, not meant to equip the disciples with knowledge of foreign languages. Hereafter the speaking in tongues, according to Bavinck, was no longer a speaking in foreign languages, but an unintelligible speech. Bavinck's article was also published by Polman, who apparently agreed with Bavinck, in *Spade Regen*.[16]

From the Lutheran church, which saw a number of its members joining the early Pentecostal meetings at Amsterdam, no official reaction is known. But according to Elize Scharten the Pentecostal gatherings were considered "spiritistic meetings" by the elders of her church.[17] The Salvation Army also refrained from taking a public stand. When asked to give his personal opinion officer J.F. Hoogesteger in a letter to Gunning (dated February 1911) expressed a careful but open attitude.[18] J.N. Voorhoeve, foreman of the (Plymouth) Brethren and editor of their periodical *De Bode des Heils in Christus*, once discussed the Pentecostals in 1919. After diminishing the value of gifts as miracles, healings and tongues, Voorhoeve denounced the movement because it allowed for female ministry, which he regarded to be "diametrically opposed to the instructions of the apostle":

> Females receive so-called revelations and speak so-called in strange languages. But the same Spirit, who has spoken about these gifts in 1 Cor. 12, has said it so clearly in 1 Cor. 14: "Let your women keep silence in the churches; for it is not permitted unto them to speak . . . for it is a shame for a woman to speak in the church." The Spirit cannot be divided against Himself! Prohibit females to speak in the church, and then have these women exercising gifts in public![19]

Meanwhile Voorhoeve and his fellow Brethren ignored the clear implication of 1 Cor. 11:5, that does allow women to pray and prophesy in public.

Revaluation by G.A. Wumkes

The Netherlands Reformed minister Dr. G.A. Wumkes was the first to write a positive account of the Dutch Pentecostals.

Geert Aeilco Wumkes (1869-1954) was a known historian and advocate of the Frisian cause (Friesland being a province in the Netherlands with a distinct language and culture). His writings on Frisian culture and church history are numerous. In 1912 he wrote a detailed account of the rise and development of the Baptists in the Netherlands. Through Polman he became interested in doing the same with the Pentecostal movement. Late in 1914 Polman met Wumkes in the minister's home in Sneek. In the years following Polman stayed there frequently and once Wumkes briefly visited Polman in Amsterdam (1917). Wumkes' description of the Pentecostals *De Pinksterbeweging voornamelijk in Nederland*, published in 1916, was the best recommendation for the movement that Polman could have wished. It first appeared in *Stemmen des Tijds* (Voices of the time), a monthly publication for Christianity and culture, after which Polman had it published as a separate brochure.[20]

Wumkes based his writing upon the many conversations with Polman and the Pentecostal literature he received from him. He gave a short historical introduction followed by a biographical sketch of Polman and a description of the Dutch movement. Wumkes stressed the international and interdenominational character and the zeal for foreign mission. His brief discussion of the Dutch movement concerned the following items: liturgy, water baptism, communion, church discipline, church government, sanctification, Spirit baptism, glossolalia, physical healing, unity of the body of Christ, and eschatology. Sanctification was considered most important: "If justification by faith stood at the centre of the 16th century Reformation, in this revival the central thought is sanctification."[21] Wumkes noticed the fear of the Pentecostals to organize themselves, but felt it would have to come to some sort of organization in order to reach something positive and lasting. In his conclusion he wrote:

> The dangers to which the movement is exposed are on the one side the falling back into the routine of formal Christianity, and on the other side a being carried away into superspirituality, a being taken up in emotion. The latter occurs as soon as spiritual gifts and revelations are placed above the obedience

to the will of God. The meaning of the Pentecostal movement is mainly in this, that she by renewal has demonstrated, that miraculous spiritual depths open up and extraordinary energies awake, when a human experiences the Spirit baptism.[22]

Wumkes' writing did not fail to arouse a lot of response. The Christian daily newspaper *De Nederlander* printed large portions of it in four consecutive articles.[23] The Evangelical papers that had stigmatized the Pentecostal movement as false were annoyed. In *Maran-Atha*, organ of the Nederlandsche Tentzending, Wumkes article was called "an important historical overview," but instead of a serious review it was followed by repeating the old arguments taken from Germany to repudiate the movement once more.[24] A. Winckel in the "Vrije Evangelische" paper *Ons Orgaan* did a better job by at least discussing the content of Wumkes' publication.[25] Winckel accused Wumkes for having written an unreliable sketch and concluded:

Dr. Wumkes demonstrates in his article that he does not know the area in which he moves sufficiently, and that he only in part understands the subject he deals with. And it does seem, that he is informed in a one-sided and superficial way."[26]

The Baptists, who were much indebted to Wumkes, were left somewhat embarrassed. They shared the objections of Winckel, but were more cautious in expressing them.[27] Dr. J. van Dorp in the Reformed church paper *Nieuwe Nederlandsche Kerkbode* wrote a sympathetic review and remarked: "One would do good to read his book and follow his example by not immediately, unseen, repudiating this movement. Probably one would get, like we did, some more appreciation."[28] The Christian newspaper *De Amsterdammer* printed an extensive summary of Wumkes' brochure in June 1917.[29]

The criticism from Winckel that Wumkes' information was one-sided seems justified. Nowhere did Wumkes reflect knowledge of the voluminous anti-Pentecostal literature. But the accusation of one-sidedness would likewise apply to the Evangelical opponents, who on the basis of the information from their German colleagues had condemned the Dutch

Pentecostals. Wumkes must be credited for introducing a new approach by allowing the Dutch Pentecostals to speak for themselves.

Diagnosis from a Roman Catholic Student

Whereas Wumkes' survey provoked a lot of response, another interesting article from a Roman Catholic went by unnoticed. Medical student H.L.M. v.d. Hoff's " 't Wonder der glossolalie" appeared in *Annuarium*, a publication of a Roman Catholic students association, in 1918.[30] As a Catholic believer V.d. Hoff resisted the prevailing view in medical circles that held all miracles to be sickly processes. This view was a threat not only to the miracle stories of the Bible, but also to the legends of the Catholic saints. In an attempt to establish a model to discern between a miracle and a sickly condition, V.d. Hoff looked for a miracle with a comparable example of a sickly deviation. For this purpose he chose to compare the miracle of glossolalia among the apostles on the day of Pentecost, with the glossolalia "that since a decade goes round the world like an epidemic."[31]

After criticizing the Pentecostal movement for its passion to imitate the first Christian era, artificial glossolalia, meaningless prophecies, hysteria, and spiritual freebooting, he concluded that the movement was sickly in all its elements. Yet, the possibility of it being a miracle was not denied on basis of its pathological character, since V.d. Hoff felt that sickness and miracle do not exclude each other. The reason that the movement could not be considered a miracle was "because it had no result, that fits with a direct intervention of God."[32] V.d. Hoff predicted that the movement would not last. His final argument to reject Pentecostalism was, "And moreover, we as Roman Catholics cannot accept it, because we do not acknowledge any new 'Church,' as long as we consider Catholicism as the historical Christianity."[33]

Although V.d. Hoff largely relied on secondary sources (Wumkes, Beukenhorst, and Mohr) and only discussed the Pentecostals because he needed a negative example, his writing is noteworthy as it is the sole description of the

Pentecostal movement from the Catholic side during this period. He was original when he critically examined two prophecies of Mrs. Polman, which supposedly announced the beginning and the end of the World War. V.d. Hoff demonstrated from the content that nothing startling was revealed.[34] His own prediction that the movement would soon end, however, has in the meantime proven false.

J.H. Gunning J.Hz. Encounters the Pentecostals

Another sympathetic sound, again from a Netherlands Reformed minister, was articulated by Dr. Johannes Hermanus Gunning J.Hz. (1858-1940), son of the known theologian J.H. Gunning Jr. Besides his ministerial duties Gunning edited the weekly *Pniël* and showed a warm interest in exploring the various expressions of Christianity.[35] Already in 1910 he corresponded with Polman and others about the Pentecostal movement.[36] In spite of the many warnings he received against the movement, he maintained an open attitude. His own sister Caroline, married to Jonkheer Dr. J.W. van Lennep, was in sympathy with the Pentecostals.[37] In *Pniël* Gunning at least once quoted from *Spade Regen* and twice he visited Polman in Amsterdam.[38] Gunning did not leave us with a rounded description of the Pentecostal movement, but did share some of his impressions:

> Since I have been the guest of brother and sister Polman in Amsterdam for a couple of days in February 1920, and there also met the known Pastor Paul, has the "Pentecostal thought" maintained a place in my heart and prayer. In the hall "Immanuel" and in the house of brother Polman I have heard and experienced things, that I cannot get away from. These people have something, that I lack, and that I'd so much like to possess.[39]

Gunning was not particularly impressed with the tongues or the visions he had heard, nor by the mutual meetings he attended. Besides he held theological objections against searching for a separate "baptism." But he was stirred by the joy, enthusiasm, and spirituality of Polman and considered the Pentecostal movement to be a "serious call of God to the quarreling, torn, spiritually dry and sunken-low Christianity of these days."[40]

H. Bakker Reanimates the Kassel Spirits

In 1924 *Stroomingen en sekten van onzen tijd* (Trends and sects of our time) by H. Bakker, orthodox Netherlands Reformed minister at Amsterdam, appeared. It included a short description of the Pentecostals. Although Bakker lived in the same city he failed to personally investigate the Pentecostal meetings. His repudiation was based on information from Germany. A wild story from Kassel served to characterize the beginning of the movement. Bakker saw signs that the movement had passed its pinnacle: "After all, who would succeed, when one has already started with so much excitement and display, to maintain the climax for years and years?"[41] As for the Amsterdam assembly he wrote:

> Those that got acquainted with her say, that in this Pentecostal assembly there is but little speaking in tongues; and moreover the leader is immediately present to "interpret" and then to call up to the service of the Lord. This assembly therefore seems to have been reduced to yet another of the many free assembly.[42]

In summary Bakker held the following objections against the Pentecostals: making subordinate matters (i.e., glossolalia) the main issue; forcing the spirit of prophecy; ignoring the spiritual development in the church; not bringing the sermon into prominence, but suggestion, excitement, and fanaticism, while these excited scenes are destructive for both soul and body.[43]

Most of these objections, however, concerned the Kassel episode. For a fair treatment of the Dutch Pentecostals Bakker should have investigated the matter further, even more so because he had received information that the Dutch were more down to earth. Yet, in spite of his conclusion that God was not in this dangerous imitation and excitement of the Pentecostal movement, Bakker closed with a constructive remark:

> At the same time I think of the "unpaid bills" of the church. In this Pentecostal movement there speaks an accusation, that the church must take to heart. It can be so lukewarm and deadly and worldly in the assembly of the Lord. We cannot accept, that we are only in appearance or are only "a little" Christian. Pentecostal fire and Pentecostal Christians belong to each other. Where is the holy zeal, that moves the church of our days?[44]

Bakker's book was widely read and saw several reprints. To this day it is a popular source for those who want to repudiate the Pentecostal movement. The decline of the movement around 1930 seemed to vindicate Bakker's judgement. In his *Onder buitenkerkelijken, sekte-mensen en anderen* (Among unchurched, sectarians, and others) from 1935, he was even more venomous in his remarks: "A religion of shaking, springing, rolling, crying and shouting, is good for harlequins and acrobats."[45] Here he described the Pentecostal movement as a slip from an American plant, that would not grow in Dutch soil. "The Pentecostal assembly belongs in California, the land of the most luxurious plant growth and surfeited film-stars; in the erotic Los Angeles."[46]

The above survey reveals that with the exception of Wumkes and Gunning all interpreters of the Dutch Pentecostal movement arrived at negative conclusions. Upon examination it appears that usually these repudiations were based on secondary information from Germany and not on a serious personal research. Van Meerloo did attend the meetings, but with the attitude of an opponent, for which reason he was refused admittance to the mutual meetings. Polman's complaint that the movement was judged without a proper personal investigation was therefore justified. Those that took the trouble to enter into a personal relation with the Pentecostals with an open attitude like Wumkes and Gunning came to a sympathetic and constructive evaluation. Both were orthodox ministers with a common interest in dissenters. They demonstrated a flexibility in thinking that is not often found among orthodox circles. In general the churches regarded the Pentecostals as sectarian. Joh. Jansen's article on Pentecostalism in the authoritative *Christelijke Encyclopedie voor het Nederlandsche volk* (six volumes, published between 1925 and 1931) is representative of this prevailing assumption.[47] Completely relying on Bakker's description he presented Pentecostalism as a destructive imitation that fortunately had passed its pinnacle. Contrary to their evangelical colleagues (Baptists and Vrije Evangelischen) the Reformed and Gereformeerd ministers (Bakker and Jansen) avoided the term "demonical" in their common repudiation of the movement.

The Cross of the Rejected

Although much aware of the strong rejection the Pentecostal movement endured, Polman refrained from writings against his opponents or even mentioning their names. Only some indirect references are found in *Spade Regen*, such as Arie Kok writing in 1909, "It is not the 'tongues' that we bring to the forefront, as so many think and gladly hold against us, but it is Jesus."[48] Sometimes Polman expressed his pain that fellow Christians condemned the movement without a proper investigation, but added, "Yet, the Pentecostal blessing has given us loving hearts and has taught us to do what Jesus did, who did not revile back or threaten, but handed it over to Him, who judges rightly."[49] From his correspondence with Gunning and Wumkes it is evident that Polman was very cooperative if someone wanted to make a serious study of the movement. The same correspondence informs us a little more about his position towards opponents. Polman did not regard slander a threat and felt that if the Pentecostal movement could not endure slander, it should rather disappear.[50] As to abuses (probably referring to Kassel) he reacted:

> That in some places some things have occurred, that were wrong and not of the Holy Spirit, I affirm completely, but don't you believe yourself, that the leaders in this movement suffer the most under it, and that they have done everything

to fight such things? Why does one now take such a sole matter and deduce therefrom, that the whole movement with her thousands of earnest children of God is not right?[51]

When questioned by Gunning about his attitude towards the church, Polman replied: "I do not have grievances against the institutionalized church of our days, but I deeply regret the spiritual deadness, the insusceptibility of the revelations of God and the ignorant attitude that she seems to adopt against what God is doing in these days."[52] The Pentecostal movement was considered a divine intervention to awaken a sleeping church.

Polman realized that his understanding and that of single assemblies was partial and needed replenishment: "Only the entire body of Christ can contain the foulness."[53] His readiness to be taught by someone from outside the movement becomes evident from his correspondence with G. A. Wumkes. When Wumkes accused the Pentecostals of using Scripture at variance, Polman thanked him for the correction and begged him to help them further in this matter.[54] Polman agreed with Wumkes, that in order to lose its one-sidedness the Pentecostal movement needed to penetrate into the various denominations.[55] Alas, Wumkes was only one of the very few clergy who responded in such a constructive manner. In general the Pentecostals were either ignored or repudiated as sectarian, which crushed Polman's hope for an ecumenical revival. During 1929 to 1930 *Spade Regen* published two apologetic articles translated from *Redemption Tidings*. The second contained a clear attack on the church: "The pulpits are filled with doubters and higher critics, who carefully follow the steps of their critical teachers. One cannot say, that the church is deviating from God; she has already deviated from Him."[56] In February 1930 Polman himself wrote:

> During my experience of nearly 22 years in this blessing, I have never doubted its genuineness, although I have seen much that was not genuine, but I have tried to bring the people to a sound understanding of the work of the Spirit. The indignity that came upon the Pentecostal movement as a

result of that, I have carried with gladness before God, for the sake of the souls, who sought the good and were upright. I feel a thousand times safer on the side of those, who unknowingly err and are willing to be taught, than on the side of those, who exercise nothing but criticism and often attribute more honour to the Devil, than to God. One will not help the people by making them afraid of the Devil; to cast the Devil out, that is our calling.[57]

In particular the allegation of being false (or even demonical) must have been hurting for Polman. His religious rebirth had liberated him from the stigma of being an "onecht" (illegitimate, or "not-genuine") child, carried with him since the day he was born. As a Pentecostal he was again branded as "onecht," this time by his brothers and sisters in the family of God. No doubt Polman and other Pentecostals have made their mistakes, but Polman's writings certainly do not reveal any sectarian spirit. As so many dissenters before him Polman was made a sectarian against his will.

NOTES

1. Johan de Heer, "Op den uitkijk," *Jeruël*, April 1907. Quoted in *Ermelosch Zendingsblad* 48/5 (May 1907),1-4.
2. Ibid., *Jeruël*, February 1908. Quoted in *Ermelosch Zendingsblad* 49/2 (February 1908),5-11.
3. The sources mentioned by Johan de Heer are: H. Dallmeyer, *Sonderbare Heilige*; E. Schrenk, *Was lehrt uns die Kasseler Bewegung*; A. Dallmeyer, *Satan unter den Heiligen*; Joh. Seitz etc., *In kritischer Stunde*; J. Rubanowitsch, *Das heutige Zungenreden*; *Auf der Warte*, 5 January 1908; *Ev. Allianzblatt*, 22 December 1907.
    In a following article De Heer quoted portions of the Azusa Street paper *The Apostolic Faith*, added with a repudiation of the movement by S.C. Todd, missionary in Macao, China, taken from the Keswich paper *The Life of Faith*. Johan de Heer, "Tongen en Zending," *Jeruël*, February 1908. Quoted in *Ermelosch Zendingsblad* 49/3 (March 1908),2-10.
4. Winckel, "Buitenland: Noorwegen," *De Heraut van de Gereformeerde Kerken in Nederland* no. 1525 (24 March 1907),3; Idem, "Buitenland: Dr. Pierson over het spreken in tongen," *De Heraut* no. 1533 (19 May 1907),3.
5. Winckel, "Buitenland: De leiders der Gemeinschaftsbewegung over de Pinksterbeweging," *De Heraut* no. 1661 (31 October 1909),3.
6. That Winckel was aware of the existence of a Dutch Pentecostal movement is evident from a remark he once added to a report from

abroad: "We feel that the men and women, also in our nation, who follow the so-called Pentecostal movement, should consider this word of Philip Mauro. We feel it is sufficient." Winckel, "Buitenland: Philip Mauro over het spreken in tongen," *De Heraut* no. 1725 (22 November 1911),3.

7. M.J. Beukenhorst, "Het spreken in 'tongen,' " *Stemmen voor Waarheid en Vrede: Evangelisch tijdschrift voor de Protestantse Kerken* 45 (1908),295-318.
   Another example of unawareness of the Dutch Pentecostals is J.L. Wagemaker, *De glossolalie in het N.T.* (Thesis, Amsterdam: Kweekschool Algemeene Doopsgezinde Sociëteit, 1913).

8. "Verklaring," *Ermelosch Zendingsblad* 50/11 (November 1909),2-8; cf. "De Tongen-beweging in Zuid-Afrika," 51/5 (May 1910),12-14.

9. J.D. Root Jr. to J.H. Gunning J.Hz., Amsterdam, 19 October 1910; 24 October 1910; 20 March 1911. These and other letters to Gunning are present in the library of the Rijksuniversiteit Utrecht, section "Handschriften."
   Root had also published one issue of the anti-Pentecostal paper *Nieuwe Spade Regen.* In his first letter to Gunning Root felt that his public meeting at Amsterdam was very successful and had been a death-blow to Polman. However, a certain H. Meijer, who had attended the said meeting, gave a different report in his letter to Gunning dated 30 August 1911. Meyer, not a Pentecostal himself, wrote that the opponents ridiculed the issue. They gave no sufficient evidence against it and refused the word to those in favor of it. The meeting ended in a chaos and the hall had to be cleared!

10. Cf. chapter 7, "Sneek and Harlingen" section.

11. *De Christen* 28/1174 (28 October 1909),343.

12. *De Christen* 30/1266 (3 August 1911),245.

13. F.J. van Meerloo, *Over de Pinkster—of Tongenbeweging* (Apeldoorn: Neerlandia Drukkerij, 1912), pp. 8-9.

14. H. Bavinck, "De glossolalie of gave der vreemde talen," *De Christen* 31/1309 (31 May 1912),171-73. From H. Bavinck, *Magnalia Dei* (Kampen: Kok, 1912). One reader's letter from Jan R. Fijn, Maastricht, reacted against Van Meerloo and recommended reading Bavinck's article again. *De Christen* 31/1326 (27 September 1912),309; cf. *De Christen* 31/1327 (4 October 1912),317.

15. Van Meerloo, pp. 5-7.

16. *Spade Regen* no. 29 (March-May 1912),3-4.

17. E. Scharten "Gaat dan heen in de gehele wereld en predikt het evangelie aan alle schepselen," *Volle Evangelie Koerier* 10/9 (March 1948).
    In *Spade Regen* Polman several times mentioned Lutherans among those attending the early meetings. Among the letters Gunning received concerning the Pentecostals was one from two Lutheran ladies. They had attended some of the Pentecostal meetings and were favorably impressed. Some of their circle of acquaintances had been baptized in the Spirit, including Elize Scharten, and had become better

Christians. Miss C.P. Siebeles and friend to J.H. Gunning J.Hz., Amsterdam, 20 March 1911.

18. J.F. Hoogesteger to J.H. Gunning J.Hz., Amsterdam, 13 February 1911.

19. [J.N. Voorhoeve] "Correspondentie: E.J. te N.B. vraagt iets over de 'Pinksterbeweging,' " *Bode des Heils in Christus* 62 (1919),45-46.

20. G.A. Wumkes "De Pinksterbeweging voornamelijk in Nederland," *Stemmen des Tijds* 5/11 (September 1916),251-71; Idem, *De Pinksterbeweging voornamelijk in Nederland* (Utrecht: G.J.A. Ruys, 1916); Idem, *De Pinksterbeweging voornamelijk in Nederland*, 2d printing, Serie Pinksteruitgaven, no. 1 (Amsterdam: G.R. Polman, 1917).

21. Wumkes, *Pinksterbeweging* (1917), p. 19.

22. Ibid., p. 23.

23. "De Pinksterbeweging," *De Nederlander* 23/7032-23/7035 (19 September 1916—22 September 1916),4.

24. "De Pinksterbeweging," *Maran-Atha* 7/8 (November 1916),58-59.

25. A. Winckel, "De Pinksterbeweging," *Ons Orgaan* 12/164 (12 January 1917),5-6; 12/165 (26 January 1917),11-12; 12/167 (23 February 1917),29.

26. Ibid., 12/165 (26 January 1917),12.

27. N. v. B., "Van de boekentafel," *De Christen* 36 (1917),83-85.

28. J. van Dorp, "De Pinksterbeweging voornamelijk in Nederland," *Nieuwe Nederlandsche Kerkbode* 2/22 (2 March 1917),2.

29. "De Pinksterbeweging en haar leider G.R. Polman," *De Amsterdammer*, 16 June 1917. Cf. "De Pinksterbeweging," *De Amsterdammer*, 7 July 1917, for a friendly review of T.B. Barratt's *De waarheid inzake de Pinksterbeweging* (Amsterdam: G.R. Polman, 1917).

30. H.L.M. v.d. Hoff, " 't Wonder der glossolalie," *Annuarium* (1918),268-91.

31. Ibid., p. 271. The sources V.d. Hoff mentioned are Beukenhorst, "Het spreken in tongen," *Stemmen voor waarheid en vrede* (1908); Wumkes, *De Pinksterbeweging voornamelijk in Nederland*; F. Mohr, "Das moderne Zungenreden," *Psychiatrisch-neurologische Wochenschrift* 10 (1908),61.

32. V.d. Hoff, p. 289. V.d. Hoff admitted that the glossolalia among the apostles could likewise be explained in pathological terms. Although he would not accept such an explanation, the event would still remain a miracle because it had a result that fits with a direct intervention of God (p. 290-91).

33. Ibid., p. 289.

34. Ibid., p. 280-81. Cf. *Spade Regen* no. 38 (December 1914),4.

35. Dr. J.H. Gunning J.Hz., *Herinneringen uit mijn leven* (Amsterdam: H.J. Spruyt, 1940; A. Brom Jr., "Dr. J.H. Gunning J.Hz.," *Jaarboek Maatschappij der Nederlandsche Letterkunde* (Leiden, 1941).

36. Six letters from Polman to Gunning and two from Gunning to Polman were found dating between 1910 and 1919.

37. Gunning to Polman, Haarlem, 31 March 1917. A. d'Ablaing to Gunning, Velp, 30 November 1918.

38. In *Pniël* 26/1334 (21 July 1917), 229, Gunning quoted a portion from *Spade Regen* 10/2 (May 1917). From the correspondence between Polman and Gunning it follows that Gunning visited Polman for the first time during 1917. Another visit dated February 1920 and was reported in *Pniël*.

39. *Pniël* 31/1604 (23 September 1922),303.

40. Ibid.

41. H. Bakker, *Stroomingen en sekten van onzen tijd* (Utrecht: Kemink & Zoon, 1924), p. 109.

42. Ibid., p. 108.

43. Ibid., pp. 110-11.

44. Ibid., p. 112.

45. H. Bakker, *Onder buitenkerkelijken, sekte-mensen en anderen* (Wageningen: H. Veenman & Zonen, 1935), p. 179. Bakker gladly quoted from Upton Sinclair's *Petroleum* (Dutch translation) the rather sensational description of an American Pentecostal farmer.

46. Ibid., p. 175.

47. Joh. Jansen, "Pinksterbeweging," in *Christelijke Encyclopedie voor het Nederlandsche Volk*, vol. 4 (Kampen: J.H. Kok, 1925-1931), pp. 573-74. Cf. W.J.J. Velders, "Gebedsgenezing" in vol. 6, pp. 182-84. Another publication (which in fact concerned the Gemeente des Heeren) from the Gereformeerd side falls just beyond the period covered by this present study: *De Pinkstergemeente en hare dwalingen getoetst aan Gods Woord*, Rapport van de commissie inzake de "Pinksterbeweging" aan de Classis Meppel der Gereformeerde Kerken (Hoogeveen: R. Slingenberg, 1932).

48. Arie Kok, "Wien zal Ik zenden," *Spade Regen* no. 12 (November 1909),2.

49. G.R. Polman, "De Heere heeft groote dingen bij ons gedaan: Dies zijn wij verblijd!" *Spade Regen* no. 29 (March-May 1912),2.

50. G.R. Polman to J.H. Gunning J.Hz., Amsterdam, 7 January 1913.

51. Ibid.

52. Polman to Gunning, Amsterdam, 12 March 1910.

53. G.R. Polman, "Pinksteren," *Spade Regen* 16/2 (May 1923),21. In *Spade Regen* 15/4 (July 1922), 52, Polman wrote, "We do not think that we only have the truth and that others have to believe the same as what we believe."

54. G.R. Polman to G.A. Wumkes, Amsterdam, 6 March 1917.

55. G.R. Polman to G.A. Wumkes, Amsterdam, 20 October 1916.

56. "Dit (of 1930 na Chr.) is het (of 30 na Chr.)," *Spade Regen* 23/3 (June 1930),35-39. Translated from *Redemption Tidings* and probably written by Donald Gee. The other article was Donald Gee, "Waarom wordt 'Pinksteren' tegengestaan?" *Spade Regen* 22/5 (August 1929),67-71.

57. G.R. Polman, "Wat Pinksteren voor ons moet zijn," *Spade Regen* 22/11 (February 1930),165.

CONCLUSION

Relation to Church and Society

At the end of this study of Dutch Pentecostalism it is now appropriate to summarize some of the findings and to assess their significance in relation to church and society. The Dutch Pentecostal movement began as an ecumenical renewal movement, generated by influences from abroad, but gradually developed into a separate denomination consisting of loosely organized independent local assemblies with a more or less congregational structure. It started with an independent circle of believers at Amsterdam receptive to the experience of receiving more power in their spiritual life, among whom many had belonged to the Salvation Army. At first mainly the more serious believers from other denominations or free circles were drawn. Thereafter the Pentecostals recruited the majority of their members from among those alienated from the church.

Since about 90 percent of the population belonged to a church (95 percent in 1909 and 85 percent in 1930), it is no surprise that most of the Pentecostals had a churchly background. Often they had only nominally belonged to a church and were by becoming Pentecostal rescued from joining the unchurched. Available information supports that many of these came from a Netherlands Reformed background, which church suffered the greatest loss in membership during this period (their percentage of the Dutch population dropped from 44 percent in 1909 to 34 percent in 1930). From the other churches or religious organizations, a disproportionately large number came from the Salvation Army. Pentecostalism could not crack the Roman "pillar"; only few with a Roman Catholic background were won.

During 1920 to 1930 the national figure of Pentecostals

(including their children), estimated by this survey, reached about 2,000. In Amsterdam where the percentage of unchurchliness was more than twice the national figure (11.6 percent in 1909, 21.3 percent in 1920, and 34.9 percent in 1930) probably one quarter of the Pentecostal members came from among the unchurched.[1] A survey among members of the Amsterdam Pentecostal assembly indicated that nearly two-thirds of the members were added through conversion. Pentecostalism had more success in urban than in provincial areas. The members mostly came from the working class, supplemented with some from the middle class (shopkeepers and tradespeople), and hardly any from the upper class. Pentecostal liturgy with its appeal to human emotion and emphasis on equality in fellowship (all are brothers and sisters) was more inviting to members of the working class than the traditional church services, and was better fitted to meet the need of those who felt alienated from church and society. Urbanization, social dissatisfaction, and the loss of function of the traditional churches most likely have been contributing factors in the decision of people to become Pentecostal. Through conversion and Spirit baptism they became members of a new community. The warm fellowship and encouragement (irrespective of education or social status) to fully participate in worship compensated for their adverse social circumstances.

Like early socialism in the Netherlands, the Pentecostals refrained from alcohol and tobacco. Since they expected a new order to be established by divine intervention, they had little interest in political issues (although Polman, according to his children, voted for Kuyper's Anti-Revolutionaire Partij). The turbulent period at the end of World War I (outside the Dutch border, the Bolshevik revolution and the replacement of monarchies by democracies, and inside the Dutch border, the introduction of universal suffrage and the call of socialist leader Troelstra for a revolt) only led the Pentecostals to intensify their eschatological expectations. In the few known cases of a socialist becoming Pentecostal, this each time involved a radical break with socialism. On the other hand, Polman, like many of the early Pentecostals, was a pacifist and visited conscientious objectors in prison to encourage them. On a modest scale the Pentecostals were involved in charitable endeavors. In Amsterdam there was a sewing school for young girls and special evenings for factory girls were held. A "mothers circle" and female workers in uniform helped the sick with small domestic duties. Parcels with food and clothing were sent to the poor in Bulgaria and Germany. Mrs. Polman was cited by the Austrian government for her contribution to a relief program for undernourished Austrian children.

Significance of Polman

Gerrit Roelof Polman and his wife Wilhelmine Blekkink were the undisputed leaders during this period (1907-1930) and to a great extent they were responsible for the shape the movement took. Both were ardent preachers who poured out all their energy and talents to obey the call of their heavenly Master in the way they understood it. Their house became a pilgrim's home, where countless people found spiritual and physical relief. Mrs. Polman exercised gifts of healing, tongues and interpretation, visions and prophecy. She was very effective in leading people to receive the Spirit baptism, particularly females and children. Her tendency towards ultra-spirituality with perfectionistic traits was partly balanced by her somewhat more sober-headed husband.

Gerrit Polman was an evangelist and charismatic leader. He exercised gifts of healing and the discerning of spirits used with exorcism. His limited formal education was compensated by self-tuition (he kept an impressive library), and even more by his spirituality. He favorably impressed people from higher as well as from lower strata of society. J.H. Gunning J.Hz. described the time spent with Polman as "holy moments." Under the dynamic and charismatic leadership of the Polmans the Dutch movement kept close contact with Pentecostals from neighboring countries. The couple were much appreciated speakers of international conferences and contributed to Pentecostalism in Great Britain, Germany, Switzerland, Belgium, and France. Polman was part of the International Pentecostal Advisory Council that during 1912 to 1914 held meetings in Sunderland and Amsterdam. During and after the First World War Polman played a significant mediating role between the German and British Pentecostals culminating in the international conference in Amsterdam in 1921, where the German and British brethren met for the first time since the war. These international contacts, together with a considerable foreign mission program, gave the Dutch Pentecostals the self-respect needed in the face of blunt disapproval at home. It strengthened their unity and confirmed their desire to be loyal to the great commission of Christ.

When Polman entered the Pentecostal movement during 1907 he was already 39 years old, 18 years of which he had spent as an evangelist. His many years with the Salvation Army and the time with Dowie were not shaken off in his Spirit baptism. The Salvation Army and Dowie clearly influenced the way Polman organized and conducted the Pentecostal movement in the Netherlands. Through the Salvation Army he had become used to female ministry and had accepted the Methodist understanding of salvation and sanctification, while becoming aware of belonging to an international force. Booth-Clibborn had shown him the Quaker virtue of pacifism. Dowie had taught him about divine healing; water baptism by threefold immersion; the imminent premillennial coming of Jesus and the anticipation of the restoration of the New Testament spiritual gifts. The "advanced truths" of Dowie were simply added to what he already had learned as a Salvationist. Likewise, most elements of the Pentecostal teaching and practice concerning Spirit baptism and the exercise of spiritual gifts could easily be integrated into his existing religious understanding. Each time his view was reformed, but not revolutionized. Most interesting therefore is the one element in the Pentecostal message that did revolutionize his attitude: the ecumenical dimension. When Polman returned to the Netherlands in 1906 he planned to found (or restore) Dutch branches of Dowie's Christian Catholic Apostolic Church, which purposed to "smash every other church in existence." After his Spirit baptism Polman wrote, "This blessing of God has filled my heart with overflowing love for my fellow-Christians and I cannot but love them all." The purpose of the Pentecostal revival as he saw it was not to build up a church, but to build up all churches.

Polman's life story resembles that of the Pentecostal movement. As an infant of 15 days old he was marked "onecht" (illegitimate) in the baptismal record of the church where he was baptized. Forty years later the Pentecostal movement in its infancy period was similarly labeled "onecht" by clergy from different denominations. For some Pentecostalism had to be false or even demonical because of its suspect origin; other critics doubted its authenticity because it allowed for female ministry. Nearly all opponents were heavily biased against the physical manifestations and the appeal to human emotion. Of course there were also theological rebuttals. If only the Pentecostals had been taken seriously, these objections might have been negotiable. Instead they were used to hastily repudiate the Pentecostals as sectarian. It would take another 50 years before the Netherlands Reformed Church (as the first church in the Netherlands) was able to positively respond to the Pentecostal claims and to enter into a sincere dialogue.

Sectarian Against His Will

Polman suffered bitterly under the condemnations by his fellow Christians, but refused to enter into arguments. His hope for the Pentecostal revival to be a channel of blessing for all churches and to see the fulfillment of Joel's prophecy "His Spirit upon all flesh" proved unattainable. This was partly due to difficulties inherent to his Pentecostal theology. On the one hand the unity in Christ of all believers was stressed, but on the other hand a division between the Spirit-baptized and the not-Spirit-baptized believers was encouraged. The temptation to view Spirit baptism as the mark of a spiritual elite was great to Pentecostals who in general belonged to the underdogs of society. Although not intended by the leaders, it prompted undesirable behavior by some members who, often by lack of "natural" gifts, prided themselves on their "supernatural" gifts.

Another dividing line was the concept of rebirth. For the Pentecostals rebirth was the sole entrance into the universal body of Christ. But their understanding of rebirth pre-supposed a crisis experience based on Methodist theology. This made it hard for them to accept church members without such an experience as fellow believers. In specific cases Pentecostals were prepared to make adjustments, as Polman did with clergy friendly to him, but not in general ideology. An ecclesiology tied to such a limited concept of rebirth fails to appreciate the variety in human personality and the theological diversity of the New Testament. Above all, it does not recognize the creative and kaleidoscopic ways in which the Spirit works. It might be wholesome in a particular setting, but is ill-fated in an ecumenical context. These deficiencies in theology would, combined with sociological factors, eventually lead to a deficient spiritual attitude.

Polman's ecumenical heart collided with his fundamentalis-tic Evangelical head. His Spirit baptism had generated a loving attitude towards all fellow Christians, but he was unable to fully assimilate this ecumenical experience into his thinking. In fact, this was a general problem among the Pentecostals in Western Europe and North America. Their lack of theological training and of self-criticism made them incapable of bringing their theology in line with their authentic ecumenical experience. The human tendency to compensate a felt loss or disadvantage in comparison with others (deprivation), was a serious threat to the ecumenicity of the movement. As the churches represented much of what many Pentecostals lacked, such as education, income, and status, they were in danger of developing an anti-church attitude, especially after being repudiated by most clergy. This explains why they often uncritically repeated an array of anti-ecumenical statements from fundamentalistic Evangeli-cals. Polman was more faithful to his Pentecostal experience when he with the introduction of church membership in 1925 deliberately did not copy the British Assemblies of God "Statement of Fundamental Truths." Instead he designed a brief declaration of faith in the form of a testimony, which, by omitting reference to water baptism and by not requiring an "initial evidence" of Spirit baptism, still kept the door open to the churches. But also Polman was not equipped with the tools to develop a theology in which inconsistencies are acceptable and ended up as a sectarian against his will. Surely this was not his fault alone. He received no help from his Evangelical colleagues nor from the academic theologians. The ecclesiastical situation in the Netherlands just was not ripe for the revolutionary ecumenical aspects of Pentecost and neither were the Pentecostals themselves.

Church and Sect Reconsidered

The term "sect" generally has an unfavorable connotation, in particular among church members, who use it to reject religious movements outside their church. However, if they would attempt to define the term, it would be hard to prevent their own church from falling under the same category. Usually one's own theology is made normative and anything deviating is branded sectarian. F. Boerwinkel in his *Kerk en Secte* dared to make his own theology relative and wondered, "Is there rightly any church, or are we in fact all sectarians, no church excluded?"[2] Sociologist L. Layendecker in *Religie en Conflict* tried to view the "church-sect" issue as a manifestation of conflict, which makes the distinction between church and sect less relevant. Layendecker argued that conflicts are unavoidable, because of the universality of institutionalization, elective affinity, and social change.[3]

The story of Pentecostalism confirms that an orientation of theology towards a sociology of conflict would be beneficial for the entire church. Conflicts should not be suppressed, but regulated. Such an orientation need not be taken as neglecting the spiritual realm of the church, but as one concerned to encourage a spiritual realm with recognition of human shortcomings. This requires an ecclesiology in which pluriformity becomes a hall-mark of the church; a dynamic pluriformity that allows room for conflict and change. It calls for a theology that refuses to make its own position normative; a theology that partakes in an intercultural global learning process. A true Pentecostal-charismatic theology should welcome conflicts as being essential for the continuous work of the Spirit. Conflicts provide the context in which the charismata operate. A gift of healing only functions when someone is sick; a prophetic voice is heard in times of crisis; a gift of discernment is effective when judgement is needed.[4] Though the Netherlands Reformed Church did allow for opposing parties to exist separately from each other within the same church (with the emphasis on separately), no church in the Netherlands during 1900 to 1930 could envision a structure this tolerant of conflicts. The smaller denominations (orthodox-Reformed and Evangelical) and the so-called sects generally experienced the most difficulty in appreciating conflicting or alternative views. With this in mind the initial position of the Pentecostals becomes the more remarkable. The early Pentecostals attempted to reach across racial, cultural, and ecclesiastical barriers. Restoring original Christianity by means of a special Spirit baptism would enable them—as they thought—to evangelize the world and to prepare the church for its role as the bride at the eschatological wedding feast. The promising ecumenical start failed, because on the one side the Pentecostals did have the right heart for the matter, but lacked the means to develop an adequate corresponding theology, while on the other side the churches possessed the means, but lacked the necessary ecumenical heart.

NOTES

1. Stichting Noordholland Provinciaal Opbouworgaan, *Sociale atlas Noord-Holland* (Haarlem: Stichting Noordholland Provinciaal Opbouworgaan, 1963), table "Percentages kerkelijke gezindten per gemeente."
2. F. Boerwinkel, *Kerk en secte* 2d ed. (The Hague: Boekencentrum, 1956), p. 7.
3. L. Layendecker, *Religie en conflict* (Meppel: J.A. Boom, 1967).
4. J.-J. Suurmond, "Een charismatische kijk op konflicten," *Bulletin voor Charismatische Theologie* no. 19 (1987),10-21.

APPENDIX 1

Geographical Distribution of Pentecostal Assemblies, 1907-1930

APPENDIX 2

Statistics

Table 1

Estimated number of Pentecostals in the Netherlands during 1920 to 1930
according to present survey

Amsterdam	500	Delfzijl	80
Haarlem	200	Groningen	60
Rotterdam	150	Stadskanaal	20
The Hague	150	Meppel	50
Leiden	30	Zwolle	50
Gouda	30	Apeldoorn	20
Hilversum	100	Heerlen	70
Utrecht	50		1650
Terschelling	50	Remainder	350
Sneek	40	Total	2000

Remainder is formed by scattered believers and by the Gemeente des
Heeren.

Table 2

Number of Pentecostals specified by province according to national census of 1930 compared with present survey

	Census 1930	This Survey
Noord Holland	230	700
Zuid Holland	66	360
Utrecht	10	150
Friesland	3	90
Groningen	40	160
Drente	7	50
Overijssel	0	50
Gelderland	8	20
Limburg	15	70
Noord Brabant	0	0
Zeeland	0	0
	379	1650
Remainder	129	350
Total	508	2000

In the specification by province and by size of municipality, the publication of the census of December 1930 did not include the 99 members from the Gemeente des Heeren nor the 30 Pentecostals with a double church membership, giving a total of 379 instead of 508. In this present survey the number during 1920 to 1930 is estimated at 2,000. For a proper comparison with the specification given by the census, the 350 belonging to scattered believers and the Gemeente des Heeren is left out.

Volkstelling 31 December 1930, vol. 3: *Kerkelijke Gezindte* (The Hague: C.B.S., 1933), pp. 184-85, 188-91, 193-94.

Table 3

Number of Pentecostals specified by size of municipality according to
national census of 1930

Municipalities with number of inhabitants	Pentecostals
0– 2,000	0
2,001– 5,000	24
5,001– 10,000	39
10,001– 20,000	15
20,001– 50,000	20
50,001–100,000	31
Above 100,000	250
Total	379

The cities above 100,000 include Amsterdam, Rotterdam, The Hague,
Utrecht, Haarlem, and Groningen.

Volkstelling 31 December 1930, vol. 3: *Kerkelijke Gezindte* (The Hague:
C.B.S., 1933), p. 184.

APPENDIX 3

Membership Application—Pentecostal Assembly, Amsterdam, 1925

VERZOEK TOT OPNAME IN DE
PINKSTERGEMEENTE.

Aan het
Bestuur der Pinkstergemeente
te Amsterdam.

Gedrongen door een innerlijke over-
tuiging en door een werkelijk verlangen
naar de gemeenschap der heiligen, deel
ik U mede, dat ik gaarne wensch op-
genomen te worden in de gemeenschap
der Pinkstergemeente.

Door genade heb ik het getuigenis
in mijn hart een kind van God te zijn,
en den Heer Jezus te kennen als mijn
persoonlijken Verlosser en Zaligmaker.

Ik geloof in de Heilige Schrift als
het onfeilbaar woord van God en in
de algenoegzaamheid der Schrift als
regel voor geloof en wandel. En in de
volle verlossing door het dierbaar bloed
van Christus, die ons in de Schrift
wordt getoond, en in den doop met
den Heiligen Geest met Schriftuurlijke
teekenen en gaven, en in het werk
Gods, dat Hij door dien Geest in de
Pinkstergemeente gedaan heeft en nog
doet, en strek mij uit naar den vollen
zegen des Geestes, die God ons wil
geven vóór Christus wederkomst.

Mijn wensch is geheel God toe te
behooren, gewijd aan Hem te leven tot
verheerlijking van Zijn naam. Daarom
zal ik mij ook gaarne persoonlijk onder-
werpen aan den geestelijken tucht, die
in de gemeente naar het Woord Gods
wordt uitgeoefend om zoo mede opge-
bouwd te worden tot een woonstede
Gods in den Geest, en met al de Zijnen
te deelen in den vollen zegen des
Evangelies, en tezamen te verbeiden de
wederkomst van onzen Heer en Heiland

APPENDIX 4

Declarations—International Pentecostal Council, 1912-1914

A Consultative International Pentecostal Council.

At the Sunderland Convention it was felt that the time had come that, in order to protect this work from wrong teaching, or false teachers, the chief Leaders in different lands should meet together, once or twice a year, to take counsel together. The next Meeting is arranged (if the Lord tarry) for December 4th and 5th, at Amsterdam.

* * *

Those LEADERS in the Pentecostal Revival who were assembled at the Fifth International Convention at Sunderland, May 28th to 31st, 1912, agreed to the following Statement :—We believe that—

The Baptism of the Holy Ghost and Fire is the coming upon and within of the Holy Spirit to indwell the believer in His fulness, and is always borne witness to by the fruit of the Spirit and the outward manifestation, so that we may receive the same gift as the disciples on the Day of Pentecost. Matt. iii., 11. Acts i., 5, 8; ii., 1-4, 38, 39. 1 Cor. xii., 7-13. Compare also Acts xi., 15-18: "And as I began to speak, the Holy Ghost fell on them, even as on us at the beginning. And I remembered the word of the Lord, how that He said, 'John indeed baptized with water, but ye shall be baptized with the Holy Ghost.' If then God gave unto them *the like gift* as He did also unto us, when we believed on the Lord Jesus Christ, who was I, that I could withstand God ? And when they heard these things, they held their peace, and glorified God, saying, 'Then to the Gentiles also hath God granted repentance unto life.' "

(Signed)
T. B. BARRATT (Norway).
ALEXANDER A. BODDY (Sunderland).
J. PAUL   ⎫
B. SCHILLING ⎬ Germany.
E. HUMBURG   ⎭
JOSEPH HILLERY KING (U.S.A.).
G. R. POLMAN (Holland).
CECIL POLHILL (London & Bedford).

Sunderland, May 31st, 1912.

Confidence 5/6 (June 1912),133.

DECLARATION.

INTERNATIONAL PENTECOSTAL CONSULTATIVE COUNCIL,
Amsterdam, 4th and 5th December, 1912.

I. The Council emphasizes its position as an Advisory Council only, not as a Legislative Council.

The resident Brother, where the Council is being held, is *ex-officio* the Chairman of it. He may, with the consent of the Brethren, appoint a member of the Council to preside in his stead.

(Accordingly Pastor Paul, invited by Pastor Polman, takes the chair for this Session.)

II. The Council feels that as an Advisory Council it must be self-elected, and not subject to the control of votes of Assemblies.

III. The following DECLARATION is agreed upon:—

Brethren representing the so-called Pentecostal Movement in different countries of Europe, gathered together in Amsterdam for an International Advisory Council, wish to state to their brethren within and outside this "Movement" their convictions concerning

GOD'S PLAN AS TO THIS REVIVAL, viz.:—

1. The present outpouring of the Holy Spirit as it is characterized by the manifestation of spiritual gifts (1 Cor. xii., 7-11) we consider to have been granted by the Lord in these last days before His coming for the edifying and perfecting of the Body of Christ, and its preparation for the "Rapture" (Eph. v., 12; 1 Thess. iv., 17).

Recognizing this fact, we believe that the Holy Spirit seeks to bring about true unity among all the people of God, according to the valedictory prayer of our Lord Jesus Christ (John xvii.). Not a unity in which uniformity prevails as to methods of work and doctrines that have long divided the Church, but a unity in spirit and fraternity which recognizes the vital doctrines of Christianity.

2. We further believe the Lord's object in carrying out this purpose with the Body of Christ to include and demand the presentation of the full Gospel of the Lord Jesus Christ in the power of the Holy Ghost, accompanied by signs as in the days of the Apostles, to the whole wide world in the shortest possible time.

In full sympathy, therefore, with the urgent appeal for an increase of evangelistic and missionary zeal, as given, *e.g.*, by the Edinburgh Missionary General Conference, we should train our churches and circles to a more intelligent interest and active participation in this great work.

3. The Baptism of the Holy Ghost and Fire we hold to be the coming upon and within of the Holy Spirit to indwell the believer in His fulness, and is always borne witness to by the fruit of the Spirit and the outward manifestation, so that we may receive the same gift as the disciples on the Day of Pentecost. (Matt. iii., 11; Acts i., 5-8; ii., 1-4, 38, 39; 1 Cor. xii., 7-13; Acts xi., 15-18.)

We do not teach that all who have been baptized in the Holy Ghost, even if they should speak in tongues, have already received the fulness of the blessing of Christ implied in this Baptism. There may be, and in most cases will be, a progressive entering in of the believer into this fulness, according to the measure of faith, obedience, and knowledge of the recipient.

4. The believer, so far as he is fully yielded (the Holy Ghost having come upon him in this Baptism) will attain unto a perfect man, unto the measure of the stature of the fulness of Christ. (Heb. vi., 11; vi., 1; Eph. iv., 12-14; 1 John ii., 12-14.)

This will normally result in a greater development of the fruit of the Spirit, and His gifts and His guidance in all things.

5. While we encourage all believers to seek the same full Baptism as recorded in the Acts of the Apostles, together with its manifestations, yet we would earnestly warn against merely seeking soulish experiences or fleshly demonstrations, which not a few have mistaken for the work of the Spirit.

Men and women who, not realizing that God has given us the spirit of power, and love, and of a sound mind, and who, instead of holding fast the Head, from whom all the Body being supplied and knit together through the joints and bands, increases with the increase of God, dwell in things which they have seen, and delight in feelings and mystical experiences, give opportunity for the evil one to deceive them by his wiles, and easily become subjects of false prophecies and of revelations or manifestations which are not of the Holy Spirit, but of the flesh, if not of the devil. (2 Cor. v., 16; 2 Tim. i., 7; Col. ii., 18, 19; 1 Tim. iv., 1, etc.)

6. The true deepening of the work of God in our midst is not to be brought about by any merely human or self-originated efforts, but by the Spirit of the Lord Himself (Zech. iv., 6), Who is always ready to impart all necessary guidance and power and wisdom for all the emergencies of our personal daily life, as well as in our gatherings and assemblies, if only we would recognize His presence in childlike simplicity of faith, and heed His directions, subjecting ourselves one to another in the fear of Christ (Eph. v., 21).

7. Some have failed to obtain the continued guidance, presence, and power of the Holy Spirit, even though they earnestly sought for it, because—

a. They did not obey the Scriptural rules laid down by the Apostle Paul for the exercising of the gifts of the Spirit (1 Cor. xii.-xiv.; Rom. xii.; 1 Thess. v.).

b. They did not discern the Body of Christ, in which the Lord has given all the ministrations necessary for the perfecting of the saints (Eph. iv., 11, 12).

In the light of these unmistakable directions and principles of the Holy Scriptures we feel it our duty to emphatically state that the genuine guidance of the Holy Spirit operates in perfect harmony with the different offices which God has appointed in the Body of Christ, e.g., pastors, teachers, helps, governments, etc. (1 Cor. xii., 28; Eph. iv., 11, 12), and cannot accept the notions of some who claim to be taught of the Holy Ghost in such a way as not to need counsel, instructions, admonition, reproof, or correction from other members of the Body.

ENGLAND........	ALEX. A. BODDY.	GERMANY........	EMIL HUMBURG.
	CECIL POLHILL.		J. PAUL.
HOLLAND........	G. R. POLMAN.		C. O. VOGET.
NORWAY........	T. B. BARRATT.	SWITZERLAND....	ANTON B. REUSS.

DECLARATION.

INTERNATIONAL ADVISORY PENTECOSTAL COUNCIL.
3rd Session at Sunderland, May 13th to 15th, 1913.

From hearts overflowing with thanksgiving the Members of the Council gathered at Sunderland send loving greeting to those who are baptised in the Holy Ghost or are seeking to know the Lord.

Grace, mercy and peace from God our Father and
from the Lord Jesus Christ.

If you will bear with us, Beloved Brothren, we will write to you of the things which the Lord has brought before us at this time. We will address ourselves to three things:—

1. The members of the Council emphatically advise the assemblies to be very careful in the matter of admitting unknown strangers to teach in their gatherings. It would prevent sinful actions and unscriptural teaching, if it was insisted that those who come should bear recently dated letters of cordial commendation from those well known in Pentecostal circles. They need have no difficulty in obtaining such, though, of course, no one should give such letters without really knowing them thoroughly.*

In our papers we have already before warned against unknown teachers coming in our circles, because they may bring false doctrines, and so cause divisions and difficulties amongst the believers. We feel led to repeat our counsel not to admit such unknown persons as teachers in our meetings, but to ask of them letters of commendation. (Titus i., 9.)

UNSCRIPTURAL TEACHING AS TO THE EUNUCH LIFE.

2. Somewhat recently a teaching has been brought in from America, pointing out that we will not be prepared for the rapture if we are not living an eunuch life (Matt. xix., 12). And this teaching is brought to the married people as well as to the unmarried; but they do not see that Paul in 1 Cor. vii., 7, says: "Each man has his *own* gift from God." So it may be that the Holy Spirit leads some people to live an eunuch life. It is *their gift from God* in this case. Others may be led by the same Spirit to marry, and so they have this gift from God, to be married. We see the Apostle does not say that only such people will be raptured that are living an eunuch life, therefore we warn earnestly against such teaching.

"Forbidding to marry" is a seducing doctrine (1 Tim. iv., 3), and practically is such teaching of an eunuch life for unmarried people a *forbidding to marry*, and it has brought for married people great difficulties, for women, willing to live an eunuch life, were caused to abandon their husbands, in spite of the cleàr statements given by Paul in 1 Cor. vii., 3-5, 10-15; and men also were carried away in the same error. But the Bible states in 1 Tim. ii., 15, concerning the woman, that she shall be saved through the child-bearing, if they continue in faith and love and sanctification with sobriety. Here we have the scriptural proof that the child-bearing does not hinder any

---

*The German teachers and leaders have, through their paper, "Pfingstgrusse," warned their people concerning a certain Bro. Kahrs and his party (speaking German and English), whose teaching is referred to in the next paragraph.

from being raptured when Jesus comes, granted that such people live in sanctification with sobriety.

God's will for all believers is not an eunuch life, but their sanctification, that each one know how to possess himself of his own vessel in sanctification and honour, not in the passion of lust. (1 Thess. iv., 3-5.)

Oh, *such* teaching of an eunuch life is a very dangerous thing, and yet the more because the same teachers tell their listeners that brothers and sisters may kiss one another, and that the curse of God (Gen. iii., 19): "In the sweat of thy face shalt thou eat bread," is abolished, and that therefore we are no more to work with our own hands in spite of the exhortation given by Paul in 2 Thess. iii., 10, 11. But we ought to hold on the Word of God, and it is our duty to do according to the saying of the apostle (2 Thess. iii., 14, 15): "If any men obeyeth not our word by this epistle, *note that man*, that ye have no company with him, to the end that he may be ashamed. And yet count him not as an enemy, but admonish him as a brother."

WRONG TEACHING AS TO DEMONS AND THE BAPTISM OF THE HOLY GHOST.

3. In dealing with the book, "War on the Saints," we want to state that the view about receiving the Baptism of the Holy Ghost and Fire is not scriptural. We think it will be helpful to give some of the main thoughts, and meet them with the Word of God.

Sentences from "War on the Saints."

1. There are many deceived ones amongst the most devoted teachers to-day, because they do not recognise that an army of teaching spirits have come. These spirits are whispering their lies to all who are spiritual, *i.e.,* open to spiritual things. Satan needs good men to float his lies under the guise of truth. A beautiful life is not the infallible test, for Satan's ministers can be ministers of righteousness. (2 Cor. xi., 13-15.)

The first scriptural word that the Writer quotes in order to prove that the most devoted teachers may be deceived by evil spirits is Gal. ii., 11-14, where Paul tells us that Peter was carried away, and did not walk uprightly according to the truth of the Gospel.

The second word of God is taken from Dan. xi., 35, and it is suggested that, according to this word, some of the teachers will fall. She thinks that this is fulfilled in our days.

2. The Writer considers *passivity* as the primary cause of deception and possession. In order to prove this she argues: "God requires co-operation with His Spirit, and the full use of every faculty of the whole man."

"Passivity of brain is an essential condition for the presentation to the mind of things by evil spirits. At night the brain is passive, and whilst activity of the mind in the daytime hinders, they have their occasion at night when the passivity is more pronounced in sleep."

3. The Writer points out that some baptised people will be deceived or possessed by evil spirits in seeking the presence of God. She writes about it:—"The true presence of God is not felt by the physical senses, but in the spirit. The counterfeit presence of God is an influence from outside upon the believer. All exterior manifestations to the believer coming from without upon the body have the characteristics of obsession, because they may come from deceiving spirits (Presence filling the room and felt by the physical senses—waves of power pouring upon and through the psychical being, or feeling of wind or a breathing upon the auto-man)."

4. The counterfeit presence of God is nearly always manifested as love, to which the believer opens himself without hesitation, and finds it fills and satiates his innermost being, but the deceived one does not know that he has opened himself to evil spirits, in the deepest need of his inner life.

The Scriptural Truth.

1. This teaching is not according to Scripture. Paul does not say in 2 Cor. ii. that Satans *can be* ministers of righteousness, but they *fashion* themselves as ministers of righteousness; and that is the same as Jesus says in Matt. vii., 15, about the false prophets, that they are coming in sheep's clothing, but inwardly are ravening wolves. By their fruits ye shall know them. Therefore the teachers are to be known by their fruits.

In this case of Peter we find no scriptural word proving that he was deceived by an evil spirit. On the contrary he points out that Peter did this because that he feared them, that were of the circumcision. It was not an evil spirit that caused Peter to do so, but it was his own spirit.

We find it best always to read every word of the Bible with its context. In this case we find that the context clearly shows that these teachers do not fall through being deceived by Satan. We read in Dan. xi., xxxiii.: "They that be wise among the people shall instruct many; yet they shall fall by the sword," and therefore we see that the quoted 35th verse is to be understood in the same way: "Some of them that be wise shall fall, to refine them, and to purify and to make them white, even to the time of the end."

2. The Bible shows us that God is always working upon men; they may be passive or active. He can work in either state. In many places we find that dreams are given by God in a state of passivity. So God is working in a state of passivity as well as the devil. Surely Paul was in a state of passivity when he received his wonderful revelation in 2 Cor. xii., 1-4; and when the Writer supposes that the night-time gives occasion to evil spirits, the Word of God is stating (Job. xxxiii., 14-16): "God speaketh once, yea twice, though men regardeth it not. In a dream, in a vision of the night, when deep sleep falleth upon men, in slumberings upon the bed, then He openeth the ears of men."

3. We are told in the Bible: "Seek ye My face," and Jesus promised "I will manifest Myself"; and oftentimes instances are given where the presence of God is felt by the physical sense. When God was with Moses in the burning bush, he looked and said: "I will turn aside now and see this great sight, why the bush is not burned." The presence of the Holy Ghost was manifested too in such a way that it was felt by the physical sense, for it is written: "Suddenly there came from heaven a sound as of the rushing of a mighty wind, and it filled the whole house where they were sitting; and there appeared unto them tongues parting asunder like as a fire, and it sat upon each one of them." This manifestation of the presence of God was really touching the outer man. The sound of the wind was heard, the wind itself was felt, the tongues of fire were seen, and so the physical senses were the means to perceive this exterior manifestation. If the Writer is right, we must ascribe the whole Pentecostal outpouring to the working of the evil spirits.

4. We never find in the Bible reason to believe that evil spirits may bring love, but Paul says about the Baptism of the Holy Ghost in Rom. v., 5, that "*the love of God has been shed abroad in our hearts through the Holy Ghost which was given unto us.*" Love that we need for our inner life is a fruit of the Spirit (Gal. v., 22), and Jesus tells us that we know by the fruits whom we have to deal with.

As John Wesley cried on his death-bed, so the Pentecostal Brethren too can cry to-day: "Best of all, GOD IS WITH US." He is teaching us and deepening His work in all willing hearts. Hallelujah!   We remain, your servants for Jesus' sake and the Gospel's,

England—ALEX. A. BODDY.	*Germany*—J. PAUL.	*Holland*—G. R. POLMAN.
CECIL POLHILL.	E. EDEL.	*Switzerland*—R. GEYER.

A Warning from the Advisory Council.

"BOOKS OF MESSAGES," ETC.

The International Advisory Council, assembled during the Seventh International Pentecostal Convention at Sunderland, Whitsuntide, 1914, feels led to send forth the following warnings of love to all who are with us in this precious faith.

Concerning Spurious Literature.

Attempts are being made to spread a kind of literature among Pentecostal circles, which claims to be given by direct inspiration, equal to the Infallible Word. We refer to the "Leaves of Healing from Jesus," "Fragrance from Heaven," "In School with the Holy Ghost," " Honey out of the Rock," "Letters from Jesus," and all books of like character. Jesus Himself is being introduced as sending forth these messages to His loved ones.

Since we have many simple-hearted people among us who might be deceived by the imitation of the language of the Bible in these booklets, we feel it our duty to earnestly and lovingly point out the danger of this kind of literature. It has really nothing to do with our true Scriptural Pentecost. Long before the Pentecostal blessing was given, books of a similar character had been abroad in America, England, Germany, and other countries. If they are not directly Spiritualistic, they are at least strangely and dangerously tinged with Spiritualism, and of a soulish character. They are now appearing in the disguise of "Pentecost," to find, if possible, admission among our beloved Pentecostal people. But they do not afford wholesome spiritual food. They will draw away from the Bible. Those who are regular students of the Word of God will readily discern that the Spirit of the Holy Scriptures is altogether different from the spirit in these pamphlets. The strange and touching effect such writings often produce upon the mind, heart, and soul is not a sufficient evidence of their divine origin. People who are being affected by them in this way have not yet learned to discern between the spirit and the soul. They need a more thorough application of the power of the Word of God in the power of the Holy Ghost to the dividing of soul and spirit according to Heb. iv., 12, 13.

England—A. A. Boddy.   *Holland*—G. R. Polman.   *Germany*—E. Humburg.
        C. Polhill.   J. Paul.
                                                             C. O. Voget.

APPENDIX 5

Financial Report—
Properties Owned by G.R. Polman

The church building was owned by Polman, not by the church. In 1911 Polman had bought the premises in Kerkstraat 342-344, Amsterdam, where the Immanuel Hall was to be build. The Polman family lived upstairs. In 1919 Polman bought a second house in Zandvoort, which was used as a rest home and named Lydia. All deeds of purchase, sale, and mortgage were found in governmental archives and archives of the land registry office. From these documents, from references in *Confidence*, *Pfingstgrüsse*, *The Latter Rain*, from Cecil Polhill's private bookkeeping record (kept by the Bedford County Records Office), and from the memorandum of succession, the following information was gathered.

IMMANUEL HALL, AMSTERDAM

The premises were sold by auction on 20 February 1911. Johannes Visser, a member of the Pentecostal assembly, purchased them for ƒ16,750 on behalf of Polman. Including costs this amounted to ƒ18,000. The costs for demolishing the old front premises and for building the Immanuel Hall with four floors amounted to ƒ30,000 giving a total of ƒ48,000. According to Polhill's private bookkeeping Polman had borrowed ƒ9,600 (£800) during 1911 and another ƒ30,000 (£2,500) during 1912. Only the latter amount was registered as a deed of mortgage, namely, ƒ30,175 in July 1912. The same month ƒ10,000 was borrowed from Elize Scharten. Whether the first ƒ9,600 was repaid to Polhill could not be ascertained. The mortgage of ƒ30,175 was redeemed in 1918 by borrowing ƒ30,000 from Adriaan Nijman, a timber-merchant from Nieuwer Amstel, who is otherwise not known. This mortgage was redeemed in 1928 by borrowing ƒ35,000 from the Nationale Levensverzekering Bank (National Life Insurance Bank). In 1931 this amount was raised to ƒ38,000. In the meantime the mortgage of ƒ10,000 to Elize Scharten had been renewed several times. When Polman died in 1932 there still was a debt of at least ƒ48,000. Over all the years the mortgage was never cleared; only the interest had been paid.

Home Lydia, Zandvoort

In January 1919 Polman bought a house in Zandvoort from a certain G. Meppelink, combined with a long-lease contract of a private strip on the nearby beach, for the amount of ƒ10,000. At the same time Polman borrowed ƒ5,000 from another life insurance company and ƒ2,000 from Dorethea Meppelink from Haarlem. A third amount borrowed in 1927 of ƒ850 was repaid in 1929. The mortgage of ƒ5,000 was taken over by a bank in 1931, while the mortgage of ƒ2,000 was renewed the same year. When Polman died the debt of ƒ7,000 was not cleared; only the interest had been paid.

Profits and Losses

The memorandum of succession revealed that when Polman died the total assets amounted to ƒ65,000 and the debts amounted to ƒ61,000. The mortgage of ƒ38,000 was thereafter brought down to ƒ35,900. Mrs. Polman had to sell some of the furniture, including the large library, to make ends meet. Because the Pentecostal assembly at Amsterdam no longer wished to make use of the Immanuel building, Mrs. Polman in the end was not able to pay the interest of the mortgage. Her position was even worsened when the prices of property dropped during the years of crisis. In 1938 she was forced to sell the house to the Nationale Levensverzekering Bank for ƒ28,000. The remainder of the debt as well as the back interest was remitted. Elize Scharten likewise remitted the debt of ƒ10,000 as well as the back interest.

In 1941 the Levensverzekering Bank sold the building to a broker without making profit. This broker sold the building in 1947 to another broker for ƒ65,000, who in his turn sold it the same day to the Nederlandse Middenstands Bank for ƒ125,000! In 1941 the hall had been used for Jewish services of the Liberaal Joodsche Gemeente (an excellent photo of the hall fitted up as a synagogue has been preserved). During the war the hall was again used for Pentecostal meetings, which continued until it was bought by the bank in 1947. When the Middenstands Bank wanted to sell the building in 1969 it was first offered to the Pentecostal assembly. The offer was turned down because the Pentecostal assembly had already purchased another building in 1961. Finally the Immanuel Hall was sold to the Evangelische Broedergemeente (Moravian Brethren) for ƒ200,000 and since then has again been used as a church.

Conclusion

The above reveals that the financial management of the Pentecostal assembly was wanting. Large sums of money were given towards the foreign mission program, while the mortgage was never cleared. Apparently it was felt sufficient to pay the interest and not to worry about redeeming the debt. Presumably this conduct was prompted by the expectation of a speedy return of the Lord. In the latter days it was considered more important to bring the gospel to the uttermost parts of the earth than to pay for a building. After the resignation and death of Polman the Pentecostal assembly was faced with the problem that the building was owned by Polman and not by the assembly. Emotionally it was hard for the assembly to accept that they were dependent on the Polman family for the use of "their building." Yet, the above reveals that Polman had not enriched himself at the cost of the assembly. The ownership of the property came down to owning a similar debt. Polman never collected large sums of money for himself as is evident from the above report. Of course it would have been far better if the building had been owned by the church. But, when the property was bought in 1911 Pentecostalism was still an ecumenical renewal movement, rather than an assembly, and subsequently did not have corporate capacity.

Deeds of purchase and sale:
Amsterdam Register Hypotheek no. 4: 1962/117; 3079/45; 3201/49; 3201/50; 3428/10; 3428/11; 4454/23; *Haarlem Register Hypotheek no. 4*: 1039/77.

Deeds of mortgage:
Amsterdam Register Hypotheek no. 3: 700/52; 734/8; 734/20; 895/154; 899/53; 1251/142; 1372/114; 1374/27; 1518/110; 1520/34; *Haarlem Register Hypotheek no. 3*: 401/49; 402/33; 678/29; 818/73; 1126/71; 1133/2.

Other references:
Confidence 4/5 (May 1911):116; 4/12 (December 1911):272; *Pfingstgrüsse* 3/46 (13 August 1911):368; *The Latter Rain Evangel* (July 1929):4; Cecil Polhill "Payments August 1910-December 1914," present in Bedford County Records Office (with thanks to Desmond Cartwright); "Testament G.R. Polman," (Zwolle: Notaris G.P. Vroom, 15 October 1903, no. 6212); P.W. van der Ploeg & S.H. Charbon, "Memorie van aangifte voor het recht van successie, betreffende de nalatenschap van den Heer Gerrit Roelof Polman" (Zandvoort, 29 July 1932); Catalogue of public sale: "Boekverkooping 20-26 September 1932," (Amsterdam: G. Theod. Bom & Zoon), 1932.

SOURCES CONSULTED

Select Bibliography

Aalders, C. *Lot en Illusie.* Amsterdam: Holland, 1939.

Algemene Geschiedenis van Nederland. 15 vols. Haarlem: Fibula-Van Dishoeck, 1977-1983.

Algra, H. *Het wonder van de negentiende eeuw.* 6th ed. Franeker: T. Wever, 1976.

Alt, M.A. *Herinneringen uit mijn leven.* 2d ed. Velp: Pinksterzending, 1971.

[Amerom, H.N. van.] *65 jaar Pinkstergemeente Immanuel.* Haarlem: Pinkstergemeente, [1973].

Anderson, Robert Mapes. *Vision of the Disinherited.* New York/Oxford: Oxford University Press, 1979.

Bakker, H. *Onder buitenkerkelijken, sekte-mensen en anderen.* Wageningen: H. Veenman & Zonen, 1935.

————. *Stroomingen en sekten van onze tijd.* Utrecht: Kemink & Zoon, 1924.

Barr, James. *Escaping from Fundamentalism.* London: SCM Press, 1984.

————. *Fundamentalism.* 2d ed. London: SCM Press, 1981.

Barratt, Thomas B. *In the Days of the Latter Rain.* rev. ed. London: Elim Publishing Co., 1928.

————. *When the Fire Fell, and an Outline of My Life.* Oslo: Alfons Hansen & Sonner, 1927.

————. *De waarheid inzake de pinksteropwekking.* Pinksteruitgaven, no. 2. Amsterdam: G.R. Polman, 1917.

————. "An Urgent Plea for Unity and Charity," *Confidence* 4/2 (February 1911),29-31; 4/3 (March 1911),63-65.

Barrett, David B. "The Twentieth-Century Pentecostal/Charismatic Renewal in the Holy Spirit, with Its Goal of World Evangelization," *International Bulletin for Missionary Research* 12 (1988),1-9.

————. *World Christian Encyclopedia.* Nairobi: Oxford University Press, 1982.

Bartleman, Frank. *Azusa Street*. Foreword by Vinson Synan. Plainfield, NJ: Logos Int., 1980. Originally published in 1925 as *"Pentecost" Came to Los Angeles: How It Was in the Beginning*.

———. *Two Years Mission Work in Europe*. Los Angeles: By the author, n.d.

———. *Around the World by Faith*. Los Angeles: By the author, n.d.

Bavinck, H. "De glossolalie of gave der vreemde talen," *Spade Regen* no. 29 (March-May 1912),3-4. Quoting H. Bavinck, *Magnalia Dei*, Kampen: J.H. Kok, 1912.

Bavinck, H.; Prins, P.; and Brillenburg Wurth, G., eds. *De Heilige Geest*. Kampen: J.H. Kok, 1949.

Beaman, Jay. "Pacifism and the World View of Early Pentecostalism." Paper presented at the 13th annual meeting of the Society of Pentecostal Studies, November 1983.

———. "Pentecostal Pacifism: The Origin, Development, and Rejection of Pacifistic Belief Among Pentecostals." M.Div. thesis, North American Baptist Seminary, Sioux Falls, 1982.

Begbie, Harold. *Life of William Booth*. 2 vols. London: Macmillan and Co., 1920.

Berg, J. van den; Schram, P.L.; and Verheus, S.L., eds. *Aspecten van Het Réveil*. Kampen: J.H. Kok, 1980.

Berkhof, H. *Christelijk geloof*. 4th ed. Nijkerk: G.F. Callenbach, 1979.

———. *De leer van de Heilige Geest*. Nijkerk: G.F. Callenbach, 1964.

Beukenhorst, M.H. "Het spreken in tongen," *Stemmen voor Waarheid en Vrede* 45 (1908),295-318.

Beumer, J. *De Geloofsgenezing door R.R. Posthuma*. Utrecht: n.p., 1907.

Beversluis, M. *Spiritualisme en Spiritisme*. Kerk en Secte, no. 56. Baarn: Hollandia, 1909.

———. *De Heilige Geest en zijne werkingen volgens de Schriften des Nieuwen Verbonds*. Utrecht: C.H.E. Breijer, 1896.

Bloch-Hoell, Nils. *The Pentecostal Movement*. Oslo: Universitetsforlaget, 1964.

Blumhofer, Edith L. "A Pentecostal Branch Grows in Dowie's Zion," *Heritage* 6/3 (Fall 1986),3-5.

———. "Alexander Boddy and the Rise of Pentecostalism in Great Britain," *Pneuma* 8/1 (Spring 1986),31-40.

———. "The Christian Catholic Church and the Apostolic Faith." Paper presented at the 12th annual meeting of the Society of Pentecostal Studies, Pasadena, CA, November 1982.

Boer-Wildeboer, M. de. "Verslag van het onstaan en groei van de 'Pinkstergemeente' te Delfzijl." Delfzijl, 1981.

Boerwinkel, F. *Kerk en secte.* 2d ed. The Hague: Boekencentrum, 1956.

———. "De Pinkstergroepen." *Oekumenische Leergang,* no. 5. The Hague: Plein, n.d.

Boissevain, H.D.J., ed. *De Zending in Oost en West.* 2 vols. The Hague: Algemeene boekhandel voor inwendige en uitwendige zending, 1934; and Hoederloo: Stichting Hoenderloo, 1945, for the Zendingsstudieraad.

Bolton, Robert. "South of the Clouds: Church Planting in Yunnan Province Through Lisu People Movements (1906-1949)." Term Paper, Fuller Theological Seminary, Pasadena, CA, 1974.

Bommel, J.P. *De Charismatische opwekking als verdere reformatie.* Kampen: J.H. Kok, 1985.

Bonger, W.A. "Geloof en ongeloof in Nederland (1909-1920)," *Socialistische Gids,* 9 (1924),705-30.

———. "Geloof en ongeloof in Nederland," *De Nieuwe Tijd,* 16 (1911),941-70.

Booth, William. *Orders en Reglementen voor Veld-Officieren van het Leger des Heils.* 2 vols. Amsterdam: Nationaal Hoofdkwartier, 1894-1908.

———. *In Engelands Donkerste Wildernissen en De Weg ter Ontkoming.* Translated by C.S. Adama van Scheltema. Amsterdam: S.L. van Looy, 1891.

———. *Orders and Regulations for Field Officers of the Salvation Army.* London: Int. Headquarters, 1886.

———. *The Doctrines and Disciplines of the Salvation Army.* London: Headquarters, 1881.

Booth-Clibborn, Arthur Sydney. *Bloed tegen bloed.* Rotterdam: Vereeniging voor religieus en maatschappelijk werk, 1918.

———. *Blood Against Blood.* 3rd ed. New York: Charles Cook, n.d.

———. *Broederschap met de Noodlijdenden.* Amsterdam: Leger des Heils, n.d.

———. "Eenige bijzonderheden uit het leven van Komm. Booth-Clibborn," *Oorlogskreet* 10/24 (13 June 1896),1-3.

Booth-Clibborn, Catherine [The Maréchale]. *A Poet of Praise.* London: Marshall, Morgan & Scott, 1939.

Booth-Clibborn, William. *The Baptism in the Holy Spirit.* 3rd ed. Portland, OR: Ryder Printing Co., 1944.

———. "My Personal Testimony," *Redemption Tidings* 5/4 (April 1929),2-5; 5/5 (May 1929),3-4; 5/6 (June 1929),2-4.

Booth-Tucker, F. de. *The Life of Catherine Booth.* 2 vols. London: Int. Headquarters, [1892].

Borgdorff, J.C.; Dijk, M. van; and Fokkens, H. *De Pinkstergemeente en hare dwalingen getoetst aan Gods Woord.* Rapport van de commissie inzake de "Pinksterbeweging" aan de Classis Meppel der Gereformeerde Kerken. Hoogeveen: R. Slingenberg, 1932.

Brandt-Bessire, Daniel. *Aux sources de la spiritualité pentecôstiste.* Geneva: Labor et Fides, 1986.

Brillenburg Wurth, G., and Lindeboom, G.A. *Geloofs- en gebedsgenezing.* Rotterdam: J.H. Donner, 1937.

Britten, Emma Hardinge. *Nineteenth Century Miracles.* New York: William Britten, 1884.

Bruner, F.D. *A Theology of the Holy Spirit.* Grand Rapids: William B. Eerdmans, 1980.

Broederschap van Pinkstergemeenten. *Het zal zijn in de laatste dagen.* The Hague: Broederschap van Pinkstergemeenten, 1968.

———. *De Pi   meente en de Kerk.* Rotterdam: Volle Evangelie Lectuur, [⌐ ⌐].

Broek, M. ten. *De Geestelijke Opwekking in Holland.* 2d ed. Ermelo: Gebr. Mooij, 1905.

Brugmans, I.J. "Onderwijspolitiek." In *Geld en geweten: Een bundel opstellen over anderhalve eeuw Nederlands bestuur in de Indonesische archipel.* Vol. 2, pp. 187-202. The Hague: Martinus Nijhoff, 1980.

———. *Paardenkracht en mensenmacht.* The Hague: Martinus Nijhoff, 1976.

Buffinga, N., ed. *Beproeft de Geesten.* Culemborg: De Pauw, 1934.

Bundy, David D. "Pentecostalism in Belgium," *Pneuma* 8 (1986),41-56.

Cartwright, Desmond W. *The Great Evangelists.* Hants: Marshall Pickering, 1986.

Centraal Bureau voor de Statistiek. *Volkstelling 31 december 1930.* Vol. 3: *Kerkelijke gezindte.* The Hague: CBS, 1933.

———. *Volkstelling 31 december 1920.* Vol. 3: *Kerkelijke gezindte.* The Hague: CBS, 1922.

———. *Uitkomsten der negende tienjaarlijksche Volkstelling 31 december 1909.* Vol. 3. The Hague: CBS, 1911.

———. *Uitkomsten der achtste tienjaarlijksche Volkstelling 31 december 1899.* Vol. 12, no. 3. The Hague: CBS, 1901.

Clasen, P.A. *Der Salutismus.* Jena: Eugen Diederichs, 1913.

Clercq, Tom le. *Een protest tegen het Leger des Heils.* Amsterdam: Jacques Dusseau & Co., 1892.

Clercq, Tom le; Vellema, E.J.; Nonhebel, J; Wegkamp, K.; Veen,

Jacques van; Vellema, D.J.; and Bonthuis, G.A. *Het Kerkleger.* Open brief aan de heeren predikanten en leden der Nederlandsch Hervormde Kerk in Nederland. Amsterdam: Jacques Dusseau & Co., [1892].

Collier, Richard. *Leger zonder vijand.* Amsterdam: H.J.W. Becht, 1965.

Cook, Philip Lee. "Zion City, Illinois: Twentieth Century Utopia." Ph.D. thesis, University of Colorado, 1965.

Corry, Percy N. "De Doop des Heiligen Geestes en daarna," *Spade Regen* 16/10 (January 1924),154-56.

————. "1 Korinthe 14," *Spade Regen* 18/10-18/12 (January-March 1926),150-52; 166-69; 183-88.

————. "Goddelijke genezing door de verzoening," *Spade Regen* 19/5 (August 1926),69-70.

Couvée, H.J. *Het standpunt van den Ned. Chr. Gemeenschapsbond tegenover de Kerk enz..* Zeist: Boekhandel Ned. Chr. Gemeenschapsbond, 1932.

————. *Is de Gemeenschapsbeweging nodig?* N.p.: Chr. Gemeenschapsbond, 1927.

————. *De Nederlandsche Christelijke Gemeenschapsbond zijn ontstaan, zijn, bedoeling en zijn beginselen.* Amerongen: Ned. Chr. Gemeenschapsbond, n.d.

————. *Niet-Kerkelijke Evangelisatie een Eisch van onzen Tijd.* Utrecht: Boekhandel der Nederlandsche Tentzending, 1911.

Cutten, George Barton. *Speaking with Tongues.* Hew Haven: Yale University Press, 1927.

Dallmeyer, Heinrich. *Die Zungenbewegung.* Lindhorst: Udastra Verlag, n.d.

Dam, J. van. *Geschiedenis van het Baptisme in Nederland.* 2d ed. Bosch en Duin: Unie van Baptisten Gemeenten in Nederland, 1979.

Darms, Anton. *Life and Work of John Alexander Dowie.* Zion: Christian Catholic Church, n.d.

Dayton, Donald. "The Rise of the Evangelical Healing Movement in Nineteenth Century America," *Pneuma* 4/1 (Spring 1982),1-18.

————, gen. ed. *"The Higher Christian Life": Sources for the Study of the Holiness, Pentecostal and Keswick Movement.* 48 vols. New York: Garland Publishing, 1984-1985.

Ditthardt, H. and Koch, T. *Velbert 50 Jahre mit Vollem Evangelium.* Erzhausen: Leuchter Verlag, 1960.

Domela Niewenhuis, F. *"Generaal" Booth van het Heilsleger en zijn "plan."* Amsterdam, [1891].

Dunn, James, D.G. *Baptism in the Holy Spirit*. London: SCM Press, 1970.

Edel, Eugen. *Der Kampf um die Pfingstbewegung*. Mülheim-Ruhr: Emil Humburg, [1949].

———. *Das Buch der Offenbarung*. 4th ed. Mülheim: Christl. Kolportage-Gesellschaft, 1914.

———. *Die Pfingstbewegung im Lichte der Kirchengeschichte*. Brieg: By the author, 1910.

Eisenlöffel, Ludwig. *. . . bis alle eins werden: Siebzig Jahre Berliner Erklärung und ihre Folgen*. Erzhausen: Leuchter Verlag, 1979.

Endedijk, H.C.; Kornet, A.G.; Vellenga, G.Y.; and Ridderbos, H.N. *Het Werk van de Heilige Geest in de Gemeente*. Voorlichtend geschrift over de Pinkstergroepen uitgegeven in opdracht van de Generale Synode van de Gereformeerde Kerken. Kampen: J.H. Kok, 1968.

Engelen van der Veen, G.A.J. van; Kuile, G.J. ter; and Schuiling, R., eds. *Overijssel*. Deventer: A.E. Kluwer, 1931.

Evans, Eifion. *The Welsh Revival of 1904*. Bridgend: Evangelical Press of Wales, 1969.

Faber, H.; Have, T.T. ten; Dijk, R. van; Goddijn, W.; and Kruijt, J.P. *Ontkerkelijking en buitenkerkelijkheid in Nederland, tot 1960*. Assen: Van Gorcum & Comp., 1970.

Faupel, William. "Glossolalia as Foreign Language: An Historical Survey of the Twentieth Century Claim." Paper presented at the 12th annual meeting of the Society for Pentecostal Studies, Pasadena, CA, 1982.

Filius, J. and Lissenburg, D. *Gered om te redden*. 2d ed. Carillon reeks no. 25. Amsterdam: W. ten Have, 1962.

Fleisch, Paul. *Die Pfingstbewegung in Deutschland*. Hannover: Heinr. Feesche Verlag, 1957.

———. *Die Moderne Gemeinschaftsbewegung in Deutschland*. Vol. 2: *Die deutsche Gemeinschaftsbewegung seit Auftreten des Zungenredens*. Part 1: Die Zungenbewegung in Deutschland. Leipzig: H.G. Wallman, 1914.

———. *Die Moderne Gemeinschaftsbewegung in Deutschland*. Vol 1: *Die Geschichte der deutschen Gemeinschaftsbewegung bis zum Auftreten des Zungenredens, 1875-1907*. 3rd ed. Leipzig: H.G. Wallman, 1912.

———. *Die innere Entwicklung der deutschen Gemeinschaftsbewegung in den Jahren 1906 unde 1907*. Leipzig: H.G. Wallman, 1908.

Fokkens, H. "De Pinksterbeweging," *Gereformeerd Theologisch Tijdschrift* 32 (1932),520-40.

Fonteyn, Henk. "Johannes de Heer: Een theologisch portret," *Soteria* 3/3 (September 1985),19-22.

————. "Johannes de Heer: Prediker van de parousie." *Religieuze bewegingen in Nederland*, no. 9. R. Kranenborg, gen. ed. Amsterdam: VU, 1984.

Frodsman, Stanley. *With Signs Following.* Springfield, MO: Gospel Publishing House, 1926.

Fuller, Daniel P. *Gospel & Law: Contrast or Continuum?* Grand Rapids: William B. Eerdmans, 1980.

Gee, Donald. *These Men I Knew.* Nottingham: Assemblies of God, 1980.

————. *Wind and Flame.* Croydon: Heath Press, 1967.

————. "The Challenge of Yunnan," *Pentecostal Evangel,* 5-3-1930, 4-5.

Gemeente Gods Rotterdam. *40 jaar Pinksterwerk in Rotterdam.* Rotterdam: Gemeente Gods, 1972.

Generale Synode der Nederlandse Hervormde Kerk. *De Kerk en de Pinkstergroepen.* Herdelijk schrijven van de Generale Synode der Nederlandse Hervormde Kerk. The Hague: Boekencentrum, 1960.

Giese, Ernst. *Und flicken die Netze.* Marburg: By the author, 1976.

————. *Jonathan Paul: Ein Knecht Jesu Christi.* Altdorf: Missionsbuchhandlung und Verlag, 1965.

Golverdinge, J. van, Jr. *Wat we weten van "Het Leger des Heils."* Leiden: D. Donner, 1883. For the Provinciale Commissie voor Inwendige Zending in Noord-Holland.

Goudsmit, Jaap. *Anderhalve eeuw doktoren aan de arts.* Amsterdam: SUA, 1978.

Grosheide, F.W. "Iets over de glossolalie," *Gereformeerd Theologisch Tijdschrift* 19 (1918),1-24.

————. "Glossolalie." In *Christelijke Encyclopedie voor het Nederlandsche volk*, vol. 2, pp. 339-40. Kampen: J.H. Kok, 1925-31.

Gunning, J.H., J.Hz. *Herinneringen uit mijn leven.* Edited by A. Brom Jr. Amsterdam: H.J. Spruyt, 1940.

————. *William Booth.* Amsterdam: H.J. Spruyt, [1936].

Haaren, W.T.M. van. "Een religieus-anthropologisch onderzoek naar de 'Gemeente des Heeren' te Elim." Kandidaats thesis, University of Leiden, 1981.

Hagoort, R. *De Christelijke Sociale Beweging.* Franeker: T. Wever, 1955.

Haitjema, Th. L., *De richtingen in de Nederlandse Hervormde Kerk.* 2d ed. Wageningen: H. Veenmans & Zonen, 1953.

Harlan, Rolvix. *John Alexander Dowie and the Christian Catholic Apostolic Church in Zion.* Evansville, WI: Press of R.M. Antes, 1906.

Hartog, Jan de. *Herinneringen aan Amsterdam.* Amsterdam/Brussel: Elsevier, 1981.

Hazenberg, W. *Jezus de Geneesheer of De Kranken door Christus genezen.* Veendam: J. van Petegem, [1893].

―――. *Bijbelleer der Genezing des Lichaams op het Gebed des Geloofs met Getuigenissen van Genezingen in Nederland.* Veendam: J. van Petegem, [1892].

―――. *De Tweeërlei Rust.* Utrecht: Joh. de Liefde, n.d.

Heer, Johannes de. *'K zal gedenken.* The Hague: J.N. Voorhoeve, 1949.

―――. *Het duizendjarig vrederijk.* Zeist: Zoeklicht, 1934.

―――, ed. *Zangbundel.* 13th ed. Rotterdam: Joh. de Heer & Zn., 1933.

―――. "Op den Uitkijk," *Jeruël* April 1907; and February 1908. Quoted in *Ermelosch Zendingsblad* 48/5 (May 1907),1-4; and 49/2 (February 1908),5-11.

Hervormde Raad voor Kerk en Ziekenzorg. *Vragen rondom de gebedsgenezing.* The Hague: Lectuurbureau der Nederlands Hervormde Kerk, 1959.

Hette Abma, G; Balke, W.; Biesbroek, G.; Boer, C. den; Bouw, W.J.; Broekhuis, J.; Exalto, K.; Graaf, J. van der; Roon, J.P. van; and Tukker, C.A. *Profetie of fantasie?* Amersfoort: Echo, 1978.

Hof, H.L.M. v.d. " 't Wonder der glossolalie." In *Annuarium der Roomsch-Katholieke Studenten in Nederland—1918,* pp. 268-91. Bussum: Paul Brand, 1918.

Hofman, John. "De Pinksterbeweging in Nederland: Onstaan, verspreiding en invloed." An annotated bibliography. Rotterdam, 1986.

Hofstee, E.W., *Korte demografische geschiedenis van Nederland van 1800 tot heden.* Haarlem: Fibula-Van Dishoeck, 1981.

Hogenraad, F.J. *Gebedsgenezing en Pinksterbeweging.* 3rd ed. Groningen: Vuurbaak, 1975.

Hollenweger, Walter J. "After Twenty Years' Research on Pentecostalism," *International Review of Mission* 75/297 (1986),3-12.

―――. *Erfahrungen der Leibhaftigkeit.* Interkulturelle Theologie 1. Munich: Chr. Kaiser, 1979.

―――. *Umgang mit Mythen.* Interkulturelle Theologie 2. Munich: Chr. Kaiser, 1982.

―――. "Roots and Fruits of the Charismatic Renewal in the Third

World: Implications for Mission," *Theological Renewal* no. 14 (February 1980),11-28.

―――. *The Pentecostals*. London: SCM Press, 1972.

―――. "The Social and Ecumenical Significance of Pentecostal Liturgy," *Studia Liturgica* 8/4 (1971-72),207-15.

―――. *Enthusiastisches Christentum*. Zurich: Zwingli Verlag, 1969.

―――. "Handbuch der Pfingstbewegung." 10 vols. Th.D. dissertation, University of Zurich, 1965-67.

―――. "Literatur von und ᵗᵐber die Pfingstbewegung," *Nederlands Theologisch Tijdschrift* 18 (1964),289-306.

―――, ed. *Pentecostal Research in Europe: Problems, Promises and People*. Frankfurt/Bern: Peter Lang, forthcoming.

―――, ed. *Die Pfingstkirchen*. Die Kirchen der Welt vol. 7. Stuttgart: Ev. Verlagswerk, 1971.

Hulzen, A. van. *De wereld van eergisteren: Nederland tussen de jaren 1900-1920*. The Hague: Kruseman, 1983.

Jansen, Joh. "Pinksterbeweging." In *Christelijke Encyclopedie voor het Nederlandsche volk*, vol 4, pp. 573-74. Kampen: J.H. Kok, 1925-31.

Jong, Otto de. *Nederlandse Kerk Geschiedenis*. 2d ed. Nijkerk: G.F. Callenbach, 1978.

Jonge, Hendrik de. "Geschiedenis in telegramstijl." Delfzijl, 1981.

Jonker, W., Jr. *Een Nederlander als baanbreker der zending in Tibet*. Rotterdam: Nederlandsche Zendingsvereeniging, 1917.

Karelse, J. *Zijn takken over de muur*. Utrecht: Bond van Vrije Evangelische Gemeente en Erven J. Bijleveld, 1956.

Kelsey, Morton T. *Healing and Chistianity*. New York: Harper & Row, 1973.

Ketel, N. "Hij heeft onze krankheden op zich genomen," *Elthetho* 72 (1918), 171-80.

King, James Gorden, Jr. "An Examination of Prevailing Beliefs Regarding Gifts of the Spirit Immediately Preceding the 20th Century Pentecostal Revival." Presented at the 12th annual meeting of the Society for Pentecostal Studies, Pasadena, CA, 1982.

Klaver, Piet. "Herinneringen van een Pinksterpionier," *Kracht van Omhoog* 28/12 (18 December 1964),18-19; 28/13 (1 January 1965),4-6; 28/14 (15 January 1965),8-9; 28/16 (12 February 1965),8-9; 28/19 (26 March 1965),8-9; 28/21 (23 April 1965),14-15.

Kluit, M. Elisabeth. *Het Protestantse Réveil in Nederland en daarbuiten 1815-1865*. Amsterdam: Paris, 1970.

————. *Nader over het Réveil.* Kampen: J.H. Kok, n.d.

Knox, Ronald A. *Enthusiasm.* Oxford: Oxford University Press, 1950; Collins Flame Classics, 1987.

Kok, A.B.W.M. *Waarheid en Dwaling.* Amsterdam: S.J.P. Bakker, n.d.

————. *Verleidende Geesten.* Kampen: J.H. Kok, 1939.

Kok, C.A. "How God Protected Christian Chinese from Bandits," *The Latter Rain,* June 1925, 18-19.

Kornet, A.G. *De Pinksterbeweging en de Bijbel.* Kampen: J.H. Kok, 1963.

Kossmann, E.H. *The Low Countries 1780-1940.* Oxford History of Modern Europe. Oxford: Clarendon Press, 1978.

Kraan, K.J. *Ruimte voor de Geest?* Kampen: J.H. Kok, 1970.

————. *Opdat u genezing ontvangt.* 3rd ed. Hoornaar: Gideon, 1974.

Kraemer, P.E. "Enig materiaal over sectarisme in een achtergebleven gebied," *Sociologisch Bulletin* 13 (1959),98-108.

Kruijt, J.P. "Kerkelijkheid en onkerkelijkheid in Nederland (1930)," *De Socialistische Gids* 20 (1935),323-39; 426-51.

————. *De ontkerkelijkheid in Nederland.* Groningen: P. Noordhoff, 1933.

Krust, Chr. *50 Jahre Deutsche Pfingstbewegung Mülheimer Richtung.* Altdorff: Missionsbuchhandlung und Verlag, 1958.

Kühn, B., ed. *Die Pfingstbewegung.* Gotha: Missionbuchhandlung P. Ott, n.d.

Kuiper, J. *Geschiedenis van het Godsdienstig en Kerkelijk leven van het Nederlandsche volk.* Utrecht: A.H. ten Bokkel Huinink, 1900.

Kuyper, A. *Het Werk van den Heiligen Geest.* 3 vols. Amsterdam: J.A. Wormser, 1889-89.

Laan, Cornelis van der. "The Proceedings of the Leaders' Meetings (1908-1911) and of the International Pentecostal Council (1912-1914)," *EPTA Bulletin* 6/2 (1987),76-96.

————. "Een pinksterdame van bijna tachtig jaar," *Parakleet* 5/17 (Winter 1985),8-13.

————. "Early Pentecostalism in Western Europe: Lessons for Today." Paper presented at the Conference on Pentecostal and Charismatic Research in Europe, University of Birmingham, April 1984.

————. "The Pentecostal Movement in Holland, Its Origin and Its International Position," *Pneuma* 5/1 (Fall 1983),30-38.

Laan, C. van der, and Laan, Paul van der. *Pinksteren in beweging.* Kampen: J.H. Kok, 1982.

Laan, P.N. van der. "The Question of Spiritual Unity: The Dutch

Pentecostal Movement in Ecumenical Perspective." Ph.D. thesis, University of Birmingham, 1988.

————. "Dynamics in Pentecostal Mission: A Dutch Perspective," *International Review of Mission* 75/297 (January 1986),47-50.

LaBerge, Agnes N.O. *What God Hath Wrought.* Chicago: Herald Publishing Co., 1921.

Layendecker, L. *Orde, verandering, ongelijkheid.* Meppel: J.A. Boom, 1981.

————. *Religie en conflict.* Meppel: J.A. Boom, 1967.

Leeuwen, C.R. van. *Ziekte . . . en hoe te genezen.* Amsterdam: J. Clausen, 1901.

Leger des Heils. "Leger des Heils Reglementen voor Secretarissen en Penningmeesters." Amsterdam: Leger des Heils, 1907.

————. "Jaarverslag en Staat van Inkomsten en Uitgaven van het Leger des Heils in Nederland van 1 mei 1891-1 juni 1892." Amsterdam: Leger des Heils, 1892.

————. "Antwoord op 'Een protest tegen het Leger des Heils.' " Amsterdam: Leger des Heils, 1892.

Lieftinck, W.H. *'Geloofsgenezing' (protest-voorlichting waarschuwing).* Naarden: Gooische Drukkerij, 1911.

Like as of Fire. A reprint of the old Azusa Street Papers collected by Fred T. Corum. Wilmington, MA: By the compiler, 1981.

Lindeboom, J. *Stiefkinderen van het Christendom.* Arnhem: Gijbers & Van Loon, 1973 (reprint of 1929).

Lindsay, Gordon. *John Alexander Dowie.* Dallas, TX: Christ for the Nations, reprint 1980.

McConkey, James. *The Threefold Secret of the Holy Spirit.* Chicago: Moody Press, n.d. (first printed 1897).

McDonnel, Killian, ed. *Presence, Power, Praise.* 3 vols. Collegeville, MN: The Liturgical Press, 1980.

MacPherson, D. *The Incredible Cover Up.* Plainfield, NJ: Logos Int., 1975.

MacRobert, Ian. "The Spirit and the World: The Black Roots and White Racism of Early Pentecostalism in the U.S.A." M.A. thesis, University of Birmingham, 1985.

Malony, H. Newton, and Lovekin, A. Adams. *Glossolalia: Behavioral Science Perspectives on Speaking in Tongues.* New York/Oxford: Oxford University Press, 1985.

Manussen, A. "De z.g. 'Tongenbeweging,' " *Ons Maandblaadje* 3/35 (December 1916),1-5.

Marle, Ida van. *Zij volgde haar roeping.* The Hague: Gazon, 1976.

Marijs-Visser, M. "De Pinksterbeweging," *Witte Velden,* 20/4-5

(July-August 1950),13-14; 20/7 (October 1950),10-11; 20/8 (November 1950),6-7.

Meerloo, F.J. van. *Pinkster- of Tongenbeweging*. Apeldoorn: Neerlandia Drukkerij, 1912.

Meiden, Anne van der. *Welzalig het volk*. Baarn: Ten Have, 1981.

Mills, Watson E. *Speaking in Tongues: A Guide to Research on Glossolalia*. Grand Rapids: William B. Eerdmans, 1986.

Missen, Alfred F. *The Sound of a Going*. Nottingham: Assemblies of God Publishing House, 1973.

Molenaar, D.G. *De doop met de Heilige Geest*. 2d ed. Kampen: J.H. Kok, 1973.

Möller, F.P. *Die diskussie oor die Charismata soos wat dit in die Pinksterbeweging geleer en beoefen word*. Braamfontein: Evangelie Uitgewers, 1975.

Mosiman, Eddison. *Das Zungenreden*. Tübingen: J.C.B. Mohr, 1911.

Mulder, L.H. *Revolte der fijnen*. Kampen: J.H. Kok, 1973.

Muller, J.G. "Leven en werken van wijlen Ds. Jan van Petegem verteld door zijn kleinzoon J.G. Muller." N.p., n.d.

Murray, Andrew. *De Volle Pinksterszegen*. Nijmegen: P.J. Milborn, n.d.

————. *Jezus, de Geneesheer der kranken*. Amsterdam: Hveker & Zoon, n.d.

————. *De kracht van Jezus' bloed*. Amsterdam: Jacques Dusseau, [1894].

Nelson, Douglas. "For Such a Time as This: The Story of Bishop William J. Seymour and the Azusa Street Revival." Ph.D. thesis, University of Birmingham, 1981.

Nes, W. van. *Een Geestelijke en Maatschappelijke Woekerplant of De Stichting van Generaal Booth*. Utrecht: Kemik & Zoon, 1896.

Nijkamp, H., ed. *Ten antwoord op een stem*. Kampen: J.H. Kok, 1981.

"Onze Strijders in het Veld: Kapitein Polman," *Oorlogskreet*, 1 December 1894, pp. 6-8.

Oosbree, R. van. *Valiants for Truth We Have Known*. Pasadena, CA: RavanO, 1986.

Ouweneel, W.J. *Gij zijt allen broeders*. Apeldoorn: H. Medema, 1980.

Parham, Charles F. *A Voice Crying in the Wilderness*. Baxter Springs, KS: Apostolic Faith Bible College, n.d.

————. *The Everlasting Gospel*. Baxter Springs, KS: Apostolic Faith Bible College, n.d.

Parham, Sarah E. *The Life of Charles E. Parham Founder of the*

Apostolic Faith Movement. Birmingham, AL: Commercial Printing Co., 1930.

Paul, J. *De oplossing van het wereldraadsel.* Pinksteruitgaven no. 3. Amsterdam: G.R. Polman, 1920.

————. *Zur Dämonenfrage.* Mülheim-Ruhr: Emil Humburg, 1912.

Penn Lewis, Jessie. *The Awakening in Wales and Some of the Hidden Springs.* London: Marshall Brothers, 1905.

Penn Lewis, Jessie, and Roberts, Evan. *War on the Saints.* 9th ed. New York: Thomas E. Lowe, 1973.

Pethrus, Lewi. *A Spiritual Memoir.* Plainfield, NJ: Logos Int., 1973.

————. "The Revival in Sweden," *Elim Evangel* 8/18 (September 1927),281-84.

Polman, Gerrit Roelof, ed. *Spade Regen* April 1908-March 1931.

————, ed. *Klanken des Vredes* June 1915-May 1928.

Polman-Blekkink, W.J.H. *Dauwdruppels.* Amsterdam: G.R. Polman, 1927.

Praamsma, L. *De Kerk van alle tijden.* Vol. 4. Franeker: T. Wever, 1981.

Rasker, A.J. *De Nederlandse Hervormde Kerk vanaf 1795.* Kampen: J.H. Kok, 1974.

Ritter, P.H., Jr. *Over Joh. de Heer.* Baarn: Hollandia, [1936].

Robinson, Martin. "The Charismatic Anglican—Historical and Contemporary: A Comparison Between the Life and Work of Alexander Boddy (1854-1930) and Michael Harper." M.Litt. thesis, University of Birmingham, 1976.

Romein, January. *Op het breukvlak van twee eeuwen.* 2 vols. Leiden: E.J. Brill, 1967.

Romein, Jan, and Romein, Annie. *Erflaters van onze beschaving.* Amsterdam: Em. Querido, 1979.

————. *De lage landen bij de zee.* Amsterdam: Em. Querido, 1977.

Rullmann, J.C. *Abraham Kuyper: Een levensschets.* Kampen: J.H. Kok, 1928.

————. *Kuyper-Bibliografie.* Vol. 1: *(1860-1879).* Den Haag: Js. Bootsma, 1923.

Rutke, Fem, ed. *Charismatisch Nederland.* Serie Nieuw Leven. Kampen: J.H. Kok, 1977.

Rijken, H. *De Pinksterbeweging en . . . .* Middelburg: Reveil, n.d.

Rijkhoek, D. *De Geestelijke opwekking van 1905 en haar gevolgen in een mensenleven.* N.p., [1947].

Samarin, William J. *Tongues of Men and Angels.* New York: Macmillan, 1972.

Sandall, Robert. *The History of the Salvation Army.* 3 vols. London:

Thomas Nelson & Sons, 1947-55. Continued by Arch R. Wiggens.

Sandeen, Ernst R. *The Roots of Fundamentalism.* Grand Rapids: Baker Book House, 1978.

Scharten, Elize. "Gaat heen in de gehele wereld en predikt het evangelie aan alle schepselen," *Volle Evangelie Koerier* 10/9 (March 1948)—13/1 (July 1950).

————. *Uit het binnenland van China.* Pinksteruitgaven no. 4. Amsterdam: G.R. Polman, 1922.

————. *Tot eer van God.* Amsterdam: By the author, [1908].

Scharten, K. "Genealogie van de familie Scharten," *Gens Nostra* 34 (1979), 49-60.

Schep, J.A. *Geestesdoop en tongentaal.* 2d ed. Franeker: T. Wever, n.d.

Schrenk, Elias. *Die Pfingstbewegung.* Stuttgart: Buchhandlung des Deutschen Philadelphiavereins, 1910.

————. *Was lehrt uns die Kasseler Bewegung?* Kassel: Ernst Röttgers Verlag, 1907.

[Schuurman, E.] *De hoofdstad vat vlam.* Amsterdam: Pinkstergemeente, 1966.

Schuurman, E. *Behoud den rechten weg.* Zwolle: By the author, 1929.

————. *Wat zegt Gods Woord.* Zwolle: By the author, 1928.

Shaw, S.B. *The Great Revival in Wales.* Chicago: By the author, 1905.

Sheppard, Gerald T. "Pentecostalism and the Hermeneutics of Dispensationalism: Anatomy of an Uneasy Relationship," *Pneuma* 6/2 (Fall 1984),5-33.

Slicher van Bath, B.H. *Een samenleving onder spanning: Geschiedenis van het platteland in Overijssel.* Assen: Van Gorcum & Comp., 1957.

Smeeton, Donald Dean. "Holiness Hymns and Pentecostal Power: A Theologian Looks at Pentecostal Hymnody," *The Hymn* 31 (July 1980),183-85; 193.

Spijker, W. van 't. *De Charismatische beweging.* The Hague: Willem de Zwijgerstichting, 1977.

Spittler, Russel P., ed. *Perspectives on the New Pentecostalism.* Grand Rapids: Baker Book House, 1976.

Steiner, L. *Mit Folgenden Zeichen.* Bazel: Mission für das Volle Evangelium, 1954.

Stichting Noordholland Provinciaal Opbouworgaan. *Sociale atlas Noord-Holland.* Haarlem: Stichting Noordholland Provinciaal Opbouworgaan, 1963.

Stichting Ozewold Derk. *De Parenteel Huetink-Wanrooy.* Wychen: Stichting Ozewold Derk, 1982.

Stotts, George Raymond. "The History of the Modern Pentecostal Movement in France." Ph.D. thesis, Texas Tech Unversity, 1973.

Strachan, Gordon. *The Pentecostal Theology of Edward Irving.* London: Darton, Longman & Todd, 1973.

Strahan, James. *The Maréchale.* London: Hodder and Stoughton, n.d.

Stuijvenberg, J.H. van. *De economische geschiedenis van Nederland.* Groningen: Wolters Noordhoff, 1977.

Stuurman, Siep, *Verzuiling, kapitalisme en patriarchaat.* Nijmegen: SUN, 1983.

Suurmond, J.-J. "Een charismatische kijk op konflicten." *Bulletin voor Charismatische Theologie* 19 (1987),10-21.

Tang, M.J. *Het Apostolische werk in Nederland.* The Hague: Boekencentrum, 1982.

Thiessen, H. *Het Gouden Jubileum van de Pinksterbeweging.* The Hague: By the author, 1978.

Timmerman, J. *Straatprediking: Jaarverslag der Bijbeltent voor straatevangelisatie en colportage in Nederland.* Amsterdam: By the author, 1909.

Torrey, R.A. *De Heilige Geest.* Frankfurt: Elmer Klassen, 1966.

Tukker, C.A. *Het Chiliasme van Reformatie tot Réveil.* Apeldoorn: Willem de Zwijgerstichting, 1981.

Veen, S.D. van. *Eene eeuw van worsteling.* Groningen: J.B. Wolters, 1904.

Veenhof, J. "Internationale diskussie over de charismatische beweging," *Bulletin voor Charismatische Theologie* no. 13 (1984),3-14.

———. "Wat de charismatische beweging ons te zeggen heeft," *Bulletin voor de charismatische Theologie* no. 11 (1983),3-9.

Veenhof, J.; Versteeg, J.P.; Hartveld, G.P.; Kraan, K.J.; Firet, J. *Op het spoor van de Geest.* Kampen: J.H. Kok, 1978.

Veenstra, S.L. *Het Leger des Heils.* Kerk en Secte, no. 38. Baarn: Hollandia, 1910.

Velders, W.J.J. "Gebedsgenezing." In *Christelijke Encyclopedie voor het Nederlandsche volk* vol. 6, pp. 182-84. Kampen: J.H. Kok, 1931.

Verdoorn, J.A. *Het gezondsheidswezen te Amsterdam in de 19e eeuw.* Nijmegen: SUN, 1981.

Vinson, Synan. *The Holiness-Pentecostal Movement in the United States.* Grand Rapids: William B. Eerdmans, 1971.

———, ed. *Aspects of Pentecostal-Charismatic Origins.* Plainfield, NJ: Logos Int., 1975.

[Voorhoeve, J.N.] "Correspondentie: E.J. te N.B. vraagt iets over de 'Pinksterbeweging,'" *Bode des Heils in Christus* 62 (1919),45-46.

Vries, Joh. de. *De Nederlandse economie tijdens de 20e eeuw*. Haarlem: Fibulan-Van Dishoeck, 1978.

Wacker, Grant. "Marching to Zion," *Heritage* 6/2 (Summer 1986),6-9; 6/3 (Fall 1986),7-9.

Wagemaker, J.L. *De glossolalie in het N.T.* Thesis, Kweekschool Algemeene Doopsgezinde Societeit, 1913.

Wesselig, J. *De Afscheiding van 1834 in Overijssel 1834-'69*. Vol. 1: *De classis Zwolle*. Groningen: De Vuurbaak, 1984.

Whittaker, Colin C. *Seven Pentecostal Pioneers*. Basingstoke: Marshall Morgan & Scott, 1983.

Wichers, A.J.; Kraemer, P.E.; and Koning, J.W. de. *Leven en werken te Elim-Hollandscheveld*. Assen: Van Gorcum & Comp., 1959.

Wielenga, B. "De genezing op het gebed." *Schild en Pijl* 1/5 (1918),1-35.

Wiggens, Arch R. *The History of The Salvation Army*. 2 vols. London: Thomas Nelson & Sons, 1964-68.

Williams, J. Rodman. *The Era of the Spirit*. Plainfield, NJ: Logos Int., 1971.

Wilson, Bryan R. *Sects and Society*. London: William Heinemann, 1961.

Winckel, W.F.A. *Leven en Arbeid van Dr. A. Kuyper*. Amsterdam: W. ten Have, 1919.

Windmuller, J.P.; Galan, C. de; and Zweden, A.F. van. *Arbeidsverhoudingen in Nederland*. 4th ed. Aula pocket 731. Utrecht: Het Spectrum, 1983.

Wumkes, G.A. *Nei Sawntich Jier*. Boalsert: A.J. Osinga, 1949.

————. *De Pinksterbeweging voornamelijk in Nederland*. Pinksteruitgaven, no. 1. Amsterdam: G.R. Polman, 1917.

————. *De Pinksterbeweging voornamelijk in Nederland*. Utrecht: G.J.A. Ruys, 1916.

————. "De Pinksterbeweging voornamelijk in Nederland," *Stemmen des Tijds* 5/3 (September 1916),251-71.

————. *Tussen Flie en Borne*. Wester-Schelling: J. Oepkes, 1900.

Zeegers, J.L. *De Geloofsgenezing, hare leer en hare waarde*. The Hague: W.A. Beschoor, 1886.

Zeehuisen, J. "Statistische bijdrage tot den kennis in het kwartier Salland, provincie Overijssel." In *Tijdschrift voor Staathuishoudkunde en Statistiek* vol. 6, ed. by R.W.A. Sloet tot Oldhuis. Zwolle: W.E.J. Tjeenk Willink, 1851.

Zendingsstudieraad. *Nederlansch Zendingsjaarboek voor 1937-1939.* Zeist: Zendingsstudieraad, 1938.

————. *Nederlandsch Zendingsjaarboek Supplement voor 1937.* Zeist: Zendingsstudieraad, 1937.

————. *Nederlandsch Zendingsjaarboek voor 1933-'34—1935-'36.* Zeist: Zendingsstudieraad, 1935.

————. *Nederlandsch Zendingsjaarboek voor 1930-'31—1931-'32.* Zeist: Zendingsstudieraad, 1931.

————. *Nederlandsch Zendingsjaarboek voor 1928/29.* Zeist: Zendingsstudieraad, 1928.

————. *Nederlandsch Zendingsjaarboekje voor 1924/25.* De Bilt: Zendingsstudieraad, 1924.

Zijp, A. *De dwaling van de Pinkstergemeente te Amsterdam.* Amsterdam: By the author, 1929.

————. *Om het behoud van den zegen.* Amsterdam: By the author, 1926.

————. *Moeten of mogen wij onze kindertjes laten doopen?* Bezwaarschrift ingezonden aan de Generale Synode der Gereformeerde Kerken, met het antwoord der Synode. Amsterdam: By the author, [1926].

Foreign Pentecostal Periodicals

Articles, letters, or references in foreign Pentecostal periodicals directly relating to Dutch Pentecostalism.

ENGLAND

Confidence

Boddy, A.A.
"A Visit to Holland," no. 6 (September 1908),6-9; 11-12; 16-17; "The German Conference," 2/1 (January 1909),7; "The German Conference," 2/2 (February 1909),33-34; "Midday Prayer Meeting in the City," 2/2 (February 1909),49; "Sunderland International Pentecostal Congress," 2/6 (June 1909),131, 134; "Swansea Conference," 2/9 (September 1909),212-15; "Holland," 3/10 (October 1910),242-43; "Pentecostal Items," 4/3 (March 1911),62; "A Brief History of the Sunderland Conventions," 4/6 (June 1911),128; "The Place of Tongues in the Pentecostal Movement," 4/8 (August 1911),176-78; "Amsterdam," 4/12 (December 1911),270-72; "London Conference," 5/2 (February 1912),30-33; "At Amsterdam," 5/12 (December 1912), 275, 283-84 "Pentecostal Items," 8/4 (April 1915),78; "Notes of the London Pentecostal Conference," 8/6 (June 1915),108; "The Amsterdam International Conference: Notes by Visitors," no. 125 (April-June 1921),19-21; "Pentecostal Items," no. 127 (October-December 1921),59.

Coppini, Oreste
"Switzerland," 8/5 (May 1915),93-94.

Corry, Percy N.
"Holland: Dedication of Mission Home," 5/11 (November 1912),259-60.

Jeffreys, T.M.
"Conference at Mülheim-on-Rhor, Germany," 2/8 (August 1909), 189; "The Recent Conference at Mülheim," 2/9 (September 1909),200-200b.

Mogridge, H.
"Holland and Antwerp," 3/10 (October 1910),243-45.

Niblock, M.
"A Third German Conference," 3/1 (January 1910),19-20.

Polman, G.R.
"Letter," no. 2 (May 1908),14; "Testimony from Pastor Polman," no. 5 (August 1908),16-18; "Spade Regen," no. 6 (September 1908),19-20; "Amongst the Ice-floes of the Zuyder Zee," 2/2 (February 1909),51-52; "Letter from Pastor Polman," 2/9 (September 1909),208; "Farewell Meetings with Mr. & Mrs. Kok at Amsterdam," 2/9 (September 1909), 208a-208b; "Switzerland," 2/12 (December

1909),280-81; "Through Dutch Eyes," 3/4 (April 1910),94-95; "A Letter from Pastor Polman," 4/6 (June 1911),138; "Testimony by Pastor Polman," 5/8 (August 1912),174-75; "The Work in Holland," 6/8 (August 1913),163-64; "The Pentecostal Bible School in Holland," 7/4 (April 1914),78; "Soulish not Spiritual," 7/7 (July 1914),136-37; "Letter," 7/11 (November 1914),204-05; "Letter," 8/2 (February 1915),29; "Pastor Polman's Journey," 8/5 (May 1915),92-93; "Holland," 8/7 (July 1915),134-35; "Holland," 8/12 (December 1915),235-36; "Holland: News from the Island of Terschelling," 9/9 (September 1916),152- 54; "Invitation to the International Pentecostal Convention in Amsterdam, 1921," 13/4 (October-December 1920),57.

Polman, Wilhelmine
"Subsequent Blessing in Holland," no. 5 (August 1908), 18-19; "Continued Blessing," no. 9 (December 1908),21; "The Strange Baptism of Sister Kok at Amsterdam," no. 9 (December 1908),22-24; "Holland," 2/4 (April 1909),91-92; "Our Children's Page," 4/7 (July 1911),163; "The Victory of the Lord," 4/11 (November 1911),250-51, 254; "Speaking in Tongues," 6/8 (August 1913),151-52; "The Secret of the Lord," 7/3 (March 1914),47; "A Vision and a Life Story," 7/10 (October 1914),186-89.

The Elim Evangel

Jeffreys, George
"Pentecost in Scandinavia," 4/11 (November 1923),230-31.
Polman, G.R.
"Invitation to the International Pentecostal Convention in Amsterdam 1921," 2/1 (December 1920),21.
Polman, W.
"What God Is Doing in Holland," 2/1 (December 1920),18-19.
Potma, C.T.
"The Foursquare Gospel in Belgium," 7/13 (1 July 1926),153.
Thiessen, Hank, and Thiessen, John
"The Garden of the East," 9/16 (1 September 1928),245; "Missionaries from Java," 10/23 (4 October 1929),355.
Wood Moorehead, Max
"Notes and Impressions of the International Convention at Amsterdam, Holland, January 8-17, 1921," 2/2 (March 1921),35-36.

Flames of Fire

Editorial
no. 2 (November 1911),1; July 1920, 4.

Klaver, Piet
Letter, no. 34 (January 1916),4; September 1916, 5-6; November 1916, 7-8; October 1917, 7; January 1918, 7-9; March 1918, 4-6; October 1918, 3-5; April 1919, 8; March 1920, 7-8; May 1920, 5; July 1920, 4-5; August 1920, 6; November 1920, 4-7; December 1921, 5-7; February 1922, 6-7; October-November 1923, 4-5.
Klaver, Rose
Letter, May 1920, 5-6; June 1921, 11; June 1922, 5-6.
Kok, Arie
Letter, no. 5 (April 1912),2-4; no. 7 (October 1912),3-4; "Tiding from Tibet and Other Lands," no. 10 (February 1913),3-4; no. 11 (May 1913),3-4; no. 12 (July 1913),3-4; no. 13 (August 1913),3-4; no. 15 (December 1913),6; no. 18 (July 1914),2-4; Letter, no. 25 (March 1915),5-6; no. 29 (July 1915),4; no. 31 (September 1915),3-5; no. 33 (November-December 1915),4-6; no. 35 (February 1916),4-5; no. 36 (March 1916),3-5; September 1916, 5; May 1917, 8-10; July 1917, 2-4; February 1918, 3; March 1918, 4; May 1918, 2-6; June 1918, 6-8; August 1918, 5-8.
Polman, G.R.
"The Pentecostal Revival," no. 4 (March 1912),3-4; "The Gospel to All Nations," no. 30 (August 1915),2-4.
Scharten, Elize
"For the Children," no. 8 (November 1912),4; Letter, no. 32 (October 1915),3-4; no. 34 (January 1916),5-7; October 1916, 3-5; June 1917, 4-6; May 1919, 5; April 1922, 8.
Vries, Ida
Letter, no. 23 (January 1915),5-5;

Redemption Tidings

Corry, Percy N.
"Holland," 2/1 (January 1926),11; "Revival in Holland," 2/2 (February 1926),9; "Holland," 2/5 (May 1926),9; "Holland," 2/6 (June 1926),11.
Gee, Donald
"Mr. G.R. Polman (Holland) with the Lord," 8/4 (April 1932), 20.

GERMANY

Pfingstgrüsse

As of 11/20 (5 October 1919): *Grüsse aus dem Heiligtum*
As of 14/7 (July 1922): *Die Pfingstbotschaft*
As of 22/1 (1 January 1930): *Heilszeugnisse*

Editorial
"Die Hamburger Dezember-Konferenz," 1/1 (February 1909),4-9; 13; 1/2 (April 1909),4-6; "Vorwärts!" 3/26 (26 March 1911),205-06;

"Von Arbeitsfeld," 3/46 (13 August 1911),368; "Von Nah und fern," 4/32 (5 May 1912),256; 4/33 (12 May 1912),264; "Ein Einweihungsfeier des neuen Saales in Amsterdam," 4/40 (30 June 1912),318; "Aus der Arbeit," 5/6 (10 November 1912),47; "Internationale Pfingstkonferenzen," 5/15 (12 January 1913), 113-15; "Für das Missionshaus von Bruder Kok," 6/45 (9 August 1914),358; 6/52 (27 September 1914),388; "Die diesjährige Mülheimer Konferenz," 10/27 (22 September 1918),106; "Nachricht über Geschwister Wieneke," 12/12 (9 June 1920),48; "Von der Mülheimer Konferenz," 12/17-18 (1 September 1920),68; "Erste Internationale Glaubenskonferenz," 13/2 (February 1921),15; "Die Erste Internationale Pfingstkonferenz in Amsterdam," 13/3 (March 1921), 18-19; "über die Internationale Pfingstkonderenz in Amsterdam," 13/4 (April 1921),26-29; "Antwerpen, Belgien," 14/7 (July 1922),13; "Aus Holland," 15/2 (February 1923),28; "Pfingsten in aller Welt," 17/4 (April 1925),61; 17/8 (August 1925),128; "Schwester Polman teilt uns ein Gesicht mit," 21/7 (July 1929),108; "Br. Metz, Haag, Holland," 21/9 (September 1929),139-40; "Nachruf," 24/7 (April 1932),99.

Kok, Arie
  "In denselben Tagen," 3/13 (25 December 1910),97-99; "Wen soll Ich senden?" 3/28 (9 April 1911),220-21; "Von Missionfeld," 4/28 (7 April 1912), 229-30; 4/43 (21 July 1912),343-44; 4/45 (4 August 1912),359; 5/5 (3 November 1912),39; 6/43 (26 July 1914),340-41; Letter, 8/44 (30 July 1916), supplement.

Polman, G.R.
  "Wer Ohren hat, der hre, was der Geist der Gemeinde sagt," 3/8 (20 November 1910),59; "Lebendiges Wasser," 3/24 (12 March 1911),185-86; "Des Christen Kampf," 3/27 (2 April 1911),209; "Lebensgemeinschaft mit Jesus," 5/52 (28 September 1913),411-12; Letter, 7/7 (15 November 1914),54; "Unsere Versammlungen zu Ihm," 11/5 (9 March 1919),21-22; "Die Kraft der Ruhe in Gott," 12/19-20 (1 October 1920),76-77; "Christus in mir," 14/2 (February 1922),11-12; "Br. Polman, Amsterdam," 20/10 (October 1928),172-73.

Polman, W.
  "Das Lebendiges Wasser," 3/12 (18 December 1910),95.

Scharten, Elize
  "Von Missionsfelde," 5/35 (1 June 1913).

SWEDEN

Evangelii Härold

Pethrus, Lewi
  "Pa resanda fot," 13 January 1921; "Berlin-Amsterdam," 20 January 1921; "Den internationalla pingstkonferensen i Amsterdam," 27 January 1921; "Amsterdam-Wien," 3 February 1921.

SWITZERLAND

Die Verheissung des Vaters
As of no. 42 (December 1913): *Die Verheissung des Vaters und der Sieg des Kreuzes*

Polman, G.R.
"Die Verständigen," 8/3 (March 1915),2-6; "Aus Bruder Polman Reisebericht," 8/6 (June 1915),1-3; Photo, 9/11-12 (November-December 1916),1; "Der Quell der Gaben," 10/8-9 (August-September 1917),31-34; "Das Geheimnis Gottes," 12/3 (March 1919),7-10; "Nach einer Predigt von Bruder Polmann, Amsterdam," 15/3-5 (March-May 1922),7-10.
Polman, W.
"Sprechen im Zungen," no. 38 (August 1913),9-11; "Des Geheimnis des Herrn," 6/10 (15-5-1914),6-7; "Die letzte Stunde," 14/3 (March 1921),10-13.

UNITED STATES

The Apostolic Faith (Portland, OR)

[Polman, G.R.]
"Amsterdam, Holland," no. 18 (January 1909),1.

The Latter Rain Evangel

Booth-Clibborn, W.E.
"Some Glimpses of the European Pentecostal Fields," July 1929, 14-15.
Polman, G.R.
"Pentecost in Holland," February 1910, 5.
Polman, W.
"Faith, Floods and Flowers," foreword by W.E. Booth-Clibborn, July 1929, 3-5.

The Pentecostal Evangel

Booth-Clibborn, A.S.
"The International Pentecostal Convention, Amsterdam, Holland," 2 April 1921.
Polman, G.R.
"Oneness, Love and Power," 1 December 1923, 12-13, 21; "The Pentecostal Work in Holland," 29 May 1926, 2-3; "Mighty Movings in Holland," 4 December 1926.

Trust

"Pentecostal Items," March 1921, 9-11; "The International Pentecostal Convention at Amsterdam, Holland," April 1921, 9, 14; "Pentecostal Items," December 1921, 9-10.

The Weekly Evangel

Polman, G.R.
  "As the Spirit Gave Them Utterance," 24 February 1917, 5-6.

Personal Correspondence

Collection J.H. Gunning J.Hz.
Present in Rijksuniverstiteit Utrecht,
algemene bibliotheek, afdeling Handschriften

A. *d'Alblaing to Gunning:* 30 November 1918.
J.R. Fijn to Gunning: 12 August 1911; 21 August 1911; 6 November 1911; 13 November 1913.
Joh. de Groot to Gunning: 22 August 1919; 28 August 1919; 17 September 1919; 27 September 1919.
J.H. Gunning J.Hz. to G.R. Polman: 31 March 1917; 2 April 1917.
J.F. Hoogesteger to Gunning: 13 February 1911.
H. Meijer to Gunning: 30 August 1911.
Pauline Oltmann-Pause to J. de Weile: 16 November 1908; undated.
G.R. Polman to Gunning: 12 March 1910; 7 January 1913; 1 April 1917; 5 April 1917; 9 May 1919; 3 June 1919.
J.D. Root Jr. to Gunning: 19 October 1910; 24 October 1910; 20 March 1911.
C.P. Siebeles and friend to Gunning: 20 March 1911.
J. Timmerman to Gunning: 12 September 1911.
J. de Weile to Gunning: 23 March 1911.

Collection G.A. Wumkes
Present in Fries Letterkundig Museum en
Dokumentatiecentrum, Leeuwarden

G.R. Polman to Wumkes: 14 November 1914; 7 December 1914; 8 February 1915; 20 February 1915; 27 February 1915; 27 July 1915; 8 December 1915; 4 January 1916; 8 March 1916; 15 May 1916; 23 May 1916; 10 June 1916; 29 August 1916; 23 September 1916; 29 September 1916; 10 October 1916; 20 October 1916; 8 November 1916; 23 November 1916; 1 December 1916; 29 January 1917; 6 March 1917; 27 March 1917; 19 April 1917; 6 May 1917; 8 May 1917; 25 June 1917; 10 July 1917; 16 July 1917; 22 July 1917; 17 May 1918; 23 October 1918; 1 April 1919; 10 January 1920; 22 February 1922.
G.R. Polman to believers in Sneek: 5 October 1908; 15 January 1909; 19 January 1909; 27 March 1909; 19 December 1911; 17 July 1912; 31 January 1913; 26 March 1914; 14 August 1914; 8 February 1915; 26 June 1915; 29 April 1916; 20 August 1917; 3 May 1926.
G.R. Polman to Drukkerij Hollandia, Baarn: 12 March 1915.
W. Polman to Van Tuinen, Sneek: 18 July 1917.
G. Roos to Wumkes: 8 July 1924.
A. van der Veen-Hiemstra to believers in Sneek: 3 July 1923.

COLLECTION MARTHA VISSER
Present with Cornelis van der Laan

Jo and Ko Andrea to M. Visser: 26 November 1923; 2 December 1923; 31 December 1931;18 February 1932; 29 February 1932; 20 April 1932; 30 November 1932; 7 January 1934; 11 March 1937.
A.K. Evers to M. Visser: 24 November 1921; 16 January 1922.
B. Kedde to M. Visser: March 1923.
W. Polman to Andrea and Visser: 17 February 1932; 2 March 1932.
M. Visser to Andrea: 30 November 1923; November 1923; 4 December 1923; December 1923; March 1937.
M. Visser to Evers: November 1921.
M. Visser to Gretha: 10 April [1921].
M. Visser to Joh. de Heer: 23 April 1920; 26 August 1921.
M. Visser to Jansen: 3 December 1920.
M. Visser to believers at The Hague: 20 December 1921.
M. Visser to Miss Jonker: November 1921.
M. Visser to H. Plokker: 10 April 1922.
M. Visser to Polman: 27 January 1921; 30 January 1921; February 1921; undated; Summer 1923; 2 October 1923; 1923.
M. Visser to Miss Van der Weide: 24 January 1923.
Notes taken by M. Visser: "Vergadering Traktaatverspreiding, 20 April 1920."

Interviews

Eyewitnesses and children of eyewitnesses
interviewed by Cornelis van der Laan

Names	Born	Date of Interview
Allan, A.J.	1912	3/18 March 1987
Bakker, Trijntje	1891	29 October 1978
Berg, Hendrikus Jacobus	1899	12 July 1984
Berg-Kleefman, Sien v.d.	1886	12 July 1984
Bins-van Hugten, Catherina Johanna	1913	12 July 1984
Boerma, Gees	1921	11 October 1986
Booy, Simon	1923	11 October 1986
Bredijk, Lena	1915	20 November 1985
Brink, Marie van den	1907	13 August 1983
Eleveld-de Vries, Pietje	1912	21 August 1986
Gagel-Verhoef, Jeanette	1905	4 March 1987
Geest, Johannes Huibert de[2]	1927	16 February 1987
Geest, Leendert de	1896	Questionnaire 1984[1]
Jong-Polman, Lydia de	1917	29 December 1983
Klerk-Helgering, Truus	1909	11 October 1986
Kuiper-de Jonge, Harmina	1906	14 August 1986
Marijs-Visser, Martha	1896	17 August 1984
Mije-ter Haak, A.M.C. van der	1919	22 August 1986
Mik, Gerrit Roelof	1921	22 August 1986
Neumeier, Carl Ludwig Mozes	1908	27 August 1986
Oltman, Carl	1906	12 October 1986
Polman, Theo	1915	26 June 1984
Pronk-Hutte, Maria Rebecca	1919	21 February 1987
Ravenzwaay-van Caspel, Lydia van	1921	2 April 1987
Rieke-Stokker, Maria Gerardina	1914	4 July 1986
Rusticus, Ibe Sjoerd	1905	12 October 1987
Schaap, Simon	1900	3 December 1984
		5 March 1985
Schipper-Kamp, Jantje	1901	14 August 1986
Schuurman, Emmanuel	1908	16 August 1986
Staalman, IJs[2]	1926	11 March 1987
Stokker, Adriana Hendrika	1904	4 July 1986
Stokker, Jacoba Alexandra	1901	4 July 1986
Strijland-van Ravenzwaay, Hendrika van	1912	16 August 1986
Thiessen, Henk	1908	8 June 1981
Tieman-Hacquebard, Suza Th.	1896	12 July 1984
Vries, Janke de	1902	12 October 1986

1. Questionnaire filled out with the help of his son Johannes Huibert
2. Children of eyewitnesses

Names	*Born*	*Date of Interview*
Vries, Walter de	1906	28 December 1983
		4 March 1987
Wilde, Gerrit de[2]	1929	15 August 1986
Wild-Booy, Hillegonda E. de[2]	1928	15 August 1986
Willems-Uittenbosch, G.W.J.	1902	15 November 1984
Zijp, Dieuwertje[2]	1926	29 November 1984

2. Children of eyewitnesses

INDEX

Jonge, Jan de, 142
Jong-Polman, Lydia Catherina de, 110
Jonker, Miss, 156

Kamp, Roelof, 141, 143
Kedde, Bernard, 152, 154, 206-07, 269-70
King, J.H., 100, 199
Klaver, Jan, 182
Klaver, Piet, 138, 140, 145, 181-85, 187, 212
Klaver-Waters, Rose, 182
Kleefman, Sientje, 132
Knippel, Hermann, 106
Kok, Annie, 182-83
Kok, Arie, 42, 93-94, 97-98, 105-06, 146, 179-80, 182-83, 286,
    294
Kok-Aldenberg, Elsje, 93, 146, 179-80
Kraan, K.J., 246
Krol, Bram, 2
Kruijt, J.P., 16
Kühn, B., 62
Kuijlman, E., 39
Kuiper, 152
Kuyper, Abraham, 6, 9-11, 36-37, 301

Laan, C. van der, xi-xii
Laan, P.N. van der, xv
Layendecker, L., 306
Leeuwen, C.R. van, 34-35, 246
Lennep, Jonkheer J.W. van, 291
Lennep-Gunning, Caroline van, 291
Leroux, de, 107
Lettau, K., 238
Lieftinck, W.H., 35
Linthout, H., 74
Lip, G. van der, 153-55
Looi, Els van, 132
Looi, Suus van, 132
Lord's Supper, 22, 28, 55, 72, 102, 140, 206, 220, 268, 279-80, 288
Lovekin, A. Adams, 239
Lum, Clara, 230
Luther, Martin, 247
Lutherans, 5, 40-41, 60, 82, 156-57, 180-81, 202, 274, 277, 279,
    287

DATE DUE

HIGHSMITH 45-220